Supporting SAP™ R/3™

Send Us Your Comments:

To comment on this book or any other PRIMA TECH title, visit Prima's reader response page on the Web at **www.primapublishing.com/comments.**

How to Order:

For information on quantity discounts, contact the publisher: Prima Publishing, P.O. Box 1260BK, Rocklin, CA 95677-1260; (916) 632-4400. On your letterhead, include information concerning the intended use of the books and the number of books you wish to purchase. For individual orders, turn to the back of this book for more information, or visit Prima's Web site at **www.primapublishing.com.**

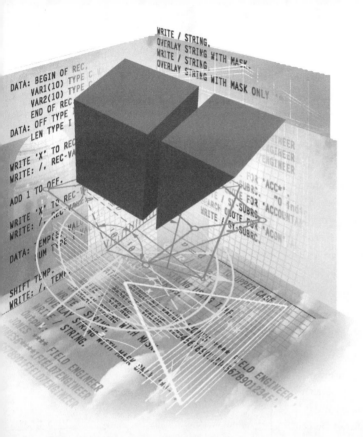

Supporting
SAP™ *R/3*™

Dennis L. Prince

SERIES EDITORS:

Gareth M. de Bruyn
Robert Lyfareff

A Division of Prima Publishing

A Division of Prima Publishing
Prima Publishing and colophon are registered
trademarks of Prima Communications, Inc.,
Rocklin, California 95677.

SAP, R/3, and ABAP/4 are either registered trademarks or
trademarks of SAP Aktiengesellschaft, Systems, Applications
and Products in Data Processing, Neurottstrasse 16, 69190
Walldorf, Germany. SAP AG is not the publisher of this book
and is not responsible for it under any aspect of press law.

Prima Publishing and the author have attempted throughout
this book to distinguish proprietary trademarks from descriptive terms by following the capitalization style used by the
manufacturers.

Information contained in this book has been obtained by
Prima Publishing from sources believed to be reliable.
However, because of the possibility of human or mechanical
error by our sources, Prima Publishing, or others, the Publisher
does not guarantee the accuracy, adequacy, or completeness of
any information and is not responsible for any errors or omissions or the results obtained from the use of such information.
Readers should be particularly aware of the fact that the
Internet is an ever-changing entity. Some facts may have
changed since this book went to press.

ISBN: 0-7615-1750-2

Library of Congress Catalog Card Number: 98-66993

Printed in the United States of America

98 99 00 01 HH 10 9 8 7 6 5 4 3 2

Publisher:
Matthew H. Carleson

Managing Editor:
Dan J. Foster

Acquisitions Editor:
Deborah F. Abshier

Senior Editor:
Kelli R. Crump

Assistant Project Editor:
Kim V. Benbow

Copy Editor:
June Waldman

Technical Reviewer:
Melissa Eskelsen

Editorial Assistant:
Rebecca Fong

Interior Layout:
Jimmie Young

Cover Design:
Prima Design Team

Indexer:
Sharon Hilgenberg

Dedications

I gratefully dedicate this book to my wife, Diane. I couldn't ask for a better wife, partner, and friend. You were so supportive, cooperative, and patient as I worked on this project. Thank you for helping me make it a reality.

And, for Eric and Alex: Look what Dad did! I hope you are both proud of my accomplishment. Thanks for not growing up too much while I worked on this book. I'm ready to play now.

Acknowledgments

There are many people I wish to thank for their contributions and participation in the making of this book. First, I wish to thank my Series Editors: Gareth M. de Bruyn and Robert Lyfareff. Thank you both for giving me the opportunity to write this book. Your continued encouragement and reassurance were the key elements to my success.

I would also like to thank Debbie Abshier, Kelli Crump, Dan Foster, and the rest of the folks at Prima Publishing. Your continued guidance, assistance, and tireless efforts are very much appreciated. You're a terrific team to work with.

Additionally, I wish to thank those individuals who were instrumental in reviewing my early treatments of this book: June Waldman, Melissa Eskelsen, and Mike Stevenson. Your comments, suggestions, and observations are most appreciated and contributed to improve the content and quality of this book.

I would also like to thank Linda McCarthy and Danny Nelson for their support of this effort and for enabling me to bring this project to fruition.

Finally, I would like to thank SAP America.

Contents at a Glance

Introduction xxi

PART I   **BUILDING YOUR
FOUNDATION FOR SUPPORT** **1**
  1   Learning about Support 3
  2   Understanding Integration within SAP 21
  3   Integrating the Support Organization 37
  4   Establishing an Overall Support Strategy 53

PART II   **THE SAP LIFE CYCLE.** **71**
  5   Supporting the Evaluation and Start-Up Phase 73
  6   Supporting the Design Phase 91
  7   Supporting the Development Phase 113
  8   Supporting the Testing and Training Phase 139
  9   Supporting the Implementation 155

PART III   **TRANSITIONING SUPPORT.** **169**
  10   Comparing a Legacy Environment to a
  New SAP Environment 171
  11   Building a Winning Support Team 185
  12   Stabilizing and Preparing for the Handoff 199
  13   The Handoff and Migration of Support 213
  14   Establishing the Support Domain 225

PART IV   **SUPPORTING THE LIVE ENVIRONMENT.** . **237**
  15   Maintaining System Security 239
  16   Creating and Maintaining Background
  Job Schedules 265
  17   Resolving Common Problems 289

18 Managing Changes in the SAP Environment 303
19 Supporting Customizations in the SAP Environment . . .317
20 Supporting Reports 337
21 Transaction and Performance Support 351
22 Developing and Maintaining User Confidence 363
23 Disaster Recovery Planning (DRP) 375
24 Archiving SAP Data 387
25 Documenting for Support 399
26 The Evolution of Support 413

PART IV   APPENDIXES 421

A   A Brief History of SAP 423
B   An Overview of the SAP GUI 427
C   Additional Tips, Transactions,
    and Tools 433
D   Finding Additional Information 441
E   SAP Training Programs and Facilities 449

Index 453

About the Author

Dennis L. Prince has an accomplished educational background in business application programming, specializing in materials management. With over four years of SAP R/3 experience, he has supported a first-time implementation for one of the industry's Fortune 50 companies. His expertise extends into SAP development utilizing ABAP/4 programming and dialog sessions. Dennis has actively provided technical support for a live SAP business environment while simultaneously participating in the implementation of R/3 at several other business sites. He is currently assigned to supporting one of the most technically complex SAP environments in today's business industry.

About the Series Editors

Gareth de Bruyn's background includes chemical engineering, UNIX site administration, and network installations. His experience with SAP began shortly after the technology became available, and he currently works as an independent SAP consultant with a Fortune 50 company. A native of South Africa, who was raised and educated in the United States, de Bruyn believes SAP technology is revolutionizing international business. He plans to earn a law degree to unite his technical and international business skills to capitalize on this global opportunity. You can contact Gareth at debcor@bigfoot.com.

Robert Lyfareff is a veteran of several successful SAP installation teams over the past four years. Coupled with his formal training in computer science and electrical engineering, this unique SAP experience enables him to write about real-world business situations and issues. What excites and challenges him about his work is the integration and modification of business practices with the new technology. Currently, he works as an independent SAP consultant and author. You can contact Robert at rlyf@bigfoot.com.

Contents

Introduction . . . .**xxi**

PART I   **BUILDING YOUR**
                FOUNDATION FOR SUPPORT **1**

Chapter 1   **Learning about Support** **3**
                In This Chapter 4
                What Does Support Mean? 4
                The Support Model 6
                The Different Kinds of Support 12
                    The Old Face of Support .15
                    The Support Makeover 15
                The Elements of Exceptional Support 16
                What Is Your Contribution? 18
                    The New Support Person .18
                    The Veteran Support Person 19
                Summary 19

Chapter 2   **Understanding Integration within SAP** . .**21**
                In This Chapter 22
                The Integrated SAP Model 22
                Understanding Integrated Data 24
                    Master Data 26
                    Transactional Data 29
                Understanding Integrated Processes 31
                The Pros and Cons of Integration 33
                Summary 35

Chapter 3   **Integrating the Support Organization** . . .**37**
                In This Chapter 38
                Developing an Integrated Support Team 39
                    Using a Common Terminology Language 40

Establishing Business Support Assignments 41
Controlling Access and Tool Use 42
Establishing a Physical Environment 44
Developing Good Communication Tools
and Forums 46
Developing Support Partnerships 47
Developing User Partnerships 49
Developing Yourself 50
Summary 52

Chapter 4   **Establishing an Overall Support
Strategy** **53**
In This Chapter 54
Elements of Success 54
The Right Size of the Support Team 55
The Right Mix of Resource Skills 56
The Natural Areas of Resource Focus 56
The Ability to Obtain and Maintain Technology 57
The Proper Amount of Control 58
The Need for Simplicity 59
The Clarity of Direction and Priorities 60
The General Mood and Tone of the Group 60
Communicating with the Customers 61
Establishing a Backup Strategy and
Cross-Training Plan 62
The Various Work Environments 63
The Development Instance 64
The Quality Assurance Instance 65
The Live Business Instance 66
The Training Instance 66
The Disaster Recovery Instance 66
Maintaining a Clean Environment 67
Summary 68

PART II   **THE SAP LIFE CYCLE.** **71**

Chapter 5   **Supporting the Evaluation and
Start-Up Phase** **73**

In This Chapter 74

Entering This Phase 75

Understanding the Objective 76

Understanding the Implementation Team Structure
and Membership 79

Roles and Responsibilities 82

Adopting a Common Tool Set and
Development Environment 82

The First SAP GUI Installation 84

Learning SAP 85

Understanding Specific Areas of Control 86

Starting Good Documentation Habits 87

Exiting This Phase 88

Summary 89

Chapter 6   **Supporting the Design Phase** . . . . **.91**

In This Chapter 92

Project Scope and High-Level Process
Migration Plans 93

Incorporating the Project Work Plan 96

Current System and Process Analysis 97

Establishing the Development Instance 100

    Process Development Client 101

    Interface Development Client 102

    The Instance Master Client 103

Constructing the Future Environment Landscape 103

Early Prototypes 105

    Setting Boundaries of Project Scope
    vs. Project Timeline 107

Communicating Results 108

Documenting This Phase 109

Obtaining Design Approval 110

Exiting This Phase 110

Summary 111

Chapter 7   **Supporting the Development Phase** . . **.113**

In This Chapter 114

Entering This Phase 115

Early System Builds 116
Establishing Logon and Access Policies 117
Working with Naming Conventions 118
Working with Customizations 119
Working with Master Data Policies 122
Mapping Legacy Data to SAP 123
Identifying and Investigating Gaps and Issues 124
Reengineering Processes 127
Early Data Loads 129
Developing Interfaces 131
Developing Reports 132
Iterations of Design 133
Freezing the Design Specifications 135
Documenting This Phase 136
Exiting This Phase 136
Summary 137

**Chapter 8   Supporting the Testing and
                Training Phase** **139**
In This Chapter 140
Entering This Phase 141
Building the Test and Training Instances 141
Working with a Dedicated Test Area 144
Supporting Final Unit Testing 144
Supporting Integration Testing 147
Supporting Pilot Testing 147
Supporting the Training Approach 149
Documenting This Phase 151
The Go/No-Go Review 152
Exiting This Phase 153
Summary 153

Chapter 9   Supporting the Implementation **155**
In This Chapter 156
Entering This Phase 157
Developing and Supporting a Live Cutover Plan 158
Ensuring a Viable Contingency Plan 160
Initiating a Blackout 161

Enabling the Turn-On 162
Providing Visible Support 163
Tracking, Resolving, and Communicating Issues 165
Stabilization, Postmortem Feedback, and Next Steps 166
Summary 167

PART III   **TRANSITIONING SUPPORT 169**

Chapter 10 **Comparing a Legacy Environment to a New SAP Environment 171**
In This Chapter 172
Integrated Processes vs. Isolated Processes 173
Differences in Security and User Groups 177
Differences in Business Exposure 178
Differences in Data Recovery and Data Manipulation . . .180
Differences in Solution Leveragability 181
Summary 183

Chapter 11 **Building a Winning Support Team 185**
In This Chapter 186
Determining Your Personal Transition 187
Assembling and Sizing the Team 191
Preparing the Team for the New Environment 193
Engaging the Business Areas 194
The Continued Use of Consultants 195
Summary 196

Chapter 12 **Stabilizing and Preparing for the Handoff .199**
In This Chapter 200
Understanding Changing Roles and Responsibilities 201
    The New SAP Instance Environment 201
    The New Implementation Team Role 203
    The Current Support Team Role 205
    Shared Roles and Responsibilities 205
Enabling Temporary Co-Support 206
Developing Handoff Criteria 208
    The Stabilization Window 208

Useful Stabilization Metrics .209
Additional Stabilization Considerations 210
Tracking Progress to Stabilization 211
Stable and Ready for Handoff .212
Summary 212

Chapter 13 The Handoff and Migration
          of Support **213**
In This Chapter 214
Getting the Long-Term Support Team in Place 215
Support Team Deployment and
Business Area Assignment 216
Determining All Elements Requiring Long-Term
Support 217
Establishing Backup Support Linkages 218
Executing Knowledge Transfer 218
Documentation Deliverables .219
Handoff Acceptance 222
Introducing the New Support Team 223
Summary 223

Chapter 14 Establishing the Support Domain **225**
In This Chapter 226
Revisiting Company Controls and Culture 227
Identifying Key Points of Control 228
Revisiting Separation of Duty .229
Reestablishing System Backup, Refresh, and Recovery . . .230
Ensuring Audit Readiness and ISO Compliance 232
Cleaning Up the System 234
Summary 236

PART IV   SUPPORTING THE LIVE ENVIRONMENT. . 237

Chapter 15 Maintaining System Security **239**
In This Chapter 240
Developing System Security Policies 241
Establishing a Controlled and Consistent Security
Process 243

SAP Logon IDs 244
Passwords 251
Protecting User Logon IDs and Passwords 253
Creating Model Logon IDs 254
Reviewing and Maintaining Logon IDs 255
Understanding the Authorization Profile 255
    Administering Authorization Profiles 258
Additional SAP Security Tools .258
Sharing Security Ownership with the Business Areas . . .260
Summary 262

Chapter 16 Creating and Maintaining
Background Job Schedules 265
In This Chapter 266
Job Scheduling: An Overview .266
Job Scheduling Tools 268
Job Schedule Status 278
Monitoring Job Schedules 279
Securing Job Schedules 281
Job Alerts and Notification 282
Recovering Job Schedules 284
Best Practices for Job Scheduling and
Supporting Job Schedules 285
Summary 286

Chapter 17 Resolving Common Problems 289
In This Chapter 290
Categorizing Common Problem Areas 291
    System Access and Authorization Problems 292
    Data Access and Contention Problems 293
    System Performance and Resources Problems 296
    Data Integrity Problems .296
    Program and Process-Specification Problems 297
Responding to the Situation 297
Useful Basis Tools 298
    Update Monitoring 298
    System Log 299
    Dump Analyses 299

Output Controller 300

Summary 300

Chapter 18 Managing Changes
in the SAP Environment 303

In This Chapter 304

Developing a Change Process 305

Different Kinds of Changes in SAP 307

SAP-Provided ABAP Programs, Screens,
Transactions, and Data Dictionary Elements 308

Customizations 310

Master Data Elements 311

Customer-Defined Objects .312

The Transport Tool 312

Communicating Changes 314

Summary 315

Chapter 19 Supporting Customizations in
the SAP Environment 317

In This Chapter 318

SAP Customizations: A Support Overview 319

High-Level Customization Management 320

Customization Update Tools 324

Using Existing Customizations and References 328

Transporting Customizations .330

Using Naming Conventions 334

Tracking Customization Activity 334

Summary 335

Chapter 20 Supporting Reports 337

In This Chapter 338

Informational Needs and Scale 339

Reporting Tools 340

One-Dimensional Table Extracts 340

ABAP/Query 341

ABAP/4 Programs 344

Third-Party Query Tools 344

Report Elements 345

Determining Useful Reports 345
Working with Report Results 347
Matters of Efficiency 347
Supporting Reports 348
Additional Resources 349
Summary 350

Chapter 21 Transaction and
Performance Support 351
In This Chapter 352
What Is Transaction and Performance Support? 353
Reviewing the Work Processes .353
Data Contention Revisited 357
SAP Performance Tools and Methods 358
  User and Process Load Balancing 358
  Synchronous and Asynchronous Updating 358
  Database Locks 359
  Database Performance Tuning 359
Maintaining Ease of Use in SAP 359
When to Enable Automated Processes 360
Summary 361

Chapter 22 Developing and Maintaining
User Confidence 363
In This Chapter 364
Determining Your Customer Base 365
Establishing and Maintaining the Partnership 367
Communicate! 368
Helping Users Help Themselves 369
Engaging the User Base 371
Grooming Expert Users 372
Damage Control 373
Summary 373

Chapter 23 Disaster Recovery Planning (DRP) 375
In This Chapter 376
Developing a Disaster Recovery Plan 377

Identifying the Critical Elements 378
Identifying the Geographic Location of Tools 378
Identifying the Disaster Recovery Timetable 379
Identifying the Recovery Team 379
Identifying the Response Method 380
Approval 380
The SAP Instance Structure and DRP Readiness 381
SAP System Backups 382
Backup Retention 383
Locating the DRP Instance and the System
Backup Storage 384
Rehearsing the Plan 384
Maintaining Your DRP 385
Summary 385

Chapter 24   Archiving SAP Data 387
In This Chapter 388
Why Archive? 389
Developing Your Archiving Strategy 390
What to Archive 390
When to Archive 390
Understanding Business Requirements
for Archiving 391
SAP Archiving Tools 392
SAP Archive Overview 392
Archiving Authorization .393
Archive Objects 393
Archive Management 395
Archive Development Kit (ADK) 395
ArchiveLink 396
Additional Archiving Considerations 397
Third-Party Archiving Solutions 397
Determining the Appropriate Elegance of Archiving 397
Summary 398

Chapter 25   Documenting for Support 399
In This Chapter 400
Why Document? 400

Types of Documentation 402
Establishing a Documentation Habit 403
Documenting Code 404
Maintaining the Support Reference Guide 409
Document Storage, Reference, and
Sharing Techniques 410
Measuring Successful Documentation 411
Summary 411

Chapter 26 The Evolution of Support 413
In This Chapter 414
Looking Back 414
Recalling How SAP Will Change Your
Work Environment 417
Developing Confidence in Yourself 418

PART V   APPENDIXES .421

Appendix A A Brief History of SAP 423

Appendix B An Overview of the SAP GUI 427
The SAP Main Screen and Issuance of
Transaction Codes 428
The Data Table Selection and Result Screens 429
Commonly Used SAP GUI Icons 429

**Appendix C Additional Tips, Transactions,
and Tools 433**
SAP Transaction Code Quick Reference 434
Using the Command Field 438
Custom SAP Job Link to Job Schedule
Location Program 439
Echoing Sessions in SAP 440
Customizing the Data Browser 440

Appendix D Finding Additional Information 441
Official SAP User Groups and Organizations 442
Americas' SAP Users' Group (ASUG) 442

Multinational User Groups 443
SAP Labs, Inc. 443
Conferences and Expositions .443
Sapphire 444
SAP Technical Education 444
Consulting Organizations 444
Ernst & Young LLP 444
Deloitte and Touche Consulting Group/ICS 445
CaRD America Inc. 445
Origin 445
Bureau van Dijk 445
SAP-Related Web Sites 446
SAP-AG Official Company Web Site 446
SAP Frequently Asked Questions Web Site 447
The SAP Fan Club and User Forum 447

**Appendix E SAP Training Programs and
Facilities** **449**
Traditional Courses 450
Additional Training Resources 452
On-Site Delivery of Education 452
Portable Classrooms 452
Information Database 452

Index **453**

Introduction

Welcome to *Supporting SAP R/3*. If you're reading this book, then you are in good company. SAP has emerged as one of the most widely used software solutions for businesses around the globe. With its unheralded market proliferation, SAP has generated overwhelming demand for individuals who understand the application and can effectively use it to support the many facets of an SAP environment.

The Purpose of This Book

As the title implies, this book discusses the elements of supporting SAP in terms of the SAP life cycle and SAP's daily, ongoing use and maintenance. First, you may ask, Why this book? Why is it the best source of information? Well, if you've done much research of your own, you might have discovered this sort of information is neither readily available nor easily obtained. The few current books about SAP focus on other aspects of the SAP environment, such as ABAP/4 programming or particular SAP business modules, or are just overviews of the whole SAP application. This book is different because it approaches the subject of actually working with SAP from the perspective of an administrator—the person who works with the application from a supporting role, ensuring the system is up and operational and that the users can get their work done. After all, someone has to get the system up and running, right? That might be you. And, once the system's up, who's going to take care of it and make sure it stays that way? You, again.

Even as prevalent as SAP has become, very little useful information focuses on the aspect of support. SAP development teams, as well as alliance partners, simply have not been willing or able to provide comprehensive, coherent documentation that approaches the scope of information you'll find in these pages. I have written this book to fill a noticeable void and to provide the kind of firsthand knowledge that cannot be generated by development or marketing teams and that can best be provided by a person "in the trenches."

This book is the culmination of real-world, daily experiences and observations acquired from four years (and counting) of supporting an SAP environment. I've been through and supported several SAP installations, some on a global scale. I've learned, tried, laughed, and cried. I've had the wonderful opportunity to work with professionals from around the globe. I've worked with some of the best out there, and we all learned about SAP and each other. I look back and find that it has been the most productive period of my professional career. I'd like to share it with you. My goal is to provide information in an organized, easy-to-understand, and economically attainable format.

Because of the high market demand for this information, businesses have had to turn to consulting firms for guidance in enabling and supporting SAP. Although the consulting solution is very viable and useful, it also carries a significant price tag. I believe this information should be more readily available, and at a cost that is much easier to absorb.

The other alternative a business can exercise is trial-and-error learning. Although this method can produce deeper levels of familiarity with SAP (usually by accident), it is typically very time intensive. Given the dynamic business environment of today, a business would generally miss major market opportunities, or give up on the SAP application, usually at a loss of time and resources.

I want to give you and your team a head start in the world of SAP support and, hopefully, save you some time and effort along the way. I expect the information presented to stand the test of time. Developing internal support infrastructures that can determine a vision and realize profits and efficiencies, all before the market shifts and internal goals become realigned, has become a challenge to the business world. The information in this book will be useful for immediate application and will be durable enough to build on throughout your SAP experience.

Intended Audience

If you're reading this book, you have possibly found yourself in one of the following situations:

- ◆ You support an organization that is actively using SAP to manage its business.

- ◆ You support an organization that is actively pursuing the installation of SAP to manage its business.

- ◆ You desire to work with and support the SAP application and are eager to learn more about its architecture and upkeep.

- ◆ You have a team that is or will be supporting SAP, and you need to know just what it is you are asking of them.

If you fit one of these descriptions, then you're in luck. This book will give you the insight and assistance you desire. Moreover, you'll find that this book will examine both technical and business aspects of supporting SAP. Why both? The answer can be summed up with a single word—integration. SAP's design is based on a hub of integration. So to understand how to better support an application like SAP, it is helpful for you to understand a better way to define support for yourself and the organization in which you may work. Integration, you will find, is your key to success. You will get the most from this material if your background includes the following items:

◆ **General usage of SAP.** You have seen the application, have learned to maneuver within it, and are somewhat familiar with the different areas of business functionality.

◆ **Basic concept of the support role.** You have worked in a supporting capacity for an organization, or you are preparing to do so, understanding the general services and functions of such a role.

◆ **Basic business fundamentals.** You understand the basic functions of the various segments of a business operation—purchasing, finance, warehouse management, and so on. Although you don't have to understand the intricacies of each, you should have an overall grasp of their high-level deliverables and interconnections.

◆ **Basic understanding of a business application.** You understand what business applications are, in general, and what they do to enable an ongoing business concern. You might not necessarily understand the actual programming of a business application, but you recognize its various components such as databases, data tables, application programs, and user interfaces.

Although I take the time to explain how each method or tool meets one of these needs to a certain degree, your own expertise will help you apply the information much more quickly and in a more meaningful way.

How This Book Is Organized

Although I assume some knowledge on your part, I still stop to explain important concepts along the way. The beginning of the book develops a strong foundation of what support is as well as more of what SAP is and does. As the book progresses, the pace and complexity of the presentation increases, and the examples match the increase in your knowledge.

This book is structured in a series of chronological parts:

Part I: Building Your Foundation for Support

This Part starts by examining the support role in an organization and by identifying characteristics that are conducive to successful support. Next, there is a review of SAP's integrated architecture to help you understand how that integration affects a support environment. Finally, the text applies what you've learned to that point and will proceed to develop an overall support strategy that works.

Part II: The SAP Life Cycle

This Part examines what it means to support SAP during its phases of introduction and readiness and explains how the support role is so vital throughout the cycle. As the information builds on itself, the text will guide you through the actual support of an SAP installation.

Part III: Transitioning Support

In this Part, the text will show you how SAP has affected the support team and changed the roles of each member. You'll discover the necessary ingredients for establishing an effective support team, managing the differences associated with supporting an SAP environment in comparison to any previous automated environment, accepting the handoff of SAP support from the SAP implementation team, and ensuring the redefinition of the support environment to successfully maintain the new system and its users.

Part IV: Supporting the Live Environment

Here, you'll learn the tools of the trade. You'll see what enables a support team member to do his or her job and learn how to establish a secure environment, automate data processing, and identify common problem situations.

In addition, you'll gain knowledge about the broad spectrum of support activities that range from managing change to describing how best to work with your user base. You'll also find vital information that describes how to maintain a clean, well-documented, and recoverable SAP environment.

Appendixes

The appendixes include additional details that will answer some of the specific questions you may have about SAP, its use, and where you can turn for even more information. Appendix C, for example, covers tips and tricks that are helpful to anyone supporting SAP.

Although the Parts are arranged in chronological order, you can also reference the information as you need it. For instance, if you really need to know about a specific SAP support function or phase, you can refer to the Part directly and read more about that particular information.

How to Use This Book

As SAP is a tool to help manage your business, this book is a tool to help manage the SAP environment that runs your business. If you are relatively new to SAP and the concept of supporting it, you may wish to read this book from start to finish. You'll have a better understanding of SAP in a business environment, and you'll be able to virtually witness the progression of SAP into a business's infrastructure.

If you're more experienced with SAP or well ingrained in a support role, you might choose to bounce around in the presentation. A review of the table of contents or the book's index can help you locate the exact information you need.

You Are Not Alone

Supporting SAP can sometimes be intimidating and overwhelming. Think about it: You're now responsible for managing a reasonably new business application, and you're learning more about it each day while concluding there is so much you don't yet understand. Still you're the support person, and the business is looking to you for answers, confidence, and stability. Well, I've been through the whole growth process, and am still growing, and I decided to include a helpful feature in this book.

> In these virtual thought bubbles, I share some of my thoughts and experiences relative to the point of discussion. Maybe you'll identify with them. Maybe you'll scratch your head and ponder. Maybe you'll laugh. In these asides, I give you my personal slices of experience, in a way that lets you read between the lines and share some of the unsaid aspects of SAP support.

Working with SAP can be quite mysterious, baffling, overwhelming, and frustrating at times. It is a very ambitious application and is extremely complex. Consider this book as your working *companion* or *partner*. Most people tend to work well when they have another person to bounce ideas off of or turn to for a helping hand. This book strives to be that silent partner, that voice of reassurance, that slice of wisdom that says, "Yes, I've seen that before. Let me show you what I did."

Even though I *suggest* many solutions and alternatives, I refrain from dictating absolutes unless clearly necessary. Why? SAP is a system that excels through its adaptability. All businesses are unique in some way, and one solution rarely fits all. Therefore, some of the methods or options I present may not exactly suit your immediate needs, and you may elect not to use them. Or you may find an idea that comes close to meeting your needs but could be better fitted to your situation after a minor tweak here or there. Again, this book aims to be a partner and helping hand. In the business world today, there seems to be more alternatives than absolutes.

Contacting the Author

I'm always interested in discussing SAP support issues with other business professionals. If you have questions that haven't been covered in this book, information you believe can be useful to me and others, or some suggestions about how I can make this book better, please feel free to send an e-mail message to **dlprince@bigfoot.com.**

1 **Learning about Support**

2 **Understanding Integration within SAP**

3 **Integrating the Support Organization**

4 **Establishing an Overall Support Strategy**

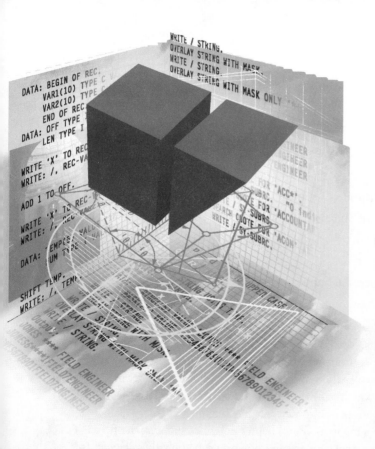

Chapter 1

Learning about Support

In This Chapter

- ◆ What Does Support Mean?
- ◆ The Support Model
- ◆ Working within the Business Culture
- ◆ The Different Kinds of Support
- ◆ The Old Face of Support
- ◆ The Support Makeover
- ◆ The Elements of Successful Support
- ◆ What Is Your Contribution?

This chapter starts with the development of your base of knowledge and serves as the footing for successive chapters. You'll notice that the following chapters and Parts incorporate concepts and terms from previous content. Therefore, the best way to begin this book is with a full explanation of the term *support*. Support comes in many methods and styles, most of which can be applied and adapted to fit your business environment. Although support can be somewhat mutable, there are core elements that define the heart of what support is. This chapter describes support, the fundamental elements of truly exceptional support, and how you can apply these elements to become a successful support team member.

What Does Support Mean?

In the context of this book, *support* refers to an individual or organization that is chartered to monitor, maintain, and frequently improve a particular business environment. Companies develop support organizations to provide many services—to act as sentries to ensure that all systems stay online; to guard against unwelcome situations that could compromise business activity or information integrity; and to proactively seek out better tools that will improve the environment's reliability, throughput cycles, and overall business productivity. A support organization is a virtual technical and informational body that responds to practically any situation or question that may arise. It's part technical wizard, part guidance counselor, and always on duty.

The support role is born when a business understands the need for help in establishing and maintaining an automated environment. The business people need to focus on providing their products or services, whatever those may be. Yet, to be competitive in today's marketplace, business people need to utilize current technology and processes in strategic and reliable ways. While applying technology is a boost to business capacity, it comes with a price. It is necessary that someone is continually monitoring the technical aspects of the business environment. This allows the business people to concentrate on their business, leaving the technical concerns in someone else's able hands. Those able hands belong to the support team.

To serve business needs, a support team must be established and properly staffed in proportion to the business it will sustain. It must be appropriately sized to respond to the anticipated volume of activity required to keep the business online. And, there must be a stable and reliable backbone of automation that will support and enable the volume of expected business activity. As a company grows, so does its reliance on core business technology and the support team that manages the technology. To properly support informational and transactional needs, a support team and the environment it manages must grow in-line with a business's growth. A business is continually changing its activities and needs; a support team needs to provide dynamic levels of technology and personnel to provide for the ever-changing business.

TIP

Balance and tuning of the support team is required for success. The support team should be balanced in relation to the business activity and business people it must uphold; the technology must be tuned so it enables business activity and doesn't impede efforts.

The complement to an organization's recognition of the need for a support team is the dedication and commitment of each support team member. This is the beginning of a relationship between the support team and the business people. This relationship requires that you play an active and contributing role in several ways. Naturally, your first responsibility is to work with the other members of your support team in a communicative and cooperative manner. All members of a support team must understand what each other is doing in the overall support of the business entity. This provides a consistent delivery of services to the company by ensuring all support team members are well informed and supportive of the common business needs. Equally important will be for you to work directly with the business people, business teams, management teams, and even external organizations and business concerns. You'll find the support team is most effective when it can provide technical expertise and advice in ways that help shape business direction, develop business processes, and facilitate the realization of business goals. This applied expertise can help a company break down limiting situations, overcome technical hurdles, and forge ahead in more effective business execution. The support role is evolving in a way that support team members need to become more involved in business process development at earlier stages. The evolution is achieved through the dedicated effort of each support team member.

It all boils down to the support team being responsible for satisfying the business customer and providing a recognizable and quantifiable level of service. Invariably, the support team is funded by the company to provide the services described here. Support costs, including staff and equipment, can be expensive and make for a significant portion of a company's annual budget. The business wants to know their investment is a good one. The primary goal of the support team, then, must be to meet and exceed the business expectations set forth, always with an eye on cost-effectiveness and return on the original business investment.

> Does this sound like the same old organizational drivel? It's not. Especially when you add SAP to the equation. SAP isn't some creature intent upon upsetting the environment, but it does challenge much of what was comfortable and recognizable to a company—this being the processes and automation tools once used by the company. You might find yourself, as did I, in the position of promoting the need for support in your organization. It's costly, and sometimes seemingly intangible, which makes it not so eagerly funded by a business organization. So, be aware that you will need to exemplify the support role, providing as much visibility to your contributions and how they provide good return to the business's support investment. This helps assure the company of your intent, commitment, and value.

The Support Model

To effectively provide services that match the company investment, the support team must adopt a definition of itself and its services—the *support model*. The following development of a support model defines support by illustrating how a support organization is constructed, what services it provides, and how it interacts with its customers and partners.

Support Model—The logical definition of a support organization that includes how the support team is constructed, how the team might be subdivided for focused business area management, and how the customer or business user interacts with the team.

The support model describes what the support services and deliverables should be. It enables you to define the points of input to the team and the resultant output of services. This model also defines the proactive methods of the support organization—essentially how the support team will work ahead to ensure business services are uninterrupted and technically evolutionary. You'll see that there are different ways to construct the model, as illustrated in Figures 1-1 and 1-2.

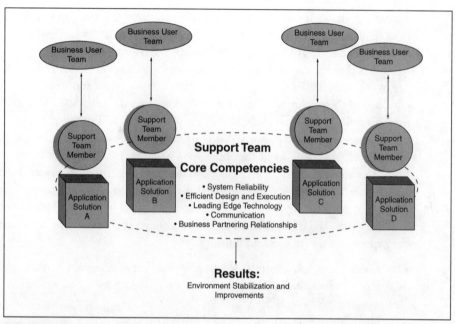

FIGURE 1-1 *Support model 1*

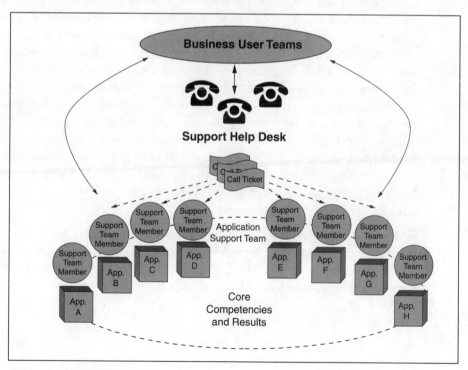

FIGURE 1-2 *Support model 2*

Figure 1-1 shows the core construct and methodology of the support team. Notice how the business customers (or *users*) can establish direct contact with the support team members. In this example, the business customer has a support team member to contact directly, and this support team member is directly responsible for responding to the customer, evaluating their situation, enabling a solution, and informing the customer of the resolution. The business customer needs to work with a support team member quickly and effectively, and this model is very well suited to enable that sort of business/support relationship. With this model, the customer is talking to the most knowledgeable person about the application or process that requires attention. Most likely, this support contact can evaluate and resolve the situation quickly because his or her main responsibility is to manage the application or process in question on a day-to-day basis. Aside from providing excellent customer response methods, Figure 1-1 also shows the internal activities, sometimes referred to as *core competencies*, that the support team manages and nurtures.

Core Competency—Major areas of strength, usually a combination of technical aptitude and strategic vision, actively demonstrated by the support team that will drive positive change to an organization's benefit.

The core competencies act as the support engine that is continually tuned to provide better performance to the demands of the customers and partners. The model defines the output, other than direct customer support, that the support team generates for its organization; it is a combination of good customer response teamed with the application of the core competencies. This particular model is usually applicable to a small or moderate-size organization. The user base is estimated to be between 100 and 300 individuals. A user base of this size enables the support team members to be quite accessible and responsive most of the time. In addition, the number of applications supported and transactions processed is expected to be modest. The system infrastructure, that is the core automation environment, is also of a manageable size, with only a moderate level of significant process and technical migrations (upgrades). The actual size of the support team would be scaled to provide maximum return on business funding; the team would be staffed in relation to the business size, activity level, and core infrastructure required to support it.

For a larger business organization, Figure 1-2 illustrates a support model in which the user base is expected to range from 300 to 600 individuals. In contrast to the support model in Figure 1-1, the core infrastructure here would typically be significantly more complex and interconnected. This sort of environment obviously necessitates a larger support team.

> Just for grins, I remember a team member looking at the oncoming SAP project and the level of support it would require; the core infrastructure and business activity to be supported was significant. His remark: "You're gonna need a bigger boat."

One new feature of support model 2 is that it incorporates the use of a support *hot line* or *help desk,* which is a front-line individual or team responsible for handling incoming user inquiries and trouble calls. This help desk is typically administered 24 hours a day, or as dictated by a business's hours of operation. Many help desks are responsible for users in multiple time zones, and hours of service may need to be adjusted to serve times of regular user activity.

The job of the help desk is to characterize any problem or situation via a direct and immediate conversation with the caller. If a system problem occurs, the help desk staff captures the problem details and routes them in the form of a *call ticket* to the appropriate support team member or support subteam for further evaluation and resolution. When the problem is resolved, the support team member contacts both the customer and the help desk. The customer is informed of the fix, and the help desk is informed to close the call ticket. All detailed information of the problem is captured and documented by the support team member—it might be useful should the same or similar problem occur in the future.

At first glance, this model might appear to have an extra layer of contact that a customer or organization would not prefer. The additional layer of interaction—the help desk—could present the model as being potentially slow in responding to customer needs. However, when applied to a larger and more complex organization, this model tends to be quite efficient for the customer. The real feature of this model, as referenced in the diagram, is that the help desk functions as a *single point of contact* for the business customer.

Single Point of Contact—*An initial contact individual or organization that clarifies the customer's situation and routes any trouble call to the right support team member or subteam. The single point of contact is often referred to as a hot line or help desk.*

This model is highly effective for larger organizations with very complex core infrastructures. The availability of a help desk frees business customers from having to determine for themselves what their actual system difficulty might be and which support team member would be the best one to contact for help. In a complex technical environment, users are not likely to know the true source of their trouble. Without knowing the true problem, they probably won't know who to turn to in the support team. For large, dynamic organizations, support assignments may alternate and a customer might make initial contact with a support team member who has moved on to a different assignment or focused area of support. If the customer does make contact with some member of the support team, albeit not the one who can be of immediate assistance, the customer could begin to be forwarded from person to person, hoping to eventually find the proper support team member. In this situation, customers often get lost in a phone-forwarding nightmare and rarely feel satisfied. The help desk can be instrumental in seeing that the customer finds the right support team member who can help.

To be effective—that is, to isolate the problem and to route it properly—the help desk must be ready to ask the user various questions about the problem they are reporting. In some cases, a few well-chosen leading questions can resolve the problem during this initial contact. As an aid, the support team can supply the help desk with a list of questions to ask at the beginning of each trouble call. These questions should work like a decision tree, branching into a narrowed area of problem identification. This approach assumes the help desk team has enough technical and process knowledge necessary to properly identify simple problems. Use of leading questions, possible problem identification, and instructions for potential corrective action might be enough to solve the customer's problem. If the situation is not immediately curable, at least it will be more likely to be routed to the most appropriate support team member.

> Well, you think you've seen them all? I received a call from a user who insisted that the SAP application he was using was completely inoperative. The screen wouldn't accept any of his input, and the cursor was bouncing around the screen in fits. Know what the problem was? This customer was an adept 10-key (keypad) user, but his Num Lock key was off. He was maneuvering about the screen with the keypad arrows! Don't get me wrong, he is one of my brightest users. This incident just goes to show that almost anything can happen, and a help desk might have been able to head this one off quickly.

The help desk should also have immediate access to the most current information about the business organization's applications, processes, and support team structure. This approach assures that the most up-to-date information is available at the time the customer call comes in and facilitates the help desk's proper routing of the call. This simple yet frequently overlooked aspect can make the help desk most useful to the customer. If information is always kept current and readily available to the help desk, it will be able to best serve the function for which it was intended. Further, when the help desk has use of the current information described here, it relieves the customer and his or her business department from having to manage it for themselves.

One final model applies directly to the support team's internal team structure. This model explores a concept termed *tiered support*, as shown in Figure 1-3.

Tiered Support—*The internal structuring of a support team into areas of various expertise.*

The premise of tiered support is that the best way to serve customers is to enable them to speak to someone who can best understand the problem as described by the user. This would allow a user to work directly with a support team member that is well-versed in the business processes and the automated functionality that enables them. To use an SAP example, assume that a customer is having a problem executing a business function within SAP screens. Asking that customer to talk directly to a support programmer who manages deeper levels of programmatic function might not be advisable. A better plan might be for the customer to interact with someone who understands how SAP functionality has been applied to the business process and focuses on this aspect of support in a daily manner. This preferred customer/support contact method represents a first-line interaction and is identified as *tier 1 support*. Later, if the problem turns out to be more complex and if the solution resides deeper within the SAP system or programmatic architecture, the tier 1 support team member can involve the programmer who can work through the intricate programmatic details. For example, the programmer might have to modify program code in order to provide a solution, thus providing *tier 2 support*. A benefit of this model is that the customer can work with one support team member who can quickly and easily interpret the customer's situation. The customer doesn't have to try to re-explain

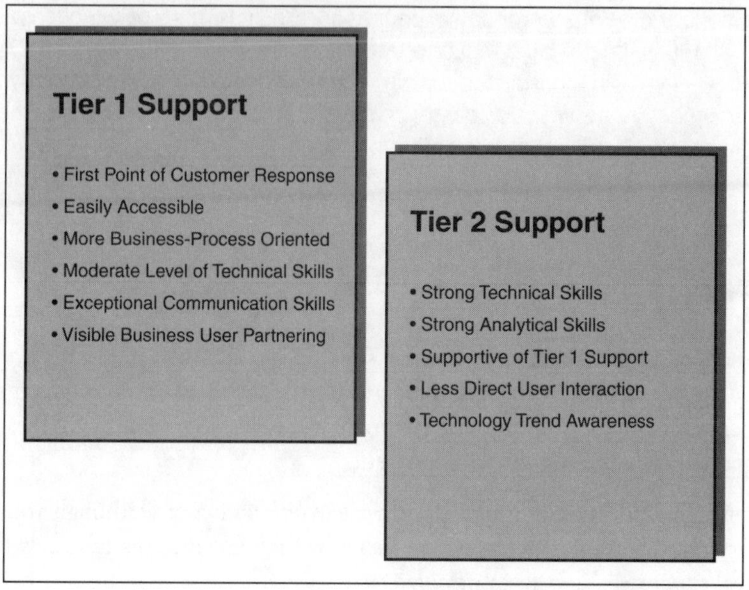

Tier 1 Support

- First Point of Customer Response
- Easily Accessible
- More Business-Process Oriented
- Moderate Level of Technical Skills
- Exceptional Communication Skills
- Visible Business User Partnering

Tier 2 Support

- Strong Technical Skills
- Strong Analytical Skills
- Supportive of Tier 1 Support
- Less Direct User Interaction
- Technology Trend Awareness

FIGURE 1-3

Tiered support model

the situation to a programmer or anyone else on the support team. This helps ensure the customer's interaction is direct, understood, and does not require restating. The customer feels comfortable that the problem was well understood by the tier 1 support team member, and that support team member will ensure the problem is properly resolved.

Business Culture

Regardless of the support model that you have envisioned and developed, you also want to ensure that you've stayed within any explicit or implicit business culture practices. Business culture can sometimes be seen as the main belief system exercised within your company. Typically, these business culture practices or beliefs could include, but not be limited to, the following principles:

◆ Providing leading-edge technology and solutions

◆ Being 100 percent customer driven

◆ Respecting individuals and their contributions

◆ Fostering collaborative business relationships

◆ Thinking in a flexible and progressive manner

Sure, you may hear this sort of rhetoric in your company meetings or read it in a corporate mission statement. However, organizations and the people within them are most comfortable when they receive consistent messages. If the highest level of a company expounds such beliefs, then each organization and individual should strive to operate in a manner that is supportive and reflective of the business directives. Be sure the support team, and you as a member, represent yourself in a manner that promotes and upholds the stated company culture and its philosophies.

The Different Kinds of Support

Now that you have a clearer idea of what support is and how it might be modeled in a support environment, this section focuses on the different ways in which support can operate within an SAP-specific environment. Here, you see how SAP can influence and enhance the support environment.

The common understanding of support is as *technical support*. Although you may be familiar with this support term, notice also how SAP has introduced a new flavor of technical support—*business technical support*.

Business Technical Support—A form of support that focuses on technical application and system environment issues, providing in-depth knowledge and identifiable support of particular business processes used by a business department or user group.

By definition, business technical support subdivides the support team into focused subteams, each providing support to a recognized business area. Working with the construct of SAP's modular design, which you'll learn about more in Chapter 2, each support subteam can focus itself on the needs and activities of a particular part of the business and its use of SAP to meet that team's business objectives. This would include teams focused on Engineering support, Purchasing support, Planning support, and so on. The depth of SAP's functionality in these concentrated business disciplines makes it advisable to develop your support organization using this subteam approach.

In this approach, the business areas now have their direct technical/business support, but you may wonder who is minding the core infrastructure of the system environment within which all business transactions are being conducted? That job falls to an infrastructure support subteam, or in SAP terminology, *basis support*.

Basis Support—The form of support that focuses on the establishment and maintenance of the overall technical environment, including hardware, software applications, and systematic linkages.

Basis support entails maintaining the central processing functions of the SAP environment. This includes monitoring how many users are logged on to the system and what they may be doing, monitoring how the system is responding to the various user sessions and processing requests that are being managed, and guarding against situations where processing slows down noticeably and process failure could occur. Typically, this team's direct customers are the business technical support teams, not the end users. Although end users might be the first to notice processing slow downs or failures, they should be instructed to contact their identified support team member or the help desk. If a problem tends to be related to basis issues, the support team member will act as a liaison to bring the situation to the basis team's attention. This follows the philosophy of the tier 1/tier 2 support interaction.

The basis support team interacts with the database software manufacturer, as well as with the SAP company. This team is also intimately involved in the operation of the physical hardware that powers the environment and determines whether additions and modifications are required to ensure suitable application response time and reliability.

You now understand more about the technical support team and its structure. At this time, you should be aware of a new quasi-support role that is developing through the use of SAP. This is the *business process support* role.

Business Process Support—A form of support that focuses on the methods by which an organization works to tactically and strategically meet its business function. It is directly focused upon business procedure as opposed to technical issues.

As its name suggests, the business process support team concentrates on the processes that the company uses to enable the business people to accomplish their day-to-day activities. This is the sort of support function that is staffed directly within the business teams, not in the technical support team that has been previously discussed. Business organizations sometimes overlook the importance of this highly valuable team. The business process support goal is to enable, maintain, and improve the interactive methods utilized by the business departments. This role is very visible and much needed within an SAP environment. SAP's methods and styles may be significantly different from those applications previously used by a company or factory. To respond to the changes that SAP will bring to a company, business organizations require strategic process experts who can clearly define the business activities and identify the SAP tools and functions that will manage the business needs. The business process team must frequently identify a migration path for a previously used business process, working to find a suitable SAP equivalent. More important, if an SAP equivalent does not seem to exist, the business process team will work to develop a creative solution that can meet the business need while maintaining an integrated linkage into the overall SAP environment. It should be expected that most companies will have some of their own unique methods and processes that are not readily supported by SAP. This could be a unique process developed around an older legacy application, and it could be a process that is entirely unique to the company. When SAP is introduced, these unique processes will need to be migrated somehow, and a qualified team of business support people will need to assess and resolve the situation. The significance of this task should not be underestimated in terms of importance or inherent value to the business areas.

> My initial background was in the area of business process support. I was brought into an SAP project team because I could represent the business activities that had been used in my company. My work with SAP expanded my knowledge of the business area I worked in and helped me gain a combined knowledge of the business and technical aspects required to manage the business activities. My point is that you don't necessarily have to be a technical wizard to make a valuable contribution to an SAP environment.

The Old Face of Support

When the information world was moving at a somewhat slower pace, and computer and software development was managed by fewer suppliers, the support environment was often less time-pressured than today. To the support role, the reduced pressure allowed more time for pondering problems and more time for enabling resolutions. However, in an age of information access at record speeds, any inhibitor to that access can go from inconvenient to annoying to unacceptable in a matter of seconds. Many customers in both the public and private sector have high demands for products and services and a low tolerance for delay.

In the case of a business environment, a down system can mean the loss of significant customer sales (and even future sales) at any given time. A faster business pace equates to more urgency in times of trouble and requires a more expedient response from a support team. This statement is not meant to suggest that support teams from the past have been ineffective or unresponsive. Rather, it is a statement of how the business climate has changed and how each company and the various teams within it must rally together to alleviate problems in record time. Remember your corporate objectives. A slowdown to an internal activity inevitably equates to a slowdown to the external customer.

The Support Makeover

You may wonder whether a rapid business pace implies that support teams are a bunch of firefighters (a common industry buzzword, by the way), leaping into action whenever a dire situation arises seldom with time to take more deliberate steps to long-term goals, be it organizational or personal in nature. On the contrary, the support role today is one of the more involved, more visible, and more opportunistic roles within an organization. The support role, working to fulfill market needs for current technology knowledge, emerges as one of the most advantageous points from which to gain a depth and breadth of desirable business support knowledge. Support teams have the opportunity to work from both process-centric and technical-centric positions. In a situation where an integrated solution like SAP has seen great successes, teams and individuals who have the complementary mix of business and technical knowledge that mirrors the SAP model are poised to achieve success and be in high market demand. Figure 1-4 illustrates this point.

This simple illustration shows the two disciplines of support, each with their large area of focus and expertise. It also shows the area of overlap that enables efficiency rates to increase. At this point of convergence, technical teams become more adept

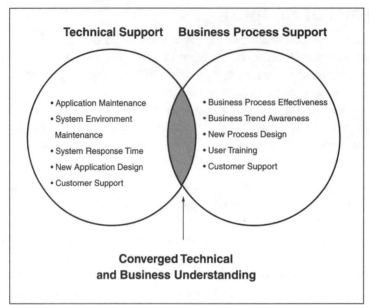

FIGURE 1-4

Process and technical support have a natural area of convergence.

The figure contains:

Technical Support   **Business Process Support**

Technical Support:
- Application Maintenance
- System Environment Maintenance
- System Response Time
- New Application Design
- Customer Support

Business Process Support:
- Business Process Effectiveness
- Business Trend Awareness
- New Process Design
- User Training
- Customer Support

Converged Technical and Business Understanding

in characterizing and resolving technical issues because they have a better understanding of the business process and what sorts of technical solutions will best enable a more effective business process. Equally, through support convergence, the business process teams become more cognizant of developing processes that are systematically efficient and durable, better enabling ongoing functionality that can be easily implemented, stabilized, and supported day after day. Each team has the opportunity to better understand the other's roles and responsibilities, and, through interactive partnering and knowledge sharing, emerge able to represent a business situation from a procedural and technical perspective. That's synergistic and that's of high value in today's business marketplace.

The Elements of Exceptional Support

Everyone wants to excel, and everyone wants to be considered exceptional. I believe, therefore, that the topic of exceptional customer support is most relevant to the subject of this chapter. How can you and your team reach this level of recognition, especially within an environment as complex as SAP? The following points review the core elements of exceptional support:

1. Clearly define your roles and responsibilities. A sure way to enable yourself and your team is to tell your customers what you do. This statement helps customers know who can help them and what they can expect when they have a need.

2. Understand and restate the problem. When a customer has a problem, be sure you clearly understand it and can repeat it to the customer You'd be surprised at how often the customer and the support team member do not communicate effectively. The usual result of this sort of miscommunication is a misinterpretation of the situation and a solution that rarely meets the true need. A good example would be a problem with data entry—both the user and the support individual need to be completely clear what data is being entered, where it is being entered, why it is being entered, and what problem is occurring. If both the customer and the support team member can state the problem in a consistent manner, the problem is well on the way to resolution.

3. Establish an open line of communication. As much as is feasible, be accessible to your customers, both formally and informally. Your customers will appreciate it, and you will establish partnering relationships that tend to be more collaborative. Users tend to be bashful at times, feeling as if they ask stupid questions. They also fear being bothersome. Be open to their inquiries, and encourage their questions. They'll be more apt to contact you, and could be extremely valuable in calling your attention to a potentially serious situation.

4. Know your customer. Understand your customer's basic responsibilities and any relevant conditions and constraints. This information helps you to understand what motivates your customer, what pleases him or her, and what may cause concern or stress.

5. Empathize with your customer. This rule piggy-backs the previous item. Show your customer that you understand the immediate situation. If the customer is angry, you might choose to mirror that anger. In psychological terms, this behavior is called pacing, and it enables you to visibly reflect your customer's attitude and demeanor, initially, in a way that will diffuse any worries or anger. Once the anger is diffused, the two of you can work together to further identify and solve the customer's problem. Sometimes people just need to vent.

6. Show your commitment. Nothing pleases customers more than your willingness to go the extra distance to resolve their problems. The occasional after-hours work and communication shows your customer that you have made their problem yours. The intent is not to manipulate here, but when

you are able to show this sort of conviction, a customer will usually be better satisfied and less likely to cry "wolf."

7. State yourself in 25 words or less. This rule is really an act of courtesy; you should be able to provide an analysis, update, or resolution in terms that are concise and useful. While word count isn't truly at issue here, deliver your information as succinctly as possible. Overused jargon merely confuses, and rarely impresses, your customer.

8. Never let the customer see you sweat. Sure, this rule may sound trite, but it's more a tool of reassurance than a manifestation of your ego. Your display of confidence can encourage your customer that the problems they experience with the system will be solved. Conversely, a customer will undoubtedly magnify any worries and concerns that you express, which is likely to make him or her less productive.

Perhaps you might be thinking: Big deal. Everyone knows these principles are the basis for customer support in any service organization. True, but, if you're considering a migration to SAP and the resulting changes to support, your customers and funding organizations will be nervous, wary, and skeptical that they will be in good care in the new system environment. By going back to the basics and clearly behaving in a traditional support role, you begin to provide assurance that not *everything* is changing. Customers can still rely upon their support team.

What Is Your Contribution?

Everyone has a contribution to make to the support team. The goal of this section is to help you determine how you can use your personal experience and expertise to make the best contribution to the team.

The New Support Person

Regardless of whether your background is technical or business process in nature, you must quickly determine which of your skills can be of greatest initial benefit to the support team. When approaching SAP, your concern may be how much you *don't* understand. The simple fact here is that you are not alone. Even the most experienced SAP user or support team member doesn't know everything about SAP. Practically everyone who interacts with SAP learns something new about it every day. You should seek out formal training opportunities to get a jump start. And, of course, the more you use the application and work within it, the more you will know about it. If you are new to support, the greatest initial contribution you can make is to understand and internalize your responsibility to the customer and organization. If you begin by visibly displaying this attitude, you are well on your way.

> I have a running bet with myself: I'll wager I can go through at least one full day without learning something new about SAP or my job. In four years, I've consistently lost this bet. I might try dog racing instead.

The Veteran Support Person

If you have been in a support role for many years, your task may be as challenging, and sometimes more so, than that of the relative novice. In this veteran's capacity, in both technical or business process support, you must now migrate to a whole new approach of supporting the company's daily, monthly, and yearly business objectives. This readjustment can be difficult; it typically means your expert status will erode, and you will be faced with learning a whole new system, rebuilding your expertise from the ground up. Your greatest immediate contribution, though, is your past experience. You can apply lessons learned with past applications and processes and help to develop and support a strategy that is more effective than ever before. You can use the migration to SAP as an opportunity to throw away ineffective methods that somehow seem to proliferate year after year.

Summary

You and I should now be on the same wavelength regarding the concept of support. You should recognize how the support role functions within an organization, as well as what the support team member's key services and deliverables should be. If this chapter reviewed familiar material, all the better. Support principles and philosophies require regular review to ensure that the support team goals are still understood and that the business needs are still being met. More important, from the SAP perspective, you should now see how the various support roles can differ and how, regardless of your background, you can help your support organization achieve its goals and satisfy its customers.

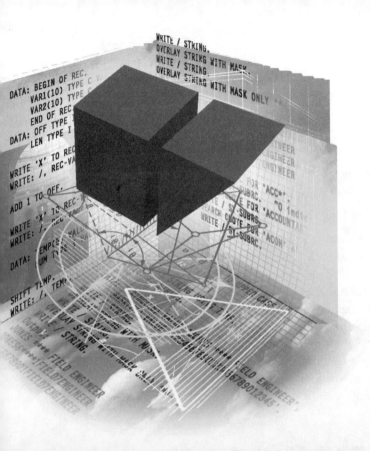

Chapter 2

Understanding Integration within SAP

In This Chapter

- ◆ The Integrated SAP Model
- ◆ Understanding Integrated Data
- ◆ Understanding Integrated Processes
- ◆ The Pros and Cons of Integration

Integration is the feature that gives SAP its power and sets it apart from other business applications. In fact, integration is a theme that appears throughout this book. It's key to your SAP environment. This chapter describes the concept of integration, explains its benefit to you and your business, identifies the core elements of SAP's integration methodology, and explores how integration defines the roles and responsibilities of work teams within an SAP-enabled company. The chapter also discusses how you will benefit from SAP integration, and of what you should beware. And, finally, this chapter will suggest ways that you can work with SAP integration to bolster your overall knowledge of how SAP works and how it will affect the multiple business areas in your company.

The Integrated SAP Model

The SAP application was developed specifically for business processes. Because SAP works in an integrated fashion, a business can manage its complete process flow from one end to the other. This is frequently referred to as the *supply chain*, and SAP is highly tuned to manage these end-to-end processes in its integrated approach.

Supply Chain—the logical and connected business events that mark the cause-and-effect relationship: receiving a customer order, responding by securing material and resources in a company, and eventually delivering to a customer's original specification.

SAP can effectively achieve this supply-chain management through the extensive use of information and process linkages. These linkages act as the keys to the dimensional power of SAP. To support SAP, you need to be keenly aware of this linking strategy and how to use it to support the SAP environment.

SAP has achieved its strength primarily through the development and use of a number of business application units or *modules*. Each logical module facilitates the activities of a particular business team within a company. For example, the company's finance team operates with SAP functionality designed for the team's specific business needs and contained within a dedicated module. The purchasing team works with a module that holds that team's specific functional needs. The same goes for other logical business areas, each with modules dedicated to their specific business needs.

Equipped with an array of business modules, the SAP application assembles them on a common operational platform, or database structure. Each module on the platform can be used independently from the others, as suggested in the previous paragraph, but the true benefit of SAP emerges when modules are used in concert with one another. SAP integration allows the modules to work with one another; each module's output is immediately available to the other modules in the system in a real-time manner. This supports the supply chain concept: activities in one area of the chain will immediately effect activities further along.

Now, the real bonus here is that you are not forced to implement the entire suite of SAP modules to create an effective automated environment. SAP allows you to decide for yourself exactly which modules to utilize within the system, and when. Remember, the modules can work independently of one another if desired. A module's output doesn't necessarily need to be provided to another within the system; the output can be used outside of SAP if required. This is key to allowing businesses to use SAP in an incremental fashion, easing into the use of SAP and disabling previous systematic solutions. This concept is known as *scalability*.

Scalability—SAP is often characterized as being scalable. This description means that SAP's modules can be enabled independently of one another. Businesses have the choice of determining how much or how little SAP functionality they wish to enable at a given time. Additional modules can be added to the environment when the business deems appropriate. A business, therefore, can choose its scale of SAP enabling and integration.

The feature that makes SAP unique in the marketplace is that in addition to being able to stand independently, each of its business modules can also achieve cause-and-effect results across the other modules—across the entire database platform—that work to mirror a business process flow. Figure 2-1 illustrates the different business modules SAP delivers and further illuminates the scalability of SAP. This visual model is inspired by the one that SAP uses to illustrate its integrated module approach.

This illustration should help you understand the overall SAP solution. It's literally a collection of plug-in components that can help manage a business. From this illustration, you can also see the ambition of the SAP application. Not only has SAP developed management solutions for common business areas such as materials management, finance, and warehouse management, but it also provides modules for plant management and human resources to actually manage business assets and the business workforce. Include the remaining modules, and you can essentially run an *entire* business with this single integrated application.

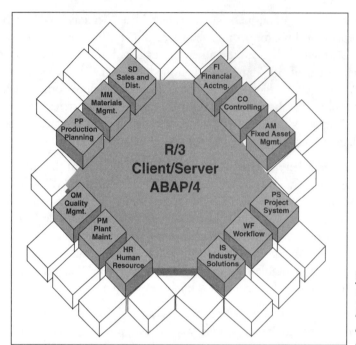

FIGURE 2-1

The SAP Architecture— business modules assembled on a common database platform.

From the support perspective, remember that you must understand SAP's functional integrated philosophy to know what you are supporting and the best approach to supporting SAP. The following section takes you deeper into the structure of the integrated elements. Understanding this information is an important prerequisite to working within the SAP framework.

Understanding Integrated Data

By definition, *integrated data* is information that is linked by a common element or elements, easily referenced and retrievable from a central data repository. SAP manages its integrated approach through the extensive use of a large database that is broken into logical tables of information. The two major types of tables in SAP relevant to this discussion are tables of *master data* and tables of *transactional data*.

Master Data Table—A table of business information that describes the more static attributes of a business concern.

Transactional Data Table—*A table of business information that captures and describes the unique combination of master and situational data, tracing a business's executed activity.*

The terms, master data and transactional data, don't actually provide the technical definition of the SAP tables but, rather, define the type of data that is stored within the tables. You'll better understand the differences between the two data types shortly. First, it is useful for you to understand how data tables are linked within SAP. Each table has identifiable elements that act as hooks into the table of information. Many tables within SAP share similarly defined data hooks that provide for logical informational linkages. These hooks are defined as *key data elements*.

Key Data Element—*The identified data elements that act as reference points into a data table and can be used to join information from other related data tables.*

The key data elements act as informational hooks by which you will navigate through the database in search of additional related information. One table within SAP might have an element such as a part number. The table it resides in has information that pertains to the part number and supports the activity the table serves within a business module. A table in the Finance module might have a part number as a key field and also contain financial information about the part number such as cost, key accounts, settlement rules, and so forth. That information tells more about the part number from a financial perspective. The part number is also a key element in a table that stores purchase order information. In that table, the part number is the key and additional data is available in the table that describes purchase order activity concerning the part number. This would be a data table that could be found in the Materials Management module. The payoff here is that the financial table can be accessed by the part number as the key identifier. Then, the part number can be used as the same key to retrieve purchase order information in the purchase order table. The result is that both sets of supporting business data can be retrieved, sorted, and reported on the same key element. The key elements will actually help you find information in what is sometimes referred to as *data mining*. The logical table links take you from one table of information to another table of related information and allow you to *mine* deep within SAP for the data you seek.

You need to understand this so-called data mining and how key elements will help you in your efforts because data research will become one of the more prevalent activities you will engage in as you support the SAP environment and its users. Your role is one of data caretaker, and you will continually need to delve deep into the SAP data tables and retrieve the information that helps solve business problems or characterizes troublesome situations within the application. This book doesn't expect you to understand the intricacies of data element properties such as how key data elements are defined in tables, but you should at least be able to recognize the different characteristics of the integrated data—master data, transactional data, and key data elements. If you want to learn more about data structures and properties and how to effectively create and use them in programming and reporting, refer to Prima Publishing's *Introduction to ABAP/4 Programming for SAP, Revised and Expanded Edition.* The important point here is that you understand the existence of key data elements, that they will link tables of related data, and that these links will enable to you search and retrieve information within SAP. The data, therefore, has been stored to work in an integrated fashion with other data within SAP.

Master Data

The master data is the static information that the SAP modules draw upon to execute systematic activity. The master data is where a company loads its profile of business information, which includes the company's organizational data such as entity definition, geography, native language information, financial chart of accounts, and warehouse identification. Organizational data is the virtual thumbprint of the company, and it's referred to as master data.

Another component of master data is the company's unique product or service information. This information includes the identification of part numbers, product bills of material, costs of goods and services, and engineering specifications. The company's product catalog is also captured as master data in SAP.

The master data also specifies the company's business relationships; for example, its material suppliers, subcontracted manufacturing or sales sites, and customer information. The internal storage of the company's business relationship profile will join the other information to round out the company's business information. Again, this is considered master data and is stored in master data tables within SAP. Table 2-1 is an abbreviated listing of fields in a master data table. The records reflect part numbers stored in SAP.

Table 2-1 *Master Data Records in SAP Table MARA (Material Master)*

MANDT	MATNR	ERSDA	ERNAM	LAEDA	AENAM
099	1234-0373BC	10/31/1995	BATCHUSER	01/23/1998	SNEADS
099	1234-4148BC	11/18/1995	BATCHUSER	09/19/1997	SNEADS
099	9000-47A	09/01/1995	ADMINIST	01/23/1998	SMITHL
099	9001-B6A9	09/13/1995	ADMINIST	01/23/1998	SMITHL

The SAP naming conventions in the columns in Table 2-1 signify:

◆ Client number (MANDT)

◆ Material number (MATNR)

◆ Created on (ERSDA)

◆ Created by (ERNAM)

◆ Last change (LAEDA)

◆ Last changed by (AENAM)

 NOTE

German is SAP's native language because the application is designed in Germany. Although much of SAP's content has been modified for the countries using it, some information remains in German. In Table 2-1, you can see SAP's field names are actually abbreviations for the German words that translate as shown above. Don't worry. You'll get used to those pretty quickly.

Besides learning a bit of German, you'll no doubt find some fun in these naming conventions. Abbreviations are not always the most politically-correct names you might encounter in any language. Wait until you and your team find the KAKA transaction; it's always a crowd pleaser.

To summarize: The company's master data is stored in SAP's master data tables, which are a collection of related business information that is used during business processing. Within each table, certain data elements have been identified as key elements, which means they will be used in accessing additional related, or linked, business data in other tables. Figure 2-2 reinforces this concept.

This example shows that the key data acts as the internal references—those hooks—to additional data within the database. The linked data tables further describe the detailed information about an aspect of a company's business. The key data enables you to quickly find the information you seek, or that is needed at the time of a business transaction, by briskly locating it within the data structures. Later in the book, you will see how the key data works in your favor and, by understanding key data, you'll be able to better support the environment and customer. It goes back to data mining—the faster and more effective you are at locating and tracing information within SAP, the better service you'll provide to your customers.

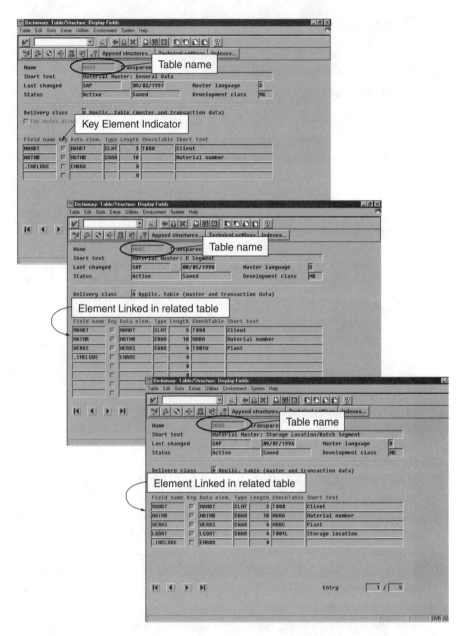

FIGURE 2-2 *SAP key data elements link to other related table structures.*

Master data is the core of the business's information pool. It acts as the pivotal point by which business activity begins. Every SAP business module contains master data. It is static in nature, meaning it will not change very frequently. Master data is the core collection of information with which business transactions are conducted.

Transactional Data

Transactional data represents activities initiated within the various business areas of the company. It is the history of your company's day-to-day business and is fundamental in monitoring business progress and trends and in providing historical audit trails. When the business users perform an activity within SAP that uses master data to effect a transaction—launching an order for material, receiving new material, disbursing funds for material received—the result of that activity is recorded in the transactional data. In SAP, the transactional data is captured in the form of *business documents*.

Business Document—SAP terminology that describes the recording of a business transaction by means of creating a record of the information and conditions specified at the time of posting.

Table 2-2 displays an abbreviated listing of the fields in transactional data table entries.

Table 2-2 *Transactional Data Records in SAP Table EKPO (Purchasing Document Item*

MANDT	EBELN	EBELP	AEDAT	MATNR	BUKRS
099	1235789901	00001	12/01/1997	1234-0373BC	0001
099	1235789902	00001	12/01/1997	1234-4148BC	0001
099	1235789908	00003	12/07/1997	9000-47A	0001
099	1235789910	00002	01/23/1998	9001-B6A9	0001

This table extract, using SAP naming conventions, provides the following information:

- ◆ Client number (MANDT)
- ◆ Purchasing document (EBELN)
- ◆ Item (EBELP)
- ◆ Change date (AEDAT)

◆ Material number (MATNR)

◆ Company code (BUKRS)

The business document in this table was created at the time an order was placed for a specific part number. It combines master data (MATNR) with situational information (AEDAT) to establish a record of activity, which is captured in the business document (EBELN). So the first line in Table 2-2 tells you that part number 1234-0373BC was ordered on 12/01/1997; the purchase order (business document) that records the order is 1235789901. All the transactional data in this example is stored in the EKPO table—a transactional data table—in SAP. For the discussion following, I'll continue to use a purchase order activity as an example to illustrate how the transactional data is used through a business process.

The information in Table 2-2 is only a portion of the information that describes the business document; it is shown in abbreviated form here solely for illustration. Other master data has been assembled to further define the purchase order business transaction—supplier, quantity, cost, pricing conditions, and so on. The result is a uniquely numbered business document—the purchase order. The other data you might seek about this document is available in other linked data tables.

 NOTE

The data field MATNR is a key field between the two sample tables, MARA and EKPO.

Continuing with the purchase order example and further illustrating the creation of transactional data, assume the goods that have been ordered are delivered, and the receiving team references the purchase order as a means to verify and validate the supplier's delivery. This verification process ensures that the proper goods have arrived in the requested quantity and by the approved delivery method. If all checks out, the goods are received in the factory, capturing unique information of the quantity of materials received, the date of receipt, the location where they were received, and the delivery method. This information is captured in another uniquely numbered business document—the material document.

Material Document—A record of a material transaction within SAP. Examples are inventory receipts, movements, and issues.

Later in the example process, when payment is to be made to the original material supplier, the finance team reviews the purchase order and material document to verify the transactions and confirm that goods were received. Finance then enters unique information of the material being paid for, the quantity, the total payment amount, and any applied discounts. This activity is captured and recorded in a third type of uniquely numbered document—the accounting document.

Accounting Document—A record of a financial transaction, for example, an issue of funds, receipt of funds, or transfer of funds.

These examples depict only one type of business flow but are a useful way to explain how the linked data comes into play throughout the sequential chain of events, or supply chain. SAP provides many interface screens that enable general users to easily query and display the information within the tables but will do so through the use of easy-to-understand screen displays. In contrast, the support team must often access the same data, but through use of the actual tables directly as opposed to the front-end screens that business users might utilize, to retrieve and review such data. The transactional data that is recorded during the business steps is done in a way that utilizes key data and table linkages. As this example shows, the original purchase order document is a key element that can be used to retrieve specific purchasing, receiving, and finance data. The example also shows how this data storage method and sequential processing provide a detailed audit trail of the business activity.

One other item to note is that the volume of transactional data will dwarf the volume of master data. Remember, these transactional data records are created at the time of a saved, or posted, business transaction. Transactional data quickly grows to a size and proportion that requires it to be managed (archived) in order to preserve system response times and efficient business analysis (see Chapter 24). From your support perspective, these data concepts—master data, transactional data, and key data elements—are important because you will need to review and retrieve this data from the database on a regular basis. You must understand the data's location and linkages to be certain that you are capturing the right data in the most efficient manner.

Understanding Integrated Processes

At this point, you have a good understanding of SAP's integrated structure and its method of data structuring, storage, and referencing. It's time to further apply this knowledge to the actual business processes. Figure 2-3 should help you apply the models and terms you have learned in a way that might make more sense to you and the business environment you will support.

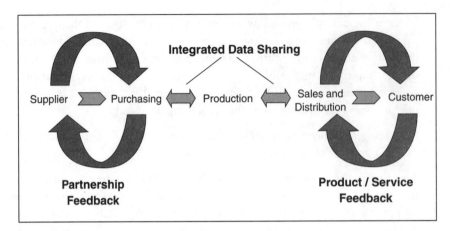

FIGURE 2-3 *The SAP Integrated Business Flow Model*

Figure 2-3 depicts the common flow of business activity that you would expect to see in any successful organization—supply chain management. This figure shows how information flows through a business or production facility. The double arrows in the middle show how the business processes share each other's information during the process. The two ends of the flow show additional information loops that involve the external customers and suppliers in the integrated information chain. In the past, this information flow was achieved by linking, or daisy-chaining, individual applications in a complex, interfaced environment. This approach typically required master data to be manipulated or massaged in some way, making the data from one application acceptable and readable by the next. In the SAP approach, the master data and transactional data are all defined and stored with consistent attributes throughout the system, which allows effective business flow to occur more easily than ever before. Previous application environments might have the same data element defined in different ways, and by different names, within the different applications.

The other benefit here is that, through the integrated system and using integrated data structures, business transactions and processes occur in real time. In other words, at the time master data is created and saved, it is immediately available for use by a business team or user. For example, during a phone conversation with a user, you could resolve some sort of data inconsistency within SAP and the user can provide immediate verification of your actions. Now that's effective support! Equally, transactional data that is posted during the course of a business process is immediately available for use and analysis elsewhere within the process. Often the posting of transactional data will effect real-time, often automatic, responses elsewhere within the system and process flow. This was exemplified in the previous illustration of a purchase order flow and how the information posted within it, and in response to it, became immediately available to the other business areas. This flow means that a business will rarely be required to wait for information to be reviewed, manipulated, and passed along to other dependent areas or applications.

One other key feature of SAP is that it is capable of providing front-end data validation and verification. This means data entered in a specific input screen can be checked for proper formatting, as well as against a list of valid values—a *check table*. In addition, some screens can be designed to require certain information be entered before allowing the data to be saved and posted; these are referred to as *required entries*. Although stand-alone application systems can also perform a similar function, the situation can be problematic if the data requirements and formatting of one application do not match the requirements and formatting of another. At the time of an interfaced data transfer, inconsistencies can occur, usually resulting in corrupt data or unwritable data records. With SAP, front-end validation ensures data consistency and rule adherence from the beginning, allowing immediate use throughout the integrated environment.

The Pros and Cons of Integration

Integration, as you can see, is at the hub of this activity. This chapter concludes with an example of how integration within SAP works well, and, conversely, how it can work against you. This example refers to a typical business activity: the purchasing of some goods.

The process usually starts when an order is received from a customer. Upon entry of that order, SAP's internal business processes recognize the order and create the need for material or services to satisfy the demand. This step triggers the purchasing department to procure the necessary materials. The purchase order posts visibility of a pending change to material levels within a company's factory, thus alerting the warehouse and finance teams. More importantly, the purchase order also informs the production team that material will be arriving soon to be used in the production process. Upon receipt of the material that was ordered, the receiving activity notifies the factory that material is now available, notifies the purchasing department that the pending order has been received, and notifies the finance team that payment to the supplier is now due. During all phases of this activity, the team that manages the customer's order can track the progress of meeting the demand by witnessing the activities being recorded within the system and can ensure that the customer's order will be delivered on time. To this end, the factory works as an integrated team, using integrated data, all within the same integrated business application. This is a simple illustration of supply chain management within an integrated application environment. The process described takes a customer order, creates a product or other deliverable good, and converts that to a sale for the company.

Despite the clear benefits of this integrated application, there can also be a negative impact if the integration is not properly understood and managed. Because all the activity takes place within a single application, everyone is working with common master data and transactional data. You'll see how processing is immediate and how common data is used across the integrated processes and what happens when these principles are mismanaged.

At the start of the process, when the customer order is received, the purchasing department launches into action to procure the necessary materials. However, the engineering team has recently flagged this material as obsolete (possibly even deleting the part number from the database). The business cannot launch the material order because the master data is in a state that prevents any progress. But the customer is waiting and the clock is ticking.

Now assume the purchase order does get created and is communicated to the supplier. Imagine that the purchase order that was launched is later deleted for some reason, but the supplier, being a good supplier, ships the material. Unfortunately, the warehouse will not be able to receive the material because it references an order that is no longer usable in the system.

Finally, suppose that the finance team enacts payment of funds to the material supplier. In this case, however, the supplier has been marked as no longer used by your company; therefore, the payment transaction will not be able to complete and the supplier won't get paid. As you can see, the scenario can get quite messy in a hurry.

The illustration here is provided to show how information in an integrated environment must be highly respected. The data must be managed very carefully and deliberately. One action in the system can have an immediate reaction elsewhere in the system. You'll likely become involved when these principles are overlooked and processes are adversely affected.

> Thus ends the days of "that's not my application's fault, it was yours."
> 'Nuff said?

One other point needs to be made regarding the real-time posting of information. As you know, data entered into SAP becomes real and usable immediately. In the days of linked applications, some data-migrating interfaces might have operated at specific times during the day or night. Although this timing was frequently a hindrance to downstream processes, it did provide one sort of safety net—inaccurate data or transactions could often be caught and filtered out of the application's data file before the information was passed along to the next transaction. SAP does not have this safety net. Provided all screen and field validations are passed, the information flows as soon as it is posted. Therefore, information must be entered as accurately as possible. Any errors will require manual handling within SAP and will leave evidence of their presence.

Although the examples of mismanaged data presented here might seem a bit extreme, they're real accounts. Of prime importance is the fact that in the SAP environment data flows within a single integrated system. Rarely are there any "filters" that might massage data from one business process to the next, as may have been the case in any previous environment made up of various interfaced business applications. If the integrated flow is broken in any way, the result will be most unwelcome.

> Understanding the whole concept of integration gave me a good amount of confidence. It's a base tenet of SAP philosophy and works nicely with the concept of supply-chain management. The terms in this chapter probably lend themselves to concepts you work with daily. If so, feel good that this portion of SAP is already familiar to you. It won't seem so cold and strange, and you'll begin to look for other parallels to your current business systems or processes. It's a good start.

Summary

Now you understand how SAP has been assembled from the modular business designs to the integration of these modules to the core of how the data within the application relates to its components. You've also seen how this integration works to enable the flow of the business that you support. Most importantly, you realize that, although integration is a true benefit, it can also be the source of business nightmares when not properly managed. In the next chapter, you will learn how this integrated architecture can influence the support environment.

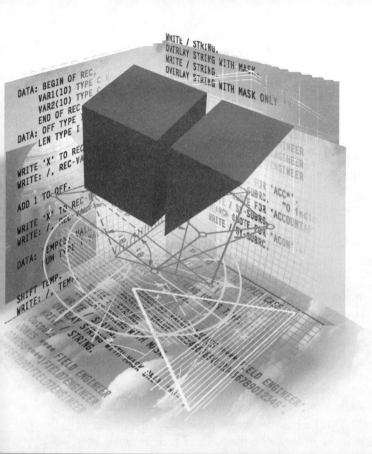

Chapter 3

Integrating the Support Organization

In This Chapter

- ◆ Developing an Integrated Support Team
- ◆ Developing Support Partnerships
- ◆ Developing User Partnerships
- ◆ Developing Yourself

This chapter continues the explanation of integration and SAP that began in Chapter 2. This time, however, the focus is on how SAP's integration methodology can influence the actual structure of the support team. Within the context of integration, you'll see how to assemble a support team and learn how that team can best serve the SAP application environment as well as the business people who use it. Integration within SAP is so pervasive that it actually guides how the business and support teams structure their internal organizations; you'll see how and why that will occur.

The chapter begins by showing how a company's business teams might organize themselves in a way that reflects the SAP modular architecture introduced to you in Chapter 2 (see Figure 2-1). The business teams' organizational structure—how they subdivide to manage business processes—is fundamental to determining how your support team will assemble itself to service these business teams. With your support team's core competencies and customer service goals in mind, you'll see how your support team can align its service approach to uphold the support team charter, which will maintain the SAP environment and should serve the overall business teams' charter. In the end, you'll find that working within the philosophy of integration will achieve more than developing organizational structures in your company; it will develop a core understanding within you. You will understand more about SAP and more about the business you support when you align the system and the business in a logical and effective way.

How SAP integration drives the formation of business teams is of tremendous benefit to all members of a business organization, from service-level employees to their managers. SAP brings much change to an organization, and all people who use it—strategically and tactically—need to understand what the potential changes entail and affect. It's one thing for a service team to understand SAP and how to manage its aspects of use, but it is just as important that a guiding management team understands how to properly apply resources to maintain the SAP environment and how to make the best strategic use of SAP's business solutions. In short, everyone needs to get involved.

Developing an Integrated Support Team

Understanding how SAP integrates master and transactional data can help you understand how to organize your team. From the explanation of the SAP business module in Chapter 2, you probably began to realize that business teams would form around each module. Your finance team works with the FI (Finance) module, the planning team works with the PP (Production Planning) module, the sales team works with the SD (Sales & Distribution) module, and so on. When a business implements SAP, the business may need to realign its workforce to the logical construction of SAP. (Part II of this book discusses realignment in more detail.) Working within the modules is what makes SAP scalable. Recall that scalability is the concept that allows a company to implement selected portions of SAP as the company sees fit. A company should only enable the SAP modules that will be properly managed and supported within the company's organizational structure.

Just as the business teams align to their respective SAP modules, your support team will serve the activities of each business team and the SAP module each team will use on a daily basis. The analysis of the integrated data flow in Chapter 2 demonstrated how business areas must work together to ensure smooth information flow within the system. The support team will establish linkages, or partnerships, to the different teams it supports. These linkages enable the business teams and the respective support team members to work together in a way that fosters proper use and support of SAP functionality. The topic of building partnerships with your customers is discussed a little later in this chapter. First, however, it is best to focus on the other partnership you must cultivate before you can satisfy your end users, that is, your internal team partnership. An internal team partnership occurs *within* the support team itself. The team needs to be sure it interacts well and that internal support team activity is understood by each team member.

If you're adept at reading between the lines, you can see this discussion involves the age-old key to success—*communication*. Integration applies not only to the business teams; it applies equally, and often more, to the support team. Some of the most critical communication that occurs in an SAP environment occurs within the support team. If the different support team members are not aware of each others' activities in the system, the system will surely fail.

In Figure 3-1, you can see how the lines of communication flow among the business teams and how their communication flows into the support team. More directly, notice how the support team members need to share their knowledge and activity with each other and how that information can then be communicated back to the business teams.

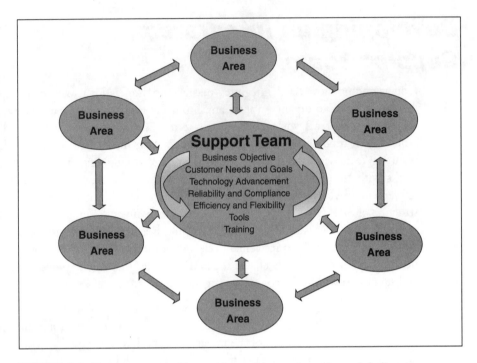

FIGURE 3-1 *The support team should communicate well between its members and also its customers.*

The task is to assemble a support team that can best serve the using community, enable the support team with the proper application access and tools, locate the support team in a communication-friendly environment, and ensure the support team is using a variety of information-sharing tools and forums. All players on the support team must understand how their actions (and the subsequent systematic actions) can affect results, both positive and negative, throughout the SAP environment. The following sections provide further detail.

Using a Common Terminology Language

The best start you and your team can have is to use the same terminology, especially to describe SAP elements and concepts. If you say the MSEG data table requires attention and possible reorganization, the other members of your team need to know what you mean and how the action, in this integrated data environment, might affect other business customers. You'll discuss bringing the system down, flushing the buffers, transporting changes, modifying the system profile, and so many other terms and phrases that represent SAP actions. SAP terminology abounds in your support teams, and you'll want to make every effort to help your team talk fluently within its own ranks.

Because you're among peers with the same duty, the use of application-specific language is rampant, but it actually enables a support team to converse more precisely and effectively. You might even get a thrill out of it as it helps you hone your SAP expertise. Understanding SAP terminology will make you better informed of the various activities you will support. Just remember, switch back to regular English when you work with your customers. Some terminology is appropriate during customer discussions, but keep those discussions simple and as business-relevant as possible.

> I quickly found that I could carry on a conversation with a peer using mainly SAP terms, buzzwords, and acronyms. I was communicating effectively, and my peer understood what I was saying. Learning to use SAP terminology might not sound important, but it further develops of your SAP fluency.

Establishing Business Support Assignments

To the greatest extent possible, you'll want to establish a support team that will mirror the method in which SAP has developed its logical areas and the business teams that are using them. This approach makes for clean and easy-to-identify boundaries. Nevertheless, in some situations the best way to manage a module, or some of its functionality, might be to further divide the activities within an SAP module and develop multiple subteams to manage those segregated activities. For example, SAP's Materials Management (MM) module contains activities such as procurement, inventory management, and engineering specifications. These activities can easily represent three different, distinct, and sizable business teams. Depending on the size and scope of the business you support, the volume of activity might be more than one individual or subteam can effectively handle. It might make sense to parse the activities into smaller functional portions than what has been presented within SAP. But be sure you can determine the logical separations within the module, as well as the interdependencies—sometimes referred as *hand-off points*. If this sort of module parsing is enabled, be sure there are no gaps in function use or support within the overall module. Table 3-1 better describes this concept.

Table 3-1 Logical Division of Functions within the Same SAP Module

Module: MM—Materials Management (Business Area)

Part Data/Specs	Purchasing	Inventory
Basic Part Data	Purchasing Part Data	Warehouse Data
Engineering Drawings	Information Records	Inventory Levels
Bills of Material	Supplier Data	Replenishment Triggers

From this table, you can see how all the information relates to the global module classification of Materials Management. You can also see the logical subdivision of the information within the module. Whether a single team can manage all the information depends on the overall size of the business. However, through this illustration of logical subdivisions within the MM module, you could feasibly assign three different business groups, and the compliment of three support groups, to manage all of the functionality within the module.

Workload balancing and separation of duties are all at issue here. First, the workload must be distributed in a way that business people can successfully manage the activities within an area of SAP, and a support team can successfully manage that group of business people. If the task list is too great, there will likely be an overload of work task and support effort. Second, if a person was in a position to manage all aspects within the MM module, they could essentially set up their own materials, purchase them, and receive them. They could even arrange for materials to be delivered to an alternative address—their home, for instance. This is an area of business control which could raise questions during a company audit. For this reason, I believe the MM module provides a good example of how activity within an SAP module could require further segregation—both from the perspectives of balancing and separation of duty.

Controlling Access and Tool Use

For the support team to perform its duties, it needs proper access to the system and the proper tools to support the environment. The use of the word *proper* implies that access and tools should be granted to the extent that they enable a support team member to maintain the portion of SAP for which the team member is responsible.

This ensures that the support team manages who has access to which information within SAP and when each of the SAP tools should be used. This is important because, in an integrated environment, you know that one action is likely to cause one or more reactions. Just as it is necessary for business people to concentrate on their area of business focus, so too must the support team: each member must manage their area of focus. Therefore, it is useful to thoughtfully limit access to SAP within the support team. One approach is to delegate any particular tool's use to a single support team member or limited number of members. This plan ensures points of control and makes potential system and data conflicts more visible and avoidable. The following support-level activities should be considered good candidates for control and limited access:

◆ SAP logon administration
◆ Transporting changes
◆ Customization
◆ System parameters
◆ Locked data entries
◆ Job scheduling

Again, the idea is not to keep the support team from performing its duties, nor is the intent to overload certain team members with global task maintenance. However, you can avoid many collisions of functionality and data by having strategically enabled control points within the group.

Also refrain from establishing control for control's sake. It becomes easy to assign each part of SAP to a different support team member, but you can end up with a fragmented, nonintegrated support methodology. You should strive to allow as much common access to all team members whenever possible. This is another area of balance and tuning within SAP: establish control where appropriate, but understand that controls can limit the actions of some support team members.

If too much control is introduced, the support team might find it frustrating and unable to make good use of SAP's tools. On the other hand, support team members are usually quite adept at finding other methods to access information within a systematic environment. Sometimes asserting too much control over a support team can result in even less control within the system.

Establishing a Physical Environment

As the old adage goes—location, location, location. Believe it or not, physical environment becomes an important point of team effectiveness and synergy. But in some respects, the importance of physical location is a difficult point to sell. Instant electronic communication tools, virtual conference rooms, and telecommuting enable team members to function as a unit without being physically adjacent to one another. In many business environments, though, a great deal of information sharing occurs between individuals during informal encounters in hallways, cafeterias, and cubicles. This doesn't negate electronic communication and virtual teams, but please give physical co-location every consideration. You may already understand how electronic communication limits informal and spontaneous interaction, but it may also reduce the actual bonding that a good team needs. Physical interaction, especially in a service-oriented organization, helps the team members work together and develop a better sense of shared results. You and your team should be located in a comfortable environment. Position yourselves in connected cubicles, expanded office areas, or adjoining floor space. The key here is to allow immediate, impromptu information sharing—it's a vital support ingredient.

If your business uses cubicles, see if you can get lower walls. You'll be surprised how many times you'll need to pop up and share something with one or more of your colleagues. Lower cubicle walls also enable you to see who is in the immediate area if you need to forward a call or quickly ask the help of a more experienced peer. And sometimes just seeing a colleague can remind you to discuss an important topic. Expanded office areas are extremely functional and sometimes referred to as "bullpens." This type of environment tends to be less private, but it encourages team members to turn to one another and discuss important activities. When possible, try to include a round table for informal meetings. Adjoining floor space also encourages open discussion. There can be many situations when overhearing a bit of information helps support team members recognize a potentially troublesome problem. Being within earshot of some discussion or activity, support team members can react in a timely manner to minimize damage and disruption to their business team's activity.

The location models in Figures 3-2, 3-3, and 3-4 apply the concept of SAP module construction when arranging the work spaces of support team members. These are three of the most common physical environments for support teams. The example shown in Figure 3-2 could be considered the best physical arrangement; it allows a team close proximity for communication while providing a relatively quiet and private work area for activities that require higher levels of concentration. The examples in Figures 3-3 and 3-4 are fine for open and informal communication, but might be more noisy and distracting to some individuals.

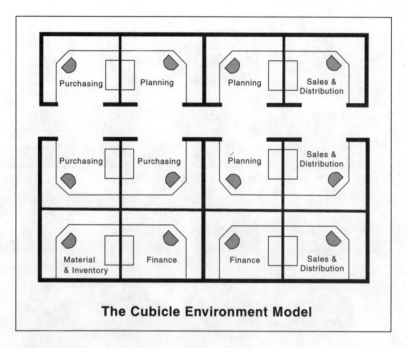

The Cubicle Environment Model

FIGURE 3-2 *Support Team Location Model 1—The Cubicled Environment*

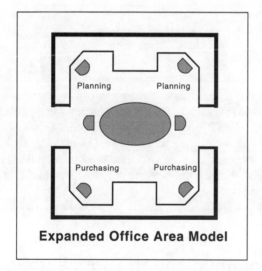

Expanded Office Area Model

FIGURE 3-3

Support Team Location Model 2—The Expanded Office Area

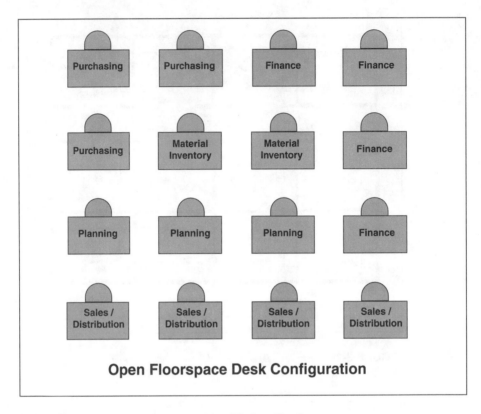

FIGURE 3-4 *Support Team Location Model 3—The Open Floor Space*

Whenever possible, involve yourself and team members in the development of a physical layout plan. Face it, you're going spend a lot of time together, and you're going to be accomplishing a lot together. The physical environment can be a positive influence on your work and the work of the team. Let your wishes and ideas be known to others who may be responsible for providing physical work spaces.

Developing Good Communication Tools and Forums

In addition to engaging in impromptu communication, team members should meet on a regular basis to discuss support issues in a more formal setting. Team meetings provide an opportunity for all members to assemble and work through larger issues that might affect the entire team or their customers. Team meetings provide an opportunity to harness the experience and knowledge of the whole team in a way that enables everyone to learn something and walk away wiser. Meetings, as you know, can become mundane and begin to lose effectiveness if not properly mediated. Be sure you work from a published agenda and avoid tangents that do not add value to the subject matter. If the quality of your meetings degrades, team members will stop attending, thus defeating the entire purpose of the communication.

In addition, you can use e-mail and voicemail messages to stay in touch with team members, but use these two mediums with discretion. *Junk mail* is easy to publish and proliferate. Check with your team to ensure the information that is being forwarded is useful and concise.

Web sites are extremely useful in communicating information. These days, more than ever, Web presence is being fine-tuned for a variety of business uses. In an intradepartmental Web site, be sure you include hot topics such as:

◆ System status

◆ News flashes and updates

◆ Projects and initiatives

◆ Team members and their support assignments

◆ Departmental documentation

◆ Links to business team Web sites

◆ Feedback forms

◆ Search utilities

Using Web sites can be as simple as installing a Web browser. And information can be published to one Web site rather than tripling efforts by saving it in a file folder, sharing it for other users to review, and possibly sending several e-mails as well.

Finally, make use of a commercial pop-up type of communication tool such as Microsoft Chat. This utility acts likes a virtual note that you can send to and display on someone else's monitor. It's another useful way to provide quick information, queries, and even a bit of fun to lighten the day.

Developing Support Partnerships

Now your team is in place and has all the right tools to do the job. How can you and your team leverage each others' roles into partnerships that further integrate and empower the whole group? This section describes how you can combine various individual technical expertise with business process knowledge, all within your support team. The sum of this synergistic knowledge will far outweigh each member's independent contribution.

Recall how a support team can develop Tier 1 and Tier 2 team members, and you'll understand that the major ingredient for knowledge synergy already exists within a support team. Figure 3-5 illustrates how the Tier 1–Tier 2 example from Chapter 1

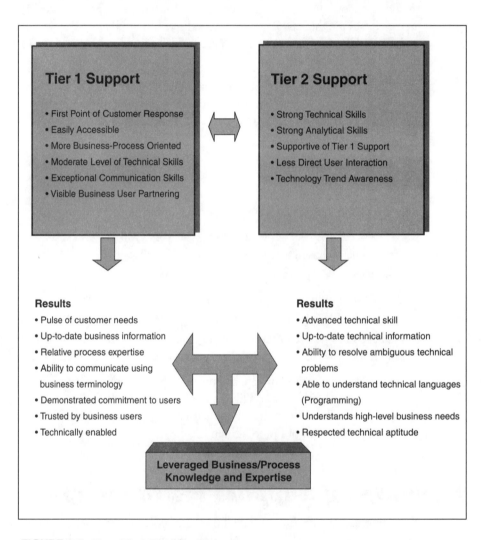

FIGURE 3-5 *Tier 1–Tier 2 Knowledge Sharing*

results in greater communication and improved knowledge development within the support team.

In this manner, the support team members are able to exchange vital and complementary information and insight. In fact, your team members will *want* to know more about all aspects of the environment they support so that they feel more confident in the actions they take. It's natural for support team members to ask one another about business experiences and technical solutions that work to better enable the system environment and the users working with it. The result is a team of technical experts who work to improve their process and technical knowledge, sharpening their ability to design solutions with business sense, technical finesse, and ease of use in mind. A support team that works within this setting encourages communication and mentorship, and is especially effective when a new member joins the team.

It's easy to see, then, that in collaborative efforts, the team's win is each member's win and vice versa. Conversely, if one aspect of the team fails, the whole team fails. This can be called *team ego*, and it's very effective. Essentially, when the team functions as a cohesive unit, members step forward to help achieve and exceed the goals set before them. Even more importantly, if a member or segment of the team is faltering, other members come to help, sometimes to their own detriment, to ensure that the whole team is as successful as it can be. It's an infectious attitude, and it really works.

Developing User Partnerships

User partnerships are extremely beneficial and fruitful, especially in a complex environment powered by SAP. Users tend to put the system through rigors you only wish you could achieve in a test environment. They're really a superb team of test technicians disguised as a business team. They have the propensity to find and experiment with just about every button, check box, and executable routine within SAP—and SAP gives them plenty to choose from! Their daily activities can be a great benefit to you, helping you better understand what they need to achieve and how they will use SAP to do so.

Your first goal is to become known by your users. Don't hide at your desk every day. Walk around the area they occupy and understand what they are doing. You'll be surprised by the number of questions they'll ask when you stroll about in their area. Usually, these are questions they might not think to call you about. You'll become aware of potential problems, or solutions, that you might not have otherwise encountered, and they'll feel good knowing that you'll make yourself immediately available to them in this way. As you spend more time with your users, you'll become aware of common trouble areas they may be experiencing. This feedback can pinpoint a problem with the application or give you the opportunity to suggest additional training materials or forums that can help to clear up certain aspects of the application. When the opportunity presents itself, ask users how they like SAP. Ask what takes them the most effort to achieve or how *they* might make the system or accompanying process better.

> There is no such thing as a stupid user. If someone's action caused a problem in the system, then first look to yourself—you may have left a functionality unchecked that perhaps should have been restricted from use.

While you're spending this time with your users, be sure to tell them how helpful they are to you. Most users, especially newer SAP users, express apologies for "bothering you so much" or asking "such stupid questions." Let them know that you appreciate their questions. After all, these users are providing your livelihood.

It's true that they will do things that might seem to defy logic and common sense. However, it's a safe bet that some contributing factor either enabled or led them to their actions. Your role is to understand why something has been done within SAP, especially if it has negative results, and work with the user and others to rectify the situation. Never, never, never openly admonish or embarrass anyone. First, it's clearly not in alignment with your support organization's creed, Second, such behavior will invariable fly in the face of any basic company principles or corporate culture and will only buy you trouble. You run the risk of diminishing your test-and-debug team, and the loss is yours.

If you can work in a positive, approachable fashion, you'll find your users will be pleased and generally supportive of your efforts. They will respond to your desire to help them. This attitude can come in the form of increased tolerance during difficult times, added patience when waiting for your responses and resolutions, and even supportive communication to your superiors. In essence, you have formed a bond with this team, and you will all be working together. Again, the sum of the whole is greater than the sum of each part.

Developing Yourself

So you've found yourself on a support team, maintaining an SAP environment. Congratulations! You're in the select ranks of professionals who work with this ambitious and desirable application. You're working with its functionality and understanding its overall architecture. As you experience each new situation a day brings, you walk away with another piece of the puzzle. The more pieces you have, the clearer the picture becomes. Occasionally, you look back and take note of where you began, what you have learned, and what you want to learn next.

You are assigned to a team to meet specific business objectives, and you learn how crucial your role is to the company's goals. You understand how SAP has been chosen to promote your company's success. In doing so, you learn about SAP's modularity, applicability, and scalability. You are exposed to other companies that are using SAP and learn how they work with it to meet their specific objectives. You're also working with other support team members, each of whom brings unique experiences and knowledge to the table.

You team up with another group of experts who focus on the processes the business uses to effectively reach its stated goals. Many of these experts firsthand knowledge of how the business and its tool set have evolved.

Then you are assigned to work with a set of business customers—your users. They come with all levels of experience, and they bring a different perspective to SAP. They work with it day in and day out, and see things you may never have dreamed of. They find little bugs in the corners of the application, and call out when the application isn't meeting the process design. They are the masses—the audience—for which SAP has been designed. They are the value-added workforce that keeps the business running and are deep enough in the trenches to know when something is amiss.

Then you go home at the end of the day and ponder all you've learned and experienced over the past 8 to 10 hours. You'll be anxious to get back to some of the situations you think you can quickly and easily solve, some of which you've seen before. Other problems that are not so easily resolved will motivate you to dig deeper into SAP and even consult other information sources. This is your opportunity to increase your knowledge of SAP. Of course, you'll contact the user who brought the original situation to your attention so they'll know you're actively working on the problem. When you arrive at a solution, you and the user can both test the solution together. The user will be pleased, and you'll feel satisfied that you were able to help.

Although so much of what you have been exposed to revolved around developing structure, organizational practices, and partnerships, it's important that you note the by-product of all of this effort: it has helped to develop your own skills, knowledge, and motivation—essentially developing *yourself*. Good job!

I firmly believe you need to look back once in a while and take inventory of your skills. SAP is HUGE! You can forever be clawing your way uphill trying to understand it all. You may never achieve complete understanding of SAP, but pat yourself on the back for what you do know. There's always tomorrow to learn a little more.

Summary

This chapter explained how SAP, in its integrated fashion, can guide the definition and construction of a support organization. Here, you have applied the SAP architecture in a way that cleanly meets the support needs. You learned how to establish and enable a support team regarding membership, responsibilities, and practices. Most notably, you learned how your business users can become your partners and how that business relationship can be rich and results oriented. In the end, it all works to enhance your understanding and application of SAP methods and philosophies.

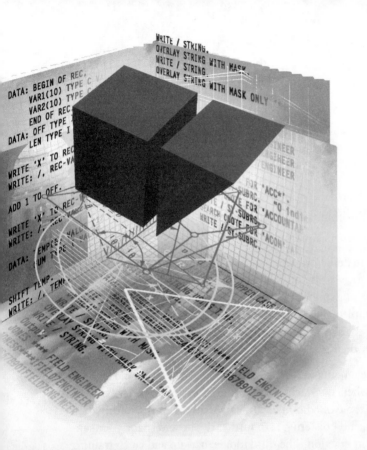

Chapter 4

**Establishing an
Overall Support
Strategy**

In This Chapter

- ◆ Elements of Success
- ◆ Communication
- ◆ Backup Strategy and Cross-Training
- ◆ The Various Work Environments
- ◆ Maintaining a Clean Environment

This chapter works with the material presented in the previous three chapters of this book—the concept of support, aspects of SAP, and the power of integration—to demonstrate the development of a support *strategy*. The support strategy will work as the glue for your pieces. The pieces alone are essential to have and understand, but they are not representative of the support picture you're trying to perfect until you can logically and usefully connect them.

The chapter starts with the elements that make a support organization most effective within itself as well as when interfacing with external customers and partners. The next section revisits the topic of communication, working with the information presented earlier in the book, and bolstering it to further define and shape your support team's methods of team interaction. The third topic—backup and cross-training strategies—is extremely important; it ensures uninterrupted service from you and your team. Finally, you will learn how to set up your overall SAP environment to meet your strategic goals, both from the support perspective as well as from a business service perspective.

Elements of Success

To begin, you'll want to understand what tools and opportunities you have at your disposal. These can be elements that range from tangible hardware and equipment to less tangible elements like experience and aptitude. No matter, it is important to determine every resource available to you when constructing, and being a part of, a successful support organization. Then it becomes even more important to apply, and even exploit, every resource to its greatest potential. Using the familiar integrated approach, you'll see how the following list of critical elements will cause you and your support organization to rise to a state of excellence. These elements are defined as follows:

- ◆ The right size of the support team
- ◆ The right mix of resource skills
- ◆ The natural areas of resource focus

◆ The ability to obtain and maintain technology

◆ The proper amount of control

◆ The need for simplicity

◆ The clarity of direction and priorities

◆ The general mood and tone of the group

The following sections cover each element in detail so that you may begin to apply these principles to your support team.

The Right Size of the Support Team

Sizing the support team is a continual act of balance and precision. The dynamics of workload, business opportunities, times of peak activity, and personnel turnover can all contribute to upset the team's balance. It is important to properly staff the organization from two perspectives—support team members need to feel that they are properly suited and assigned to successfully meet their service goals. The business users need to believe the support staff is large enough to respond promptly to problems or requests.

When the team is proportionally too small for the workload or user base, the team might thrash about in feelings of confusion, instability, inadequacy, panic, and frustration. Obviously, that state of mind works against the team's effectiveness and presents an unpleasant representation to the rest of the business organization. During an occasional period of high activity—a *peak* period—a well-integrated team will typically see the task through, knowing there is relief once the activity resumes to a normal level. However, if peak activity is sustained, even to the point where it becomes the new level of expectation, then the team will start to tire and burn out. Balance gives team members the opportunity to breathe a bit, be more reflective when working through situations, and generally be more creative and satisfied with their work.

When you bring SAP into the mix, you need to take into account that it consumes resources as fast as they can be applied. Support teams are eager and willing to work with SAP, but the team size must fit the task. Businesses are eager to unlock every mystery and opportunity within SAP, but caution must be exercised to ensure the investment to be made is worth the result it will have on the business.

Be careful on this point. SAP can and has been often misinterpreted as being a virtual servant—capable of performing to every business whim. All we need to do is throw a switch and watch it perform. Not true. SAP is integrated and powerful, but it is not entirely self-operative and self-maintaining. Do not understaff your support team; they'll likely wither under the pressure.

Another potential problem arises when the support team is too large. Initially, this situation suggests that all work would be done on or ahead of schedule. The team would have ample time to work out analyses that would improve many aspects of the business. The support processes would run cleanly, and audits would be met with a yawn and immediate certification of compliance. Wrong. Actually, an oversized team tends to be relatively inefficient. When the team is too large, tasks are often too subdivided and responsibility becomes obscured. Relatively simple tasks or processes become arduous and overburdened as they expand to fill the available time. Support personnel usually like to stay active and sometimes continue to enhance a task until it is no longer effective or useful.

Last, when the team is too large, people have trouble retaining a common group understanding and working toward well-understood goals. Group meetings become difficult, and communication becomes filtered and strained as it's passed from person to person. It usually ends up that milestones are missed because, "I thought you were in charge of doing that." Again, balance is the key to properly sizing a support team.

The Right Mix of Resource Skills

The next element is to ensure the proper and complementary mix of skills and knowledge. You will want to know that your team is truly integrated and that the contributions of individual members build on one another. For example, if you want to code a business procedure in SAP, you wouldn't assign two members of the team who might not be familiar with the functions of the SAP ABAP/4 language. As well, you wouldn't assign two fully versed programmers to tackle the project, knowing that neither one has much business experience and would not be able to represent at least the basic business needs.

Members of a well-balanced support team are likely to find more successes and task completions through a balancing of skill mix than if they were improperly staffed and trained. They'll enjoy more job satisfaction when working in cooperative efforts that meet customer expectations and learn more about the environment they service by working within a support team that promotes knowledge sharing and teamwork.

The Natural Areas of Resource Focus

This point actually extends the previous point, but speaks to the individuality of each team member. Each member has a different and valuable contribution to make. Your goal here, as well as that of the team's leader or manager, is to identify the various aptitudes of each member and to put that individual into a role in which he or she can make the most positive impact to the team and its objectives. This point makes a lot of sense but is frequently forgotten. It is forgotten because sometimes organizations put individuals in organizational slots, not always matching the individual's skill and aptitude to the role assigned to them. This is sometimes the case when organizations need to quickly fill team positions, and maybe forsake a good fit for a quick fix.

It's clear that all members in an organization have the responsibility for performing the duties assigned to them. After all, that's why they're here—to work. But you should take into account that individuals see things differently and approach situations from different directions; use these differences to your team's benefit. It makes sense that a team's more technically-minded programmers wouldn't perform to the best of their abilities if their core duties revolved around design and presentation of process flow charts. Equally, it would be inappropriate if your sharpest process analyst was asked to sort through lines and lines of ABAP statements, looking for the data element that isn't being set properly.

Sometimes it is difficult to assess each member's aptitudes. However, when each person's strengths and weaknesses have been determined, some internal reshuffling of duties might be in order. It will probably take several iterations, but the result will be well worth the effort. And, remember, if the team doesn't have the luxury to work through the try-and-retry method, there is another alternative—just ask each member what he or she feels most suited to. It's really that simple.

The Ability to Obtain and Maintain Technology

Technology is the reason a team is in business. The team, with its collective members, always needs to be aware of new technology and techniques. After all, it is largely for this reason that the business funds the support team. Support teams should be constantly investigating new trends in business information management, as well as hardware advances that will make their environment more reliable in continually serving the business needs.

 NOTE

SAP has become so successful because it emerged to solve some age-old business process and information management problems. Technical teams are reading about it, learning about it, and talking to other professionals about it. Their responsibility is to determine whether it is the right solution for their company.

After a technology has been implemented within a company, the next challenge is to ensure proper maintenance of the technology. The support team needs to be continually aware of new features, releases, and known problems. New technology is great, but it's usually quite expensive. The long-term benefit is realized when it can be tuned, exercised, and enhanced to its fullest potential. The job of the support team is to work in this capacity.

The Proper Amount of Control

Control is sometimes viewed as a dirty word. It implies restriction, regulation, and potential bureaucracy. Control in this environment includes managed access to information or functionality within SAP. In an organization of system specialists and programmers, system control can sometimes be regarded as the virtual Big Brother. However, control that can be cleanly and appropriately applied will help the group define itself and allow members to know exactly when their participation is required.

Control should begin at the organization-chart level. Recall that I provided a detailed discussion of this topic when discussing support organization models and team member assignments in Chapter 3. In respect to the integration of the SAP application, with its different business modules, you want to be sure you know what information and activity you are responsible for. Further, whether you realize it or not, you will want to find your boundary to be sure your actions don't cross over into the realm of one of your teammates. Similarly, you would hope to maintain the integrity of your area of responsibility, ensuring that no one accidentally disrupts or corrupts your home base.

In some respects, the use of control can work to provide a useful method of check and balance. If system controls are so rigorous in their intent that they begin to prevent the support team from performing their necessary job duties, then control has become overly ambitious. When a support team member reports that they cannot properly support their business customers due to the support team member's lack of reasonable system access, the control methods are due to be reevaluated. In this way, control is kept as a beneficial element of preserving the system environment, and doesn't become a tool that blatantly locks people out.

There is really no black-and-white answer to the question of how much control is too much. Some support teams prefer to be overly cautious at the start and slowly let out some slack. This approach is fine, but when necessary access is blocked, support team effectiveness and customer satisfaction can deteriorate. Most critical business situations require fast action. An overly controlled environment prevents effective and timely problem resolution.

Other support teams prefer a looser environment at the outset and tightening only in high-risk areas. This, too, is a valid approach, but could expose a business to issues of data integrity, corruption, and security. If system access is too permissive, serious effects upon data protection and accuracy can be enacted before the situation can be recognized and corrected.

From my experience with SAP, neither is the right answer. The best answer often combines both schools of thought and the team develops and tests control methods before putting them into widespread use. There is no definitive answer to the question: How much control is right? My advice is to simply keep your eyes open, remain flexible to suggestions, and be prepared to react in a critical control-related situation.

The Need for Simplicity

Simplicity and complex environments, on the surface, appear to be mutually exclusive elements. If the system environment is complex, how could it really be simplified? However, simplicity should be a driving goal when working the environment and making it more supportable for you and your team. Simplicity works to enable all of the elements of success that are discussed in this section. With simplicity, you and your team can better ensure consistency and clarity throughout the system environment.

Starting with the team itself, the simpler the team is structured, the more likely it will produce desired results. This concept goes back to the modular design of SAP and takes advantage of that design. Keep team members focused on their respective modules so they may best understand the content of each and best represent the functionality to peers and customers alike. Although the workload should be distributed to take advantage of the team's capabilities, be careful not to fragment assignments to a level that makes work disjointed and difficult to represent on an organization chart.

Simplicity also works in communication. Information should always be presented in a way that is clear, concise, and to the degree that meets the team's needs. The information should be applicable to the team's responsibilities and span of control. Simplicity in communication should be exercised during interdepartmental information sharing. Team members are responsible for communicating their actions and for ensuring that the other support team members understand what those actions entail and could affect.

In addition, always keep customer communication simple. The team needs to be able to communicate with its customers using the customer's language. This concept is all part of knowing the audience and being able to relate a relevant and appropriate message. Simplicity also lends itself well in the system environment. Later in this chapter, you will learn how a potentially complex infrastructure can be streamlined into a very direct, front-to-back flow.

The Clarity of Direction and Priorities

A support team should always understand what it is being asked to do and how any assigned task supports the company's higher goals. This aspect is easy to miss, but it works at the core of good business sense and effective application of resources to a business need. The support team should engage in activities that clearly support a strategic goal of the support team, the business teams, or the overall company itself.

Support team members work more effectively when they understand the reason for their assignments, and can clearly understand how their efforts will be of benefit to a higher level of strategic achievement. If the team members can gain a solid grasp of the reasoning behind their tasks, they will be more likely to provide a higher lever of commitment and enthusiasm in their work.

The General Mood and Tone of the Group

This point takes the team's attitude into account. Working in a support team is demanding and exacting. It requires sharpness and dedication from each team member. Sometimes it can be a bit thankless—for example, when the only time someone contacts his or her assigned support team member is to report a problem. Sometimes, no news really is good news. Alas, news happens every day, doesn't it?

So to round out the list of elements for success, it's important to take the team's pulse and to assess its stamina and overall level of satisfaction. Keeping one's nose to the grindstone only produces a ground nose. The team needs to have certain freedoms to be direct participants in key decisions. Ideas need to be considered and valued—often supported to fruition—to show members that they are valued and valuable. And the team needs to have fun. Blowing off steam on a somewhat regular basis is good for cleaning the thoughts and refreshing the minds.

I believe that a team has tremendous strength. Although what I've written here is of general use to all teams, it is of highest importance when dealing with SAP. Again, this application has the capability to overturn the way your business operates. That power can be bad, or it can be good. I've seen mostly good come of it, largely because I've worked with an outstanding and committed team. The team was regularly recognized for its achievements, which worked to feed its enthusiasm.

Communicating with the Customers

The importance of communication can never be emphasized enough, and the way it is used—or abused—on a support team can be crucial to the team strategy. The support team is assigned with managing the business's information storage and flow. The team is also in the business of sharing information, internally and externally, to position the team for success. Remember, always keep the communication simple and applicable.

Whereas the preceding section covered aspects of internal communication, this section covers external communication—*intercommunication*, if you will—with the business teams. Begin with the support team's charter and vision. This should be effectively communicated to the business first. The stated intent and role of the support team helps the business areas—the areas that fund the support team—understand why the support team is so important to daily business. The challenge here is to share enough information so that the business knows the core competencies of the support team, sees who is on the team, and understands who is responsible for what. The support team should also show some additional services it can provide.

Next, as the support models in Figures 1-1 and 1-2 described, you want to communicate how the support team will interact with the customers. Clearly explain your team's model to the business areas and let them know how to get in contact with the team in the most efficient, and user-friendly, manner. Most business teams want to know how to work with the support team and are usually very amenable to following stated guidelines.

Your customer needs an escalation path—an emergency contact—to use in times of critical need, and you should provide that for them as well. Sometimes, business teams will consider the use of an escalation path as the way to climb the support team's ranking ladder when they want to report unacceptable or unwarranted behavior—the adage of "going straight to the person in charge." But the recommended use of the escalation path is when you, the support team member, are not available and a customer must get in contact with someone to resolve a critical problem. Customers get frustrated quickly when they don't know where to turn in emergency situations. They have a problem, and they need a quick solution. Provide them with additional avenues of getting help from the support team in your absence.

Your customer also wants to be informed of pending changes, enhancements, or times of system unavailability. Surprises don't always sit well in this business relationship. Your customers want regular methods of gathering information—rather, receiving information—which will be of use to them. Be sure to provide effective methods of voicemail, e-mail, marquee displays, and user-friendly Web pages. Often, this forward-thinking communication can answer a customer's question before he or she places a call to you. Although you may not hear about it directly, your customer usually is very appreciative of this proactive effort.

Remember that your customers have ideas about the business and process flow, too. Be sure to provide some sort of repository for their questions or suggestions. Good tools to use here include Web page forms, dedicated e-mail nodes, and even the old-fashioned suggestion box. You'll be surprised by some of their ideas, and you'll want to be sure to respond to them.

All in all, the more methods of communication you make available to your customers, the more likely you'll continue to foster a positive partnership. Just about everyone has a question, idea, or gripe. Give them some way to let you know about what's on their mind.

Establishing a Backup Strategy and Cross-Training Plan

This topic is somewhat related to the subjects of department sizing as well as escalation paths. This section explains how support teams can use interdepartmental backups to step in when a primary contact (perhaps the tier 1 individual) is unavailable. Support teams can also use cross-training to build and maintain their overall knowledge base.

Starting with the backup strategy, it's only realistic to agree that you as a primary support contact will be unavailable from time to time. It could be due to a meeting, training opportunity, or even lunch or a vacation. One way or another, you will be away when the phone rings or the call ticket comes in. If you have a designated backup, the support process can remain relatively transparent to the customer, and resolution can flow as easily as if you were there yourself.

Now, the caveat here is to know that the backup plan is successful only when your backup is properly versed in your regular activities and responsibilities—hence the need for cross-training. For your customer's sake, for your backup's sake, and even for your own sake, be certain that the person stepping in for you can help out in an educated and effective manner. Otherwise, a backup might end up doing more harm than good, or will confuse and alarm a customer if the backup appears inept in providing support for one of your areas of responsibility.

Cross-training with SAP actually becomes easier and more natural, again due to the integration of the system; there is an inherent desire to understand how other processes work with those you directly support. This can naturally lead you to probing into areas that other support team members are responsible for supporting. You might be responsible for making sure the inventory receipts are able to occur properly within SAP's MM module, but you begin to get curious about those purchase orders and how and why the buyers enter the information they do. The easiest form of cross-training in this case is to ask the support team member who is responsible for supporting purchase order activity to explain the job to you. The more you learn about SAP and the different processes managed within it, the better equipped you are to make sound business and technical decisions as well as to get to the root of problems quickly.

The most important point here is to be sure that you and your team are properly cross-trained so that no single individual holds all of the knowledge for any process that requires supporting. When only one person understands the ins and outs of a process or technological aspect of the system, he or she becomes very valuable and very risky. You can refer to these situations as *knowledge silos* because they rise up as a columnar container of vital goods. In some instances, team members may enjoy the prestige of being the only one in the know, but that ego trip is at the expense of the team and should be viewed as a dangerous situation. Don't forget the bus factor—if this individual is struck down tomorrow by a bus, does that leave a gaping knowledge hole in the organization. This type of vulnerability is definitely a point you should consider and mitigate.

Cross-training is also an innate activity among support team members for more personal reasons. Everyone would like to get away from the office once in a while. Some folks, find this difficult, though, when they believe they are the only ones intimately knowledgeable about any process they support. Cross-training is in your best interest. Working with your colleagues, you soon develop a buddy system—your buddy can cover for you when you're away and vice versa.

Finally, cross-training provides variety for support team members because it enables them to rotate assignments from time to time. If the business climate will allow it, an attempt should be made to develop a rotational support process. This approach can sometimes be seen as a risky endeavor because it can involve learning curves while team members become acquainted with new business customers and processes to support. But if the investment can be made, the payoff is a more knowledgeable team that will have a more integrated understanding, and experience, with the SAP system.

The Various Work Environments

The next topic relating to your support strategy is the actual system environment, or the various working environments in which the support team does its work. SAP environments can be much like planes in flight. Sometimes a minor tweak—usually within the cockpit—can be performed safely while the plane is in the air. Sometimes, more significant modifications need to be made and tested. For this, it's best to land the plane and work on it in the hangar. SAP uses the terms *instances* and *clients* to describe and identify installations.

Instance—*The highest level of SAP installation identification. The instance represents the resources allocated, such as processing events and allocated memory, which will enable operation on a server (hardware).*

Client—*The subdivision of an SAP instance into separate, virtual work environments. This use of the word client is not the same as the "client" in a client/server relationship. A client is a means to define a business concern, such as a company, and that client will work with its own distinctive master records and information tables.*

Again, simplicity is essential when establishing and managing your system environment. Of course, you'll need your Live Business or Production instance— where the business conducts its work every day. You'll also need a Quality Assurance (QA) instance—where new modifications, settings, interfaces, and so on are tested in a Live Business-like environment. Further, you'll need a Development instance— where new functionality is first implemented, unit tested, and initially evaluated for eventual live business or production use.

Figure 4-1 shows the instances already mentioned (Development, Quality Assurance, and Live Business) plus two additional instances, Training and Disaster Recovery instance (which are covered next).

The Development Instance

The Development instance is where all the ideas, innovations, and bug fixes begin. It's often referred to as the *crash and burn machine*. Access to this instance is usually quite loose. Liberal access to the Development instance allows the support team to work with detailed system settings, customizations, ABAP code, and master data. This instance is also where the development of entirely new functionality, such as add-on functions (bolt-ons) and interfaces to external files or applications, occurs. Unit testing should be conducted here to prove that the proposed change or solution achieves the desired results. Also, some initial integration testing—often known as *regression testing*—can occur in the Development instance. The results will probably not be 100 percent accurate and reflective of the Live Business instance, but initial regression testing can be useful in the development environment. The Development instance should contain the base code and settings of the Live Business instance; it's a copy of the Live Business environment.

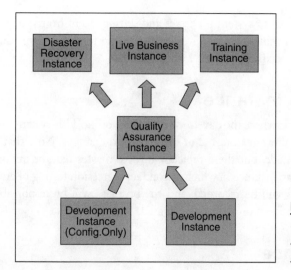

FIGURE 4-1

The landscape of the different SAP working instances within the greater system environment

This instance may also be where your team requests an additional client for customizations and configurations to be mastered. Access to this client would generally be more restrictive, and it would be used for maintaining a source of reference for the active Live Business environment settings. Because so much change can take place on the general Development instance, including customizations and configurations, you may save a lot of recovery time and effort by having this specially designated client around.

But a word of warning: Too many clients will create a refresh nightmare. Keep clients to a minimum. Simplicity should drive your environment whenever possible.

The Quality Assurance Instance

This instance is used to conduct more business-like or production-like testing. It is often called *full regression testing*. This type of testing occurs within an environment that is a virtual mirror image of a Live Business instance, and helps ensure that changes or new functionality will not have a negative effect on other stable, live business processes. This system has access controls in place similar to the Live Business instance it mirrors. It preserves the integrity of the testing environment and provides a realistic view of how changes and additions to functionality will be accessed in a live environment.

In the QA system, it is also a good idea to involve the business partners in end-to-end, full regression testing so that they may verify and validate results. Usually, changes and enhancements to system processes and settings stem from a request by the business team. The business team's involvement in the testing ensures that the outcome matches their specified criteria.

The Live Business Instance

This instance, of course, is where the day-to-day activities occur. This system must be a very secure system to prevent untested or unauthorized changes. Note that some minor changes can be made, but these typically involve master data or minor customizations. This is *not* an instance in which to conduct regression testing of any sort. Any posted transactions will be recorded, and the business will be responsible for their effect to actions initiated or audit trails created.

The Training Instance

This instance is useful when conducting user training sessions. In this instance new users can be led through a business's processes and actually perform the functions without affecting—or experimenting in—the Live Business instance. It might be a good idea to enable generic user logon names such as RECEIVE, MASTERDATA, PROCURE, and FINANCE for use in the Training instance. Generic logons will be easier to maintain, and passwords can be easily changed if ongoing access by a trained user is not desirable. This instance is a copy of the Live Business instance and is usually quite secure in terms of change control. The difference between this instance and the QA instance is that the Training instance is truly static and representative of the Live Business environment. The QA system can, and usually is, in a relative state of change because modifications to the Live Business instance are in the process of being installed and tested.

The Disaster Recovery Instance

This instance is the safety net under the Live Business instance. As the name says, this system can be enabled if the Live Business instance becomes unavailable or corrupt for an extended time. This instance is copied in full from the Live Business instance on a regular—usually weekly—basis. It is typically kept geographically distanced from the Live Business instance for obvious reasons. This is the instance you hope your business never needs to use but never wants to be without. The Disaster Recovery instance should be tested quarterly or semiannually to ensure it is fully operational, complete, and can be turned on if needed to maintain business activity. Because this instance is a disaster recovery machine, it is even more secure than the Live Business instance. Access should only be granted on an as-needed basis.

I actually witnessed a disaster recovery event. Although it wasn't SAP that was affected, the example is valid: An e-mail server used in my workgroup crashed. We were told that it would be back up in a day. This event actually lasted more than a week. We were all being pretty patient, and the e-mail support team was working frantically to restore the system. However, by the end of the week, many of us realized that we should have had a disaster recovery plan. Don't think you'll ever need to be prepared? Think again.

Maintaining a Clean Environment

As you can see, it is necessary to maintain a somewhat complex system environment when working with SAP. Much activity occurs every day within the various SAP instances. The business is constantly evolving, and the system environment needs to maintain pace with the business needs. Occasionally, though, the different instances, except the Live Business environment, need a good flushing. You'll probably refer to this activity as *refreshing* the system, and you'll want to be sure you perform it on a regular basis.

The instances require refreshing regularly to prevent them from deviating too much from the Live Business instance. As the business goes on each day, transactional data accumulates, business scenarios and trends develop, and overall load increases. To ensure your different instances can still represent the Live Business environment, which is crucial to know your testing is effective, you'll want to reestablish the instance content. Figure 4-2 provides an illustration of a usable refresh strategy.

 NOTE

The refresh strategy is important to the support team's effectiveness when designing and implementing change. (See Chapter 18 for more detail about managing change within SAP.) For now, this information is presented as another useful method to employ in your team's overall support strategy.

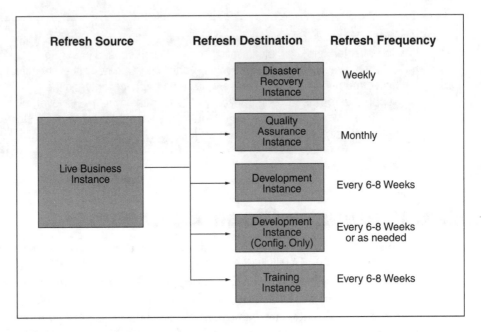

FIGURE 4-2 *SAP instance environment refresh model*

Communication again plays an important role when you are executing a refresh strategy. Other team members need to be fully and duly aware when the refreshes are scheduled to occur. A refresh, you should know, will overwrite all existing development work, including customizations, which have not yet been implemented in the Live Business environment. Special steps can be taken to capture and recover change in process, but doing so requires additional effort from the team. Nevertheless, your team needs to know that its work-in-process (including work with test data) must be captured for restoration or completed and moved along to the Live Business instances before the refresh occurs. Because any test data will be overwritten as well, you'll want to be sure lengthy test cycles can be concluded.

Summary

This chapter concludes Part I of this book. The preceding material helped you lay your foundation for supporting an SAP environment. Chapter 1 began by explaining the whole concept of support, helping you to understand what it is, what it does, and how it has evolved. Then, you saw useful models that you can employ to help establish your support team. Further, you learned how these models can be modified to fit the needs of your business and about the key elements that make for exceptional SAP support and help you to understand how you can contribute to the support team.

Chapter 2 took you deep into the concept of integration and explained how SAP has harnessed it to establish logical linkages, both with information and the overall business process flow. You read about some of the intrinsic details of how SAP stores and links data in its different table structures and how these linkages help to define and perfect integrated business processes. Along the way, you saw warnings about some of the traps you can expect to encounter when working in such an integrated environment.

In Chapter 3, you learned how SAP affects the support team and how SAP integration will actually define a team's identity. Not only did you discover how to best integrate activity with other support team members, but the discussion also helped you understand how you can best partner with your main customer base, the business users.

Chapter 4 showed you how to develop your team's overall support strategy. This strategy becomes the true picture you present to customers and partners and helps to establish your team's mission within the business organization. Communication is a key ingredient to this strategy, as is ensuring appropriate backup and cross-training strategies. Finally, you learned about the core information that describes how you can implement a strategic SAP support environment.

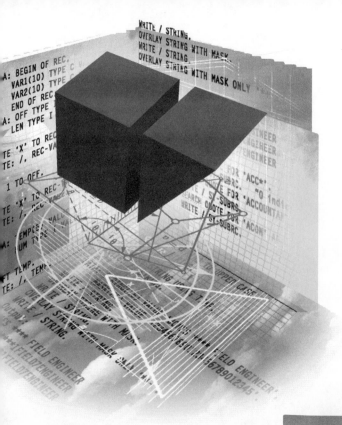

PART II

The SAP Life Cycle

5 **Supporting the Evaluation and Start-Up Phase**

6 **Supporting the Design Phase**

7 **Supporting the Development Phase**

8 **Supporting the Testing and Training Phase**

9 **Supporting the Implementation**

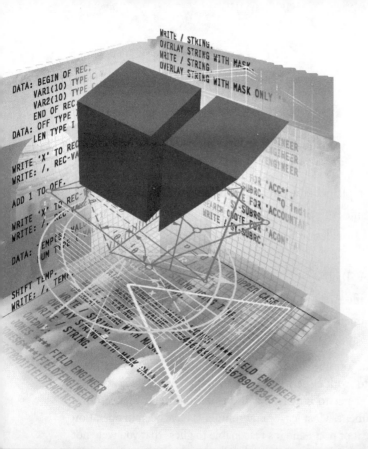

Chapter 5

Supporting the Evaluation and Start-Up Phase

In This Chapter

- ◆ Entering This Phase
- ◆ Understanding the Objective
- ◆ Understanding the Implementation Team Structure and Membership
- ◆ Roles and Responsibilities
- ◆ The First SAP GUI Installation
- ◆ Learning SAP
- ◆ Adopting a Common Tool Set and Development Environment
- ◆ Understanding Specific Areas of Control
- ◆ Starting Good Documentation Habits
- ◆ Exiting This Phase

In this chapter, you start your journey through the SAP life cycle. This life cycle is really a unique opportunity to work closely and intently with SAP. In fact, it might be the best chance you'll ever get to understand the true origin and makeup of a business's automated environment. Most legacy environments have been in operation for roughly 20 years—believe it or not—and it's reasonable to guess that you were not in any sort of support role back when the whole development of that environment began. However, if a company you work with chooses to migrate its business operations to SAP, you have the rare opportunity to be there from the start and perhaps even make the history that others will talk about 20 years from today.

Automated business tools change over the course of years, with additions and enhancements being made along the way. But there does exist a core platform—or foundation—on which those tools rest. SAP will be the new foundation for the environment you will support. If given the opportunity, you should jump at the chance to work with SAP at this stage in your company's business life. The experience and knowledge you will achieve over the course of an SAP migration and beyond cannot be easily captured any other way. From this point on, you'll have the inside knowledge, and you can proudly say, "I was there."

Your journey through the SAP life cycle starts with a tour of the beginnings of this major business shift. This first phase of the life cycle—the evaluation and start-up phase—can be quite ambiguous and even intimidating for a company that may be deciding to migrate their business environment. Although a lot of companies have made the transition—and most of them successfully—a lot of other companies still have not. If the company you work with decides to pursue the SAP environment, it will begin with a lot of poking, prodding, and probing. And, at some point—

hopefully sooner rather than later—you will be tapped on the shoulder and asked to assist in the life cycle's execution.

This chapter begins by giving you an overview of how a migration project starts up and how it works to create an internal organization all its own. It describes how you fit into this *implementation team* and whom you might find as your partners. Because you need to understand the task at hand, this chapter recounts the sorts of activities that are commonly encountered when working on this sort of project and further describes how this crucial phase positions the project for successful implementation. Then, you'll see how and when you will actively engage in your own SAP training. You'll also be introduced to the tools and methods that you will use at the start of an SAP migration.

TIP

There is a very useful tool within SAP that helps you approach and progress through the implementation effort: the SAP Procedure Model. The Procedure Model can help you and your team develop your implementation roadmap. The approach discussed in Part II is inspired by the Procedure Model, but the support team's core competencies and commitment to serving the business is added to make the Procedure Model much more useful and robust.

Entering This Phase

As you enter this first phase of the SAP life cycle, you'll probably find yourself engaged in fact finding and assessment activities. Before deciding to use SAP, a company will usually send out the "drones" to find out more about the application and what its use will mean to their business. Others in the organization may have already gathered SAP literature and information through a variety of means: directly contacting the SAP company, visiting Web sites that discuss SAP, reading commercially published works, or attending conferences and expositions that are devoted to SAP solutions. Because the company you support may have been working with its current business automation tools for up to 20 years, much of SAP will seem foreign. But taking these initial investigative steps will lead to major strides in the future to come.

As this phase begins, the discussion assumes that someone in your company has started gathering, or is currently gathering, information about SAP and is beginning to see how it can be put to good use in your business setting.

Understanding the Objective

Understanding the objective for deploying SAP becomes important as you begin to ponder your involvement in an SAP implementation team. You'll want to read as much internally published material as you can find that describes the investigation already done within your company. It will probably be a series of presentations or other informational forums that describes the potential for change to the company's intended project sponsors. Every project needs a sponsor—a management team or similar directing body—that can provide the necessary resources for the project and who will evaluate the project's goals against the company's long-term objectives. (In many cases, the sponsor actually initiates the formation of the project team.) With the business market undergoing the change and gyrations that it is, companies are facing the sometimes harsh reality that change in a business is no longer a matter of choice but now a necessity for survival. Therefore, a project team, consisting of just a few higher-level contributors, may already be in place and can present their findings to the SAP implementation project sponsors.

> We've all heard the story about the high-level worker who was "sent off to do a special project." This euphemism usually means that the individual was sent somewhere where he or she can do little or no harm. Tell people you're working on a special project, and you'll see the recognizable hint of a suppressed grin. This special project is not one of those projects. It is the project that will be setting the direction of your company for years to come. In my experience, it came as a tremendous opportunity that promotes leading-edge application knowledge and the necessary project management skills to achieve an SAP implementation.

SAP is in the company of several other Enterprise Resource Planning (ERP) tools. SAP is the leader in installed customer base and, as you're reading this, has probably been chosen by your company (see Appendix A for more details regarding SAP's history and market position). This being the assumption, the project leader or leaders will begin forming an initial team to further evaluate SAP's solutions from a technical and more detailed business perspective. And this is where you come along. You may have a role in preparing the information that will be presented to the project sponsors and other senior management of your company. Your initial assessments will help the sponsors know that SAP is the right investment and that, even though all the details are not yet in, SAP will propel your company into the next millennium.

NOTE

Your involvement in this early phase of the implementation is a terrific opportunity for some good visibility.

If you participated in the formation of the project objective, then you're well aware of the business and market climate that may have driven it. If you weren't directly involved in this phase, be sure to review the relevant information. When someone asks you why the business is migrating to SAP, you'll want to answer with confidence. For an idea of what the project objective could look like, see the sample in Figure 5-1.

The presentation of the objective becomes known as the *project charter*, and it is the keystone that drives your activities. At this phase, much of the project intent will be delivered to senior managers. They need high-level information and terminology

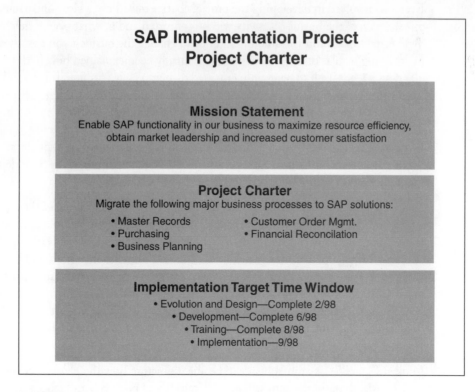

FIGURE 5-1 *The project charter statement explains the reasons for sponsoring an SAP implementation.*

that they can easily interpret into actions that uphold the high-level company goals. For example, if your company is eager to become a leader in supply chain management techniques, then the project charter should allude to how the use of SAP will enable a superior solution for managing the end-to-end business flow.

Project Charter—The starting point in the project life cycle and the development of the solution that leads to the eventual SAP implementation.

> You may hear about mission statements, company vision statements, and the Japanese term *hoshin* being used to drive top-level company directors to enact and motivate positive change in a business. Sometimes, at the reporting-line level, the connection between your daily actions and those lofty company goals is obscure. Working on such a high-visibility project as an SAP implementation gives you an opportunity to get closer than you may have ever dreamed possible to meeting those goals.

Everyone involved in developing the project charter must have a clear understanding of *how much* of the business activity will be converted and at what pace. The charter must take into account the amount and rate of change the business can absorb while maintaining regular business activity. It has already been explained how SAP's modular design lends itself to being implemented in a progressive fashion. It is a good idea to consider using a phased approach to the amount of SAP that is implemented at a business. To use a popular metaphor: Take a foundational approach to the implementation—lay the foundation, allow it to cure, and proceed to build upon it. Businesses have anxieties about change, especially change that is as potentially sweeping as a business automation overhaul. By taking a phased approach to SAP deployment, the impact can be softened and made more palatable.

Be sure you understand the approach your team is taking and the effect the amount and rate of change will have on the business. Refer to the traditional role of a support team: You must maintain control of the business environment, especially during times of change. If change becomes a risk to the business activity, change should be mitigated so that the goals and objectives of the change can be met without jeopardizing market presence or end-customer satisfaction. Don't hesitate to speak up and provide your views, comments, or recommendations; that is why you are on the team. If you don't understand any portion of the objective, ask questions. You'll want to be sure you can fully represent and support the tasks that lay ahead.

Look at Figure 5-1 again. You should be able to picture how the planned changes to a business automation system will *directly* impact and positively influence those top-level objectives.

Understanding the Implementation Team Structure and Membership

With the green flag of sponsor approval waved, the project implementation team will assemble. This is a gathering of various individual contributors who will effectively realize project milestones by demonstrating knowledge about a company's current state of automation and transferring that outdated automation to a future state reality. An implementation team is usually made up of experienced contributors who can represent the business and technical aspects of the company's automated systems. The team's first challenge is to understand that there is much ambiguity when working to migrate older automation over to SAP methods and processes. The team will need to demonstrate open mindedness and forward thinking to make the migration a success.

An implementation team can change and grow over the course of the project, but one good start is shown in Figure 5-2. In this example, the team is assembled in a multidimensional fashion. The first facet is a core team dedicated to the technical aspects of the implementation. These team members will investigate the management of the system environment, data storage and retrieval, application activity, and the all-important migration of the current business automation to SAP. The other facet of the team is those team members who are identified as leading the business process activity. These individuals are chartered with understanding the business processes, requirements, deliverables, and overall business effectiveness. But the most interesting dimension, I think, is where the two intersect. In order for the technical developments to be made, it is necessary to defer to the business process expert. In order for the business process to evolve and become more systematically robust, it is necessary to defer to the technical expert. If you refer to Figure 1-4, this phase of the life cycle marks the beginning of the integrated business/technical support methodology.

Notice, also, how there are two project leaders at the head of the implementation team. They, too, can be contributors from within the company's ranks, usually with supervisory experience. The leaders will work to manage the unique aspects of both the technically-oriented and business-focused team members. This approach enables each leader to effectively represent the needs of the two disciplines. The leaders' role would include representation within the team itself, as well as clearly and accurately representing the team and its objectives to the rest of the company. And, as the team works in an integrated, overlapping method, so, too, will these project leaders. It becomes important to note that an SAP implementation is no ordinary project, and leaders who are experienced in working with, enabling, and running interference for

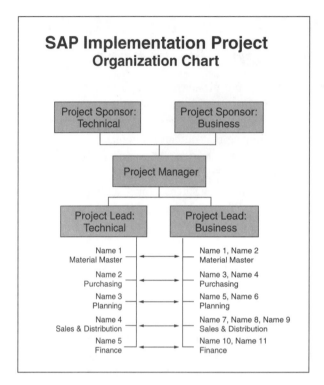

FIGURE 5-2

The initial membership of an SAP implementation team

a team will most likely succeed. Plus, as demonstrated in Figure 5-2, the team members will be organizationally linked to the project leaders. For efficiency, the leaders can act as team managers, administering guidance, development, and compensation for the individual team members.

> During an SAP implementation project, and especially after, I witnessed the effect of the integrated team approach on the team leaders. They developed a skill for working together effectively and for understanding and supporting the specific issues that were critical to one another. After the project, these leads moved back into the management ranks but operated with a more global business view. They worked and interacted with other management in a way that promoted teamwork and achieving a win for the whole organization, not just a particular department.

A final element to the team membership can be the presence of a skilled and informed SAP consultant. No doubt you've heard about consultants, the work they do, and the incredible demand for their services. In SAP terms, these are the practiced individuals who join the implementation team to provide initial guidance about the nature and operation of SAP. Many consultants have already worked with businesses migrating to an SAP-based environment and typically have much first-hand knowledge and insight to share.

The consultants will help the implementation team become familiar with SAP and can advise the team on how to begin a migration effort. Be aware, though, that your team will want to carefully select the consultants who are right for your needs. Take into account the consultants' areas of expertise and experience and match those with your implementation's scope and timeline.

With this assemblage of participants, your new implementation team has been developed by enlisting the services and expertise of individuals who have accomplished business backgrounds or strong technical skills. It is being guided by leaders who fully understand their task and can effectively and skillfully incorporate those objectives, through the use of available resources, into a positive result. To jump-start the effort, consultants have been brought into the team to help with the start-up and the implementation. All these resources should be 100 percent dedicated to this effort; no one should attempt to perform his or her role on this team on a part-time basis. In essence, the implementation team acts as a microcosm of the company itself. This team will learn, grow, and have many experiences along their journey. It will work through fun times and challenging times, and the members will bond like no other team you've seen. If you find yourself on this team, you are in good company.

> My first experience with an SAP implementation, and as a member of the implementation team, was one of the most rewarding of my 15-year professional career. It was actually an opportunity that changed my direction in a truly positive way. In fact, I believe that I learned more in that one year than I ever had in any other year of my professional service. It also worked to set the bar of achievement higher than I had dreamed, and I've now adopted that level of expectation as my baseline reference from which to further develop my skills and services.

Roles and Responsibilities

Although the preceding Part alluded to this topic, I want to just take a few more moments to discuss the development of roles and responsibilities within an implementation team. Specifically, this section focuses on your primary contribution to a team.

As Figure 5-2 shows, the team is a combination of business-disciplined and technical-disciplined contributors. Defining this separation is especially important when it comes to the issue of ownership for deliverables. You must thoroughly understand your role on this team and what deliverables you will own. If you are on the technical side, then your primary directive is to work with data definition, storage, retrieval, and systematic manipulation. Equally, you could also act as a tool expert who can install and instruct in the use of additional application tools. If this becomes your role, then you need to be clearly responsible for the associated deliverables.

Business-centric contributors are responsible for understanding and interpreting business requirements. You need to identify and classify business requirements clearly with regard to their effects and results. The business contributor also acts as a liaison to the business community when further business specifications are required or when input from the business people is solicited. Because this business-focused team member is most adept at speaking the business language, he or she should clearly be responsible for managing business-related deliverables.

The other dimension of the team, and a good structure to establish, is the further definition of implementation *subteams*. In this structure, the implementation team focuses on the specific business areas that need to be represented. This is the identical approach illustrated in Chapter 3. This sort of team structure enables a purchasing team to focus on procurement issues, and so forth. All implementation subteams should work within a common guideline of approach and responsibility during the implementation effort, but the focused subteam approach allows each subteam member to perform more detailed work and have a tighter span of control and ownership. Figure 5-3 illustrates this subteam philosophy.

Adopting a Common Tool Set and Development Environment

Now the team needs to determine what tools it will use as it works through the SAP life cycle. The tool set is very important because it begins the discipline of commonality and establishes the environment of working through change. This tool set

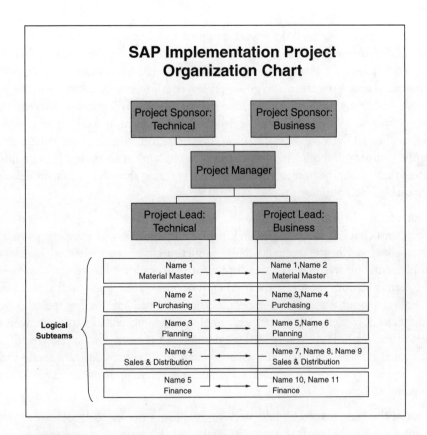

FIGURE 5-3

The SAP implementation team is now subdivided to focus on the specific needs of each business area.

includes the use of a specific e-mail application, word processing application, time-line tool, spreadsheet tool, and a graphical application that can be used to prepare presentations as well as business and systematic flow diagrams. The key for the team here is a single set of tools that will help ensure consistency of communication and tool utilization across the team.

By the team adopting a common tool set, you might find that you'll be leaving behind one or more of your favorite applications when it is replaced by an official application of the implementation team. But in the spirit of team unity and acceptance of change, you'll need to work through the temporary inconvenience of learning a different tool. If you have the opportunity, work to investigate and recommend a tool for the team's use. Most likely, the team leaders will be reviewing tools for range of functionality and how each will serve the needs of the SAP implementation. Your investigations and recommendations for tools will most likely be appreciated.

Team members also need the proper hardware to work with their software tools. If possible all members of the team should use the same hardware configuration. This approach allows for relatively easy, standardized setup, modifications, or upgrades. However, be sure your team can get an assessment of the hardware in use in the business areas. Some hardware might have differences that will effect a different result when operating SAP. An example would be a conventional PC workstation as opposed to a UNIX server workstation. If various configurations will remain in use in the company, the implementation team should work with those hardware differences throughout the implementation project, ensuring the solutions finally delivered are usable by all business people.

Lest I forget, be sure the entire project team can be effectively located in a defined office area (refer to the examples in Chapter 3 for details). All the same considerations noted in Chapter 3 should apply—sometimes more so—when establishing an implementation team's working environment. Although it's sometimes not feasible, the team can work most effectively when it occupies a single physical area. If some members of your team are at a remote location, you will have to give special consideration to how those remote members might communicate and participate with the rest of the team. However, at least 90 percent of the team should really work in a dedicated business environment where synergy and momentum can develop from the beginning. Ease of communication and team development are major keys for ongoing success.

Finally, the team leaders should work to establish a dedicated laboratory environment for the implementation team. A converted classroom or a temporary building works well. The facility should fully support multiple hardware configurations; have eventual access to the SAP application; and include other amenities such as a white board, projector, screen, and any other tools that will facilitate information development and sharing. This area can become the team's dedicated meeting quarters and can provide an opportunity for the team to gather away from their individual desks.

The First SAP GUI Installation

Well, clearly, this is *the* tool that you will be using throughout the SAP life cycle. Your team will want to have access to the SAP graphical user interface (GUI) as early as possible. Chances are that none, or very few, of the team have seen it. And it might be possible that someone on your team—maybe you—will get to work through the process of accessing and installing the GUI. The requirements for enabling SAP R/3 access begin with a network connection to the server on which SAP is installed. Then the actual GUI will be accessed by each client—the team members' workstations—so they may begin using the application. The GUI can be accessed from a shared network executable file, but in the case of PC workstations it's typically recommended that the GUI be installed directly on the hard drive of the PC. It will require adequate memory and storage area, but the GUI response time is usually better than the response time of a network-accessed GUI.

Initial access to the GUI is usually through the linkage to an official SAP training server, physically located at an SAP branch office. SAP makes a variety of development machines available to new customers. These machines enable a team to learn SAP content, navigation, and basic functionality.

Learning SAP

Learning SAP is nothing you achieve through a few hours or even a weekend of poking about in any kind of random manner. In contrast, these first experiences are usually most effective when guided by an veteran SAP user—perhaps one of your team's hired consultants. SAP is a large application, and it's easy to get lost while navigating within it. It could be compared to Web surfing: You can go lots of places, but sometimes you can end up somewhere and not exactly recall how you got there. With SAP, you might not always find a friendly trail of "go back" links to help you retrace your steps.

The task here is for the implementation team to sit down to some focused, structured training on the look, feel, and use of the SAP application. The leader of the instruction should guide you through the application areas and provide examples and exercises of core SAP functionality. For this training to be effective, it must be a hands-on experience for you.

But don't expect to emerge from this initial training session as any sort of newly accomplished SAP expert. Rather, use this first experience as another foundation of knowledge upon which you will build throughout the SAP implementation life cycle. This initial training should cover the following:

◆ GUI access and logon

◆ Overview to SAP maneuvering and icons

◆ Error, warning, and informational messages

◆ Introduction to business module functionality and where it can be found

Your first SAP experience is actually a fun time. I always remember my primary course on SAP. I was really confused, skeptical, and rather frustrated. It is one of the best experiences, I believe, that a support individual can go through. At that time, I stepped into the shoes of a business user who is faced with changing the way he manages his duties. The new tool being used is foreign, and initial usage is clumsy and cumbersome. Yet the user feels the need to master the tool as quickly as possible. The experience makes for a really useful and applicable point of reference. I keep that virtual pair of new-user shoes in my office. When I have opportunity to work with a new business user, one who is unfamiliar with the SAP environment, I grab that pair of shoes and make sure I can work with the user in a way that offers comfort and confidence.

Understanding Specific Areas of Control

This section covers the early steps in developing and establishing control in the implementation environment. Control is an area that SAP covers well, and it's most likely an important topic to your business. Through points of control, a business can protect its informational assets and ensure the security of its efforts. As you work with the implementation team, you will see how these control points work in the overall picture and how you and some of your team members might be assigned to sentry these areas.

In this context, *control* is another name for "access," and it begins with access to the SAP server. Much like any automated environment, logons and passwords need to be established to allow a potential user into an application. This activity begins as early as the start-up phase, and it is a good idea to assign the role of *Logon Administrator* to a member of the implementation team.

Logon Administrator—This role provides a central contact to establish logons and a clear line of communication for implementation team members. The basic function of the logon is to give a user access to SAP. (Chapter 7 covers the mechanics of establishing SAP logons and the necessary components of those logons.)

Other aspects of SAP also require focused maintenance and control; for example, SAP profile administration or SAP customization (two elements you will learn more about later in this book). Like logon IDs, control points preserve integrity and consistency within the SAP environment. This early phase of the life cycle provides an excellent opportunity to understand SAP control points and a time to develop policies and procedures that will evolve and eventually be used in a live business environment. For now, make it a point to begin tracking who on the team is granted an SAP logon to make sure that each member is accounted for and can begin to explore the application.

Starting Good Documentation Habits

In this phase, also, be sure you understand the importance of documenting activities and decisions right away. You'll find that an implementation life cycle requires abundant documentation, and you should prepare for that requirement from the outset. Just about everything you learn, decide, and do that affects the implementation cycle should be captured for others to review and for you to refer to later. Make the effort to establish good documentation habits early, and you'll avoid the need to "rediscover" some of the ideas you'd once had but can't exactly remember. You'll be swimming in information, so make it easy on yourself.

The project leaders require different types of documented information— information that is necessary to effect an informed, accurate, and controlled migration to SAP. So much of this information, you'll find, is in your head. You'll be asked to document it all, and provide it in an intelligible, consistent manner that can be shared with and refined by the other team members. But until the formal documentation requirements are requested, be sure you capture initial team meeting minutes, discussions, or whatever else seems pertinent at this time.

The most important suggestion that can be offered at this phase of the project is to develop a usable method of storing and retrieving all documentation that is created throughout the implementation life cycle. Lots of documentation is wonderful to have and use, but it's only truly useful when it can be accessed with regularity and ease. You may think this point is painfully obvious, and maybe not worth stating. However, you will be amazed at the amount of documentation that can be generated by an implementation team and how quickly it can get lost in a melange of storage devices and archival methods. It's recommendable to start simply by securing a readily accessible network file share that will be identified for the team's use. Take a look at the example in Figure 5-4.

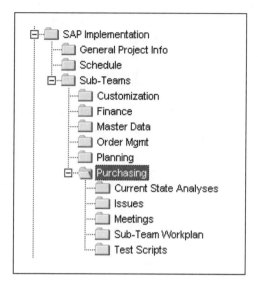

FIGURE 5-4

This sample implementation team shared documentation directory facilitates good information storage and retrieval.

Make the structure of the directory as intuitive and applicable to the team as possible. Avoid cryptic folder names that use phase code names or numbers or any other naming conventions that might require definition other than the name that appears on the folder or file. Windows NT, 95, and 98 allow for directory, folder, and file names that are longer than eight characters, so take advantage of that feature. Make sure the team has immediate access to this file structure and discuss its use at the first team meeting. If your team is appropriately staffed, it might be a good idea to designate an individual to monitor the directory's use and tidiness. Again, it will fill up quite quickly, and soon you'll lose more than you'll save if you don't take a methodical and logical approach to your document storage.

Exiting This Phase

As this phase of the life cycle completes, you and your team should now be equipped with or have achieved the following:

- ◆ Project sponsorship
- ◆ Project charter
- ◆ Project team
- ◆ Initial SAP instance
- ◆ Start-up SAP training
- ◆ Dedicated work tools and working environment

NOTE

Within each of the following four chapters that document the SAP life cycle phase entry requirements and exit results will be provided. This information should help you check your work and progress as the implementation effort moves along. These phase checklists should encourage you to think about what unique deliverables will be necessary for your business's SAP migration. You may think of elements to add as well.

Summary

This chapter started you on your journey through the SAP life cycle. During this phase, the SAP implementation team was established, and another foundation was built, upon which the SAP environment will be erected. You'll find that working with SAP is like working with a virtual box of building blocks. Your goal in this first phase of the life cycle is to establish your presence and role on the team. Your early involvement in an SAP implementation will provide you a base of knowledge to understand more about the business environment you will be supporting and how the business processes and methods will change with the advent of SAP. With the exit outcome described, you are now ready to move on to supporting the next phase.

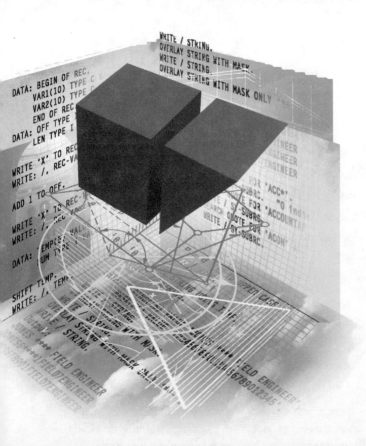

Chapter 6

Supporting the Design Phase

In This Chapter

◆ Entering This Phase

◆ Project Scope and High-Level Process Migration Plans

◆ Incorporating the Project Work Plan

◆ Current System and Process Analysis

◆ Establishing the Development Instance

◆ Constructing the Future Environment Landscape

◆ Early Prototypes

◆ Setting Boundaries of Scope vs. Timeline

◆ Communicating Results

◆ Documenting This Phase

◆ Obtaining Design Approval

◆ Exiting This Phase

The purpose of this chapter is to help you develop your implementation road map. You've been told the destination of this effort, albeit in rather high-level terms. The goal is to translate that stated target into actionable and achievable steps. Both you and the project sponsors are going to be very curious as to how the project's global objective will actually be realized. So here is where your journey through the SAP life cycle really begins to pick up speed, and you become an active team contributor, not just a team member.

In the previous phase, you understood, internalized, and aligned yourself with high-level business ideals. Any project of this scope needs to begin with that footing. But in this phase, you must roll up your sleeves and get into the finer points of how to migrate the business toward SAP. The process is very deliberate and methodical, and you'll find that a lot of structure and rigor goes into this phase. But any good roadmap is carefully researched, plotted, and prepared. Trial runs are made to ensure that the course leads to the desired destination—but maybe not directly at first.

The first step here is to translate high-level objectives into more meaningful SAP terms and concepts. That comes in the form of a first-pass *process migration plan*. Although the plan is only roughly defined, it makes use of your SAP knowledge to date and helps you gather more detail. All that you and your team assess and recommend is incorporated into a project work plan, and this plan eventually structures the tasks that must be completed to realize the implementation goal.

Process Migration Plan— *A plan that provides more detail about which existing business automation will be identified to migrate to SAP functionality.*

Soon afterward you'll determine what operates in the present time. This task entails the complete and careful scrutiny of the current business environment. You can't effectively start any journey without a strong grasp of its beginning. As you conduct your exhaustive research and review of the current environment, you may find that you'll learn more about the current processes. During current-process evaluation, the real dissection of business processes and applications begins.

If you've been supporting the company's business applications in the past, your knowledge and experience is highly valuable in determining the best migration path of those application functions into SAP. You've worked the applications, seen the problems, and identified areas for their improvement. That knowledge can only work to improve an SAP migration. On the other hand, if your experience in the previous automated environment is limited, here's where you can take up the slack by absorbing as much information as you possibly can about those business applications and their intended purposes. At the same time, you will bring fresh insight—a new set of eyes—and you might be in the advantageous position of seeing a solution from an untried perspective.

To help achieve the goal during this phase, your team begins by establishing its first SAP development environment. If you're really itching to get into SAP and start working with data and process flow, here's your entry point. But this phase concentrates on design aspects, so it would be premature to force processes into SAP without ensuring that you and your team fully understand what your results will be. SAP is extremely deep, and you probably won't be too successful traipsing about without a clear set of directions. You'll need to prepare the formal documentation that will grow and evolve throughout the life cycle. This documentation serves as your initial testing and proving ground and helps you communicate your findings and recommendations for the business migration.

Project Scope and High-Level Process Migration Plans

The first step of this phase will continue the stated vision of the project charter (as explained in Chapter 5) to develop the implementation's project scope. At this stage, it is necessary to outline the implementation team's task by using a well-defined set of project goals and deliverables. Further, the team needs to determine how the project scope's stated goals will be met while also providing boundaries under which the implementation team can operate. These boundaries ensure the project goals can be clearly defined with identifiable business solutions and an agreed level of functionality. Open-ended projects ultimately suffer from a lack of direction or ability to effectively meet project milestones; the team will never reach its goals if the goals themselves are not definitively stated. Using the project charter presented in the previous chapter (see Figure 5-1), your implementation team's project scope should resemble the example shown in Figure 6-1.

The project scope should be drafted and communicated within the implementation team. Once the project scope is developed and communicated, it's logical to develop a *project migration plan.* When developing this plan, you and your team work with the business processes that will be migrated to SAP. You match the business processes to the applicable business modules in the SAP architecture. At this point, the project scope can be tested against the original project charter: does the scope of the project—now better defined within a migration plan—enable the vision first communicated in the project charter? This exercise determines whether you are using the necessary SAP modules, whether the modules can meet the higher-level business requirements, and if SAP includes the solutions that meet your business's needs. Don't be surprised to learn that your project scope might need to include custom development of functionality.

**SAP Implementation
Project Scope**

- Based upon SAP R/3 version 3.0
- Implementation Timeframe =Q398
- Enables use of SAP MM, PP, CO, SD, and FI modules
- Legacy systems to migrate: PURCH, PLAN, FIN

Business Areas Impacted:
- Purchasing
- Planning
- Master Data Team
- Finance

Business Areas Not Impacted:
- Product Packaging
- Customer Quotes
- Warehouse

FIGURE 6-1 *An example of an implementation team's project scope.*

Project Migration Plan— *A plan that describes the steps to be taken in implementing the project scope.*

SAP provides a lot of solutions, but inevitably a company will have a specific need that cannot be accounted for within SAP's architecture. At this point in your evaluation, you should try to document the anticipated high-level process migration. Figure 6-2 gives one example of how this might be accomplished.

Don't be concerned if your analysis results in some processes that have not yet found homes on the migration path. They could emerge as processes that will be beyond the scope of the initial project charter. Also, these could be processes that might, after more detailed examination, be good candidates for discard or process reengineering. If all details are not available, just note those areas as requiring further investigation. The important point is that you've captured them somewhere at this stage. In addition, be aware that the project scope can now be more clearly understood, and it should be determined if the scope can be achieved within the time allotted to the implementation team. Sometimes, trimming a project scope begins at this early phase of the implementation. Development of the project migration plan helps the implementation team determine if the stated task can be achieved in the time allowed or if some potentially less-critical goals can be delayed for future migration.

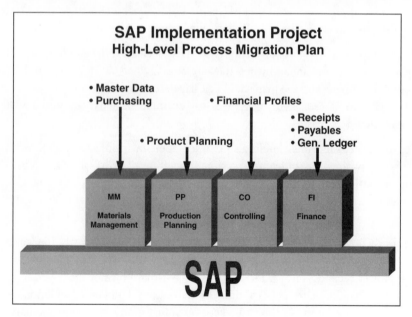

FIGURE 6-2 *An example of a high-level process migration plan*

Incorporating the Project Work Plan

The design phase now moves on to the development and ratification of a *project work plan*. This plan further clarifies what the target can and should be. Some implementation efforts may begin with a target date in mind, but the detailed drafting of the project plan usually sheds some reality on the situation and might require a review of original expectations. As with the project migration plan, a project work plan details the effort required to fulfill the project goals. Again, if the goals are too aggressive, they will need to be adjusted.

Project Work Plan—A first sketch of an interim goal and milestone list, which should include enough milestone identification and related completion dates to ensure a pace that supports the final implementation target date.

You should avoid a plan that chooses an arbitrary implementation date and then attempts to work backward to meet it. This approach rarely results in a thorough and accurate implementation, but you might be able to exploit SAP's scalability feature. If your team is required to meet a specific implementation date, it is best to utilize a phased approach to the implementation of SAP business modules. Your company might not get all the functionality initially desired, but the lagging functionality can be enabled in a follow-on phase. Look back at the high-level migration plan and determine if any areas lend themselves to scaling back or restructuring. Your main concern should always be to keep the daily business active and profitable.

More important to you personally is to have a clear understanding of what your specific deliverables are and when they are due. Ownership of tasks and deliverables is important here, and the plan should clearly define each individual's specific responsibilities and tasks. Figure 6-3 gives an example of what an initial work plan might include.

At this time, subteams should also develop their own process-specific work plans. This step enables the subteams to accurately capture all deliverables and requirements for the business areas they are representing. All subteam work plans should be delivered to the project leaders, who can roll the plans into an overall implementation team project work plan.

Project work plans need to be extremely flexible documents, to say the least. At the beginning of this phase, the plan provides the necessary structure and direction to get the project off and running. However, every twist and turn of the SAP life cycle can raise new requirements, opportunities, or restrictions. Unplanned situations will alter the plan, and a careful eye must be kept on your team's target implementation date. Your project leaders will monitor the project work plan carefully, and you will need to actively advise them of changes that may affect the target date.

	Task Name	Duration	Start	Finish
1	⊟ SAP IMPLEMENTATION MILESTONES	358 days	Tue 6/21/94	Wed 11/1/95
2				
3	Phase 1 - Evaluation and Start-Up	0 days	Tue 6/21/94	Tue 6/21/94
4	Project Charter Defined	1 day	Thu 9/1/94	Thu 9/1/94
5	Project Leads Identified	1 day	Mon 8/1/94	Mon 8/1/94
6	Project Team Members Identified	1 day	Wed 2/8/95	Wed 2/8/95
7	Project Sub-Teams Developed	1 day	Tue 6/21/94	Tue 6/21/94
8	SAP Training Instance Established	1 day	Tue 6/21/94	Tue 6/21/94
9	Project Team Tool Set Defined and Enabled	1 day	Tue 6/21/94	Tue 6/21/94
10	SAP Training for Team	1 day	Tue 6/21/94	Tue 6/21/94
11	Team Documentation Share Defined	1 day	Tue 6/21/94	Tue 6/21/94
12	Control Teams Identified and Staffed	1 day	Tue 6/21/94	Tue 6/21/94
13				
14	Phase 2 - Design	1 day	Tue 6/21/94	Tue 6/21/94
15	Project Scope Determined	1 day	Tue 6/21/94	Tue 6/21/94
16	High-Level Migration Plan Developed	1 day	Tue 6/21/94	Tue 6/21/94
17	Complete Project Work Plan	1 day	Tue 6/21/94	Tue 6/21/94
18	Assign Sub-Team Process Owners	1 day	Tue 6/21/94	Tue 6/21/94
19	Sub-Team Work Plans Developed	1 day	Tue 6/21/94	Tue 6/21/94
20	Current State Analysis	1 day	Tue 6/21/94	Tue 6/21/94
21	Development Instance Enabled	1 day	Tue 6/21/94	Tue 6/21/94
22	Future State Plan Developed	1 day	Tue 6/21/94	Tue 6/21/94
23	Perform Early Prototypes	1 day	Tue 6/21/94	Tue 6/21/94
24	Communicate Prototype Results to Sponsors, ┊	1 day	Tue 6/21/94	Tue 6/21/94

FIGURE 6-3 *An example of an Initial Implementation Project Work Plan*

Picture this concept like a spring between two blocks. You can continue to add pressure to the spring without affecting the position of the blocks. However, when enough pressure is applied, one of the blocks—I always picture the rightmost—will move outward in response to the pressure. The rightmost block represents your implementation date. If that rightmost block doesn't move with increased pressure, then what you have is a trash compactor—not a pretty sight. Luckily, the project leaders with whom I've worked have all seen the need to relieve the project pressure, adjusting the implementation date only when absolutely necessary.

Current System and Process Analysis

The first job in the design effort is to detail the current environment, also called *current state* or *legacy environment*.

Legacy Environment—An automated environment that utilizes systematic methods and applications in existence for a significant period of time. In the context of this book, legacy refers to the systems, applications, and processes that are identified as candidates for migration to SAP.

It is necessary to fully define how the current business processes work to determine how the functionality might be represented within SAP. The desired result is to reverse engineer the business processes identified as candidates for the initial SAP migration. You must not only fully define the *normal* business process that you will migrate—perhaps purchase-order creation, material receipts, or financial reconciliation—but also identify any parts of the process that aren't so normal. That is, you must faithfully capture any process nuances, quirks, or potential disconnects that might impede a complete SAP migration later.

This step requires careful documenting of your findings. This information is crucial at later design steps and ultimately saves time when you turn your attention to more SAP-focused process activity. Take your time and perform as thorough a job as possible. You might want to begin with any existing documentation that describes the current state processes to help you identify the design's input, output, and controls. Be cautious, though, because the documentation could be out of date. As stated before, many of these processes and applications you are migrating could be as much as 20 years old. Unless your company has demonstrated exceptional documentation methods, it's likely that the documentation might not accurately reflect the most current state of the processes or the applications that support them.

To best achieve this requirement, be sure your investigation yields the following details about the process:

◆ Points of input
◆ Data manipulation within the application
◆ Data storage and reference areas
◆ Expected output
◆ Business area(s) that use the process

First determine the overall business flow and where any particular process you are detailing fits within that flow. Take a look at the simple example in Figure 6-4.

This view pinpoints how the process you are focused on works within the greater picture. Although the example in Figure 6-4 is very simple, this view helps to determine where SAP functionality will replace certain portions of the current state (refer to the high-level migration plan in Figure 6-1). All process flows that will be affected by the migration of elements to SAP solutions should be documented using a process flow diagram. All members of an implementation team need to refer to the current state

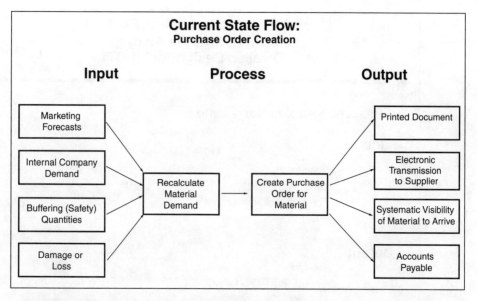

FIGURE 6-4 *A simplified example of a Current State process flow diagram*

process flow to ensure that their business processes migrated into SAP are complete and functional.

With the process view firmly in place, another tool is needed to completely capture the current state process details. This is the step in which automated process details are identified and documented to serve as a blueprint for the process migration. Figure 6-5 shows an example of a detailed design tool (DDT) template, explaining the details of a specific automated process.

Again, if you already have some documentation for your current state processes, be sure to make good use of it. Take care that what you are documenting is truly the representation of the process as it is currently used within the company. If you're not sure of all details of a process and its current use in the affected business area, work with a process-focused implementation subteam member; if necessary, that subteam member might engage the advice of one of the business people. The underlying goal is to ensure the process to be migrated is fully understood.

Don't be concerned if your analysis identifies some processes that don't seem to have a natural home on the migration plan. These could emerge as processes that are outside the definition of the initial project scope. It might be necessary to develop systematic interfaces to legacy information systems that will not be included in the initial migration to SAP. Or these could be supporting processes information systems

SAP Implementaion Project
Current Process Analysis
Detailed Design Tool (DDT)

Process / Application Name

Input:

Description:
Origin:
Format Requirements:
Event Trigger:

Output:

Description:
Format (Print, File, Other):
Recipient (Dept. or Process):
Retention:

FIGURE 6-5 *An example of a Detailed Design Tool (DDT)*

that might, after more detailed examination, be good candidates for discard or process reengineering. If all details are not available, just note those areas as requiring further investigation. The important point is that you've captured them somewhere at this stage. Don't try to develop a redesign just yet.

Establishing the Development Instance

This section focuses on another activity that should be taking place parallel to the current state investigation effort. At this point in the SAP life cycle, the implementation team should establish an SAP Development instance in which SAP process investigations will continue and where you and the rest of the implementation team will soon be developing actual process replacements for the current state activities you have been analyzing. The purpose of this slight detour from the process analysis is to help you understand how the process details you are gathering will eventually be put to use within SAP.

First, you need to understand the SAP organizational hierarchy—defined within SAP's system architecture—as well as the terminology used to describe the hierarchy. SAP's architecture uses logical subdivisions of the business information and process flows that it will maintain. As a full-scale ERP, SAP can manage many different segments of a company's business activity. Although fully integrated, the SAP architecture acknowledges the need for logical areas of business separation that allow and foster points of business control and isolate discrete business processes within the system.

The internal SAP hierarchy begins with the SAP Instance. The *instance* can be defined as the highest level of an SAP installation, and in terms of the R/3 application, refers to the server and database upon which SAP will be installed and from where the instance will be centrally managed. The instance is the virtual nerve center of your SAP installation and will become home to the core functional application software.

From the instance come the clients. (Remember, don't confuse these SAP "clients" with hardware workstations as in a client/server configuration.) The SAP clients are segments of SAP functionality that can be utilized to uniquely identify and run a business. Every instance needs at least one client, which is the top-level identity of the business that is being managed. If you're wondering whether an SAP instance can manage several companies within a single client, the answer is yes. However, what you'll most likely see is a company that will have several instances, each with a defined client, representing different development and testing versions of the business environment (see Chapter 4). With the implementation team's Development instance, it is best to establish several different clients as opposed to instances—just for now. This instance methodology is much like the system environment described earlier in which several instances support the different phases of support and enhancement of a live business. In this phase of the SAP life cycle, the scale of activity is smaller, so we can achieve the separation and control at the client level. Figure 6-6 illustrates the implementation team Development instance.

Each client will serve a unique purpose during the early stages of design and development. The following sections describe how these different clients are used.

Process Development Client

The process development client is where business processes are understood, detailed, and evaluated. The team members work in this client to:

◆ Understand SAP's approach to supporting the business process

◆ Compare and contrast the SAP solution to the business's current state solutions

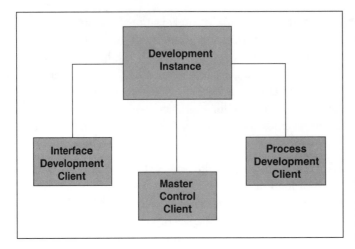

FIGURE 6-6

The Implementation Team Development instance is established.

♦ Detail the process migration plan

♦ Identify any functional process gaps

This phase is where any real-world experience you have becomes useful as you work with SAP and learn how it provides solutions to the business process needs. You should spend enough time reviewing the screens to become familiar with SAP element names, screen flow, and logical processing points.

Interface Development Client

The interface development client is where, as process details and project scope dictate, interfaces into and out of SAP are developed and tested. Interfaces import or export data in and out of SAP for use with other portions of the business process. As stated before, it might be necessary to develop interfaces to legacy information systems. Granted, SAP is a fully integrated business application, but you should not expect a business to literally turn off its legacy systems and turn on SAP. It's actually more prudent to use the phased approach, which is supported by the modular design. The size and scope of the required interfaces depend on how much or how little of the SAP functionality your team's scope allows.

SAP's ABAP/4 programming language provides good support for interfaces and is an effective way to mitigate the impact of an SAP installation. The use of interfaces allows data to be shared between SAP and a business's legacy solutions. Interfaces can also work as virtual *bookmarks*, easily identifying business processes not yet migrated to SAP and allowing a methodical process to turn off subsequent legacy solutions; SAP functionality can be enabled to replace the legacy process as well as replace the interfaces.

In the next chapter, you will find a clearer example of an interface's design. The current discussion and level of detail presented, however, is more suitable to this explanation of the design phase.

The Instance Master Client

Just as the Live Business instance maintains the integrity of an installed SAP environment, the instance master client captures and maintains master data and system configurations. Only a few team members should have access to this client. Typically, these individuals should be specifically assigned to enable, monitor, and maintain master data integrity and configuration policies. (See Chapter 3 for a discussion of limited access to some aspects of the environment. This client is your case in point for use of that methodology.)

The Instance Master Client is where the designated team members work in a controlled SAP environment and develop the ideas and practices that emerge as overall policies when the installation goes live. It could be said that the SAP environment control process is developed in this client and perfected through each step of the SAP life cycle. The implementation team members work with one another to identify base process requirements and settings. When process policy is reached, the team responsible for the master client establishes any required parameters in the master client that enable and preserve the initial process specifications. The team members that maintain the master client settings will document any required process settings as business environment policy. In Chapter 7, when actual SAP development is discussed, you'll see how the instance master client is the key element in refreshing the contents of the other development clients.

The establishment of the Development instance—and the various clients—is a necessity at this point of the SAP life cycle. Although actual SAP development hasn't yet started the Development instance provides the first tangible view of the project's goal. Chapter 7, which covers the development phase, continues the discussion about the clients and what activities occur in each. For now you just need to understand that this instance activity will probably occur parallel to the current state process analysis effort.

Constructing the Future Environment Landscape

By this time, your team has its high-level migration plan and a more detailed work plan that guides and tracks your progress. You have also spent time identifying processes that will migrate to SAP during the initial implementation, and you have sufficient documented detail that clearly defines the intrinsic attributes of each process. Continued reference is made to the phrase "initial implementation" because it is viewed as the best plan to utilize SAP's scalability and effect a modest approach to SAP deployment. Work to get SAP into your company's daily life by steps, the first and most important being the introduction of the new GUI and general SAP methodology. Follow-on projects, maybe smaller or larger, can enhance the new SAP environment and make use of the functionality.

By now your team has also secured and established a Development instance, and you may have had the opportunity to probe into it. Recall what you learned in your initial SAP training and go a bit beyond that. Exploration is encouraged at this time, and you'll learn at a faster rate if you experiment a bit. There's probably nothing you can hurt in this early environment, although expect that you will probably get lost in the GUI. The paths in SAP do not always lend themselves to the kind of backtracking you can do in a Web browser.

At this point, then, you and the members of the team should be able to draw a blueprint of what the business will look like when SAP migration occurs. You will now design the *future state environment*, which becomes helpful when communicating the proposed migration and eventual result. You play a part in the development of the future state as you investigate SAP solutions and find replacement processes for the current state activities. Remember the scope of your implementation and the high-level migration plan; use their objectives and details to guide you and the rest of the team when you determine which processes are being replaced by SAP in the future state. Use the future state design to draw your attention to interface points where legacy processes and applications will not be included in the initial migration to SAP. Don't expect to turn off the entire legacy environment and turn on SAP in a single effort. Figure 6-7 illustrates how migration to SAP can be communicated using a future state diagram.

This future state diagram is well worth the investment required to create it, and it reflects the implementation team's progress in defining the new business environment. The diagram shows the processes that you and your teammates are intending to migrate to SAP, and the diagram should give you a feel for the work that lies ahead. Furthermore, this diagram helps define areas of ownership within the implementation team and highlights processes that might require combined efforts. Finally, this type of information can be presented to the project sponsors and other senior management. Use the current state flow diagram and compare it with the future state diagram. This information will help the company executives understand your progress and prepare for the level of change that the business will experience.

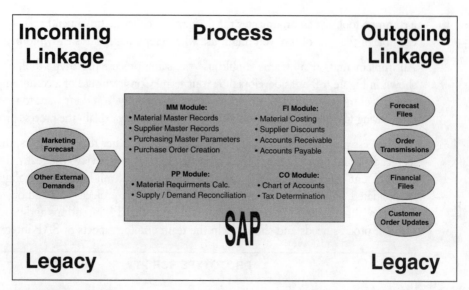

FIGURE 6-7 *This example of a future state diagram shows how legacy elements will be replaced by SAP elements.*

Early Prototypes

Prototype—A test of a new solution, process, or product that determines early on within a development effort whether the element being tested is potentially useful as intended.

You may wonder what it is you are prototyping at this phase of the SAP life cycle. You haven't been into SAP long enough or deep enough to map any of the legacy processes into SAP functionality, but you do have your collection of process details and a future state diagram. At this point, and usually with the active participation of the SAP consultants on your team, you will want to begin running through theoretical business situations. This verbal review of the intended process migration is a first chance to test the validity of the project's goals and milestones. This early review can be achieved using a *process prototype script.*

Process Prototype Script—A prepared document outlining the intended details and flow of a business process that migrates from a legacy solution to an SAP solution and contains pertinent process data and process flow descriptions.

For this exercise, your project leaders will require you to present your process findings and proposed initial migration plans. To do so effectively, your team should develop a common tool that communicates the designs in a consistent manner. Figure 6-8 is an example of the type of tool you might use when preparing for this early prototype.

All implementation subteams should use the same process prototype tool, either as shown in Figure 6-8 or as developed by your team. Consistent use of a common prototyping tool moves the review process along quite smoothly. You don't want to waste any time having to explain a review tool before you can actually explain the process proposal.

The process prototype scripts will be presented to the other team members, the project leaders, and possibly the project sponsors. During this review, the team discusses the different proposals, looks for areas where processes might be better aligned or consolidated, and ensures the overall results support the project goals and objectives. Your consultants should be on hand to advise you of SAP's intentions and provisions for your process needs and should help the team employ aspects of SAP integration.

PROTOTYPE SCRIPT

Script ID: **Script Name:**   **Subteam Owner:**

Purpose: To test the ability to create a purchase order.

Scope: The prototype will explore the following:
                     a) Condition #1
                     b) Condition #2

Upstream Process Dependencies/Assumptions:
  ◆ <identify process execution>
  ◆ <identify interactive function>
  ◆ <other parameters>

Downstream Process Dependencies/Assumptions:
  ◆ <identify processes waiting on this process' result>
  ◆ <identify automatic processes>
  ◆ <identify manual processes>
  ◆ <identify output>

Procedures:
Describe the process in SAP and Legacy Terms
  ◆ SAP Transaction ID:
  ◆ SAP menu path:
  ◆ Data Parameters:
  ◆ Legacy Process Interfaces:

FIGURE 6-8 *An example of a Process Prototype Script*

Further, the team should design a more global, end-to-end review of the different processes to ensure continuous and complete information flow. I recommend deferring this larger scale prototyping until each discrete process is tested and validated.

> Document, document, document. It gets overwhelming and a bit frustrating, and I had difficulty dealing with so much written work. Documentation is a necessary evil, though. But be careful not to mistakenly consider the amount of paper you have generated for the degree of progress you've actually made on the project. Nevertheless, well-written documentation that accurately reflects the phase intent will be very useful. Trust me.

Setting Boundaries of Project Scope vs. Project Timeline

When considering project scope in contrast to a project timeline, you to begin to make trade-offs. Scope and timeline discussions began as early as the high-level process migration plan stage, and those discussions continue as more implementation details are available. Your early prototype may have drawn attention to an aspect of SAP that has not yet been targeted but could be a terrific boon to the business. Several processes might require that the project scope be revisited, depending on the ease with which the processes can be migrated to SAP. At this point, however, the team should further consider how to balance the original scope and charter of the project, the capabilities of SAP, the amount of risk to the business processes, and the sponsored time period in which the implementation is expected to occur.

At this point, you and your teammates need to determine whether SAP has functionality that can cleanly replace an existing business process with an integrated portion of the SAP application. Although the most desirable situation is to engage SAP solutions whenever possible, you may find a process that won't cleanly migrate—perhaps because a necessary component of SAP isn't yet enabled, thus preventing a logical process transition. Or, as previously mentioned, you may find that your business has a process or requirement so specific that SAP has not discretely addressed and accounted for it. In this case, you need to assess the feasibility of creating a customized SAP process. This activity will add to the design, development, and eventual support requirements of the specific business process as well as add to the project implementation. Sometimes the best choice is to leave the process unchanged, interfacing it to or from SAP or establishing a short-term, manual process until you can enable additional SAP functionality.

As a member on the implementation team, you will continually be asked whether the migration plan can be executed within the allocated time window. After all, time is money, and companies that choose to migrate to SAP are eager to start it up and reap its benefits as quickly as possible. Your role is to continually evaluate your progress, consider any additional requests or changes that have been proposed, and if any critical milestones may be missed, possibly delaying other dependent activities. Flexibility is valuable, but occasionally you might want to establish a maximum threshold to protect the project schedule. If the project scope is too liberal, undefined, or subject to add-on requests by the business teams, the feasibility of meeting a stated implementation date can be jeopardized.

> As more business areas learn about an SAP installation project, more of them start their own independent investigations. This situation should not be discouraged because the more business people who understand how SAP works will make the implementation task easier. However, during this period, business people tend to make ad hoc requests, and the project scope begins to bubble and change. The project team needs to develop a litmus test—a relative sanity check—to determine whether the new requirements and recommendations can truly be achieved within the original time frame. Be careful. Many people are quite skilled at convincing you that their "little addition" will really save a lot in the long run. If you're not eternally vigilant, it will be raining nickels and dimes wherever you turn. From the support perspective, you'll need to sound off when you notice that the original charter and timeline might be compromised.

Communicating Results

As your team nears the end of the design phase, it should communicate its results to the rest of the business. What you are doing is of extreme interest to the rest of the company, and everyone will be anxious to learn more about SAP.

If it hasn't already been done, encourage your project leaders to host a company kick-off meeting that focuses on the implementation effort underway. This event is a great way for your project leaders to introduce the team members, describe the team's mission, explain how the members were chosen, and define the expected outcome of the implementation.

Most importantly, planting the seeds of change should begin as soon as possible. The more the business teams hear about SAP, the more curious they'll become. It will be obvious to them that a new implementation team has formed and is now occupying dedicated floor space. Folks will want to know what this team is doing and what SAP is. The implementation process is a lengthy one, and progress should be communicated whenever feasible. Eventually, the business areas will be asking "when" as opposed to "what."

Documenting This Phase

Because documentation is such an important ingredient of an SAP implementation, check to see that you and your team have the following information:

- ◆ Process migration plan
- ◆ Project work plan and timeline
- ◆ Current state process flow
- ◆ Current state process details
- ◆ Future state process flow
- ◆ Process prototype scripts

This abundant documentation is used and improved upon as the implementation progresses. By no means should the preparation of the documentation be considered make-work. It is all useful, and it is needed to proceed in the SAP migration life cycle. Be sure that the documentation is rich in content. Your future designs will only be as good as the effort you have put into the documentation at this phase. And don't forget to document all relevant decisions and discussions. Keep track of this information in electronic format whenever possible, and store it on the team's documentation file share. Even simple e-mail communications can contain important information that you will refer to in the future.

If you've been in a support role in the past, you're probably wondering what the activities described in this chapter have to do with support. You're on a specialized team, your interaction with the daily business applications has probably ceased, and you are no longer identified as a contact for the business users. It can be strange, and you may feel you've gone off to live and work in some make-believe world. However, take note that a migration like this is the ultimate support contribution. Practically everything you do on this team will eventually be used in the business environment. The way you approach and complete your duties throughout the SAP life cycle will make the bed in which you'll eventually sleep. Don't short-sheet it.

Obtaining Design Approval

Your team will need to obtain official approval during the different phases. Design approval should be considered one of the project plan's major milestones, and you should commit yourself to ensuring the designs for which you are responsible are duly approved. Approval check-point reviews allow closure to phase events and mark the entry into the next phase. Without the approval, you might never exit a stage, spiraling around in perpetual review and investigation. Equally detrimental, without the approval, you may enter a subsequent phase with an incomplete or inaccurate design.

Be sure your team can identify a point where process designs can be reviewed and approved. For example, you might seek design approval during the early prototypes. Or if a prototype wasn't completely successful due to incomplete design details, be sure to establish a time for the prototype review team to reconvene; run through the prototype a second time and obtain approval if appropriate. Whatever the timeframe, however, seeking design approval is the responsibility of the project leaders. Try to capture any approval that you do receive in some sort of electronic communication. Design approval is an important milestone that you'll want to store in the team's file share.

Exiting This Phase

As you exit this phase, you should, again, take inventory of your team's results. Be sure you can confidently report the following phase outcomes:

- Operational SAP development instance/clients
- High-level migration plan
- Project work plan and timeline
- Detailed current state process documentation
- Current state and proposed future state flow diagrams
- Early prototype process scripts
- Documentation of all major decisions
- Proof of design approval

Summary

This chapter described the rigors of working in a theoretical process design environment. At this point in the SAP life cycle, your team has made a major advancement toward securing an SAP Development instance, and the legacy processes being analyzed can be developed into future state solutions using actual SAP terms and methods. However, you must still work in a documentation-oriented environment. Although this environment may not always be familiar or comfortable for a support individual, the experience of taking a process down to its bare skeleton and rebuilding it into a proposed SAP solution makes you a more knowledgeable and efficient member of the support team. You will know every twist and turn that the information and process can take. Clear and complete documentation of this activity enables you to quickly reference information that might require additional review by yourself or other support colleagues in the future.

> Hey. Are you having fun? I'm not being sarcastic—are you and your team having fun? Face it, this stuff can be real drudgery. We found a lot of solace—and team building—by engaging in regular gaming within our group. At lunchtime and after hours, we would power up the latest version of Doom and blast each other. It was a great way to release tension. I was the newbie and usually accounted for most of the other players frags (their scores as my Doom character was obliterated). Once I got over the inherent motion sickness, I was handling the on-screen weapons with better precision. The bottom line is this: Take a break occasionally. This work can be a bit grueling, and you'll want an outlet, whatever it might be.

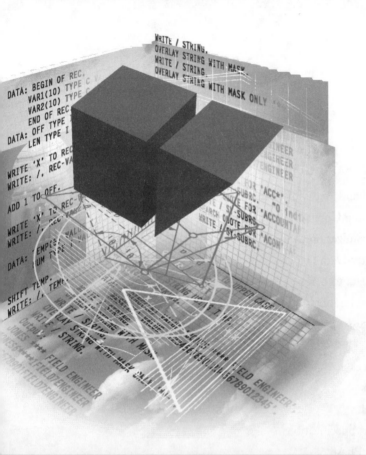

Chapter 7

Supporting the Development Phase

In This Chapter

- ◆ Entering This Phase
- ◆ Early System Builds
- ◆ Establishing Logon and Access Policies
- ◆ Working with Naming Conventions
- ◆ Working with Customizations
- ◆ Working with Master Data Policies
- ◆ Mapping Legacy Data to SAP
- ◆ Identifying and Investigating Gaps and Issues
- ◆ Reengineering Processes
- ◆ Early Data Loads
- ◆ Developing Interfaces
- ◆ Developing Reports
- ◆ Iterations of Design
- ◆ Freezing the Design Specifications
- ◆ Documenting This Phase
- ◆ Exiting This Phase

You say theory's fine and all that, but you want to see this stuff really work? Are you getting a bit impatient with all of the design review and analysis? Good. Now you're in the driver's seat, and it's time for the rubber to meet the road. This chapter takes you through the development phase of your SAP implementation. Yes, you've been developing and redeveloping your business process migration for some time in the theoretical arena, but now you'll spend the larger percentage of your time in the development instance, putting SAP to work, as opposed to working with process analyses and flow diagrams. More analysis and document preparation will still need to occur, but you're closer than ever to making SAP active. You can prove that the objectives of the implementation will be met. A key concept to bear in mind is that all of the work you put into your design documentation now acts as your roadmap for your SAP migration.

I won't mislead you—this work isn't easy. If it were, everyone would have done it by now. In fact, this stage is even more grueling than its predecessors. Your job here is to visibly support the business by demonstrating a recognizable set of solutions within SAP that will effectively and reliably support your company in the future.

In this phase, you'll see how the environment itself further develops. The evolving of the development environment includes additional levels of system structure, control, and policy setting that will need to occur to ensure the development instance and clients remain secure and usable to the team. You'll see that the evolving development environment becomes the start to a support environment that will grow into a future state maintenance model.

Then you'll discover how your early design and analysis work starts to map into SAP functionality. The actual functionality mapping will initiate the need for development naming conventions and master data policies. You'll want to be sure that you and your team are laying a consistent, reliable foundation that can support the business—and yourself—for years to come. This chapter will also begin the discussion about SAP customizations. In the customization section of this chapter, you'll see that SAP is designed to be tailored to a business's specific needs. You'll take a tour of this concept and learn about the need for policy setting and control in the customization realm.

With all of that completed, you'll get started on actually loading your legacy data into SAP so that you and your team can begin the core development work. Using and building on your process scripts, you'll conduct some early testing and find that some of your designs need to be revisited. Not to worry, though. This phase is very iterative, and the more you run and rerun your process tests, the more you'll learn and understand SAP. At this stage, you're beginning to rehearse for the pending live implementation. Therefore, the iterations are your early road tests, and you'll want to fully exercise your process designs until you're certain they are meeting the business needs. At a point, the chapter's discussion will show you how to break out of the redesign cycle and actually freeze your designs so implementation progress may continue. Analysis paralysis is very common in this phase, and you'll see how to recognize its signs and how to deal with them.

Finally, you'll get more documentation tips that will help you capture your efforts in this phase and ready yourself for the final phase. By the time you and your team complete this phase, you will all announce that all is ready, and the project leaders will herald the call that the implementation is about to commence.

Entering This Phase

Good solid design and a sound working environment are the clear prerequisites as the development phase is entered. Without them, you're already at the disadvantage of being ill-prepared. Be sure you and your team have cleanly and completely exited the design phase before progressing to the development phase. To be sure, be certain you have the following:

- ◆ SAP development instance/clients
- ◆ Detailed process design documentation
- ◆ Business process scripts
- ◆ Updated project plan/timeline
- ◆ Appropriate knowledgeable supporting resources

The line between this phase and the previous one is actually somewhat fuzzy. During the initial design phase, some minor development may already have occurred in the development instance—most likely in the master client. But most of the development activity begins after the designs are fully reviewed and approved. If you or your team have already started some development, that's great. If not, do not worry because the real enablers here are your proven and approved process designs.

In this phase, the development clients become more business-like in structure and content. In addition, other parallel activities will help establish sound and usable data and system settings, and you will further define your development processes, policies, and documentation. In this phase, tremendous advances will be made in SAP process development and support team knowledge growth. Be sure you continue to strive to document as much as possible to lay the foundation for the eventual support environment. Lessons learned, techniques used, and other pertinent discoveries should be captured to help guide and facilitate the long-term maintenance of the installed environment.

Early System Builds

A *system build* is another term for preparing the system environment. Usually, a dedicated team of individuals within the implementation team structure performs this task. It includes the global enabling and setting of system parameters. The initial build was done for your team when the development instance was established and the clients were defined. But, as with process designs, system builds are repeated again and again throughout the development stage. It all works as practice for the eventual implementation.

 NOTE

I refer to the system build process as I further explain the activities that take place in this phase. For now, I just wanted to call your attention to the concept.

Establishing Logon and Access Policies

The activity of creating SAP logon IDs was briefly mentioned in Chapter 6. Now it is necessary to be more exacting and controlling with the IDs and the system access that is granted with each. Like most any other business application, SAP provides authorization checks throughout its architecture. These checks work to help a business define clear areas of process separation as well as system administrative separation. As a business example, an individual who is authorized to purchase materials in the system would not actually "receive" those materials. These two activities should be performed by different people in different business areas: purchasing and receiving. This concept is often termed *separation of duty*. It not only enables business areas to focus clearly on their assigned duties and the execution of them but also is a major business audit concern. Most auditors, internal as well as external, would quickly raise a red flag if this separation of duty was not in place.

From a technical perspective, separation of duty is an issue as well. The easiest example to provide is that of establishing SAP logons. Usually, this procedure should be managed by a single individual—with a designated backup—who ensures that all requests for new logon IDs are properly authorized and adhere to technical separation-of-duty policies. If everyone in the support team were able to establish logons, chances are the system would quickly get out of control and consistency would be compromised. This area is also an audit concern. Technical individuals should not be able to establish logons or authorizations at will—especially for themselves.

Your team should keep these requirements in mind when establishing its logon security policies. In the previous chapter, you or someone on your team started a list of those folks on the team who had been given an SAP logon ID. At this time, the list should be expanded to include additional information (see Figure 7-1).

You can see that this spreadsheet now includes more information about the individuals who have logons and introduces the use of the SAP user profile. A *user profile* is a collection of individual authorization objects that map to SAP functionality. During the execution of SAP functions, authorizations are checked to ensure the logon ID (a.k.a. the user) is properly authorized to carry out the function. If not, an error message is returned on the screen and progress is denied.

SAP Logon ID Spreadsheet					
User Name	**Logon ID**	**Sub-Team**	**Profile**	**Phone #**	**Date Created**
John Smith	JSMITH	Purchasing	S:01:MATBUY	777-1212	2/18/98
Betty Anderson	BANDERSON	Purchasing	S:01:MATBUY	777-1215	2/18/98
Mike Michaels	MMICHAELS	Finance	S:01:FINACCT	777-1220	2/25/98

FIGURE 7-1 *The SAP Logon ID Spreadsheet should be expanded to include more detail during the development phase.*

 NOTE

Part IV provides more detail about the actual creation and assignment of profiles and authorization objects. For now, the intent is to encourage your team to begin tracking users, their logons, and the authorizations associated with them.

Working with Naming Conventions

Naming conventions are simply the identification and adherence to a common set of rules when developing SAP settings and making data entries in a business application. No doubt you have encountered naming conventions before within your legacy environment. However, as you work to migrate your business to SAP, you'll need to revisit those conventions. Some of what you used before may still be applicable and useful in SAP. However, most of your elements will need to be redefined, or mapped, to SAP terms and conditions. Definition and mapping includes working with known SAP values, field lengths, and so on. As you continue to read this chapter, you'll find that naming conventions come into play in a significant way as you prepare to migrate your processes into SAP.

SAP-provided data fields, system settings, and valid values should meet most of your business's needs. There will be times, though, when SAP hasn't provided the element or value that you need. In that case, SAP also nicely enables businesses to define their own system settings and valid values. At this point, establishing naming conventions and following them with the utmost rigor becomes especially important. SAP aids a business in defining its own settings and values by establishing the use of the "Z class" of elements as customer-defined elements. In other words, elements that are created specifically for your business start with the letter Z. For example, the following items are customer-defined elements within SAP:

- ◆ ZABC: Customer-defined data table to capture company-specific information
- ◆ ZABC-FIELD1: Customer-defined data element in company-specific table
- ◆ ZABCPROG: Customer-defined ABAP program that updates ZABC table entries

Your team should attempt to find logical links within the naming conventions that will make your specific elements easy to identify and support.

 CAUTION

> When the time comes for your company to upgrade your SAP version—say, 3.0 to 4.0—you will install revised versions of SAP code and functionality. As part of the upgrade process, SAP manages the migration of data elements and programs that it has defined. What won't be managed are the customer-defined elements that your company may have established. If you've followed a logical and consistent naming convention, any elements specifically defined for your business will be easier to identify and manage during the course of an SAP version upgrade. Of course, the easiest route is to always strive to use SAP-provided elements, but that approach isn't always possible.

Working with Customizations

Customizations are settings, elements, and fields that SAP expects your company to establish and manage. This feature is another key to SAP's core architecture and scalability. SAP is not an out-of-box product in the purest sense. You should not expect to install SAP and begin operating your business at the flick of a switch. The application needs to be tailored so it represents your company and the activities that it manages under SAP. Customization is a large effort in the SAP life cycle and eventual on-going support realm.

Customization requirements are usually encountered during the latter part of the design phase, but mainly during the development phase. Team members working to migrate processes will need to enable SAP fields or establish a collection of data settings that support the process. Therefore, customizations are necessary. However, this area requires strict SAP authorization control. Because SAP is an integrated system, customization settings that are established or changed can have an immediate effect on other processes or areas within SAP. Therefore, settings must be reviewed from a cross-functional perspective and controlled to ensure they remain consistent, functional, and nondestructive to other areas of development. To achieve this level of review and control, certain key individuals should focus on the aspect of customization and configuration. These people are the customization team, and it should include members who can effectively represent the different business areas that are migrating to SAP functionality.

The first role of the customization team is to establish the basic company parameters, or *global configurations*, that identify the company. These parameters include the following information:

- Country settings
- Tax settings
- Organizational settings
- Financial valuation settings

In addition, each member of the customization team who represents a business area needs to identify and establish base customizations that enable the initial activity of each business process. These include:

- Business calendar settings
- Material/Service type settings
- Number ranges
- Transaction code settings
- Inventory storage settings
- Financial reconciliation account settings

The list is actually quite extensive and depends on the type of business your company engages in and the degree of SAP migration your company is pursuing. Only you can define the depth of customization that is required, but the implementation team should establish some effective documentation templates that track the settings and the decisions behind them (see Figure 7-2).

The customization team can use this matrix to determine the basic settings that will make the development clients usable. By the content it captures, the matrix helps identify owners, track discussions and decisions, and identify how the particular setting is accessed. This document should be completed so that it can serve as the main tool during subsequent system builds. Initial client customization is a significant step in the system build process, and the base customizations are easier to enable if they are effectively documented.

SAP INITITIAL CUSTOMIZATION

This document is intended to capture all customizations that will be required to enable the implementation team's development instance/clients. All settings documented here have been thoroughly reviewed, tested, and approved by the Customization Team and the developers that have requested the settings. These customizations will be managed and maintained by the Customization Team, and the Customization Team will be responsible to enable these settings during each iterative system build.

Changes to these settings must be reviewed with the Customization Team, and only the Customization Team will have access to change any previously approved settings. All settings documented here will be maintained in the Master Client.

DESCRIPTION	3.0 MENU PATH & TRANSACTION CODE	AFFECTED MODULE	STATUS	DESCRIPTION OF SETTINGS	SUB-TEAM OWNER	DATE APPROVED
Client Common Settings						
Organization Settings						

FIGURE 7-2

An SAP Global Configuration Matrix is a useful tool to document and track any required base customizations.

Although a central team manages and maintains customization settings, you should establish a controlled process by which the other implementation team members can interact and submit requests for additional customizations. Figure 7-3 illustrates a tool that engages implementation team members in SAP customization.

This worksheet is more detailed than the Global Customization Matrix, and its primary users are implementation subteam members who discover and develop customization settings and policies to enable process migration. If you are responsible for the migration of a process into SAP, you'll find areas of required customization that need to be enabled to successfully complete the migration. You should be prepared to document your findings in a way that can be understood and discussed within the customization team. Because it isn't feasible for the customization team to locate every setting required of all processes being developed, this worksheet helps facilitate the communication between the customization team and the other members of the implementation team (see Figure 7-4).

If it supports your project's milestones, encourage the formation of customization team forums. In these forums, discuss requested customization settings and validate their process-specific or cross-functional effectiveness. As this is a major portion of the overall implementation cycle, be sure someone is assigned to track progress, issues, and resolutions. When specific customization proposals are to be discussed, encourage the developer making the request to attend a forum to further explain his or her findings and reasons for their recommendations. Like all other aspects of the implementation, be sure all decisions are fully documented and stored for easy retrieval and review.

This file is to be used for documenting customizations to be applied to the SAP clients. If you have any questions, please contact the appropriate Customization Team representative.

Customizations Request Worksheet

Description of Customization: Describe the customization to be made in as much detail as possible, and the business reason for this change.

Menu Path and Transaction Steps:
Menu path, including pushbuttons, field names and values.

Transaction Number:
System->Status, then press "Technical Info". Note the transaction number on the screen.

Affected SAP Modules:
Describe what SAP Module (MM, PP, etc.) is being affected by this customization

Submitted by:
Date Submitted:
Consultant Contact (if applicable):

FIGURE 7-3 *A detailed configuration worksheet helps implementation team members thoroughly communicate customization settings.*

SAP customization is a very detailed endeavor and is deserving of a treatment all its own. You want to be sure your implementation team is represented by a dedicated customization team and that the customization team members work with, establish, and adhere to good naming convention practices and good control techniques. Be sure the customization team membership is a subset of the overall implementation team and not a detached group of individuals. If supporting this effort means that your implementation team should be increased in size, then encourage that as well.

Working with Master Data Policies

Master data policies work in much the same way as customizations work. Data that is to migrate into SAP must do so in a controlled and consistent method. This process again incorporates the major points discussed thus far: control, naming conventions, and documentation. Master data policies can often be the result of a customization policy. It is feasible that a master data control team would be formed to address the cross-functional impact of master data settings. This team could have a somewhat shorter team-life than the customization team. Once the master data control team

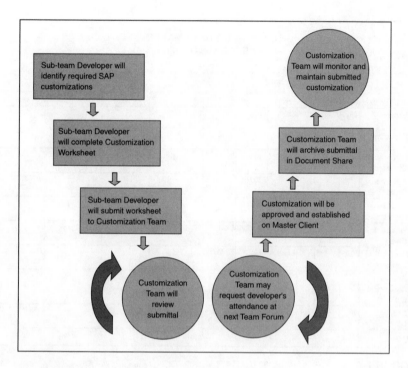

FIGURE 7-4 *This proposed customization communication flow chart shows how implementation team members can interact with the customization team.*

has effectively established master data policies, it should be expected that those policies remain in effect for the long-term use of the company.

Mapping Legacy Data to SAP

It's now time to actually define the mapping of legacy data into SAP terms and processes. The reason this task isn't part of the design phase is that the customization and master data settings cannot be defined until a valid SAP development instance and client strategy is defined for the team's use.

You begin the process of field-to-field mappings by populating the SAP development environment with your company's business data. And, as you may have guessed, you are asked to work with another document template, the Data Mapping Tool (DMT), as shown in Figure 7-5.

This tool helps you identify your current legacy data repositories and the individual elements that need to be migrated to the SAP data tables. As you review the table and process construction within SAP, you'll want to create your DMTs so they map

LEGACY >> R/3 DATA MAPPING TOOL
- PURCHASE ORDER -

	R/3					Legacy			
Description	Program	Scm #	Table	Field	Data Element	Database	Dataset	Field	Comments
Vendor	SAPMM06E	100	EKKO	LIFNR	ELIFN CHAR 10	PO_DBASE	PO_HEADER	VENDOR_ NUMBER	
Order Type			RM06E	BSART	BSART CHAR 4		N/A	N/A	DEFAULT - 'NB'
Purchase Order Date				BEDAT	BEDAT DATS 8			PO_DATE	DEFAULT TO DATE OF LOAD
Purchase Order				BSTNR	BSTNR CHAR 10			ORDER_ NUMBER	USE NUMBER RANGE 01
Purchasing Organization			EKKO	EKORG	EKORG CHAR 4				
Purchasing Group				EKGRP	BKGRP CHAR 3	PO_ITEMDB	PO_ITEM	BUYER_ NUMBER	
Item Category			RM06E	EPSTP	EPSTP CHAR 1				BLANK
Acctount Assignment Cat.				KNTTP	KNTTP CHAR 1				BLANK (STANDARD)
Delivery Date				LPEIN	LPEIN CHAR 1				DEFAULT - 'T'

FIGURE 7-5 *The Data Mapping Tool (DMT) helps facilitate the mapping of legacy data to the SAP environment.*

logical groupings of data that represent a process flow or a major collection of related data. This approach makes the actual data extractions and loads in the development phase much easier and more congruent to the overall SAP design and flow. Isolating elements outside of their process flow might lead to misinterpretation of the data's use and intention.

Identifying and Investigating Gaps and Issues

During your DMT creation, you probably found (not unexpectedly) that not all of the legacy elements were cleanly mapped. What to do? SAP, in all of its depth and breadth, could never possibly address every nuance conceivable in a business's legacy environment. It comes real close, though.

If you find yourself in this situation, it's time to draw from past experience, future vision, and a bit of creativity. The challenge here is to determine how the missing pieces of your process might migrate to the SAP environment. Consider the following questions when assessing the problem:

◆ How critical is this element to the overall process?

◆ How frequently do you use this element?

◆ Is there a business-legal need for this element?

◆ Is this element a duplication of another effort that may be better addressed in another process migration?

◆ Is there an opportunity to change the process to better fit into the SAP architecture?

First, establish a method to identify and capture development issues. Issue tracking can be done using another matrix-type design that is managed by a team member who is responsible for monitoring the issues, keeping up-to-date issue status, and rallying any actions required to resolve the issues. This matrix becomes your working to-do list to ensure that any and all limiting development and design issues are understood and can be presented to whomever is involved in the issue resolution. The matrix could include the following issues:

◆ Inconsistent business requirements

◆ Inconsistent legacy data or process flow

◆ Nonfunctional SAP processes

Be sure you categorize each issue in terms of severity. This approach will help you and your team identify the most mission-critical issues to be resolved first. Equally, give high priority to those issues that may be preventing the completion of a follow-on or dependent process elsewhere. Issues should be reviewed in an appropriate forum of developers, business process designers, consultants, and business or project leaders. Your goal in the forums is to discuss the issue, provide or poll for potential solutions, give direction to redevelopment and reverification efforts, and achieve business approval. As issues come and go, be sure to move closed issues to the end of the list—try not to remove them entirely—and to update the criticality status to reflect the current urgency of the issue.

Herein lies the inevitable trap when performing a migration to SAP—how to truly migrate to SAP style and methodology and not just re-create your legacy environment in a new business application. It can be hard to let go of cherished solutions, especially for the users, but sometimes also for the individuals who support them. However forward thinking and vision pays off in the end. If you merely move your current processes into SAP, you will probably miss the opportunity to utilize major integrated portions of the SAP methodology.

When any one of the issues appears to be a gap in process or functionality, you'll need to give it some additional design analysis effort. When you're working with a process hole or gap, see if any of the following options might apply:

♦ **Reclassify the element in SAP terms.** Evaluate the use of the orphan legacy element and see whether SAP's process has a similar field that could be used to achieve the same purpose. This option differs from the direct mapping process only in that the legacy element might have had an additional feature that SAP does not. However, if you can determine that the additional feature can be replaced elsewhere in SAP, the overall solution being migrated to SAP can be done so in an easier and more supportable manner.

♦ **Redefine and enlist the use of an existing SAP field.** This strategy is sometimes playfully referred to as, "Chuck, I'd like to buy a field." Essentially, you find another field in SAP that is nonconsequential to the SAP process and can be used to populate and store the data element your legacy process has used. Free text fields or generic check boxes are good candidates for this sort of data migration.

♦ **Retire the use of the element.** This solution is, of course, probably the easiest. If the orphaned element has been stored in the legacy process "because we always have," then use a critical eye to determine its real value. Sometimes, these elements were once critical to a particular legacy process or effort. You might find that, if a process or effort has since been discontinued or replaced, the residual data capturing might linger on. Definitely strive to remove these elements from the new process.

If the element is critical, persistent, and definitely requires active enabling within the SAP process, then it may be time to reengineer. *Reengineering* is not just a buzzword, and it shouldn't be taken lightly. However, changing to a new business environment provides a golden opportunity to challenge tradition and breathe new life and value into a legacy process.

Reengineering Processes

In its truest sense, reengineering is the opportunity and action of critically analyzing business processes and methods. You may already be familiar with this concept, but experience shows it is much easier to describe than to do.

A business can hold fast, struggle, and fight for its traditional methods. It's understandable and real. But to break new ground in the business market and achieve leadership, businesses need to break emotional ties with traditional methods and work to explore new opportunities that will promote and enable excellence. Although this may sound like the well-known business mantra, it's an aspect that, again, is much easier said than done. In fact, you might find it easier to reengineer from the support perspective than from the business perspective. Support environments are usually searching for new ways to manage the business and its applications. Business environments, however, can sometimes be reluctant to change a process that is stable and repetitive but possibly inefficient or not 100 percent effective in meeting the business requirement.

What should be the easiest question to answer during this process—what do we really need from the process?—often becomes the most elusive. It's a question to be asked every step of the way to ensure that the same old techniques don't proliferate. With regard to SAP, there is a dynamic that seems to occur when the newness and foreign nature of the SAP processes cannot be quickly embraced with the familiarity of the old process. Teams can, often to their own surprise, try to re-create the legacy processes in SAP, thus lending some familiarity to the new application. Try to avoid this trap. What will be achieved is a potentially splintered, fragmented SAP process flow, and the potential gain is unlikely to be reached.

Keep in mind, also, that the more SAP is altered, fragmented, and short-circuited, the more difficult it is to support. If a new process design includes a variety of process escapes—deviations from internal SAP process flow—the integrated SAP processes will not function as originally designed. A design approach like this works to create a potential for numerous process dependencies that can be like supporting a bowl of spaghetti. Work within SAP as much as possible.

So how do you begin to reengineer a process? From the implementation team standpoint, you will participate in the following steps:

1. Define the criticality of the process.

2. Determine the dependencies, both upstream and downstream.

3. Clearly define the process result.

4. Locate the same process result within SAP.

5. Determine the readiness and willingness of your business to reengineer to a new solution.

6. Redefine the process in SAP terms.

7. Refit other process designs accordingly.

The details depend on a particular situation, obviously. However, SAP has proved rather proficient in meeting 99 percent of the business needs ever encountered. Chances are, your means to a solution is in there. From a support role, you will probably get the chance to dive deeper into SAP in search of the solution that the business requires. And if the solution still can't be found within SAP, then the process you're trying to define might be exceptionally unique to your business. In this case, you will need to review SAP flow trade-offs in exchange for developing unique interfaces or *customer-defined solutions*.

Customer-Defined Solution—*A nonstandard SAP functionality created within SAP using the ABAP/4 Workbench tool set. Solutions can include programs, screens, transactions, and reports.*

In Chapter 6 you learned about customer-defined elements within SAP. A customer-defined solution, or bolt-on, is a process or functionality that is implemented right within SAP, but which SAP does not support from the application standpoint. These solutions can be integrated into SAP's flow but will require potential local changes to SAP-delivered code. This useful approach produces an SAP look and feel but also may require special support handling, especially during a system upgrade. Because the solution is customer defined, it needs to be manually refitted when an upgrade occurs—migrating from SAP version 3.0 to 4.0, for example. To learn more about creating customer-defined solutions in SAP, refer to Prima's *Advanced ABAP/4 Programming.*

Beware of those people slinging "reengineering" as some sort of marketing slogan. It really is an opportunity to break some paradigms and institute positive change. But you might find, as I sometimes did, that the term is often used as an attention-getting bullet or a status symbol. Until it's really exercised, it's nothing more than a catch phrase. Unfortunately, I found it to be a bit overstated and underused. You might not always be in the position to correct the situation, but don't lose faith. Real reengineering does exist, and you're sure to have a chance to see it in action. It's a neat experience. Take the plunge.

Early Data Loads

The next step to take, after the base configurations are enabled and some of the data mapping wrinkles are ironed out, is to begin populating the development clients with usable master data—that is, the business information and data used by the business on a daily basis. This step facilitates the full enabling of the developmental environment for use in testing, verifying, and refining the migrated business processes. To achieve data loads easily and effectively, it is recommended to create and use data strip-and-load programs.

The *strip program* will identify and extract data from your company's legacy systems. Programming of this sort can be achieved through the use of a common data query tool such as QUIZ, QTP, or any other sort of programming tool or language that is currently in use in your legacy environment. Then you can use the previously prepared DMTs, to extract legacy data in a way that logically maps to and populates functional flows or major groupings of SAP data tables. For example, if you want to populate material master data in SAP, develop your legacy strip program to capture all relevant information that will cleanly populate one of SAP's logical material master views, as you had previously defined in your DMT. The output of your legacy data extraction should be a space-delimited, flat, ASCII file. This file is easy to copy and later manipulate during the load process. To complete the extract process and prepare the data for loading into SAP, be sure to copy the file into an accessible UNIX file directory— /tmp/data/mtlmstr/datastrip, for example.

When loading the data into SAP, you need to prepare a custom program written in ABAP code. This program will locate and retrieve the data file from the UNIX directory and populate the various SAP tables that you specify. Be aware that the DMT should specify special circumstances where data conversion may be required. For example, some fields may require truncation, and some may require complete redefinition from legacy terms to SAP terms. The ABAP data load program can handle all these routines. Figure 7-6 is an example of a working ABAP data load routine.

Your initial data loads will probably not be 100 percent effective, and you will have to execute them until you have a clean data load. For this step, your subteam partner, representing the business process, will have to review and validate the results of the data loads. Forewarn your partner that the data review is conducted on a record-by-record basis and is very tedious. However, you must follow this initial procedure to ensure that the data mappings were defined correctly and that the data is accurately populated within SAP.

```
DATA:           BEGIN OF INT_TABLE OCCURS 10,
                    PARTNUM   TYPE C,
                    PARTUOM   TYPE C,
                        PARTTYPE   TYPE C,
DATA:           END OF INT_TABLE.

DATA:           W_DATAFILE(50) VALUE '/tmp/data/mtlmstr/datastrip'.

OPEN DATASET W_DATAFILE FOR INPUT IN TEXT MODE.

DO.
        IF SY-SUBRC NE 0.
                EXIT.
        ENDIF.

        READ DATASET W_DATAFILE INTO INT_TABLE.
        APPEND INT_TABLE.
        CLEAR INT_TABLE.

ENDDO.

CLOSE DATASET W_DATAFILE.
```

FIGURE 7-6 *Sample SAP ABAP data load program*

On future iterations, you might be able to use ABAP to write additional custom data-verification programs. A program like ABAP can greatly reduce the time required for verification and can eliminate some aspects of human error. However, you should only write and use special code like this after accurately defining and testing the potential error conditions.

 TIP

If it hasn't already been done, the technical members of the implementation team need to receive concentrated ABAP/4 training. This training ensures that they can effectively write data manipulation programs, interfaces, and reports within SAP. For more information on training, please refer to Appendix E.

The data loads are executed over and over again to ensure their accurate function. Data loaded into SAP is then used in a variety of process development iterations. The data becomes so well used, and abused, that you have to refresh it on a regular basis. Developmental data loading is also a practice effort. You will also use these programs when you make the final migration to the live business installation. Be sure your programs can be archived and retrieved safely throughout the course of the life cycle.

Developing Interfaces

At some point, you will probably need to develop interfaces into and out of SAP. The exact conditions depend on the approach your team is taking to the scope of the process migration. But, for example, you might need to pass data between SAP and a legacy information system.

The first step in developing an interface is to understand what data is required to be passed. For example, if your company is not migrating the real-time calculation of inventory balances, it is necessary to develop an interface program that can strip the information from a legacy information system and populate SAP with the data. This interface is considered an *inbound* interface, meaning the information is being transferred into SAP. Remember, SAP is your evolving hub of business information, and it should be considered as the main point of reference when passing data. So in the case of this interface, you need to strip a material number, any special attributes, and the inventory quantity information into an ASCII file. The file is then deposited into an available UNIX directory, and an SAP program is written to capture the file and populate SAP with the data.

The opposite effect is a *outbound* interface: a program that strips information from SAP and makes it available to non-SAP information systems. A good example here is a purchase order strip that provides usable data to other company offices that are not yet using SAP. For this purpose, the data is stripped from SAP and written to a UNIX file. A legacy-based program then retrieves the file, manipulates the data into a format that a legacy application can use, and loads the data into the legacy information database. Inbound interface programs are constructed much the same as your developmental data load programs; the interface needs to access a file of data and accurately populate data tables within SAP. For outbound interfaces, refer to Figure 7-7 as an example.

```
DATA:           BEGIN OF INT_TABLE OCCURS 100,
                    INCLUDE STRUCTURE EKKO.
DATA:           END OF INT_TABLE.

DATA:           W_DATAFILE(50) VALUE '/tmp/data/mtlordr/dataout'.

START-OF-SELECTION.

        SELECT * FROM EKPO INTO INT_TABLE WHERE ELIKZ NE 'X'.


        OPEN DATASET W_DATAFILE FOR OUTPUT IN TEXT MODE.

        LOOP AT INT_TABLE.
                TRANSFER INT_TABLE TO W_DATAFILE.
        ENDLOOP.

        CLOSE DATASET W_DATAFILE.
```

FIGURE 7-7 *Sample SAP Outbound interface program*

The final step in establishing your interfaces is to determine the frequency in which they will be executed. Interfaces can be run monthly, weekly, daily, or multiple times a day. It depends upon the business requirements and the availability of the data that is to be passed.

Developing Reports

Business reports will usually be included in the process specifications. Usually, these reports are strips of logical data, sometimes manipulated or calculated, and they aid the business areas in performing job duties and analyzing activity. Reports always have been a mainstay of the business community, and will most likely remain so. In your current state process details, report specifications should have been captured.

Some of the reports you'll be asked to design are direct replacements for reports that had been previously generated by legacy applications. If the application and the information contained within it are targeted for migration, a new SAP-based report needs to be written as a replacement. As with the other aspects of current state design review, reports should be closely scrutinized to determine true value and use to the business community. If nobody remembers the original intent of a report, it probably shouldn't be printed.

When developing reports in SAP, you'll use ABAP/4 programming language. You should look for opportunities to consolidate report information into more streamlined presentations (some reports that are generated might serve more than a single customer). Legacy reports may provide overlapping information because that information was stored in different applications in the legacy environment. Because SAP is integrated, you might be able to combine two reports that served two business areas and still serve the same two business areas.

SAP reporting is also very customizable, allowing the same report to run under different sets of selection and reporting criteria. A single program could provide very different information output based on the selection criteria introduced. Also, reports can be designed with a front-end screen that could serve as a custom report menu, which allows users to choose the output they require. These reports can run in background processes on SAP, still utilizing different selection criteria, and can be scheduled to execute at predefined times and intervals.

Iterations of Design

As your designs are migrated into SAP, you'll conduct very informal, ad hoc tests to see whether the processes are working as originally intended. You'll naturally wish to perform these tests just to be sure you are on the right track and that the required deliverables are well on their way to being met. But now—for any number of reasons— your process isn't working correctly. The problem can require alterations consisting of minor modifications or major overhauls. The bottom line is that your deliverable must allow the associated business activity to continue with minimal to no disruption in the overall flow.

Take a moment to put on your support hat. This is where you will more fully develop an understanding of the business processes and the SAP objects and settings that enable them. You now have an opportunity to develop deep business and SAP-technical expertise as you work through iterations of process design and development. Although this task of iteration can be laborious and redundant, the result of knowledge and expertise gained cannot be overemphasized.

Business-focused and technical-focused subteam partners need to work together through a process design migration. You should expect to encounter some hurdles or roadblocks during the design migration. Anticipate them and don't let them discourage you. After all, you've been working with limited SAP access and environmental conditions up to this point. It is in this stage that you find all sorts of interesting elements and settings within the system, so continue to work through the processes and note the points of disconnect or process impediments. Document and track these situations, developing a process issue list that you can review with other team members. Some resolutions can come quickly, but most solutions include one or more of the following requirements:

◆ Additional configurations

◆ Revised data mapping specifications and data loads

◆ Reevaluation of business requirements

◆ Process gap fillers (custom solutions)

When faced with developing solutions to the particular process barrier, ask the following questions:

◆ Is the process being analyzed fully enabled by SAP?

◆ Can the business process be modified slightly to fit within the SAP design?

◆ Should the process remain within the current legacy solution?

◆ Should the process be managed with a custom SAP solution (bolt-on)?

◆ Should the process be completely reengineered?

These questions are similar to the questions you asked when creating the initial process design in the previous phase. You might find yourself asking the same or similar questions again if the process is not mapping into SAP very cleanly. Your goal is always to work within SAP's standard set of solutions, but you want to be sure you don't attempt to force fit a process just for the sake of enabling SAP functionality. You need to remain true to your business's needs. This area requires a fine balance, and you might have to prepare several possible solution scenarios and present them to a business manager or to the project leaders.

During the redesign cycle, you'll find yourself in need of additional or revised business process specifications. If you're a business-focused subteam member, you must understand and document those needs and communicate them back to the company's business users or management. If you are a technical-focused subteam member, you are really not in the business of defining business processes, although your experience will lend itself to making sound suggestions. You will want to defer to the business process owners for making the determinations regarding the specifications under which the eventual SAP-enabled process will operate.

Be sure, when you need additional business specifications, that the reviewing business individual or individuals understand the project goals and milestone objectives. Allow the reviewers enough time and information to base their decision on solid facts, but remind them of the need to act with relative speed to ensure the project stays on track.

Whenever possible, work directly with the business teams in developing the solutions. If the review effort is slow going and becomes a potential obstacle to the overall project progress, take the problem to the project leaders.

After all the iterations of process design and redesign, the process will eventually meet the specifications, and you will be ready for your first road show. This show is another of many project checkpoints. As you did in the design phase, you will now arrange for additional show-and-tell sessions with your team members, project leaders, and sponsors. You might call this show-and-tell session your "functional prototype."

Functional Prototype—An early system test that determines if a new design functions as required and provides the expected result within the automated environment.

At this stage, the process you are prototyping will probably work only at the unit (individual process) level. However, as each process is migrated and initially validated, it becomes a good idea to ensure each process meets the requirement from the business's perspective.

Freezing the Design Specifications

This topic works with the design iterations discussed in the preceding section. In this context, it becomes necessary to assure that all aspects of a business process are fully specified in relationship to business requirements and that those requirements will remain unchanged until, at least, after the ultimate implementation has occurred. This milestone, known as *specification freeze,* can sometimes be difficult to achieve.

Specification Freeze—A point in development when process requirements are considered complete, disallowing any additional opportunistic modifications.

Specification freeze might be difficult to achieve due to the need for further design review. If, for example, a process design was reviewed and approved for migration, the process migration might not perform as expected. This situation may require specification review and revision. The reviewer(s) must understand and support the milestone objectives of the development effort. Sometimes specification freeze can be delayed simply because the process reviewer was not aware of a design completion milestone or the review has not prioritized the review activity in a way that supports the design completion milestone. Also, as the definition of specification freeze suggests, specification freeze can be delayed while reviewers continue to request additional— usually insignificant—design enhancements.

Specification freeze can also be hampered by lack of clarity in the process requirements or objectives. SAP is not a design-as-you-go application, and you want to discourage ad hoc specifications whenever possible. Otherwise, a process design can quickly get out of control or become a barrier to other process development.

Finally, specification freeze can be delayed simply because no one in the business organization is clearly responsible for the process approval. All process solutions require visible, traceable, and accountable business approval. Otherwise, it is impossible to ever determine whether the process solution was properly delivered. This sort of approval and accountability can sometimes be difficult to obtain. However, until it is, the process design can be continually in flux and most likely not meet the project milestones.

Documenting This Phase

Documentation continues to be the order of the day here. During this phase, you should have worked with the following:

- ◆ SAP user logon matrix
- ◆ Cross-functional customization matrix
- ◆ Process-specific customization worksheets
- ◆ Data mapping tool (DMT)
- ◆ Report and interface specifications
- ◆ Data strip-and-load programs
- ◆ Development issues list

Exiting This Phase

As you exit this phase, you should be able to deliver the following:

- ◆ A configured system
- ◆ Functional data strip-and-load programs
- ◆ Successful first-pass migration of legacy processes to SAP
- ◆ An issue-tracking log that identifies processes requiring further development
- ◆ Updated design documentation
- ◆ A central repository of tools used in this phase

The tool repository mentioned refers to your team's documentation share. Also, though, it can extend into the SAP data dictionary. All information regarding the properties of data elements can be found there, as can your custom ABAP programs that are used for data loads. As you went through the iterations of development, you saw the need to continually add to and refine your development tools. Also you will find that development tools such as documentation and programs that have been defined and refined could be useful to other team members. To help ensure the project progresses according to plan, take the opportunity to leverage the developmental efforts of individual team members across the team; working with existing code and documentation could save some effort along the way.

Summary

I won't summarize this chapter by congratulating you on completing the development phase. The truth is, you will be developing right up to the end of the project and beyond. Remembering that SAP is a vast, integrated system, you'll know that the project team's efforts and developments will continually be revised and modified throughout the SAP life cycle. You're fine-tuning your business engine—one turn of a screw here presents the need to turn another screw or tighten a belt elsewhere. The real goal is to act in a controlled, well-documented, well-communicated manner. Ensure that the business specifications from which you are working are complete and frozen. If not, you'll never be able to exit this phase.

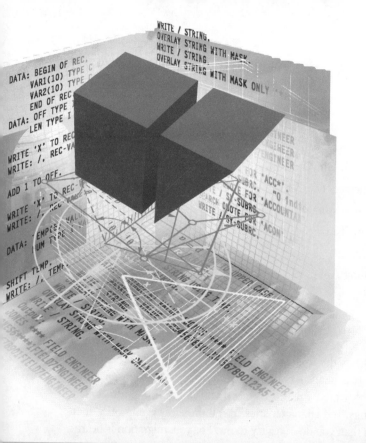

Chapter 8

Supporting the Testing and Training Phase

In This Chapter

♦ Entering This Phase

♦ Building the Test and Training Instances

♦ Working with a Dedicated Test Area

♦ Supporting Final Unit Testing

♦ Supporting Integration Testing

♦ Supporting Pilot Testing

♦ Supporting the Training Approach

♦ Documenting This Phase

♦ The Go/No-Go Review

♦ Exiting This Phase

The testing and training phase is the final step before you and your team begin the actual SAP implementation. It is here that you rigorously test your designs, both in singular fashion and in an integrated stream. By now, you've become quite skilled with SAP functionality, settings, and characteristics. You'll probably even notice that you think more in SAP terms than you do in legacy terms. For you, migration is nearly a reality. However, in this phase you will run iterative tests to ensure that your process designs are complete, accurate, and reliable. In addition, you will begin sharing and demonstrating your designs with individuals outside of your implementation team—the end user community.

Before the testing gets started, you need to perform additional system builds. This time, you and your team will prepare Testing and Training instances. The Testing instance, or Quality Assurance (QA) instance, is where the iterations of testing occur. This environment should be tightly controlled, much like the Live Business instance you will create later. In fact, this QA instance may evolve into the Live Business instance. The Training instance, on the other hand, is where your team will conduct classroom exercises to prepare the end users for the pending implementation.

Some results from your testing and training may necessitate last-minute design modifications. In the best case, these design flaws will be easy to repair and not pose a major threat to your implementation. (See the section "The Go/No Go Review" for tips on dealing with significant complications.)

If everything is on track, your next step is to get the business teams ready for the implementation, making sure that all users are identified and properly prepared for the SAP migration. Then you'll conduct your final review. This chapter explains what this review entails, who is presenting, and who is listening. If the results are in your favor, then you'll exit this phase and move on to the actual implementation.

Entering This Phase

You may have thought that this phase would never officially arrive. The development phase was one of the most enduring phases and may have seemed endless at times. However, you have exited the development phase, and you should now have the following results with which to begin the training and testing phase:

- ◆ Functional SAP business process solutions
- ◆ Defined and functional legacy interfaces and/or bolt-on solutions
- ◆ Revised and frozen business specifications and requirements
- ◆ A tool depository that contains all development work and documentation to this point
- ◆ Additional SAP-knowledgeable resources as required (for example, consultants)

You and the implementation team are nearing the end of the project. Your goal now is to work the processes that are migrating to SAP to the point of stress and potential failure. You need to test them hard and continuously. In fact, you'll want to be prepared for the end users to begin their testing; their job is to prove that reliability has been designed into the processes and that the required business results are achieved. You'll also introduce a pilot-test methodology, and test to see whether you've been successful in achieving the goals and objectives that were stated in the first phase of the life cycle.

There's still more documentation to be generated and modified now. However, you'll see how to leverage all of what you've documented up to this point, smoothing the development documentation into usable, long-term support documentation and training materials. You'll also see how the documentation has undergone a migration of its own, and how it will prove to be invaluable to you and your team.

Building the Test and Training Instances

Just as you did to prepare for the development phase, this phase requires you to establish two additional SAP instances. The first thing you should notice in Figure 8-1 is that the environment has continued to grow and evolve. This situation requires the implementation team to deal with increasing complexity and maintenance needs and to ensure proper staffing. Your team's responses to the evolving development environment is leading to the support strategy that will exist after implementation. (See

Part III for details on post-implementation support.) Your project leaders should begin evaluating the longer-term maintenance requirements of the new SAP environment.

The QA/Test instance should contain all processes that will be tested under more-formal and controlled conditions. It should be managed in much the same way as the Development instance master client—access should be limited, and specific individuals should manage the population of elements. The reason is simple: This instance is where the project team members and business process owners establish and prepare their test cases or scripts. To ensure their success, they need the assurance that their work can be set up and maintained in a protected environment. Preparation for testing can be extremely time-consuming, and it's not a task that is gleefully repeated.

The Training instance should be established in the same manner as the QA instance. In fact, it can actually be made from a copy of the QA instance. Compared to the QA instance, though, the Training instance contains less "prepared" data. The Training instance is where users work and learn, creating transactional data much as they would in their existing legacy environment; in many ways the Training instance resembles the Live Business instance.

The QA and Training instances require the customization team to make the initial settings, and the appropriate implementation subteam members to execute and verify the data loads. With your tool repository easily accessible, you'll retrieve programs and documentation to expedite this step. Preparing these two new instances is another

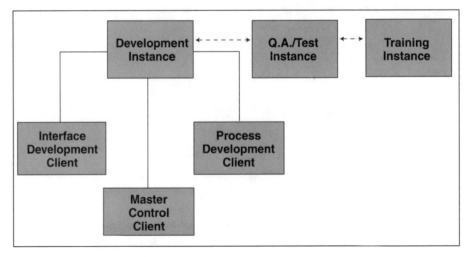

FIGURE 8-1 *The revised Development instance architecture incorporates the QA/Test instance and Training instance.*

iteration of process and tool usage and refinement. You're now fully engaged in rehearsal for implementation. This step incorporates the use of the previously created process matrix. The matrix acts as the menu from which you will select and migrate developed process solutions to the QA/Test client.

TIP

SAP also provides a tool, the Correction and Transport System (CTS), that enables the electronic capture and transmittal (transporting) of process solutions and settings from one SAP instance or client to another. There's even a tool that allows the complete copying of an SAP client. Client copying is a function found within the SAP Basis tool set and is not discussed in detail in this book. For more information about the CTS, refer to Chapter 18 of this book.

You are also ready to begin the final preparations for business access control within the SAP environment. Using the logon ID matrix you created and refined during the Design and Development phases, you can expand it in order to compile the final listing of the actual business users who will require SAP access and authorization. Look to the business specifications for the information that describes what sort of business user should be enabled to conduct which processes. You need to work directly with the business community to ensure that each user has been identified—and authorized by management—for the intended SAP access and authorization. When completing this activity, your logon ID matrix will probably look like the example in Figure 8-2.

	User Name	Logon ID	Business Area	Manager	Location	Profile	Employee ID#	Phone #	Date Created
1			SAP Business Area Logon ID Spreadsheet						
2									
3	User Name	Logon ID	Business Area	Manager	Location	Profile	Employee ID#	Phone #	Date Created
4									
5	Jerry Sampson	JSAMPSON	Purchasing	Marty Masters	Building A	S:01:MATBUY	EM55211	777-1825	8/1/98
6	Tom Martin	TMARTIN	Purchasing	Marty Masters	Building A	S:01:MATBUY	EM46588	777-2388	8/1/98
7	Al Erickson	AERICKSON	Finance	Connie Green	Building C	S:01:FINACCT	EM33456	776-1662	8/1/98
8	Terry Stevens	TSTEVENS	Finance	Connie Green	Building C	S:01:FINACCT	EM12222	776-1668	8/1/98
9	Mary Severson	MSEVERSON	Planning	Steve Samuels	Building A	S:01:MATPLN	EM33344	777-1992	8/1/98
10	Tim Sharp	TSHARP	Planning	Steve Samuels	Building A	S:01:MATPLN	EM12334	777-1811	8/1/98
11	Harry Levins	HLEVINS	Master Data	Donald Hart	Building B	S:01:MATMSTR	EM45644	775-1291	8/1/98
12	Jane Tapp	JTAPP	Master Data	Donald Hart	Building B	S:01:MATMSTR	EM34567	775-4622	8/1/98
13									
14									

FIGURE 8-2 *This business process profile matrix identifies the business users.*

During the entire testing phase, the process owners should ensure the use of restrictive profiles to further the development of this important business control tool. Testing the profiles, possibly through use of model SAP logons your team may have created, helps ensure the business processes you migrate to SAP function as expected, and can be properly controlled through the use of the logon profiles. Testing profiles in conjunction with processes is necessary to ensure the business users have adequate access to perform system tasks, but not so much access that they could affect other processes for which they are not authorized.

Working with a Dedicated Test Area

By this time, you can see that your testing is about to reach a state of formality, and the need for a dedicated test area/classroom becomes apparent. If your team has already established a laboratory environment (see Chapter 5), then this task might be a simple matter of reevaluating the room's amenities. If not, you should consider establishing a separate physical environment in which to conduct controlled, uninterrupted test cycles. This type of facility is not an absolute prerequisite to this phase, but a controlled and comfortable environment is extremely conducive to focused testing. You will be involving other team members and business representatives during the testing phase. It's not the kind of activity to conduct around a single PC at a team member's desk.

If possible, encourage your team to secure a closed room that will be large enough to accommodate the following items:

- Tables and chairs for at least 30 individuals
- PCs or workstations that are network enabled and can run the SAP GUI
- A projection system that can display transparencies as well as PC-based presentations

As you might imagine, this facility is a significant investment for your team. However, it is extremely useful and conducive to the tasks being performed during the testing phase and is essential during actual user training.

Supporting Final Unit Testing

Your final unit testing begins with specific migrated business processes that represent a single business activity or event. Your goal is to conclusively prove that the new process will yield results that are the same or better than the results achieved in the legacy environment. To achieve this goal, you need to incorporate the use of the following tools:

- ◆ QA/Test instance
- ◆ Master data
- ◆ Appropriate use of business profiles
- ◆ Detailed process event scenarios

The master data requires some additional manipulation. At this time, the QA/Test instance contains basic company data that was loaded during the data strip-and-load execution. However, you will probably need to work within the instance to establish required SAP data records that may not have existed in your legacy environment. You will create data and information that is required to mirror the legacy process. For example, you might need to create data linkages of material numbers and vendors to effectively test the purchase order creation process.

Your master data loads populated material information as well as vendor information. However, the linkage between the two might not have existed in your legacy environment similar to SAP's Information Records (a data record that represents the linkage between a material and the vendor that will supply it). You'll need to create that linkage manually within your to support the unit test of the purchase order process.

Next, be sure to identify which sort of business user is likely to perform each process to be tested. Using the business profile matrix that has been prepared and is under control, identify the specific profiles that should be associated with the logon IDs that are used when conducting the unit tests. Actually, you will probably have business profiles associated to your QA/Test logon that reflect the business process that you own or support. This approach enables you to conduct impromptu testing as you prepare the framework of your unit test. When you are ready to execute the test through the help of other partners or business representatives, you may elect to establish generic user logons that provide the desired business profile.

The last step is to revise your process design scripts so they contain the additional information that can be used in executing the unit testing. This version of the scripts incorporates the information previously specified during the design and development phase but also includes the master and conditional data parameters to be used and tested during this stage of the process validation. Figure 8-3 shows an example of a revised business process scenario.

SAP IMPLEMENTATION UNIT TEST

TEST DESCRIPTION

This unit test will exercise the migrated Purchase Order process in SAP.

Test approach: Create various purchase orders in a standard fashion.

Programs to be tested: SAPMM06E, RSNAST00

TEST CASE DEPENDENCIES

1. Q.A./Test system is available.
2. Test data exists.

TEST DATA REQUIRED

1. Valid material numbers on SAP.
2. Valid supplier master records on SAP.

TEST PROCEDURE

1. Access SAP transaction ME21.
2. Enter supplier number, order type, and delivery date.
3. Verify detailed information in second screen.
4. etc.

EXPECTED RESULTS

1. All master data will be recognized and valid.
2. SAP will validate field entries.
3. SAP will assign new purchase order number at time of posting.

ACTUAL RESULTS

1.

2.

3.

FIGURE 8-3 *An example of a revised Business Process Scenario for Unit Testing*

Supporting Integration Testing

In this phase of testing, also known as end-to-end testing, you perform sophisticated tests to simulate the larger business process and data flows. The approach to integration testing can be largely modeled after the end-to-end business process flows you created during the design phase and tested during the early prototyping effort. Essentially, you need to work with the other process developers and owners to assemble the individual processes into a logical, operational chain of events. This testing phase is complex because the data with which the different processes are working often are the result of a previous process. Consequently, this phase is the first opportunity to prove the consistency and flow of the data through SAP. You, your team, and the business representatives will now see the integration in full force. No doubt, you'll find some breaks along the way. Expect those and work to make repairs as quickly as possible.

Supporting Pilot Testing

Pilot testing is most significant in that the end users are more involved in the solution reviews. At this stage of testing, users should receive hands-on experience with the SAP processes and be asked to provide feedback regarding the overall usability and applicability of the migrated solutions. The group of end users involved in this phase of testing should represent each of the business areas. The purpose of this phase is to test the designs and to evaluate how users interact with the system and the processes that will be enabled. The pilot-testing phase is also your first opportunity to watch how the users approach SAP and how successful they might be when executing the system processes. Pay especially close attention to the rate at which the users grasp the material being presented. Pilot testing becomes a dry run for your eventual training program.

Before you actually involve your business-area representatives in pilot testing, arrange for them to have some initial SAP training—the sort of training that you received during the start-up phase. Be sure they have the opportunity to become familiar with the SAP GUI and the methods of navigation. You want to ensure that your pilot test is focused on the processes being reviewed; not the use of the SAP GUI.

Pilot testing is typically conducted by the business-focused members of the implementation subteam because the audience is more business based. This approach helps to develop confidence and trust in the material being presented. The business-focused implementation team members can usually relate to the business situations that surround a process and easily identify with and respond to questions the business audience might have. If the business-focused implementation team members can effectively relay how an SAP process will replace a legacy process, the audience of business representatives will usually feel more confident that the business requirements were thoroughly understood and represented within the new SAP processes. The business member will show—and should explain—how the legacy business process attributes were carefully considered and managed with developing the process migration.

The technical-focused implementation team members act in more of a supporting role in this test phase. They ensure the system is ready for the pilot test and work in the background to guarantee that no unforeseen technical problems creep up during the pilot presentation. This effort can include monitoring system processing response, automatic processes, output, and user logon capabilities. Clearly, the technical member will have verified all of the technical aspects in the test instance before the pilot presentation begins, but you should expect at least one surprise.

Before the pilot test, the implementation team members—both business-focused and technical-focused—should review the processes and the pilot scripts that will be executed. The business-focused members should confirm that the presentation material is applicable to and understandable by the intended audience. The business-focused members should also provide any necessary sample transactional data. The technical-focused members should verify that any required master data from the legacy applications has been loaded.

Also, all customizations that are required for the process execution should be verified. Both business-focused and technical-focused implementation team members should go into the pilot tests with fully prepared scenarios, data, and process functionality, yet be ready to react as need be.

> One very valuable yet often overlooked result of the pilot presentation is that the partnership between the business-focused and technical-focused implementation team members becomes evident to the pilot presentation audience. This partnership works to solidify the useful and beneficial working relationship that can come from the teaming of these two types of individual contributors, and the partnership further proves the power of integrated information and knowledge sharing. I have heard users favorably comment on how well the business and technical team members worked together to ensure the success of a pilot test.

To help with the flow of your pilot-test session, you might follow this sequence:

1. Introductions

2. Description of implementation project scope and goals

3. Discussion of SAP data hierarchy and legacy mapping methodology

4. Overview of customizations pertinent to the process being presented

5. Process flow overview

6. Script execution

7. Questions and wrap-up

One final idea is to ask audience members to complete a post-test survey. The information you collect will help you gauge the effectiveness of the process design as well as the effectiveness of the presentation. You will probably be supporting several pilot tests, and you should take the opportunity to incorporate any suggested improvements as might be shared on the post-test surveys. Some attendees may not wish to fill out the surveys, but most will and are usually quite conscientious yet candid in their responses. This survey becomes your presentation's report card; you should study and understand the responses you receive and share them with the rest of the implementation team. In addition, other presenting teams will benefit from the responses.

Supporting the Training Approach

The training approach is a multifaceted situation. Your approach must answer the following questions:

♦ Where will the training be conducted?

♦ Who will prepare the training material?

♦ Who will conduct the training sessions?

♦ Who will coordinate the training effort?

The first question is actually quite simple to answer. The formal training should be conducted in the same dedicated area as the pilot tests. In fact, your pilot-testing survey should have asked about the presentation facilities. If respondents mention any deficiencies, try to correct them.

The second point is a bit trickier. Although this discussion has presented the events and activities sequentially, the reality is that much of the activity will occur in parallel, especially during the iterative development and testing cycles. So the question becomes one of resource bandwidth: Is the implementation team able to manage a training effort as well? Some popular opinion asserts that, yes, they should. Nobody knows this information better than the implementation team, and nobody can represent it better than this team. But, wanting the implementation team to perform the implementation training can be easier said than done. The implementation team is working hard to ensure that all migrating processes are working and ready for the upcoming implementation. Preparing for and supporting SAP training is a very time-consuming and rigorous task. Your project leaders should help you find a balance. They need to understand the training task and the current load the implementation team members are under.

Although the use of external training teams is sometimes effective, this practice is generally discouraged for several reasons. (These teams are in the business of preparing technical training material and presenting it to company employees.) First, working with an external team often takes more time than having the implementation team prepare the training themselves. Second, external teams often have their own methods and tools that are "effective in training company employees." However, the implementation team has already developed significant documentation—process and data mappings, interface specifications, process scripts—which can (and should) be used as the basis for training material. In addition, your team will need to train the external training team. Even if the trainers are fluent in SAP usage, they are most likely not fluent in your company's business practices.

Another consideration is whether the external training team can work within the business culture that your users would expect. If the external team approaches the task with extreme professionalism, it might appear to be stilted, one sided, and inflexible. By contrast, an approach that is too casual and informal can seem to be unprepared and potentially inaccurate. Only your team will know your business users and only you, having worked within the environment, can determine the best, most effective approach to take. Consider, also, that you will need to alter your approach for different business teams—a training program presented to a financial team will probably differ in tone and style from a program presented to a material-handling team. Ask yourself whether an external team would understand and adapt to subtle audience nuances.

Finally, you'll probably find you can be more at ease, and put the audience at ease, if you are training business users you know. These are your users. They have either worked with you in the past, have associated you with the project recently, or will work with you in the future. If you are able to demonstrate the new functionality with ease and confidence, they will usually reciprocate with a general mood of acceptance.

You can see that this discussion also answered the question of who should conduct the training sessions. Much like the pilot-test presentation, the training should be conducted by the implementation team, partnering the business and technical members whenever possible. If these same people have created the training documentation, who better to actually present it?

Now, the one aspect of training that you might find amenable to external assistance is the actual coordination of the training effort. This activity is practically a project in itself. Classes need to be defined, participants need to be identified, and materials need to be prepared. Each class participant should have a class workstation—two per station at the most—and each participant should be given the course materials, including copies of slides, training scenarios, and laboratory exercises. All of this activity needs to be closely coordinated to ensure the class presenters can be allowed to focus on the course content as opposed to making student binders, arranging class schedules, and the like.

Training is often pictured as classroom-style lectures with printed manuals to refer to later. Here are some different types of training materials and delivery methods for your consideration:

◆ Access to the SAP help files and tutorials

◆ Custom-designed computer-based training programs (screen capture and processing)

◆ Customized SAP help text from within the SAP GUI

◆ Videotaped classroom presentations for later viewing

◆ CD-ROMs containing training materials

◆ Quick-reference process guides

◆ Intranet sites with process descriptions, flows, and FAQs

Documenting This Phase

This phase pretty much documented itself. This section explains how that happened and describes the current state of your project documentation.

Start with the original project charter. That original, high-level declaration of intent became a project scope. It went on to guide you and your team in the development of your high-level migration plan. Then the project scope became the work plan and timeline and eventually evolved into the implementation turn-on plan. Quite an impressive progression for something that began as a lofty company goal stated on a single slide.

Similarly, your current state analyses, consisting of process flow diagrams and process detail tools, began as a point of reference for the migrating processes. They went on to assist you in the development of the high-level migration plan and helped you prepare and conduct your early prototype scripts. That information helped develop your detailed mapping tools. Soon after you developed your future state processes and created data load programs to begin populating the SAP development instance. As the phases continued, this information fed into the creation of your unit test scripts, pilot scripts and, ultimately, into the actual training material that was presented to the business users.

Throughout all of this activity, you diligently tracked your issues. Early gap issues helped determine the actual scope of the project, and your recommendations helped to further define the project work plan. The issues you tracked along the way became the catalyst for review and change of the process development. Some of the issues drove the need for SAP customizations, legacy interfaces, and bolt-on designs. The issues further helped illuminate potential areas of risk, and better guided the development and execution of testing. As the next chapter explains, issue tracking helps you develop a contingency plan for the implementation, as well as a good method to log and track any issues that might occur when your implementation actually goes live.

Yes, you have prepared a lot of documentation—perhaps more than you've ever dealt with on a task. However, from this review you can see how all the documentation you have created serves your phase goals throughout the SAP life cycle.

Finally, each training course should conclude with a survey. Always check that the material is on track and that the course objectives are being met. Always review the survey results and use the feedback to improve the next session.

> One project team I worked with used the reward system during the courses. To encourage class participation, we offered coupons for free desserts at the local cafeteria to anyone who asked a pertinent question or made an astute observation. As a result, the students were very attentive and involved. Food is always a great motivator.

The Go/No-Go Review

The final proof of your team's efforts is the go/no-go review. It's just what the name implies. At this meeting, your project leaders meet with the original project sponsors, senior management, and business area managers (where applicable) to share the project's progress, milestones met, and degree of readiness for the implementation. The reviewing team receives high-level information regarding the success of the business migration in relation to the original project charter as well as the results of the testing and training phases. The information the implementation team leaders present during this review serves to prove whether the implementation is ready to commence.

The review may highlight potential implementation risks or draw questions from the audience regarding the business's readiness for the implementation. You may have to undertake additional development, testing, and follow-up training. It's quite feasible that a process is operational, but the concepts are so complex that more training is required to prepare the end users to work within the new environment.

Exiting This Phase

When you and your team receive the official go-ahead, the real ride begins. If you've achieved successful passage of this phase, you should have accomplished the following:

- ◆ All identified migrating processes have been fully and successfully integration tested.
- ◆ All risky or show-stopper issues have been resolved.
- ◆ All affected end users have been trained and have received training material to which they can refer during the live implementation.
- ◆ The project sponsors and other senior management have authorized the progression to implementation.

Summary

Completing the testing phase is a huge achievement. By now you're probably more tired than you ever dreamed possible, but you also should feel extreme satisfaction with your efforts. Remember, you stepped away from your traditional support role and entered this incredible think-tank arena. You started with a bare glimpse and understanding of SAP and emerged as an extremely informed individual who is actually teaching others how to use the application. Take time to pause and celebrate with your team. Few others have or will ever achieve what you have. Enjoy your accomplishment. As I said before, if this were easy, everyone would have done it already. Next stop, implementation.

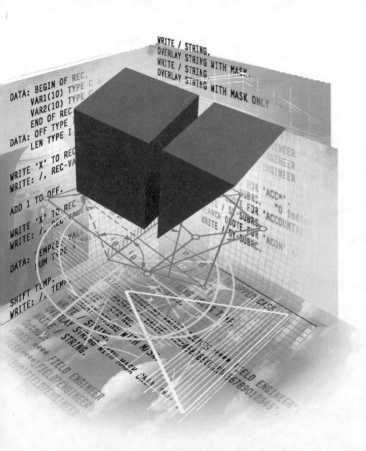

Chapter 9

Supporting the Implementation

In This Chapter

◆ Entering This Phase

◆ Developing and Supporting a Live Cutover Plan

◆ Ensuring a Viable Contingency Plan

◆ Initiating a Blackout

◆ Enabling the Turn-On

◆ Providing Visible Support

◆ Tracking, Resolving, and Communicating Issues

◆ Stabilization, Postmortem Feedback and Next Steps

It's time! You and your team have labored hard and long on internalizing a major business objective, its promise, and its plan. You've left your familiar role of support, or you've joined this team with a fresh perspective of support. Whichever it is, you have accomplished a terrific feat in that you now know more about your company's processes than anyone else, and for good reason. You've worked to decouple, dissect, and diagram how the processes currently work, should work, and could work to meet the business needs.

You are sitting on a ton of documentation and an elaborate development and test environment; you have worked with a team dedicated to performing the amazing task of migrating your business operations from a collection of legacy applications and processes to the new SAP methodology. Everything's developed, tested, and ready to go. What now?

This chapter describes the final activities you'll need to support as your team migrates the business over to SAP. It starts by showing you what the cutover plan looks like and what you are required to do to develop and execute each step in the plan. Along with this plan, you'll need a backup strategy—just in case. Then, you learn how to enable an effective business blackout. This freeze period starts your clock ticking toward implementation. It is the ultimate commitment, and it's an exhausting yet exhilarating activity.

Next this chapter covers the first days of an enabled SAP environment and shows you how you will support SAP. You'll get back to your basic customer support activity, but you'll learn the importance of providing support that is even more visible than you may have provided in the past. This chapter also explains how to monitor the new processes as your business goes live and how to identify problems and opportunities for further system tuning. Once again, you learn how to capture, track, and manage the issues that arise during this phase of the life cycle. And, finally, you learn what happens to the team after this major event has been executed. It is a time to consider where you've been and where you might go. This wild ride will take your breath away.

It's sometimes hard to believe that you and your team are really ready for the implementation. This is why it is so important to get off the merry-go-round of analysis, redesign, and testing. These are all signs of activity and progress, but remember that your ultimate deliverable is the implementation. Even more intimidating than starting up the project in the first place, your actual implementation can come as a "leap of faith" to make good on all your activities and promises. You, as an implementation team member, may have an easier time embarking on this final activity than some senior managers or project sponsors. The real eyes are on them to make good in their organization and you won't let them down.

Entering This Phase

Supporting the implementation shouldn't really be called a "phase" because it is more of an event or happening. Whereas the other phases incur iterations and cycles of design, development, or testing, this portion of the life cycle typically occurs rather quickly, in a very well-planned, strategic, and rapid course of actions. Nevertheless, to support the implementation you must have successfully achieved the following:

◆ All intended business processes are effectively migrated into future state solutions.

◆ All processes have been thoroughly tested and approved (unit and end-to-end).

◆ The Live Business instance is identified and ready for the final build.

◆ All team members have designated roles and deliverables.

◆ This activity is in congruence with the overall project plan.

◆ All user training has been completed.

◆ The business community is ready for the implementation and awaiting the cutover.

◆ All appropriate business partners—external customers, suppliers, or other company entities—are aware of the pending cutover.

You're at the point of no return—more or less. With entry into this phase, you are preparing to undertake an extreme change, perhaps one of the most extreme any business can embark upon. But at this point, you have supported this effort long enough to be eager to complete the cycle. It puts a buzz in the air, and all business eyes are on you and your team members. If you have conducted each of the previous phases faithfully and have exited each with the prescribed deliverables. You really should have nothing to fear.

> Sorry to break in again, but this really is exciting. Remember, you are in the process of making company history. You are about to achieve a near impossibility within a business environment. Essentially, you are making a major adjustment to a plane that's in flight.

Developing and Supporting a Live Cutover Plan

Your job is to complete each individual task that must be executed, in chronological order; the result is an SAP installation that can manage the business activity. If you retrace most of your life cycle steps, you can see that they were all rehearsal for this point in the project and that each would be repeated one last time as SAP is finally implemented. In addition, you, other team members, or business representatives will take other steps to communicate and prepare for the pending cutover.

Cutover Plan—The list of steps that need to occur to enable the migration of all development and process changes from the legacy environment to SAP.

Usually, the best time to perform your actual implementation is over a long holiday weekend. The reason is somewhat obvious: You want as much business downtime as possible with as little impact to regular business operations as necessary. Therefore, beginning the effort on a Friday afternoon and concluding in the late hours of a Monday holiday is extremely useful.

Well, it's the ever-present curse of the support team. Weekends and holidays are always the best times to perform system upgrades, enhancements, and SAP implementations. To support the business, you're required to make your efforts as invisible as possible to the business community. During the implementation, you'll be living like a bat, fluttering about at all hours of the night making sure implementation tasks are being completed. It is a rush of adrenaline, and you'll get some sort of strange thrill out of the whole thing. I did.

The following steps are the minimum required to effect the implementation:

1. Freeze master data updates in legacy environment.
2. Request any buffer material or replenishment to enable initial start-up.
3. Notify all partners of pending SAP implementation.
4. Release final product or service orders to business.
5. Enact final financial transactions on the legacy application (as applicable).
6. Begin implementation system build.
7. Begin disabling legacy applications targeted for migration.
8. Validate initial build settings and functionality.
9. Conduct legacy data loads in a sequential manner (assumes dependencies).
10. Validate all data loads.
11. Enable user logons and authorizations.
12. Enable all reports and background job schedules.
13. Enable all interfaces.
14. Execute any start-up SAP processing (for example, the Materials Requirement Planning [MRP] execution).
15. Monitor and verify initial system response.
16. Announce SAP availability to business areas.

As you can see, the plan works to effectively identify the actions required to disable the legacy environment and the subsequent (sometimes parallel) activities that are required to prepare the SAP system to take over. If it helps your effort, you can split the cutover plan into two separate plans: a legacy shutdown plan and an SAP build plan. Whichever method your team chooses, be sure you are fully prepared to support the activities for which you are directly and indirectly responsible.

Ensuring a Viable Contingency Plan

Although no one wants to admit it, let alone think about it, you must prepare a backup strategy. If the most unforeseen event should occur, and the lights dim when you power up the SAP instance, you'll need to gracefully retreat from the cutover and reestablish the previous legacy environment. You first presented the high level of the contingency plan during the previous phase's go/no-go review. Before the actual implementation, you'll want to ensure the contingency is fully drafted. The contingency plan should include the following specifications:

◆ Affected systems and applications that might need to be reinstated

◆ All personnel who will need to be available to carry out the contingency

◆ SAP system performance metrics and functions that are to be closely monitored

◆ A reliable method of capturing business transaction information in the event of exercising the contingency

◆ A time window to use when monitoring new system performance and to dictate when the contingency plan is no longer needed

Contingency plans are always required with an effort such as this. Chances are you and your team will never need one, but in case you do, you want to be prepared. Again, you're responsible for supporting the business operations, and a ready contingency such as this is visible reassurance that your number one directive is to always ensure minimum disruption to the business.

The development of the contingency plan comes from your earlier efforts in redesigning current state processes. Through your activities in identifying processes that are migrating to SAP, you have, in essence, blazed a trail that could lead you back to those processes and applications. In fact, knowing where all legacy data has been mapped into SAP, you can easily retrieve any of that data and update the legacy information systems.

During the initial turn-on, business areas should be equipped to capture their early SAP transactions, just in case they have to be retrofitted to a legacy process. Unfortunately, the best method for recapturing data is to do so manually. The business users should understand the need to capture the data during the prescribed contingency test period. The actual contingency test period usually lasts for 48–72 hours. It's much like buying a car.

If anything is going to be seriously wrong, you'll know quickly. The most important element of the new system to initially monitor is system performance and response time. Designated members of the implementation team should closely monitor SAP transactions and the processing time associated with each.

> Initial system performance can appear to be remarkable and encouraging. In my experience, system performance was quite good in the first day or two. However, I later learned that many users were too intimidated to work within the application. Depending on the level of user readiness and acceptance, some users may choose not to log on to SAP right away.

Contingency plans are also a final reality check for development and testing efforts. Usually, a team like yours will scoff at the need for such a retreat. You have all been working to design, debug, and prove your new SAP solutions, and you will probably not see the need for such a plan. However, the mere fact that a contingency is required causes you and your team to be doubly sure that all processes are ready and that nothing of major significance can cause a reversal of the implementation. Sometimes the very idea of disappointment or potential embarrassment is enough to keep you and your team from allowing the new system to fail.

Initiating a Blackout

A blackout is most suitable for a very large SAP migration or one that entails large amounts of legacy data that needs to be migrated. In the case of very large implementations—affecting a significant amount of business processing and data records—an extended holiday weekend might not be enough time to conduct a thorough and complete implementation. You might need to migrate a significant amount of data from your legacy systems. Master data records (for example, part numbers and supplier numbers) can be loaded into SAP rather quickly. However, if your migration includes significant amounts of transactional data, such as customer order files and linkages, or large volumes of historical data records, the data migrations can take considerably longer. If the implementation is anticipated to take longer than three days (the time period of an extended weekend), it might be a good idea to suggest a time frame in which the business areas can comfortably be blocked from performing systematic tasks. During this week, usually beginning with the preceding weekend, the implementation tasks will begin and progress until all duties are complete and the new system is ready for use.

Blackout— In this context, the term means that business activity will be suspended for a defined period of time; a few days or a week, but preferably no more than that.

If a blackout is required, be sure the team leaders can provide daily progress updates to the business areas. The business people are curious about the implementation team's efforts during this time. As the blackout period continues, the business areas should get the assurance that they can soon resume their business activities.

Enabling the Turn-On

Before beginning the implementation activities, you will likely work very closely with the business areas. The conclusion of their work marks the start of yours. When the last legacy order is processed, the last receipt has been made, and the last accounting transaction has been processed, your work begins.

The users may decide to work a little ahead, where possible, to soften the impact of the early use of SAP. This approach might mean that a production area has been adequately stocked with material or that material purchase orders have been launched a bit further ahead than usual. The business communities will, in this way, work with the implementation team to help smooth the migration and allow for gradually increasing SAP activity. The business teams might like this sort of involvement and feel as if they're part of the implementation, too.

> This interesting time is the ultimate example of work behind the scenes. It's as if a department store has closed for the weekend, but you're still inside, actively working on details that will change the appearance of each internal department when the store reopens. Your payback is the amazement and delight of the users when they return to the office, being greeted by the implementation team and SAP.

Now the users are gone, and the system is yours. Working from the cutover plan you developed, you'll begin the virtual stopwatch that tracks the implementation activities. You've rehearsed and prepared for this moment and methodically perform the steps in your turn-on plan. Each subteam member is on hand and in sight around the clock. If your turn-on plan has been developed much like your project work plan and timeline, the different subteam members will see when their activities will occur and manage their time accordingly. However, in the interest of preparedness, the plan should work as an activity chain and subteam members should be contacted as soon as their responsibilities are to be performed. In some cases, if upstream tasks in the turn-on plan are completed sooner than expected, the team can take advantage of extra review time at the end of the task list. Naturally, the more time you have at the end of the implementation activities, the better you and your team are prepared to deal with any minor slowdowns.

For good communication, develop an oversized task list that shows the different turn-on steps and dependencies. Mark off each step as it occurs so other team members can see how the effort is progressing. Celebrate acceleration in the schedule by driving even harder to complete the entire task list early.

Team members will be a bit tired. Some of them may have attended to implementation tasks for many hours into the night. Team leaders should conduct daily—or more frequent—progress meetings throughout the turn-on effort. Each subteam should share its progress and any issues that it may have encountered. Also, if an acceleration in the schedule is anticipated, that information should be communicated so others may plan for it. But, finally, the team leaders should encourage the team to get some rest before the users return to their offices. The real test is about to begin.

Providing Visible Support

The first day of SAP being online is like being on hand for the opening of a new amusement park. You're an employee of the park, and you're there greeting guests as they enter the gates. The guests feel your excitement and want to know what the buzz is all about. You're proud and confident that they will be satisfied and amazed with your work. Maybe not everyone on the implementation team will feel exactly like that (they could still be a bit tired), but each team member should be out greeting the business users and helping them get started in the new SAP system.

Implementation packets, full of information regarding the SAP turn-on, should be at each user's desk. Each packet should include reminders of the processes that have been migrated, a list of first steps to take when accessing SAP and reviewing the data, a quick-reference list that notes the most useful menu paths or transaction codes, a reaffirmation of help desk usage as well as any additional hot line or status line phone numbers, and statistics about the turn-on such as how many people were involved, how many person-hours were logged, and the average number of hours each person slept. Have a little fun, and the users will be more at ease.

You are now officially back in the traditional support role, but you're much more accessible than you were before. First, arrange to have a workstation available within the user community. The users might need help getting started with SAP and will want to know that help is close by. Wander through the business areas throughout the initial days, stopping by users' desks to see how they are doing with the new system. You may need to develop a rapport with them before they'll feel comfortable asking you for help. Sometimes they don't know what to ask, and they may just need to tell you what they want to accomplish. You can help them get started and begin to build their confidence.

One innovative communication method is the use of walkie-talkies. That might sound a bit odd, but walkie-talkies are an extremely effective way for subteam members to communicate with one another during the initial turn-on. Using walkie-talkies is much more efficient than placing phone calls or paging team members. The users will think it's a bit silly at first—even a bit extreme—but they'll quickly see the value of instant communication when they have questions and need help fast.

> Just remember that a walkie-talkie is an open line of communication. Keep the conversation relatively professional and pertinent. I won't even begin to share some of the anecdotes I have on this point.

Most of all, be extremely visible and compassionate to the users. They'll be nervous, apprehensive, and possibly skeptical. Listen to everything they have to say and take additional time to explain more of the "whys" and "what fors" to help them better understand SAP. It's also useful to conduct daily meetings with the business user teams, preferably near the end of their day, to hear about their early experiences with SAP and to air issues that might benefit everyone. The implementation subteam members should arrange the meetings. Keep them informal, possibly meeting in the business area, and encourage candid comments or suggestions. Be sure you quickly follow up on any questions that you cannot answer immediately.

Now that you're back in the support role, you will have an easier time with your business users if you display a magnified attitude of enthusiasm and commitment. They will look to you as a gauge of how successful the implementation effort has been and for a sense of how confident you are in the new system. Keep yourself at ease, have some fun, and commit yourself to their every need.

Tracking, Resolving, and Communicating Issues

Any issues that come up during the early days of SAP turn-on should be accurately captured, communicated, documented, and resolved. You and your team will need to look for recurrent problems that could pose trouble to the business areas. As mentioned in Part I, the users are your best source of strenuous system and process testing.

One of the best ways to track potential issues in the early days of an SAP turn-on is to use implementation-specific *hot line* and *status line* phone numbers. The status line can provide information about the implementation that is useful to all business users regarding system performance, common problems and resolutions, and even current activity statistics. Conversely, users should call the hot line to get immediate help from an implementation subteam member. The hot line is useful for more critical issues, and it should be fully staffed—usually by 8 to 10 team members—for at least 12 hours a day. This should be adequate to cover the hours that business users might actively use the system. The hot line phone number, hours of operation, and general information should be included in the implementation packet. Also, for times when a subteam member cannot answer the hot line, equip it to capture a voicemail message. You should also enable a message status indicator that triggers the paging of a team member for urgent messages.

While attending the hot line, subteam members should ask callers which business area they are working in, what function they are attempting to perform, and what sort of trouble they are having. Answers can often be provided over the phone—the implementation subteam members were responsible for developing the processes, right? If an answer to a user's question cannot be provided immediately, the hot line attendant should document all information about the problem and the caller who submitted it. You can use a paper form or a simple Web site that has a form design for quick and easy data entry. In this case, you should tell the caller when an answer might be available. After the call, the hot line attendant should reach a subteam member who can resolve the situation, then direct that person to the caller's desk.

Use of a call-tracking Web site can help other subteam members monitor issues that may arise in their business areas of support. Logged calls should be categorized by business areas, when possible, to assist the subteam members in determining which calls they should focus on. Calls that involve more significant problems or steps to resolution should be shared in an implementation team forum.

The implementation team should plan on meeting twice a day, at least during the first week of the turn-on. Team members should share information about the system performance, process effectiveness, and overall user acceptance of SAP. Any problems that have been captured in hot line call trackers or individual business team forums should be communicated during this meeting.

Stabilization, Postmortem Feedback, and Next Steps

As the SAP turn-on completes its first week of operation, you and your team will begin to gain a clearer picture of how the application is working. You will find areas in a day when system load is heavier. You should work to alleviate any unnecessary load during these times, for example, by rescheduling background processes, to ensure that the users can still receive acceptable system response time. Both users and their managers will want to see that SAP is superior to the previous legacy applications. Community acceptance is sometimes only achieved through your eternal vigilance and a bit of positive and honest coercion.

As SAP use continues through the first week or two, you might find that hot line calls subside and that users are finding their way relatively well. Continue the visible support and use of the tools discussed earlier, but monitor the need for each as time passes. One implementation I worked on went so well that the hot line was almost as unneeded as the contingency plan. That's good, though. It's better to be prepared for the worst and have nothing happen than the other way around.

This stage of an implementation is known as the *stabilization period*. In it, the implementation team is working closely with the system, the processes, and the users in an effort to establish an acceptable level of normal business activity. All the wrinkles will not be ironed out, and you must recall similar situations of minor process inefficiency from the legacy days. But it is necessary to prove the system is stable, and that can be done through the tracking of the following metrics:

- ◆ System uptime is consistent and reliable.
- ◆ Transaction response time is within normal, acceptable levels.
- ◆ Business processes can be routinely executed without any problems for a designated time.
- ◆ Process flow supports the business cycle and does not require special handling.

◆ Future process and program enhancements are expected, but major process and program bugs should not occur in the normal routine of the process.

Subteam members should conduct postmortem reviews, attended by business users. In these reviews, discuss the processes that are now being used and evaluate their effectiveness. Refrain from using terminology that references legacy systems unless the discussion requires it. You need to work with the users to migrate their language to that of SAP.

Open the discussion in your postmortem meetings to what the users are seeing, thinking, and feeling. Encourage them to share problems they've encountered and some of the interesting tricks or nuances they have discovered. This forum clearly lends itself to the sharing of best practices. Report all the feedback to the rest of the implementation team. If issues arise, be sure to accurately document them and follow them to resolution.

The project team leaders should then use this information to prepare reports for the business management and project sponsors. Provide them with information regarding the activity that has been conducted on SAP, statistics about the system and process stability, and general feedback received from the business users. Be generally confident that the new SAP processes are meeting and even exceeding the original goals of the project charter.

You'll now spend a good many weeks ensuring that the system is stable and that the users are getting accustomed to their new work tool. This period won't be as encompassing as the implementation you've just come through, but it will command most of your attention. However, begin thinking about where you will go from here. After all, this is where the ride slows to a stop and all passengers get off. You may choose a different attraction to experience, or you may wish to ride this one again. You'll have several options, so ask yourself what you want to do with what you've learned.

Summary

The project is wrapping up. It's been an interesting experience, and you are now more knowledgeable about your company's automated business system, SAP, than you ever could have become any other way. I hope you've noticed how much opportunity, effort, and faith has been involved throughout this unique experience.

Some of the concepts in this chapter may seem like common sense and useful in any program implementation, not just SAP. Nevertheless, you need to remember that changing a company's core business application resets much of the business environment. For the users, it can be like learning to walk again. Rarely does a business make such a sweeping change in its environment. Smaller application introductions can affect a select few users or teams, but an SAP implementation has the potential to affect all aspects of your business—potentially, if not in an initial release, surely in a follow-up implementation where additional SAP business modules and integrated functionality are introduced. Support team members often take for granted the amount of knowledge and understanding users have about the system applications they work with. Over time, their increased knowledge helps buffer some levels of support. Remember, so much of that application knowledge your users once had is now gone. The onus is back on you.

But for now, congratulate yourself and your team for a job well done. Thank all the people who helped you and partnered with you. Thank the sponsors for having faith in you to get the job done. Don't forget to thank your families, friends, and significant others. Chances are they haven't seen as much of you lately as they would like. Take a little personal time to catch your breath and reflect on the events of the past months, and then get prepared to decide what you want to do next.

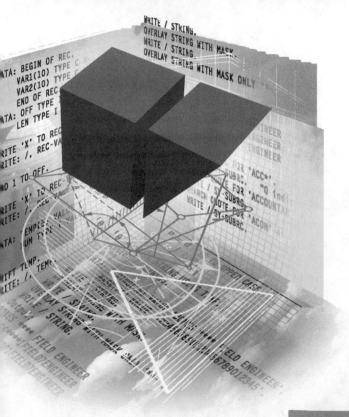

PART III

Transitioning Support

10 Comparing a Legacy Environment to
    a New SAP Environment

11 Building a Winning Support Team

12 Stabilizing and Preparing for
    the Handoff

13 The Handoff and Migration of Support

14 Establishing the Support Domain

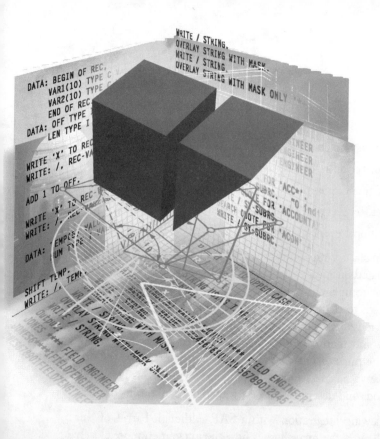

Chapter 10

Comparing a Legacy Environment to a New SAP Environment

In This Chapter

- ◆ Integrated Processes vs. Isolated Processes
- ◆ Differences in Security and User Groups
- ◆ Differences in Business Exposure
- ◆ Differences in Data Recovery and Data Manipulation
- ◆ Differences in Solution Leveragability

This discussion of transition starts with a look at where we have been and where we are now. In terms of automated business systems, this strategy means a comparative look at the legacy system environment and the new SAP system environment. Much of the support approach needs to change with this migration to SAP. Although that statement might appear obvious, SAP support really causes a sweeping change to the overall support philosophy and methodology. The use of SAP offers tremendous potential benefits, but at the price of change. The preceding chapters showed you how SAP changes a company's business processes. This chapter explains how SAP also changes support methods and describes the best way to dovetail those changes.

This chapter starts by reviewing integration within SAP. Although Part 1 of this book covered this topic at length, the focus here is how the integration more closely compares to the legacy environment that your company just left behind—either fully or in part. This chapter compares the integrated processes within SAP to the activity and information flows of the separate application methodology within most legacy processes. You'll even see how some of your existing legacy processes—assuming you are interfacing to and from SAP—look very different now and become identifiable targets for future migration.

Next this chapter compares the SAP infrastructure to your legacy environment. You'll learn how application security will need to be changed and why you may have to maintain dual security methodologies. If your company still has active legacy applications after the initial SAP migration, they need support in the new environment that includes a slight bent toward a future migration.

This chapter then explains how your business activity is changing, including the risk factors associated with the new system's availability. You need to mitigate any impact to the business areas that could be caused by an unavailable system. In addition, the SAP environment and the legacy environment require different handling, especially when it comes to data recovery and manipulation; therefore, you should pay special attention to this aspect in the new environment.

Finally, this chapter discusses how solution leveragability—utilizing common process solutions—has changed in your new SAP environment. Most successful companies use common solutions across their organization and throughout their various sites. Leveraging a legacy solution is much different from leveraging an SAP solution. In fact, depending on the size of your company, the leveraging of an SAP solution may need to be managed at the newly-implemented site by the new support team. This situation differs from the legacy environment if the older applications received central support, such as from a main office or corporate headquarters.

Integrated Processes vs. Isolated Processes

Integration is one of the major benefits of SAP's architecture, and it should be exploited to its fullest potential. (Refer to Chapter 2 for a description of the many aspects of SAP's integration.) Integration links all logical data and processes into a continuous chain of events and information. To a business, the integration supports the business flow by allowing the end-to-end streamlining of common, repeatable tasks.

The first comparison, then, is that of accelerated process throughput. Through integration, a process that starts in one area of SAP—a business module—can be immediately seen and acted on farther down the business flow. A good example is that of materials used and maintained in a factory. Materials must be procured in order to supply a factory with raw goods with which to build products and fulfill customer orders. However, before material can be procured, it must be established within SAP's material master tables. The benefit here is that, immediately upon being posted (saved) on SAP, the material master information becomes usable and enables the creation of any additional master data records that allow the procurement of the goods.

In a legacy environment, turnaround time is typically not as instantaneous. Most legacy environments require separate applications to achieve this simple result. A material master application typically contains the company's master information: a collection of material specifications, engineering data, and other data that identify the material and its use. That information is created and saved but can only be maintained within that system application—or database. There would probably also exist another system application, and database, containing much of the same information about the material, plus additional information that is applicable only to the purchasing business area. However, before the purchasing team can work with the new material, the information must be transferred to the purchasing database from the material master database. This process of transferring data is usually handled by a job that strips the data from the one information system and transfers it to the other—

overnight! Already, this step introduces a delay in your business's processing time—a delay that is passed along to the waiting customer who placed an order for your product.

In the legacy environment, the overnight wait for data processing can be a problem for the business users. All too often, schedules are crunched, and data flow is needed quickly to react to a particular business situation. For a support team, this situation often involves calls from users begging for some way to get the data from system A to system B right away, special handling, and sometimes ad hoc processing of a data transfer job. In contrast, SAP relieves the support team of this data handholding because the users handle the communication between the business areas them-selves—no data transfer is required, and the information is immediately available throughout the business chain.

The same goes for other business areas, depending on the scope of your initial imple-mentation and the degree of integration. Most legacy environments are an assemblage of separate business-focused applications that serve only a single, or selected, business user groups. The transfer of data from an application is a scheduled event that can occur sev-eral times a day. However, it is seldom done instantaneously as with SAP. Therefore, legacy environment support inevitably involves extensive data transfer support.

The one important point, and comparison, to note here is that much of the informa-tion stored in each legacy business application is duplicated. Consequently, you are managing and maintaining duplicate data—usually at some cost and effort to the company. This duplication is necessary because each business application requires some sort of identifying data, or header information, that distinguishes the informa-tion that is being managed and manipulated. You can see this overlap, and potential for duplicated data management, in Figure 10-1.

As the figure shows, data transfer sometimes requires special considerations. You can see that the material description information requires truncation when it is passed from system A to system B; the illustration's data conversion legend shows that the 30-character description will be truncated to 20-characters when passed to system B. That step constitutes additional handling and manipulation of the data.

In some cases, the data that is being truncated is not instrumental in the absolute description of the material; in other cases, the truncated information could be of vital importance. Therefore, you must inform users of the data in system A that their descriptions can only be 20 characters long, as opposed to the 30 characters that sys-tem A accommodates. From a user's perspective, this situation usually doesn't make a lot of sense. From a support standpoint, it leads to fielding the same question time and again. In contrast, SAP associates only one description field with the material

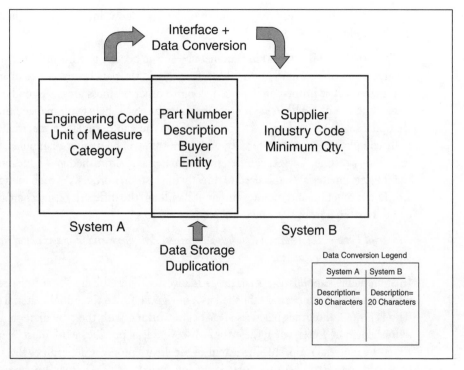

FIGURE 10-1 *Legacy data management can cause data overlap and duplication*

master and references that field throughout the system in the same manner and with the same characteristics. Your only job is to ensure that SAP is available for use and that the proper users have access to the different functions within it. The data management is handled within SAP.

Finally, consider the legacy applications that might still be in use in your company after the initial SAP migration As discussed in Chapters 7 and 8, the implementation team developed interfaces that strip and load data between the legacy applications and SAP accordingly. Now with SAP implemented, the benefits of the integrated environment are being realized, and those interfaces to your legacy systems may be bothersome bottlenecks. The support team or another specially focused team might now look for ways to enable additional SAP functionality to eliminate these remaining legacy applications. Once the functionality has been absorbed into SAP, the data flows even more continuously, and the need to support a custom interface disappears.

Another topic that I touched on in Chapter 2— the potential downside of SAP integration—bears restating in this discussion. This is the other side of how integrated data becomes immediately available, or unavailable, in an instantaneous fashion. So from a support perspective, you must understand how integration might require special attention.

First, posted data is live and instantaneous—a true benefit to a business that needs a steady stream of information flow. However, should the data be inaccurate in any way, that inaccuracy is immediately passed along to other business areas. A good example here is the use of SAP's *material type* information. SAP helps you manage materials that are raw goods and directly procurable. Or you can designate a material as partially completed—as a subassembly, perhaps—that will be further manipulated within a factory setting. Or you can designate a material as a finished good, meaning it is the top-level material that is used to directly fill customer orders. As each material has a different function and requires different handling, the different business areas manage the material from their own unique perspectives.

Material Type— *Information that helps a business determine and manage a material based on its intended use or activity.*

Imagine what happens if a material is inadvertently established as a finished good when it should have been established as a raw good. Once the initial material master data is posted, the other business areas begin working with the new material item as a finished good. Later, when the error is discovered, all previous work must be undone to set the material properly. The extent of the error's progress determines the amount of rework required. Because SAP is an integrated system, it may be necessary to rework the material in a progressive—albeit opposite—fashion. Before a material type can be changed, any open orders for the part must be canceled. Also, financial settings need to be disabled. This operation goes on down the business area chain until the material returns to its initial state. No doubt, support will be needed to identify which settings still require undoing.

Another downside to integration is the instantaneous unavailability of SAP information. Just as erroneous data can be made available for immediate use throughout the business areas in a company, so, too, can valid data be made unavailable. As SAP is integrated, if any information is flagged as deleted or removed entirely, other business area processes can be immediately halted.

Therefore, all business users and support individuals must clearly understand this point. A good example here would be of a material's obsolescence. If it is determined that a part no longer is of use, a company may choose to make that part obsolete. SAP achieves obsolescence by flagging a part as *deleted*—the actual part deletion is a separate step. When a part is flagged as deleted, other processes, such as demand planning and procurement, are halted or restricted. If a mistake is made and the wrong part is flagged, you can guess what the result will be. In this case, SAP issues a series of warnings, errors, or aborts to different business areas when they attempt to work with the part. You can expect to receive phone calls from users who had "just worked with the part only an hour ago."

The point of this discussion is twofold. First, SAP increases the speed of data availability for a company's business areas. This feature reduces process throughput time, and relieves the support team from having to manage explicit data transfers. However, all information that is enabled or modified in SAP is done so in a real-time capacity, which, of course, can be troublesome to a company if errors are introduced. The support team member typically becomes involved in any event that appears extraordinary or problematic. Consider the amount of information your company manages and the amount of systematic transactions you might support. This analysis will give you an idea of how to plan for a number of errors you might need to help resolve.

Differences in Security and User Groups

With SAP, system security is achieved with a single user logon ID and the associated authorizations granted for that logon ID. Your users are established on SAP with the knowledge of their role in the company. Their user authorizations (controlled by the logon profiles) enable them to perform their job duties as they relate to a business area. If the user's business assignment changes, you must modify that user's logon authorizations, but not their logon ID. In contrast, the legacy environment requires different logons to different applications. Each user needs to have a logon established and managed within each application to which they have access. In the legacy environment, the support team member must know and support each user at the application level, and users have to maintain multiple logon IDs and passwords.

SAP simplifies the process of user logons. A single ID establishes the user's access into the application, and the use of appropriate profiles enables the user to access and manage data specific to the business area that the user represents. The caveat here is that users must have the appropriate access via the authorizations within SAP. As a result, business users and business managers must understand exactly which activities should be enabled for each business user. Actually, for the business area manager, this may constitute a new level of involvement. In the legacy environment, single applications could usually be identified as serving distinct business areas. Therefore, it was only necessary to identify a new user in a business area and to ensure that new user gained access to the respective business application. However, the integrated nature of SAP requires management to be more closely involved in determining the types of transactions the users should be able to execute. In this scenario, business area managers become immediately and directly responsible for the teams' actions. Therefore, business activities must be identified in SAP terms, and the users must have the necessary logon and authorization level. If the authorization is too restrictive, the support team member becomes involved when the user reports SAP messages that inform of inadequate authorization. Likewise, but even more critical, is the need to control the assignment of authorizations that allow too much business user capabilities. System activities should be restricted to those duties related to a business area and authorized by the business area manager. The ability for a user to perform extraneous activities could be a business control issue and a risk to data integrity within the system.

> Just a couple of weeks into a new SAP implementation, my team was alerted to odd changes in material demand data. Knowing that our process design incorporated a single, weekly, plant-wide MRP process, the rate of demand change that some users reported didn't make sense. A review of user activity revealed that a single user had found the MRP execution function within SAP's screens and was executing it. The user reported that he "just likes to push buttons to see what happens." This situation prompted an immediate review of that user's authorizations and led to restrictions on all users. It wasn't the fault of the user. It was just an additional point of control that needed to be put in place. Chock one up to experience.

As you can see, authorization becomes an issue that is now shared between the support community and management. Management needs to clearly specify which activities their business area users should have access to within SAP. The support community must translate those needs into identifiable and manageable SAP authorizations. As user requirements change, management needs to proactively inform the support community so the logon ID authorizations may be modified. Equally, as the support community encounters areas that might not have been properly addressed and secured, it should communicate the potential for problems to management so that mutually agreed upon changes can be made.

Differences in Business Exposure

As you can see, the introduction of SAP into your business changes how a support team needs to work with the system and the business users. You can see how an integrated system requires a different approach, and a different respect level, than the legacy application environment did. For example, you know that data accuracy is more important than ever because the data is immediately usable by other business areas. Equally, you know how important it is to ensure that business area users have adequate, yet not excessive, access to functionality within SAP that is relevant to their business needs. One way to learn about supporting this environment is to compare the maintenance of the environment, and the potential exposure to the business users, under a legacy solution and under an SAP solution.

In this comparison, you could say that the legacy environment is more *forgiving* than the SAP environment. You have harnessed the power and speed of an integrated environment, and you have effectively implemented real-time processing across the company. So what happens when it becomes necessary to temporarily disable the system? All business environments require some sort of scheduled downtime, be it for special data processing, application maintenance, or hardware maintenance. There are significant differences between the two environments.

First, the legacy environment, being made up of a series of independent business applications, supports individual system maintenance quite easily. If a procurement application in a legacy environment requires an upgrade, database reorganization, or hardware modification, the single application can usually be disabled without affecting the other business areas in the company. The procurement users can be notified directly, and the downtime can be arranged to meet their specific needs and schedule. If the application suddenly stops functioning or requires an emergency shut-down, it is not possible to properly notify the business area affected in a proactive method as just described. Still, only the single area might be affected while other business activity in other applications can continue.

The same would be true for any legacy application that affects a single business area. This isolation of business impact is one advantage of a legacy environment, although it shouldn't be considered a *feature* that would overshadow the benefits of an integrated environment.

In the SAP environment, downtime is somewhat more complex. If the system is to be disabled, or *brought down*, it must be coordinated with all business areas. Downtime is not usually desired, but it can become necessary to perform routine system maintenance. All business areas need to be notified weeks in advance to ensure the downtime occurs at a time that is understood and prepared for by all area users. If the downtime is scheduled and considered routine, it can be manageable. However, it must be closely coordinated with the business areas and across the support team. Because SAP is now the core of your company's business processing, downtime needs to be kept to a minimum. But in contrast to a legacy application, the unplanned disruption of SAP availability or an emergency shut-down affects all business areas using SAP. That's just a reality of the system environment, and an eventuality that the support team must accept. Experience shows that this is typically not a rampant problem with most SAP-enabled businesses.

Differences in Data Recovery and Data Manipulation

Every automated business system requires regular backups of the system information. System backups capture the business data at a given point of time in an effort to provide for data recovery or disaster control. Backups, which are copies of the system database, control files, and other defining information, are usually stored on magnetic media. These backups are performed by the team that maintains the actual hardware on which the applications run. This team performs the scheduled backups as well as verifies the validity and completeness of each.

In a legacy environment, backups can be performed for each defined system or database that supports a business application. Sometimes, multiple applications can be managed by a single hardware configuration, but seldom, if ever, are multiple applications supported by a common database. In terms of complexity, legacy backups are quite straightforward and relatively quick. Often, full system backups are achieved on a nightly basis. SAP, on the other hand, is more complex to manage when performing system backups. Because SAP operates through a collection of relational database tables, a complete and usable backup is achieved through an entire system backup. The scope of such a backup typically requires several more hours to execute than a legacy system backup requires. SAP backups can be performed at several levels, one being an entire system backup and another being an incremental change backup. For this reason, it is usually wise to perform whole system backups on weekends, with incremental backups occurring nightly. However, the amount of magnetic media, constituting the backups, that needs to be maintained is significantly more than that of a legacy environment.

Now, although the legacy backup appears easier to achieve, restoring the information is simpler in the SAP environment. The SAP environment is restored by applying the single whole system backup. Depending on the timing of the backup, incremental backups can then be applied as necessary. By contrast, a legacy restoration includes the application of several different backups for several different systems, depending on the complexity of the environment. In addition, data may be out of sync across the applications. Depending on the time of the restoration, information in one application may not exist in other interfaced applications. The legacy recovery could entail more effort to determine where the last business activity concluded. So, if a legacy system requires restoration, it is isolated to that system and the applications that operated in it, but synchronization of information across the entire legacy environment might be more difficult to achieve. The time will occur when the support team encounters a system or application failure that requires data recovery. Business users should be notified immediately of both the failure and the recovery plan. With legacy applications, the impact might be isolated to a select business area, whereas an SAP system failure affects practically every area.

If a system problem occurs—usually a hardware failure or some sort of data corruption—you must enact a recovery from the system backup tapes. Recovery can also be required if a background job or process incorrectly manipulates data. Whatever the reason, you also need to be prepared to handle data recovery.

Data recovery in the SAP environment is significantly different from data recovery within a legacy environment. In the legacy environment, data recovery can be managed at the application level, and usually from a most recent—a previous day's—backup tape. A single table of information can often be restored quickly and easily. In SAP, however, data recovery is more complex, requiring the restoration of complete system backups. SAP does not currently provide for single-table recoveries. Therefore, to avoid overwriting all business data to achieve a recovery, it's best to perform a backup restore on one of your SAP Development instances. From there, data within a table can be extracted and imported into your Live Business instance for recovery purposes. Recovery can still be effectively achieved, but it could require restoring a Development instance to get the isolated data you require.

Finally, you should understand the difference in how the two environments—legacy and SAP—manipulate data. Although data transfer was slower in a legacy environment, that approach does allow for manipulation of data files before they are transferred to another system application. As the data is not yet in the receiving application's database, data can be modified or deleted before it has any impact on the users of the target application. SAP, as stated before, is a real-time environment, and data becomes immediately available to all areas—hence the need to pay extra attention to data accuracy.

Differences in Solution Leveragability

The final topic in this chapter is *solution leveragability*. Many businesses perform this activity as they strive for common business solutions across departments or geographically dispersed sites. The goals of leveraging solutions are to ensure application and process consistency and to reduce the need for redundant effort—recreating an existing solution—within another business department or site.

Solution Leveragability— *To take a copy of a solution from one system and apply it to another.*

Many legacy applications were designed with leveragability in mind. Often controlled from a company main office or corporate headquarters, the applications are quite generic in presentation to ensure ease of distribution and maintenance. Usually, modifiable source code is secure at the central site. Although this approach promotes consistency, it doesn't support unique requirements that occur at different business sites. Also, any requested changes must be fully reviewed, tested, and approved across all using sites to ensure the changes are not destructive or degrading in any way. This process is usually very time intensive.

SAP also has benefits and drawbacks when it comes to leveragability. The first difference is that SAP is designed for local customization. The whole intention of SAP is to allow itself to be modified to meet a business's unique needs. Although a company might provide common products or services across multiple business sites, the application requirements at the sites can differ significantly—especially for global businesses. Business customs and practices differ greatly from country to country—currency, tax rates, import and export restrictions, language requirements, and so on.

Therefore, a developed and customized business process within one of SAP's standard business modules will not necessarily be immediately leveraged to another site in a different country. The process design and system settings can largely be duplicated, but you should not expect a fully functional drop-in solution. Although this characteristic may appear as a drawback—because it requires dedicated effort to leverage a solution to another business site—customization is another of SAP's application strengths.

> The differences between SAP and a legacy environment will affect you, positively or negatively, depending on your previous support experience. If you actively support a legacy environment, it might be easy to develop a negative view the change SAP brings to the environment. If you're new to the support realm, the differences described in this chapter are academic. Either way, SAP does mean change, and, if your company is now working with SAP, you need to work with the new environment and not against it. I've watched others attempt to avoid SAP's impact on their support activities, but the new environment eventually catches up with everyone and every aspect of support. Resistance is futile.

Summary

This chapter focused on some of the more prevalent differences between SAP and a legacy environment. Since your legacy environment has probably existed for about 20 years, it's only natural that significant change is being introduced into the new support environment. Understanding these differences and the realization of the need for change is the first step in preparing to transition the support function from a legacy environment to that of a newly implemented SAP solution.

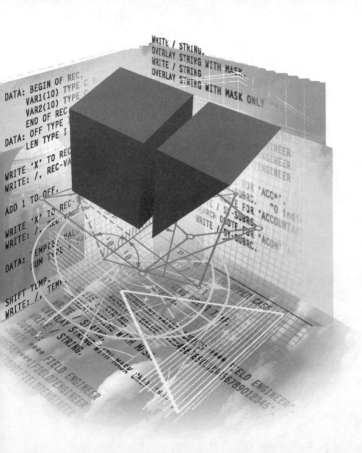

Chapter 11

Building a Winning Support Team

In This Chapter

◆ Determining Your Personal Transition

◆ Assembling and Sizing the Team

◆ Preparing the Team for the New Environment

◆ Engaging the Business Areas

◆ The Continued Use of Consultants

The purpose of this chapter is to get you thinking more about transitioning within your new SAP environment. As you learned in the last chapter, much of the automated environment has changed, and the support organization must change as well. Adopting the attitude that change is good encourages an organization and the individuals within it to reassess methods, styles, and goals—organizational and personal. The amount of change that SAP brings can overwhelm and intimidate, but it is also the best chance you and your organization will have to truly break out of old habits, ruts, and boxed thinking patterns. You can use this time to see business goals with renewed vigor and meet them head on with your newly empowered automated environment.

If you have just completed the implementation effort, this chapter shows you how your skill set has changed and points out possibilities for applying your new skills in the future. All that you learned in the implementation is priceless, and it becomes your personal pearl of wisdom. (If you didn't take part in the implementation effort, this chapter shows you how you can still take advantage of some of these opportunities for advancement.)

Then there's a discussion about the formation, or re-formation, of your company's support team in light of the changes that SAP caused in your organization, The factors that drive how the support team is assembled and then subdivided are revisited. The architecture of SAP remains at the forefront of discussion and shows you how that architecture can determine the makeup of the new support team.

After the transition team is in place, it is important to prepare them for the new support environment. In most cases, the transition team is a mix of previous support team members and implementation team members. You'll learn how the two will mix and what steps you can take to help develop a new team.

Then the focus shifts to the concept of business and technical support crossover, which was discussed in the Part I of this book. Crossover can again come into play during the transition stage in your organization's evolution. This time, when members of the business teams become your partners, you have the opportunity to engage them in a new relationship that strengthens the overall support of business processes through the bonding of both disciplines more tightly than before.

The last section of this chapter covers the role of consultants in your organization. During the implementation life cycle, consultants assisted the implementation team with process design and development. They helped the team gain better understanding about SAP and its application to your company's business. Now your organization has to decide how to make the best use of the consultants working with you, how to determine whether you still need them, and how to eventually move the organization along without them.

Determining Your Personal Transition

When an organization changes over to a new business management system, you need to understand what the change means to you and where you might best apply your talents and services. Relatively speaking, SAP is still quite new to the business industry. R/3, the application, is only six years young, which makes it practically brand new from an industry usage standpoint. Therefore, supporting it is virtually brand new to you.

If you have just come from the implementation team, you worked with that team to dissect former legacy processes and to rebuild them into newly developed SAP solutions. As you worked in that capacity, you developed an intimate understanding of the processes, their importance to the business areas, and their potential for improvement. If you worked in the implementation arena, then you are well educated about the new SAP processes. You are an expert. Your first opportunity, then, is to migrate into the support organization—maybe returning to it if you were "on loan" to the implementation team—and continue to nurture the SAP solutions you helped to develop and implement. These processes are your handiwork, and you want to ensure that they operate and are utilized as you and your team intended. You are highly valuable to the support team. You can probably assess and quickly correct any hiccups in the process or functionality of the system. In fact, upon request, you can probably provide standing dissertations about the intrinsic design details within these processes. Because you have such a deep knowledge here, you are best suited to resolve problems quickly and efficiently. A fast fix can reduce the amount of business impact, sometimes making it appear as little more than a brief respite in processing.

Your knowledge also makes you a key candidate to educate other support team members about the new SAP solutions. If you look back to your implementation experience, you see that your knowledge was achieved through multiple iterations of design, development, and testing. You found many details that were not explicitly obvious when utilizing SAP. You probably also have found several little-known SAP transactions, screens, and menu paths that were utilized to complete the process development. Although the system has been well documented, it will always be necessary to provide further explanation to others who also wish to know more about the solutions. Because you are the company expert on your processes, you have the opportunity to train others within your group, enlightening them to the SAP designs, the company-specific customizations, and the best usage and manipulation of the solution at hand. Most important, you can also explain how your process works with the other solutions in an integrated fashion. You have thoroughly tested your processes in an end-to-end manner; you know which processes feed yours and which processes are dependent on yours. Because you are no longer in an isolated application environment, special attention is needed to fully understand how the integrated processes serve one another and what potential risks exist. This is all knowledge that you can provide to your teammates. At the same time, you can and should continue to perfect your knowledge about the solution and how it works with the other integrated processes within SAP.

The next point to discuss is the extension of your solutions. During an implementation, the timeline and milestone schedule inevitably require design and development trade-offs. For example, in the interest of meeting the schedule, you might have delayed work on some of the unique enhancements you wanted to include in your process designs. Now you may have the time to enhance the performance and efficiency of your processes. You might even find more functionality and features within SAP—customizations, automatic processes, additional data linkages—than you have seen before. The implementation effort can be something of a crunch time. With the application now in active use, you might find the breathing room you need to deepen your knowledge of SAP and your company's processes. Every additional bit of knowledge and understanding you garner increases your value to the organization and the proficiency with which you utilize SAP.

The previous chapter also touched on the aspect of leveraging solutions to other departments or geographic sites. Your company may be interested in establishing consistent processes across its different entities and will require experienced and knowledgeable personnel to achieve this goal. The consultants you worked with before helped the implementation team understand more about SAP and its features and functions. During the implementation, you worked to apply that information to meet your company's specific business needs, customizing the solutions to satisfy the specific business requirements. You learned about SAP and exactly how SAP is used in your company to support the business activity. At this time, there isn't a consultant around who can provide the same level of integrated knowledge. You now have the opportunity to become an internal consultant to your company, working with other departments or sites to help them achieve the same results in less time.

You also have the opportunity to continue on the implementation path. Using the assumption that your company chose the phased approach to SAP implementation, the scope of the initial implementation worked to enable some of the SAP business modules. You can continue with the follow-on implementation efforts. Because you are the most knowledgeable resource about the newly implemented SAP processes in your company, you can make better decisions and determinations about how to apply additional functionality without undoing any of your previous work. It's a sort of momentum you can work with, and it relieves a new implementation team from having to learn about your solutions first before additional design and development can commence. Also, you understand the general philosophy of the implementation effort and may even have the opportunity to work with other former implementation team members. The result is a group momentum that springs from previous experience and newly developed SAP and business process expertise.

So, as you can see, you now have several options. The possibilities might overwhelm you, but ask yourself what your true desire is. During the implementation, you may have been exposed to something new that you had never considered before. If you came from the support team, you might have found that working with cutting-edge process technology is exciting and invigorating. You may want to seek out further advances in solution development. Or you may have enjoyed working in the support team, and you want to return to it with deeper knowledge and expertise. You will be of high service to your business customers, and you will even begin to find improvement opportunities before they do.

Finally, suppose you had not been a part of the SAP implementation at your company. Perhaps you were a member of one of the business areas and became involved with the implementation team as it developed the new processes. You might know quite a bit about the old business processes and how they were reshaped and potentially reengineered to become SAP enabled. If you now have the opportunity to work on the support team, you have great knowledge to contribute as well. Many of the business users will be looking for ways to relate the new SAP solutions to the legacy solutions they once knew. These users will be seeking guidance and reassurance; they want to know that they are still working with a process that makes sense to them and with which they can soon become proficient. If you had previously worked within one of the business areas, you can help these users understand how their processes have evolved. By supporting the new processes, you can determine whether the previous business requirements are truly being met through the ongoing use of SAP. You might find that a minor design flaw or gap exists and, using your previous business and process experience, you can drive the resolution quickly and completely. Along the way, you also become more familiar with the technical aspects of SAP and can learn how to actually enable the changes you determine are necessary.

If you have experience supporting the former legacy environment, then you have some choices as well. The clearest choice is to work with SAP in the new environment. You can approach the new environment with lessons learned from supporting the previous one. To be effective, you need to learn a great deal about SAP and the new process designs. If possible, you should attend the training sessions during the preimplementation training period. In addition, you need sufficient technical training in the use and maintenance of R/3. You can get this training directly from SAP as well as from other sources.

 TIP

For more information about some of these training opportunities, please refer to Appendix E at the back of this book.

Don't forget that you might be working with previous implementation team members in the new support team. You can learn a lot directly from them, and you should take advantage of the resident experts. In addition, if legacy applications are still in operation in your new environment, the support team still needs to provide legacy experience and expertise; you might find transition work there. You can manage and support those continuing applications while developing your knowledge of how SAP is interfaced and how the interfaces are operating. This transition to SAP support is slower than other routes, but it might be the best choice for your personal situation.

The advent of SAP into your company's infrastructure heralds inevitable change. Push yourself to not "hide" in legacy applications that still may be around. If support is to be your long-term home in the company, you will need to work with SAP sooner or later. I recommend sooner than later just due to the amount of competition you could face during times of organizational restructuring. Changes to a company's information infrastructure typically precede changes to the organizational infrastructure. Try not to leave yourself out on a limb—a legacy environment—that is destined to be pruned away in time.

Assembling and Sizing the Team

The new support team will now require refitting. With so much change having just taken place, it will be necessary to revisit the structure and membership of the support team. This procedure entails the assembly of a support team membership that can provide the necessary support for the new SAP solutions while potentially maintaining previous solutions from the legacy environment. Of equal importance is understanding the new balance of solutions, legacy versus SAP, and creating a support team that can provide the correct ratio of support services to the users in the business areas.

To start, consider the new process application landscape that is enabling the business areas. It is probably a cross section of new SAP functionality with some interfacing to legacy applications. Most likely, the implementation team has successfully migrated logical areas of business activity by using the integrated SAP business modules. The SAP architecture is extremely useful in determining not only how implementations can be managed but also how support of the businesses can logically fall into place. For example, the migration plan presented in Chapter 6 was developed from the implementation project scope and later served to establish the implementation team membership. That plan established what sort of expertise was required on the team to make the implementation a reality. In the same manner, those process and team representations can be used to determine the makeup of the support team. Therefore, if your company has implemented SAP to the scale described in Part II of this book, your support team might look like that shown in Figure 11-1.

In this example, the bulk of the team is focused on the SAP elements of the environment because they rationally outweigh the legacy elements. However, the legacy elements are still of value to the overall business environment and require the appropriate amount of support focus.

Also notice the team labeled as *Infrastructure*. This team, which could be new to your support environment, focuses on the Basis portion of SAP. From Part I of this book, recall that Basis is the part of SAP that acts to control the central functions of the system, including logon IDs, performance monitoring, backup management, and other hub activities. These activities might have been managed by the central hardware management team from your legacy environment, which may have been physically located with the rest of the support team. Alternatively, each application support member may have managed these activities. Either way, SAP requires a fully focused team to carefully monitor and maintain the central processing activity of the SAP application.

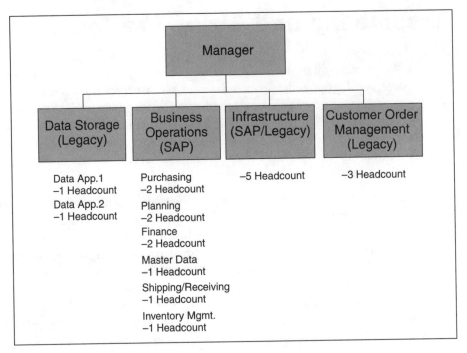

FIGURE 11-1 *A proposed support team structure would include a balance of SAP and legacy process support.*

The next element of support team development relates to the size of the team. Team size is largely driven by issues of company personnel policies or budget targets. It can sometimes be a live-and-learn effort, but be cautious not to understaff this team. Although much of the data management is handled through SAP's integrated processes, the fact remains that SAP is new and will need ongoing maintenance, modification, and adjustment. To make the support team successful, it must be properly staffed to manage the sharp learning curve that comes with settling into the new system, as well as to handle a sharp increase in business user interaction. Figure 11-1 presents an initial recommendation for support team sizing.

 NOTE

Figure 11-1 is only an example. The number of support team members should be adjusted in direct proportion to the complexity of the business processes being supported, the number of users for each process being supported, and the geographic location (including time zone concerns) of each of the users.

I once worked at one extreme where an SAP support team was grossly understaffed. The organization that implemented SAP expected it to be a whiz-bang solution that would easily reduce the need for support personnel. However, we learned that just the opposite is true, at least in the early stages of SAP use. My few colleagues and I were so busy that we had to sacrifice some standard business practices—security, audit compliance, documentation—to properly maintain the system activities. It was a very stressful situation, indeed. In the end, additional effort was required to return the business controls to standard levels of acceptability once a larger team was put in place. In my opinion, an organization should err on the side of a slightly oversized support team. I have yet to see an SAP support team member complain of being bored and underutilized.

Preparing the Team for the New Environment

This topic closely follows the previous one. After defining the new team, the organization must ensure that the support subdivisions are logical and properly staffed. Proper staffing implies that the team contains the proper mix of technical and business process knowledge to best support the solutions and the business users.

In preparing the new support team, SAP training is considered first and foremost. If any support team member is inexperienced in SAP functionality or principles, he or she requires training. In this case, partnering with experienced implementation team members can be of immediate benefit, establishing a mentoring environment. You can make good use of the tier-support concept presented in Chapter 3. Allow yourself to work closely with a support team partner who has knowledge or experience that you currently don't have. The reciprocal would be sharing your knowledge and expertise with your partner.

It is beneficial for the support team to attend the preimplementation training sessions. If that isn't possible, or as an addition to that classroom participation, the support team can review the implementation test and training documentation. The training system should still be available to and actively used by the support team. In fact, as SAP stabilization occurs and support is nearing transition, it might be a good idea for the implementation team to conduct follow-up training sessions for users and others who may have missed initial sessions or wish to review the information. If possible, team up with a classroom leader and lead the class together. You are sure to learn the subject matter.

An experience-sharing session is another useful way to prepare the new support team for its job. In this open forum session, implementation team members can describe their best practices during the implementation effort and explain what worked well and what didn't. The implementation team can offer much useful advice, especially considering they trained the using community, fine-tuned the new processes, and ensured that the system was ready and reliable for the actual turn-on.

Engaging the Business Areas

Here is where SAP's system architecture again plays a pivotal role in the development of business and support team structures. Because the information in the new system is so tightly integrated and available in a real-time manner, more responsibility rests within the business areas for data integrity and information timeliness. The business area is a stronger ally than ever before.

Again, business area involvement leverages from some ideas presented in Part I of this book. Practically everything the business users do within SAP can have an immediate effect upon other business teams. The first goal is to ensure that all users firmly understand the concept of integration and can properly execute the business processes in an accurate and timely fashion. Encourage the users to speak up if they are unclear about any of the business processes or the information for which they are responsible. Because the environment is so new, you should expect and encourage many questions. It's going to take a long time before the user base can reestablish its previous level of system and process knowledge.

One very effective method of helping the business users become more efficient and knowledgeable about SAP is to actively solicit their direct involvement with the business process maintenance. Initially, establish an identified process support team (a concept presented in Chapter 1). The process support team, preferably consisting of previous business-focused implementation team members, can act as a highly knowledgeable hub of process knowledge and analysis. The need for this sort of individual or team (sometimes referred to as "process analysts") is high in a new SAP environment. This team differs from conventional technical support in that it acts as an immediate reference point to the business users. These analysts should work near the business users for fast and informal access. They can answer quick questions regarding SAP's use or the intrinsic details of your company's processes working within SAP. The users will have many questions, but not all of them will be technical in nature. Therefore, they need a resource to answer their more process-oriented questions.

The process analysts can serve an even greater need in the form of identifying process trends both within the company and within its particular industry. Your company chose SAP to ensure that the business would continue to prosper and gain market advantage. The initial implementation was the first step in that process. Now to use SAP to its fullest capacity, your company needs to further understand SAP from the process perspective. This procedure works much like the ongoing development of the technical aspects of SAP.

Therefore, with a support team striving for further technical development and a process analysis team striving for further process development, it only makes sense for these two teams to partner and develop solutions to enhance the company's overall business process effectiveness. Just as SAP is integrated, a company should strive to integrate its technical and business expertise. Regular information-sharing should be arranged so that the trends a process analyst witnesses can be passed along to the support team. The same holds true for the support team sharing technical developments that may be of use to the process team.

> In my opinion, there has never been a better time for business area users. I have worked in an environment that supported the partnering of technical and process expertise. It is a much-valued partnership, and is fully supported by the company. The business users now have additional avenues of assistance to which they can turn. Often, through this partnering effort, technical and process support experts are able to step in for one another when answering user questions or resolving process problems. The users that I have been supporting are generally very pleased with the heightened level of support they now receive.

Direct business users can be a valuable source of SAP experience and support. Users are more comfortable and self-sufficient if they have opportunities to take ownership for portions of the business processes. Try to establish several users as "process experts." Help them to better understand the SAP solutions and intentions and then designate them as additional informational resources. If this effort is visibly rewarded, more users may take on similar process ownership roles.

The Continued Use of Consultants

And how about those consultants with whom you've been working? They were a terrific addition to the implementation team during the process design and development phases. They've been on hand to assist with the actual implementation. They've also worked with you to stabilize the new system and bring additional reliability to your business environment. Has their service come to an end, or can they continue on with your team?

Perhaps a consultant focused specifically on a single area of SAP and helped your team implement processes within that area or module; now that the purpose has been served, the consultant's services may no longer be required. Consultants like this may go on to work with other businesses implementing SAP in a similar capacity or they may acquire additional expertise and certification in other areas of SAP functionality, thus broadening their skill set that can be employable by other businesses.

If you have had the opportunity to work with a consultant who is adept in many areas of SAP, both technical and business-oriented, then that consultant may be useful to your company in an extended assignment. These consultants are highly valuable in helping to fine-tune a process that has been implemented, squeezing out every potential drop of efficiency and integration that might available. Or they can help bring other company sites up to speed in their SAP implementations. Best yet, these consultants can further train the new support team members on SAP functionality and application. A wise organization recognizes the financial benefit of developing in-house SAP consultants who can perform as well as outside consultants.

The only caution is to avoid having your organization become too reliant on a consultant's services. In this case, your company might not develop the internal confidence needed to use its own resources. Contracted resources are always temporary, and if too much reliance is placed on them, their departure could be devastating to a support organization.

Summary

As support transition nears, it is necessary to establish a support team that can continue to maintain the new system and processes as seamlessly as possible. Support's overriding goal is to ensure minimal disruption to the business, and a transition like this needs adequate preparation. The new system environment, possibly containing SAP and legacy elements, needs to be understood and staffed accordingly. Holes in support—applications or activities that are not clearly owned and maintained—could spell disaster for your company or dissatisfaction to the user community, to say the least.

This period of the SAP life cycle requires you to consider what assignment you will seek. Just as at the beginning of the book you decided whether you wished to embark on the adventure of supporting SAP, here you need to determine how you will apply your skills within your company. You will have your own level of expertise to contribute, and you will find that many other options are available. You are the only one who can decide which assignment to take.

If you migrate into the support team, you may find it operates with a different approach, commitment, and service level than you might have seen exhibited in previous support environments. Although it may be vastly different from legacy support, SAP support can bring new developmental opportunities not previously available to you.

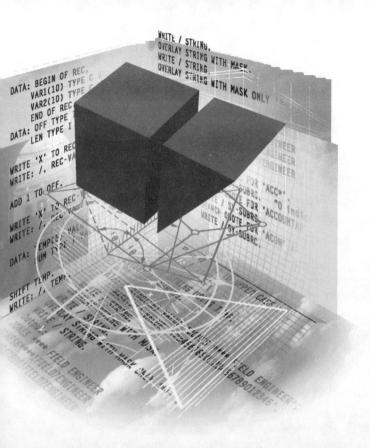

Chapter 12

Stabilizing and Preparing for the Handoff

In This Chapter

◆ Understanding Changing Roles and Responsibilities

◆ Enabling Temporary Co-Support

◆ Developing Handoff Criteria

◆ Tracking Progress to Stabilization

◆ Stable and Ready for Handoff

An SAP implementation, though largely managed by the dedicated implementation team, also includes the participation of many others within the company. Specifically, it requires the active participation of the existing business support team. Before and during the actual implementation, a business support team continued to work to manage the legacy environment.

Though the air was buzzing with the changes to come, the existing support team not only maintained the legacy applications but also increased its duties by striving to better understand the long-term effect of SAP in terms of how it will be supported. In an indirect way, the existing support team most likely partnered with the implementation team to prepare the business areas for the coming of SAP and worked to help assure the users that the changeover to SAP would occur as smoothly as possible. The existing support team was responsible for understanding the pending SAP implementation and for managing the legacy systems right up to the point when the final migration took place; in fact, the support team and the implementation team were both instrumental in the implementation. It's easy to assume that an SAP implementation is made successful solely by the efforts of the dedicated implementation team. This simply is not the case.

The major topic of this chapter is how the two teams—SAP implementation and the existing legacy support team—work together, and apart, to manage an SAP implementation and the transition period afterwards. It begins with an understanding of the roles each team plays, and how the players on each team ensure a clean migration. The teams work under different control criteria, and it is important to understand the logical blending point. This chapter explains how the two support teams work together to support the automated environment and the business users. This method of dual support promotes knowledge transfer, process understanding, and overall system stability. The two teams work together to ensure that the system stabilizes in a reasonable amount of time. The ultimate goal of the teams' partnership is a support *handoff*. The time will come that the implementation team must move on, and the long-term support team must take on the full responsibility of supporting the new system and processes. This handoff must occur as a nonevent—transparent to the business areas.

To ensure that a handoff can meet its goals, a set of rules and deliverables—*handoff criteria*—needs to be established as a measure of handoff readiness and completeness. Again, both teams work toward this effort together. The handoff criteria becomes the instrument by which system and process stabilization can be monitored and managed. Therefore, this chapter identifies the key elements of handoff criteria as they pertain to SAP and explains how to know when system stabilization is being achieved.

 NOTE

Stabilization, the point when the new processes are functional as designed and fully meet the business requirements, is the key prerequisite to effecting a support handoff. A stable system is one that can be operative with reasonable hands-on management by the support team. The handoff criteria, as you will see, determine what is reasonable.

Understanding Changing Roles and Responsibilities

When beginning to blend the two teams—the implementation team and the current business support team—it is necessary to revisit the roles and responsibilities under which each member performs. Each team, initially, has different business and schedule motivations that drive its actions. The implementation team works to complete process and system development to ensure that the SAP implementation occurs as planned and that the original business objectives are met. The implementation team's goal is to meet the ultimate milestone of implementation. The existing legacy support team, anticipating the SAP implementation, works to keep the business activities operational in the legacy environment while preparing for a smooth, nondisruptive changeover to SAP. This team is very business control oriented. Therefore, it is useful to look at the new system environment and see how these two support teams can meld their roles and motivations to start a support migration—the handoff.

The New SAP Instance Environment

After the SAP implementation occurs, the attention moves from development to support. The instance environment is no longer centered on mass development and testing, but on maintenance and modification. No doubt, some quick changes are required to ensure that the new SAP environment performs to its original design intent. Fixes and modifications need to be fast, yet controlled. Controlled maintenance starts with understanding the new system environment and the establishment of methods by which change can be carefully managed to yield the desired outcome. So, look at your SAP instance environment. It should now look much like the example in Figure 12-1.

In Chapter 8, you learned that the implementation team's QA/Test instance eventually became the Live Business instance—where the daily business activities are now occurring. The team still requires a Development (that is, a crash-and-burn) instance where changes can be made and unit-tested prior to moving to the Live Business instance. However, without the QA/Test instance, you limit the possibilities of performing true, integrated production-like testing. Therefore, another instance should be put in place to fill the void. Look at the revised diagram shown in Figure 12-2.

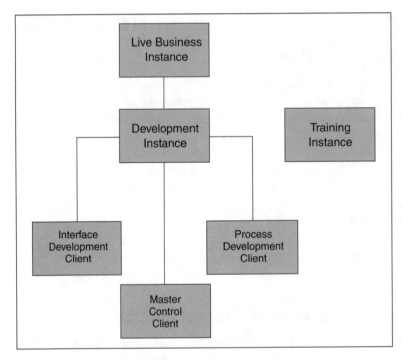

FIGURE 12-1 *The new SAP Live Business environment will require a new method to control change.*

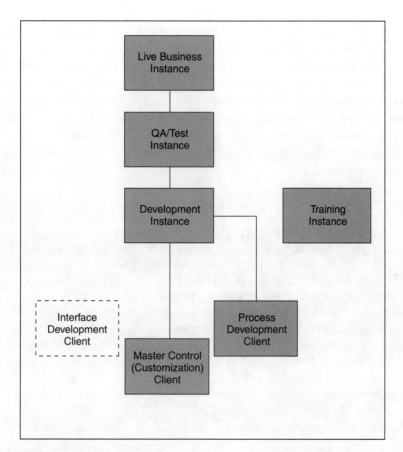

FIGURE 12-2 *The SAP Live Business environment requires the reestablishment of a QA/Test instance.*

Notice how this environment is beginning to more closely reflect the environment suggested in Figure 4-1. You see in Figure 12-2 that the interface development client is being phased out.

At this point, interface and process design development and unit testing is best accomplished in the same client. The customization master client continues to exist as a point of system refresh and reference. Chapter 9 showed the conclusion of the transformation by introducing the Disaster Recovery instance. For the immediate time, though, the Disaster Recovery instance is not yet required.

The New Implementation Team Role

The implementation team previously worked long and hard to understand SAP and how it can replace and improve your company's legacy applications. Though the team had been extremely milestone-driven, its work was still conducted in a manner that allowed for much research and testing, all in a laboratory-type environment. As the actual SAP implementation took effect, the implementation team worked closely with the system and the business users to ensure that the processes were meeting the business needs and that the system was performing in a reliable manner. The final implementation actually took the team's work out of the laboratory and put it into the live, real-time business arena. Errors or problems at this point needed to be understood and mitigated as quickly as possible. The team's actions had to be more deliberate than ever before.

> This period can be a difficult transition for the implementation team. Now you are very much in the public eye, and, unfortunately, if things go wrong, many users will be quick to tell you so. Working in a development environment provides a certain amount of protection. Your actions there usually affect only the other implementation team members. Because you're all working on the same implementation, a common understanding and patience develops. However, when the turn-on occurs, all actions now affect the different business areas, and problems can quickly escalate. This change will shift you and your teammates into the support role immediately, causing you to now consider user acceptance and confidence as a main deliverable. The business areas could become quite wary and even critical of the new SAP processes. You need to promote the new system, largely by ensuring its processes remain available and accurate.

With a revised SAP instance strategy in place, you can begin to consider the different types of problems that occur and the changes that might be required to stabilize the new SAP environment. The most significant changes the implementation team makes are actual code changes. As SAP is enabled and the business users begin to work with it, inaccuracies or minor omissions in programmed functionality become apparent. These include process decision logic, linkages to other processes or interfaced legacy applications, or incomplete process parameters.

Whatever the case, the implementation team must work rapidly to modify the code so that the business activities can continue. Remember, in an integrated environment, any erroneous information can quickly affect additional SAP business modules or the company's different business areas. Speed is of the essence here. However, it must be a controlled speed, as demonstrated in the discussion of instance testing. Try to resist the urge to make code changes directly within the Live Business instance. Even the seemingly smallest change in SAP can yield unexpected results elsewhere in the integrated environment.

Other changes might also be required. Customizations may need to be set or reset, or additional data values may need to be made available in any number of the master data tables. Whatever the situation, by now the implementation team is working in more of a reactive nature than it was before. This change is common and expected during an SAP migration despite thorough preimplementation testing. No business or organization desires to work in a reactive mode—as opposed to the more desirable proactive mode—but it is a reality and helps the team progress toward system and process stabilization.

The Current Support Team Role

The current support team continues to respond to the needs of the business users and the process performance. The business must continue, uninterrupted, and the sweeping changes introduced by the SAP implementation need to be monitored closely. The current support team, though, has also taken on a slightly different role. First, team members have become students of SAP. While this team has continued to ensure process and system functionality in the legacy environment, they have also immersed themselves into learning about SAP, its functionality, and how the company intends to migrate the legacy processes. In some cases, a legacy application a support team member maintained might have been replaced entirely by SAP functionality. That team member now needs to fully understand the replacement SAP functionality while still providing the same level of support to the business users. Equally, if a legacy application continues to be in use after the SAP migration, the support team members need to understand how SAP might be interfacing to or from that legacy application. It will be necessary to understand how the legacy data is used in SAP, how it is converted, and which business users depend on that information. If legacy data is being populated from SAP, the support team members need to understand the source of the data in SAP, often requiring the review of SAP's data tables. Either way, the current support team needs to become SAP-literate to effectively support the business users. You might even see how the current support team members have become experts in both SAP and legacy applications.

Shared Roles and Responsibilities

You may now have noticed that two teams are working together to support the live business. The implementation team needs to ensure the new processes are working as designed and that the designs are usable and effective. The business results must continue to be met, and the users must build confidence in and become familiar with SAP. Similarly, the current support team continues its role of ensuring that the automated processes are satisfying the needs of users and the overall business. The current support team must ensure that the users are receiving the SAP migration well and that management continues to receive indicators that business goals are achievable and are being met. So, in essence, the two teams are in the business of monitoring a new system environment to ensure it is up and operational when the business needs it. The system must perform in an acceptable manner, avoiding long response times or processing bottlenecks. Both teams are working closely with the users to ensure that the new SAP system and processes can be easily and reliably utilized. Users are polled to determine how well they understand and accept the new processes and at what levels user knowledge and expertise are developing.

At the same time, the implementation and current support teams are working to support one another. This is actually an outgrowth of the implementation approach— that is, a team of individuals working together to understand a company's goal and striving to make that goal a reality. Now, the new goal is settling in and stabilizaing SAP. Both teams have a vested interest in this goal. The implementation team wants to ensure that its vision of a new SAP-empowered business environment can succeed. The current support team wants to ensure that the maintenance of business automation works to enable the business teams, not restrict them. Therefore, the teams work together to make these identifiably common goals a single point of business success.

Enabling Temporary Co-Support

As both teams are so closely linked to the same business objective, it becomes apparent that the two can work together to support the company's business users and processes. It's a truly desirable situation for a company to reap benefits from this sort of combined and dedicated workforce focused on making the business activity more productive and reliable than ever before. At this point, though, you need to understand some inherent differences between the two teams and how to merge their efforts into a functional, agreeable single effort. This activity is likely to be a temporary effort, aimed at stabilizing the new environment. As Chapter 11 pointed out, the support team changes soon after stabilization is achieved, with the long-term result being a good combination of current support team members as well as previous implementation team members.

Temporary Co-Support—The result of the combined efforts of the implementation team and the current support team: Both teams are working in a cooperative effort to maintain and stabilize the new system environment. They share the same goal: ensure the business activities are properly supported and disruption to those activities is minimal.

Control becomes the keyword in making this merging of the teams happen. It's actually a point of give and take—the current support team must share system control with the implementation team. The implementation team needs to relinquish some of the freedoms it once had in the SAP development environment—the system needs to be locked down and more closely controlled than before, usually involving many new players in roles of overall system control maintenance. So the first event that needs to take place is to revisit SAP logon access for the support team. Leveraging from the organization charts of both the implementation and current support teams, align the team members into their areas of business support or infrastructure support. Subsequently, access to the Live Business instance should be granted to those areas that the team members actually support. Remove system-wide access wherever possible. This type of access might be appropriate only for the infrastructure team members.

> The onslaught of control. It's difficult to deal with, especially if, when supporting an implementation, you had the freedom to roam the entire system before. Initially, you'll believe that control slows your efforts and creates needless points of bureaucratic checkpoints. Those opinions are understandable, but try to recognize that control provides consistency and stability to the new environment. It's easy to make quick changes and modifications within SAP and then forget to tell other team members. If you are free to enter other SAP business modules, a change you make could have a negative effect on the support team members responsible for managing that functionality. Look to control as a means to better understand and focus upon the business area you support and to which you have systematic access. At the same time, understand the company's audit requirements and how your controlled actions help to make passing audits a thing of ease.

When adequate system access control is in place, all members of the combined support team must understand how to adjust their attitudes to fulfill their particular role.

For example, implementation team members need to internalize the fact that they no longer have free access within the system nor carte blanche to affect system or process changes. What these team members have achieved is phenomenal, to say the least, but an implementation effort—working in a complete laboratory environment—can distort the view of some of the rigors that come with supporting a live business. In addition, these team members need to begin mentoring the current support team members, showing them the many aspects of the SAP designs that have been developed and implemented. This is going to take some additional patience and time from the implementation team members' perspective as the current support team members work to become more familiar with the new environment. Most of all, the implementation team needs to become sensitive to the fact that a live business has many more controls than does a development environment. This concept should not be new to the implementation team members, especially if they originally came from the legacy support environment, but it's a discipline that is sometimes quickly forgotten and hard to return to.

The biggest change the existing support team needs to work with is the effects of working with an integrated, real-time system environment. SAP needs to be closely monitored, especially the functionality of the new processes. Any problems, bugs, or inconsistencies must be evaluated and resolved very quickly. The integration factor works both for and against a business. Unchecked problems can have a large-scale effect in a relatively short time. The current support team members need to react with possibly more of a sense of urgency then they had before. Communication with other team members is critical to overall business process success. A more coordinated, support team approach must be exercised as opposed to the support of a single application that affects a single business area. Also, the current support team members need to be sensitive to the fact that the implementation team members have just emerged from a high-powered, highly driven implementation effort. At times, implementation team members may appear a bit over-reactive, but it's largely because they have learned the effects of SAP's integrated architecture and move quite quickly to respond to potential issues. The current support team members will probably need to pick up their own pace a bit.

Developing Handoff Criteria

Clearly, a co-support approach is not desirable for an extended period. Although it is a very desirable combination of expertise to have in your company, it is rather expensive, too. Just the method of ensuring good communication across such a large team can become challenging. And, bottom line, the new system needs to be stabilized to the point at which the size of the support team can be reduced, and the users need to be returned to working with a traditional support team. But, no one wants to be handed a hot potato, and an unstable SAP system can be just that. Therefore, measures need to be put in place and metrics need to be established to help both teams determine when stabilization has been achieved.

The Stabilization Window

First, it's a good idea to determine how long it would take for stabilization to be achieved. The time-frame in which stabilization is expected to occur will not necessarily be exact, but it helps guide both teams to work to a date milestone by which their efforts can be measured. Depending on the level of migration in your implementation, a standard window of time to work with would be four to six weeks. To some, this might seem like a long time, especially considering the degree of testing that took place during the implementation phase. In addition, because many of the processes introduced will be repeated many times a day or week, any potential fixes that are needed should manifest themselves relatively quickly. However, every business must encounter a regular, monthly financial reconciliation period. A full stabilization team effort should be in place to see that activity through. Much will be learned with the first effort and, if possible, it is beneficial if the implementation team can be available for a second month's closing to apply what was learned from the first.

On the other hand, four to six weeks may not be enough time for an adequate SAP stabilization. After all, 20 years of application know-how has been replaced by brand new functionality. Could a business possibly exercise as much activity in such a short period of time? The answer, obviously, is no. However, there is an opportunity cost to maintaining such a large support team. Stabilizing an SAP environment should occur as quickly, effectively, and completely as possible. The nature of business support dictates that users continue to raise system-related issues and that fixes continue to be required. However, the goal of stabilization is to mitigate the volume of problem-solving activity, but not to eradicate the entire activity itself.

Useful Stabilization Metrics

To help guide your SAP environment to stabilization, you should understand what metrics are useful to establish and monitor. These can be system response time metrics, business process metrics, or a combination of both. The goal is to return your automated business process environment to a state that requires a nominal amount of unplanned support effort and virtually no unplanned system downtime. Stabilization, once realized, also marks the point when a support handoff is appropriate. Consider the following potential system and process metrics that might lead you and your team to a stable environment.

- ◆ No unplanned code changes for at least four consecutive weeks
- ◆ No unplanned or critical customizations for at least four consecutive weeks
- ◆ No background job aborts for at least five consecutive cycles
- ◆ Hands-off automated processes (no intervention required) for five consecutive cycles
- ◆ System/transaction response time is within acceptable parameters
- ◆ Any known long-term fixes (not critical) are fully characterized and staffed for resolution

These major metrics will help lead your SAP environment in the direction of stabilization. Each business area support team member should further define each metric in terms that are more specific to the business process activities. Much of the criteria needs to be defined by the unique business needs and should include control parameters that are acceptable to the business.

Additional Stabilization Considerations

Additionally, you and your team should consider at least the following two points when working through the stabilization window. First, consider the makeup of the long-term support team. It should consist of a good mix of previous implementation team members, current support team members, maybe a few newcomers, and possibly a consultant. You want to be sure that the team feels adequately confident and can demonstrate the necessary SAP and business process knowledge to provide the required amount of support. Additionally, it needs to be able to characterize and resolve problems quickly to reduce the potential for data or process corruption. If additional team training is required, it should be noted before the final handoff. Also, consider recruiting experienced resources if the team is a bit light on seasoned expertise.

Second, it is a good idea for the business areas to determine the level of process and SAP execution expertise that is being attained by the business users. As the stabilization time frame nears its end, users should be able to demonstrate significant growth in their SAP process knowledge. Within four weeks of the initial SAP implementation, the implementation/training team should offer and conduct follow-up training sessions—repeats of the original training sessions. This step encourages users to revisit some of the previously presented concepts and mechanics. Retention this time, however, should be much greater because the users now have had hands-on, real-life experience with the new processes. The support team will be relying, to a certain degree, on the users' knowledge of the new processes, ensuring that the users can execute their daily transactions accurately. Bad data or a misused SAP process can have as much negative impact as a bug in a portion of code.

The support team needs to know that the users can successfully and consistently perform their tasks within SAP and that business process analysts can answer users' process questions. Of course, this scenario can cover 100 percent of the situations, but 90 to 95 percent effectiveness should be the goal. A simple method to use in monitoring user absorption is to administer simple tests at the completion of follow-up training sessions. The outcome helps users understand where they are still unclear about aspects of a process and also helps managers understand how to best provide additional learning opportunities for the business people.

Tracking Progress to Stabilization

On the road to stabilization, most system and process problems surface within the first few weeks or the first month-end cycle. With measurable metrics established, the team will probably not be able to fully begin seeing progress to stabilization until a few weeks into the implementation. Most activity occurs in the initial weeks, and much of it is sometimes attributed to the newness of the system. Users make mistakes because they are less intimately familiar with the new processes than they once were in the legacy environment. Likewise, support team members might make mistakes or commit oversights simply because they are not yet fully familiar with the nuances of SAP or its interfaces to legacy applications. Always allow for and expect an active first month and don't assume that this activity level is an indication of the new environment to come. It's just the settling of the dust after the sweeping change that has occurred.

To ensure that all stabilization issues are properly captured, identified, prioritized, and resolved, it is a good idea to create an issue-tracking matrix similar to those you used during the implementation effort. Such matrices quickly relay information about an issue, identify responsible owners of the resolution, and help you and your team determine your rate of progress toward stabilization. During the first few weeks of SAP being live, the issue matrix should be reviewed at least weekly, maybe twice-weekly, to ensure that critical issues are resolved quickly and that lower-priority issues don't accidentally escalate.

As the weeks continue, you will see a noticeable decline in user calls, code problems, or job aborts. Your issue matrix should begin to show more closed issues than open, and with declining levels of criticality. This is because most processes are repetitive, and most have been exercised quite well by the fourth week of SAP being live. Soon you should see your stabilization metrics report progress toward a point of support handoff. However, if a problem does arise during the stabilization period, the clock for that particular metric should be reset. For example, if a process executes well for three cycles (iterations) but fails on a fourth, the metric should be reset so that the next cycle constitutes the first cycle for the next group of measurements. Remember that you need to monitor any change made to SAP, be it within code, customizations, or elsewhere, until its impact on other processes is clearly nonconsequential.

One other thing to consider during the stabilization time frame is the effect changes might have on the users or their processes. If bugs are found and corrected, determine the best method to communicate any resulting changes that need to be made. In most cases, simple information-sharing sessions with the users can be effective in discussing the impact. If a resulting change is more significant and has a truly measurable effect upon one of the new processes, it might be a good idea to conduct further training sessions.

Stable and Ready for Handoff

Much like the implementation itself, this point is another major milestone in your company's SAP migration. It is when success can again be measured. First, the company turned on SAP and began managing business activity with the new system. The system and processes have been monitored and modified as needed to ensure that the business activity continues to flow properly.

After a period of weeks when processes were performed without major upset or significant handholding, the new system is deemed stable. The keys to the new system are now ready to hand over to the long-term support team. This is significant proof of the effectiveness of your company's SAP implementation because a handoff can only be properly achieved after a period of proven accurate business results and automated process functionality. Congratulate yourself and your team and get ready for one final migration.

Summary

In this chapter, you can see that the SAP life cycle actually continues beyond the implementation and turn-on. It is a major event in the life of a business and involves many individuals to effect a functional migration. Therefore, many companies can be frightened away from an SAP implementation. As you learned in Part II of this book, an SAP implementation requires clear goals, a dedicated team, and a certain level of faith. Although one might argue that the resource needs never seem to end, you need to look back and account for all that has transpired. By this stage, your company is operating on an automated business platform that positions it for future growth and expansion. After the initial migration, the rest is relatively easy, and as your business's processes stabilize, the pending support handoff proves the validity of the original project charter. It's sometimes a test of endurance. You're in it this far, so don't give up yet.

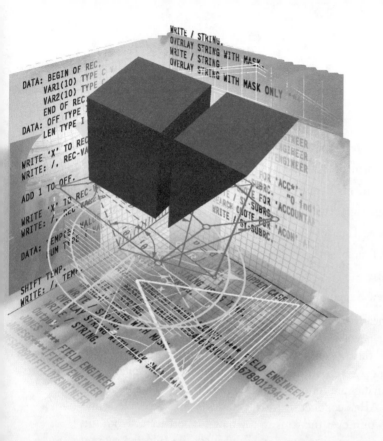

Chapter 13

The Handoff and Migration of Support

In This Chapter

- ◆ Getting the Long-Term Support Team in Place
- ◆ Support Team Deployment and Business Area Assignment
- ◆ Determining All Elements Requiring Long-Term Support
- ◆ Establishing Backup Support Linkages
- ◆ Executing Knowledge Transfer
- ◆ Documentation Deliverables
- ◆ Handoff Acceptance
- ◆ Introducing the New Support Team

The SAP life cycle is now nearly complete. As discussed in the previous chapter, you have worked to stabilize the new system and processes. Through the close monitoring of the new processes and functionality, while tracking performance against established control metrics, the new SAP environment reached a point of acceptable stabilization. The business activities are running smoothly, and the users are becoming quite settled in the use of SAP to conduct their daily duties. With the implementation goals met, it is time to turn over the reins to the new support team. From this point on, your company is now an operational SAP business site, and the support team becomes an SAP support team.

You've already seen how the handoff criteria and metrics led you to the point of actual handoff. The handoff leads to the establishment of the new support team structure, made up of a collection of technical and business process experts. This support team works with the remaining implementation team members to effect the handoff, ensuring that all new processes and functions are accounted for and have new, long-term owners on the support team. The key here becomes the identification of elements to be handed off and the assurance that a linkage can be made between the original developers and the future support team members.

Of course, the handoff is a two-way effort. It is neither a *push* effort from the implementation team nor a *pull* effort from the support team. It needs to occur using both methods. And the handoff criteria works to ensure that nothing slips between the cracks or is prematurely thrown over the wall to the new support team. The handoff is one of the last milestones to be realized in the overall implementation effort. But it's not a milestone to rush through because it is a major contributor to the long-term success of the implementation and the new team supporting the SAP environment.

The discussion in this chapter focuses on a concept known as *knowledge transfer*. Knowledge transfer is a method of ensuring that the members or the new support team have enough knowledge about the new SAP elements that are being handed off such that the support of those elements can transition smoothly and reliably. Actually, knowledge transfer itself becomes a key element in effecting an acceptable handoff. The discussion of knowledge transfer in this chapter points out how it incorporates elements of technical review, documentation deliverables, and any final requirements of technical support training. The final handoff cannot be realized until both teams believe the knowledge transfer is complete and effective. The caveat still exists, though, that not all aspects of a new SAP element can be fully reviewed. Therefore, the new support team needs to establish backup linkages to the original developers or process designers from the implementation team in an way to provide a temporary safety net of knowledge support.

After the handoff, the new support team should be redeployed and reestablished to support the business areas. Redeployment is the final step in restoring a traditional support team, although each team member's activities and long-term linkages might be different from what they possibly supported before SAP. The effort comes full circle when the new team is introduced to the business areas and is in place to provide the necessary system maintenance, enhancement, and user interaction that continue to assist in the evolution of the business environment.

Getting the Long-Term Support Team in Place

At this point, the new support team is firmly staffed with the individuals who will be a part of ongoing business support. As the support team assembles into its final form, the long-term support team management should be mindful of the mix of expertise on the team. The team needs the appropriate skill set to fully and effectively support the new SAP solutions while also being able to manage and maintain any resident legacy applications. New team members are most welcome at this time, especially if they can bring deep business experience to the support team's mix. The new team should be well balanced between technical expertise and sound business application. It might be a good idea to retain a consultant or two from the implementation effort—to help smooth out any transition issues and be available to provide further guidance and teaching to the long-term support team. Above all, the new support team must dedicate itself to the key principles and ideals of support. Going back to much of the discussion in Chapter 1 of this book, it is highly important that the new team is fully subscribed to providing the best support possible and is able to engage the business teams in a manner that will complement the new SAP environment. It's a fresh system, a fresh team, and the best time to revisit the foundation of support basics.

> Yes, I know I keep going back to the concept of support basics. I don't wish to sound like a broken record, but you'd be surprised at how easily the support organization can overlook the basics of support—your team's major core competency—during this time of change. The new SAP environment becomes so engrossing that it's easy for a support team to become overly focused on internal issues. This situation is understandable, but I have seen how a support team can become so self-absorbed that some of the basic customer service practices take a back seat. Just remember the reason your support team is in existence and that other business areas allocate the dollars for your team's services.

Support Team Deployment and Business Area Assignment

Each dedicated support team member needs to be assigned to a business area of focus. As you saw in Figure 11-1, the team should be able to provide appropriate support resources to the different business areas, including legacy application areas. Additionally, the new environment will require a team of dedicated individuals to manage the core of the new SAP environment: the infrastructure (internal operations) team.

Assembling the appropriate mix of players for your particular business needs and determining the right size of the team may be a trial-and-error process. It's never a good idea to have too many resources. Neither is it appropriate to be understaffed.

Each team member should understand his or her role and be able to manage the day's duties as clearly and completely as possible. A team that is too large may under-utilize (that is, waste) its resources. However, a team that is too small will not be able to adequately respond to support issues. Additionally, a team that is too small tends to burn out its resources quickly. If this situation leads to the departure of a seasoned resource, the company then has the cost of bringing a new player on board and training him or her.

You might want to rely temporarily on consultants who can be employed for specific periods of time. If a consultant is actively supporting a business area in a consistent manner, it's probably an indicator that your team needs an additional long-term resource. If a consultant is spending significant effort teaching and training the long-term resources, it might be wise to seek additional training opportunities for the support team members. Ideally, the support team will quickly take over all aspects of core business support and the consultants' services can be smoothly phased out.

> Beware of becoming too dependent on the consultants. If your company is concerned about overhead expenses, you'll find that consultants carry a pretty significant price tag in exchange for the service they provide. Your organization should be investing in the long-term company-employed support team members; don't allow a resident consultant to evolve into a crutch.

Determining All Elements Requiring Long-Term Support

The next task is to clearly identify all elements requiring support, including all new SAP functionality, programs, settings and any interfaces or modifications to legacy applications. It's been a flurry of activity since the SAP implementation, and the implementation team has probably started to work in a mode that tends to take even the smallest detail about the new environment for granted. But, hopefully, good communication and documentation habits have captured 99 percent of the new environment's elements.

To be sure you are identifying all handoff elements, work with the implementation team's original design documents and the subteam's detailed work plans. If constructed properly, these items identify the work done within each subteam and point to the new elements requiring support. Be sure to include SAP customizations in the review. Many of those, though seemingly small, have a major effect on the long-term support success.

As a good sanity check, it might be wise to perform an online SAP object check. Using transaction SE11 (SAP's Object Browser), perform a search on all customer-defined elements using your team's designated naming convention. This procedure should uncover any custom elements that may have somehow escaped the handoff list of elements. Although some may no longer be applicable—objects are often created during development and later abandoned before implementation—some elements may spring up as reminders that are quickly accompanied by, "Oh yeah. I almost forgot." As already implied, a lot of work went into the implementation, and you shouldn't expect that every element will be identified at the first go around. All major elements will be captured, but some secondary items my go unchecked at first. The next topic will help to soften the impact of this eventuality.

Establishing Backup Support Linkages

Inevitably, the support team will find an SAP element—typically customer defined—that was not previously shared or discussed. It's typically nothing catastrophic, but discoveries like this can pose a series of questions that beg quick answers. Rather than spend an unknown amount of time trying to determine what the element is, how it is used, and what decisions led to its use, establish linkages to the original implementation team developers.

Linkages to the original developers and designers should be expected by both the implementation team and the new support team. As each handoff element is identified, owners should also be assigned from both teams. This process creates the linkage. This linkage exists to provide ad hoc and informal support, usually relegated to a simple phone call. Questions that arise after stabilization and handoff don't imply that a poor handoff took place. They represent the reality of working with a new environment, especially one as complex as SAP. Most developers are more than willing to provide this assistance.

Executing Knowledge Transfer

Knowledge transfer is the formal event that takes place to enable a final support handoff. It is the gathering of implementation team members, technical developers, process designers, and long-term support team members. The goal is to fully review the aspects of new SAP functionality so the long-term support team member can effectively support the new design or functionality. Knowledge transfer sessions can be coordinated through the use of a simple matrix, possibly leveraging from a listing of handoff elements. Owners will be determined based on who was instrumental in the development and implementation of each element, as well as who is to be responsible for ongoing support of each element. Knowledge transfer is yet another milestone that needs to be successfully executed prior to a clean support handoff.

Formal knowledge transfer sessions should be conducted on a process-by-process basis, allowing the gathered individuals the opportunity to fully review and discuss each particular process and its support elements. This approach assumes that the sessions are attended by implementation subteam members and support team members that are of a similar business area focus. The sessions should consist of process and design review led by the original implementation team developers and designers of the new process. However, the session needs to be informal enough to allow for open discussion between the developers and the support team members.

The following design and support points should be discussed:

- Review of process specifications, deliverables, and proven results
- Review of SAP and/or legacy elements that are employed in the process functionality
- Identification of affected business areas and key process analysts supporting the new design
- System authorizations (user and support)
- Regular maintenance requirements, if any
- Stabilization metrics
- Outstanding fixes or enhancements, if applicable, and plans/resources to address them
- Known trouble areas or watch points to be aware of and to monitor
- Troubleshooting techniques
- Data or process recovery steps

The knowledge transfer sessions should be conducted with enough time to fully discuss these topics, plus additional time for further questions. Both parties—presenters and receivers—should leave the session knowing that the knowledge transfer was successful and the processes discussed can be properly supported by the new support team member. If any questions arise that cannot be fully or satisfactorily addressed within the session, those questions should be documented and resolved quickly. A knowledge transfer should not be considered complete until all outstanding issues have been resolved to the satisfaction of all session attendees.

Documentation Deliverables

During the knowledge transfer sessions, one of the logical deliverables will be the various design and support documentation. The information that guided the implementation effort by successfully capturing process design elements, specifications, methods, and results attains its highest value at the time of knowledge transfer and support handoff.

The documentation should be assembled into a comprehensive package of deliverables. Each deliverable will provide detailed information to the support team regarding the elements being handed off. The documentation can actually serve as a guide in the knowledge transfer sessions. It shows the support team members the logical progression of the new process design and cleanly links the new design to the environment from which it evolved.

Therefore, documentation deliverables should include the following set of detailed information:

◆ Original process specifications and required results

◆ Design alternatives and decisions

◆ Full development specifications including SAP data elements, tables, transactions, and screens

◆ Documentation of SAP ABAP programs that support the process, especially custom programs (bolt-on functionality)

◆ All supporting SAP customizations

◆ Full report specifications for any user output that is created and used through the execution of the process

◆ Complete documentation of legacy interfaces, including any data conversion routines that may be in use to meet the SAP and process data requirements

◆ Records of all design, development, and testing approval

At this time, you should be able to see the deliberateness of the documentation development. Developing good documentation habits early in an SAP migration project will ensure the accurate capturing of development details and decisions along the way. Envision the usefulness of documentation during this transition of support. You will see that it would be near-impossible to accurately and honestly capture the same level of detail if documentation were not being prepared from the point when the implementation project first began. With this in mind at the early stages of an SAP implementation, you'll be able to design and utilize early documentation to facilitate the final handoff.

One final piece of documentation still needs to be prepared before the handoff can be effected. This is a new document known as the *support reference guide*. This document is intended to be an initial point of reference when providing ongoing support for a live automated business process. The support reference guide contains the pertinent information that will enable the support team to quickly assess process intent, results, and problem solving. It's something of a collection of highlights from the previously provided implementation documentation. It's not a repetitive document, however. The support reference guide, sometimes known as a *troubleshooting and recovery guide*, is the tool that support team members use when they are called on to resolve a potential system or process problem. It works as a memory jogger or quick reference at times of off-hours support—for example, when a process aborts in the middle of the night—or when backup support is required in the event that primary support is not readily available.

The support reference guide should include the following information:

- Process design overview and general description
- Data specifications (naming conventions, elements, and tables)
- Hardware requirements
- Security
- Background job specifications and schedules
- File transfer or data sharing specifications
- Troubleshooting and recovery instructions
- Maintenance requirements
- Special maintenance or upgrade considerations
- Additional report specifications

This document should be the joint creation of the developers, designers, and long-term support team members. It will easily leverage from the documentation deliverables already identified, although it will be more focused on ongoing use and maintenance aspects of a process as opposed to development specifications or design alternatives. Be sure the guide adequately covers the information noted in the preceding list.

Of all of the items listed, the most important is the section focused upon troubleshooting and recovery. This section begins with information gleaned from the initial implementation and stabilization activity. Often, in this early stage of the document's life, these recovery and troubleshooting instructions can be rather sparse. However, as situations arise and require resolution throughout ongoing support, this section should be regularly updated. It becomes a basic road map for both primary and backup support team members. This document should become the cornerstone by which support activity can be guided and managed. Delivery and acceptance of this document marks the start of a virtually living support documentation methodology.

Handoff Acceptance

The rigor with which the steps and deliverables throughout this text are delivered is intentional. The goal of this chapter is to emphasize the need for thoroughness and completeness at every step in the SAP life cycle. No development is too small and no decision is too insignificant to be duly documented and internalized into the progress of the support transition. Maintaining such strict milestone deliverables can be extremely laborious and tedious. However, the final goal has now been reached.

If you have been true to the integrity of your milestone deliverables up to now, then the final support handoff should be a non-event. In fact, handoff acceptance becomes more of a final signing on the dotted line than any sort of last-minute flurry or struggle for relinquishment of support responsibility. The ensuing discussion will review how you got to this point and how the handoff is more an event in name than anything else.

The previous support team was relatively involved in the activities leading up to the SAP implementation. It was aware of the migrating processes and their effect on retiring previously used legacy applications. As the implementation effort progressed, the support team attended pilot test sessions and began to better grasp the changes that were on the horizon. Support team members who attended user training sessions got a user's eye view of the new SAP processes. As the final turn-on approached, the support team worked with the legacy applications up to the last minute, prior to their ultimate replacement.

After the implementation, the two teams—previous support and implementation— merged into a larger *co-support* team. Their common goal was to ensure system and process functionality while working side by side to stabilize the new SAP environment. If problems arose, the implementation team took the lead in providing quick resolution, probably under the curious and watchful eye of the previous support team member. Soon the dust began to settle, and stabilization goals were reached. The combined team members have considered their longer term assignments and are aligned to either support the new environment or to seek alternative assignments outside the group. But a good mix of talent and expertise remains and works to make up the new support team. When knowledge transfer occurs, much of the basic process information is already understood—thanks to the teamed approach during the stabilization period. The knowledge transfer serves to review this information while providing a comprehensive look at the process development from beginning to end. Especially pertinent is the review of process or technical details that might not be readily visible but are important to ongoing support. The handoff criteria have been reviewed, and the documentation deliverables have been met. The only thing left is to effect the handoff through the final act of official acceptance.

Introducing the New Support Team

The final step in the support handoff is to announce and introduce the new support team to the business areas. The support team management should prepare an official organization chart and distribute it to the rest of the company. At the same time, the support team goals, objectives, and core competencies should be restated, with emphasis on how the support team membership and focus might have changed to accommodate the new SAP environment.

Each support team member on the organization chart should be clearly associated with the business area he or she supports. The team members should make themselves immediately visible to the business users and begin cultivating the partnerships mentioned in some of the preceding chapters. Support team members might attend business area team meetings to discuss the teams' initial questions and concerns. From this sort of face-to-face meeting, both teams can begin to determine what issues or opportunities now exist and decide how to prioritize and effect change and advancement within the business community—now powered by SAP.

Summary

And there it is: the SAP life cycle brought full circle. Hopefully, you can see how each step has been building on the previous steps. You have seen how active and important the migration of support can be and how it clearly leverages from the previous efforts of the implementation team. To use the metaphor of a foundation, this chapter shows how the handoff criteria, along with the knowledge transfer and documentation deliverables, work to build a new footing for support of the SAP environment.

Throughout this entire journey, the importance of each step should now be clear to you. You should understand how successive progress is highly dependent on previous efforts and results. The degree to which your company is enabling SAP migration will determine the ultimate content of each phase of the SAP life cycle. Take the time to consider each element covered here to ensure that you are working in a complete and logical manner. A little extra time invested up front will save much back-end scrambling or rework.

The migration effort ends the SAP implementation, although one more topic needs to be addressed before the support transition concludes. The next chapter explains how to reestablish the aspects of support ownership and control. It is the final step to take as you and your team become a full-fledged SAP support team.

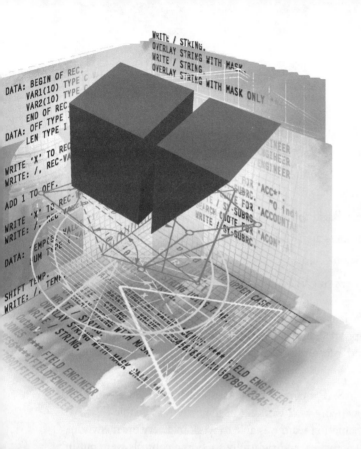

Chapter 14

Establishing the
Support Domain

In This Chapter

◆ Revisiting Company Controls and Culture

◆ Identifying Key Points of Control

◆ Revisiting Separation of Duty

◆ Reestablishing System Backup, Refresh, and Recovery

◆ Ensuring Audit Readiness and ISO Compliance

◆ Cleaning Up the System

As you can see from this chapter's title, the subject matter here concerns the new support team and its control of the new operating environment. One of the key responsibilities of the support team is ensuring that the automated business systems are secure. Consequently, the support team must be sure that appropriate controls and safeguards are in place to avoid interrupting business activity and to protect the business information.

Having just been through an SAP migration, you can see how many people get involved in the effort and how many were working in the system to enable the SAP implementation. The implementation team was able to work in a very open environment during its development activities, and rightfully so. Some controls were put in place during the development phase to protect the new SAP process designs and master data, but nothing like the control that is exercised in a live business environment. In the live environment, the systems and data must be secure and controlled not only from a business controls standpoint but also from the standpoint that protects the company's confidential information within its particular industry.

The intent of this chapter is to help you reestablish your support team's control of the new SAP environment. You start by reviewing your company's key business controls and exploring ways to ensure that the new support team is back in alignment with the overall company culture. The focus is on the key control points to ensure that the new SAP environment has not compromised any basic tenets of business activity and institutional methodology. Then you review your separation-of-duty policy, which applies to both the business users and to the support team members—sometimes even more so to the latter group. You learn about the risks to avoid within the support team and how to monitor and maintain clean, divisive lines of access.

Next you revisit your backup and recovery controls. Your environment needs to be properly protected through the active and regular capture of the environmental and business data. If any sort of emergency or data corruption occurs, you'll want to be sure you have an adequate course of recovery. Although the actual mechanics of establishing recovery methods are discussed at length in Part IV of this book, the discussion in this chapter suggests your team revisits its SAP instance landscape and makes a final amendment that provides a route for recovery.

Through all of this activity, you will ensure that your new SAP environment is secure, reliable, and under control. This process serves to make your environment audit ready; that is, you can demonstrate your levels of control when internal and external auditors examine your business systems. Much like death and taxes, audits are another of life's realities. However, this chapter shows you how you to make an audit a commonplace event that stirs no anxiety or last-minute effort. As you demonstrate this level of control, you will also be in a position to demonstrate the reliability of the business processes you support and their inherent ease of repetition.

Finally, you will examine your new environment and begin to look for areas that require some cleanup. Much like the construction of a new home, an SAP migration can leave behind some scraps and residue of the activities that have just taken place. You'll want to ensure that the environment is clean and that no elements are left lying about to distract or confuse the support and business teams.

Revisiting Company Controls and Culture

This first point goes back to the company's support strategy and the degree to which the organization believes system and process controls need to be exercised. Some businesses choose to be very stringent with control, whereas others may choose a bit looser environment. The driving force behind company controls usually stems from known audit checkpoints and areas of potential business exposure. Depending on your company's industry, these control points can vary in terms of their level of restriction.

SAP can drive the need for change to a company's control culture. For example, if a company previously operated under a looser control environment, allowing support team members to maybe conduct some business transactions on behalf of the business area they supported, the realization must be made that the environment is now highly integrated. This new environment could result in trouble for other integrated business processes if some less stringent legacy control methods are still utilized. The same holds true for business users who may have been granted some levels of system access in the previous legacy environment, perhaps in managing processing errors. The high levels of process and data integration may determine that, at least initially, this sort of freedom should be restricted. Keep in mind that most of the business community, including some of the support team members, is still learning about the new SAP processes. For this reason, a business might choose to play the conservative role for a while.

Identifying Key Points of Control

The first point of control to put in place in your new SAP system is to protect the Live Business instance from unauthorized changes. The most direct method to achieve this sort of global control is through the use of the SAP Workbench Organizer. Accessed via SAP transaction SE03, the Workbench Organizer leads to the global system change options (see Figure 14-1).

By setting the system to *not changeable*, you can protect the internal ABAP code and data dictionary elements from untested modification. This setting also protects most of the internal customizations, although some may still be open to direct updates.

Next, consider your team's access to the importing of changes into the Live Business instance. As mentioned during the discussion of the stabilization period (see Chapter 13), changes deemed necessary to the Live Business instance should first be developed

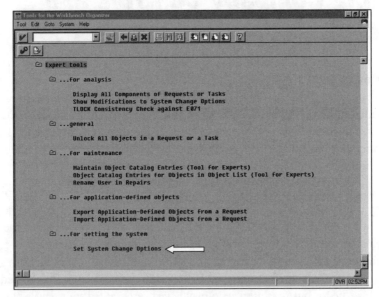

FIGURE 14-1

Use the Workbench Organizer to modify the System Change Options (SAP transaction SE03).

and unit tested in the Development instance. Next, the change is moved into the QA/Test instance for business team testing and validation. The final step is to move the approved change into the Live Business instance. Importing the changed SAP objects occurs at the UNIX level, using the *tp import* command. Your support team's infrastructure personnel are usually the best people to manage this function.

Multiple imports, attempted at the same time, can block one another and potentially corrupt the objects that are being changed. (See Chapter 18 for more on change management.)

Then, restrict access to the set up and modification of SAP logon IDs to two or three support team members. The business teams and support team need to display appropriate controls over enabling new users and their system functionality access. This step should actually be an extension of the logon ID administration methods that were established and exercised during the implementation effort. If the implementation team members who previously managed logon IDs are no longer performing that role, be sure to remove their access to this activity.

There is a final key control point that should be reviewed after the new support team is defined and the implementation effort has drawn to a close. This last control point involves restricting or removing the access previously granted to the implementation team members. Believe it or not, this point is easy to forget, but it is an exposure to the ongoing business control. Review the SAP logon IDs and methodically inspect each ID and its authorization access. All logons that belonged to team members no longer working in a support capacity should be immediately removed or the associated access reduced to display access only. Other questionable logon IDs should prompt the contacting of the logon user to determine if they have a continued need for SAP access. Finally, you should review the access of implementation team members who have migrated to ongoing support to ensure that their access complies with their new support assignments. Make any authorization changes necessary to ensure the team members have access appropriate to their new support duties.

TIP

It might be worthwhile to develop methods of continually reviewing logon IDs and their associated access profiles. This can be easily achieved by creating a report that can be run and reviewed regularly, or even a simple listing of the SAP tables that contain this information. (Hint: see SAP tables USR01, USR02, and USR03 to get started.)

Revisiting Separation of Duty

Separation of duty was first presented to you during the discussion of business controls and ensuring business users can only perform their specific, assigned system tasks. The same holds true for the support team members. It's important to ensure that support team members can effect only SAP activity that is pertinent to the support of their direct business users.

More importantly, separation of duty becomes an audit issue for the support team. Support team members having direct access to a company's business systems and business data need to be working within logical control parameters. Access restriction ensures that appropriate process and data control is maintained. Also, and not to appear paranoid, access restriction prevents support team members from manipulating business systems and data in an unauthorized fashion.

Reestablishing System Backup, Refresh, and Recovery

With the new system in place, a backup, refresh, and recovery methodology must be reinstated. This effort reestablishes reliability to the system environment. At the same time, this effort also reestablishes key control of the new system environment to the support team.

The hardware support team—that is, the team that maintains the server(s) upon which the SAP instances are established need to schedule and execute regular system backups. Even from the hardware perspective, the new SAP environment differs from the previous environment, so the hardware support team needs to be fully trained on the execution of SAP system backups. Be sure that whole system backups are performed at least once a week, with incremental backups occurring nightly.

Next, it is time to make a final modification to the SAP instance landscape. During the stabilization period, your team enabled the appropriate instances to support a development area where fixes and enhancements could be made. A new QA/Test instance was established for live businesslike testing, leading to a clean migration of a change to the Live Business instance. At this point, it is time to reestablish your team's Disaster Recovery Planning (DRP) instance. This instance is practically a mirror image of the Live Business instance. It should be an exact duplicate in terms of hardware specifications, including processing power and disk storage capacity. The DRP instance is the final instance to complete the new support instance landscape; now you should have a configuration that resembles the example shown in Figure 14-2.

Part IV of this book provides details regarding the elements of actual DRP testing and readiness. But at this point, the DRP instance should be established and identical to the Live Business instance. It should also be managed by a trained and qualified hardware support team.

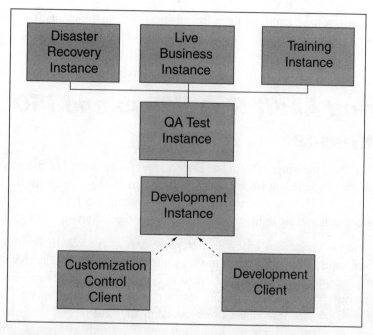

FIGURE 14-2 *The introduction of a DRP instance completes the final SAP support instance landscape.*

The DRP instance should be as far as possible from the Live Business instance (for example, in a different state). Sounds pretty obvious, but I've known of DRP machines that physically sat only a few feet away from the Live Business instance that might need to be potentially recovered. Such proximity doesn't really provide the confidence that a business' automated environment is truly recoverable in the event of a disaster.

Finally, it is necessary to establish an instance refresh strategy. This activity is probably new to the SAP environment. Not many legacy environments are managed in this way. The refresh strategy was established during the development and testing phases of the implementation cycle. This activity ensured that all development and testing was being conducted in a clean environment that reflected the intended long-term live business environment. At this time, the Live Business instance is in place, and it is exempt from refreshing, obviously. However, the backups taken from the Live Business instance will serve as the tools of refresh for the support team's development, QA/Test, and Training instances. The refreshes need to be regularly scheduled, just as during the implementation effort, to ensure the support team is developing, testing, and training in live business-like environments. The refresh cycle was previously depicted in Chapter 4. For this discussion, Figure 14-3 represents that cycle.

Ensuring Audit Readiness and ISO Compliance

At this stage, the support team has gained appropriate control of the new SAP system environment. Controls are again in place and in alignment with the company's requirements. This check determines whether the support team has enough control and demonstrated reliability to successfully meet the requirements of an audit.

The *audit* is the regular review of a business and its controls by both internal and external audit groups. These groups visit company sites and carefully review the operations. The auditors are looking for areas of business weakness or exposure that could compromise the business's ongoing interests. Equally, auditors may be looking for business exposures that could affect the company's customers. Auditors, although sometimes regarded with the same amount of warmth as lawyers and used-car

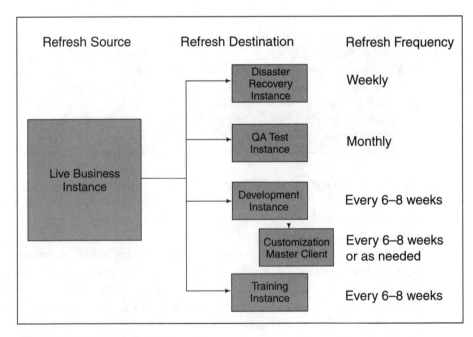

FIGURE 14-3 *SAP instance refresh model*

salespeople, actually guide a company to see its weaknesses in execution and provide suggestions and guidance to reduce risk and exposure.

To be audit compliant, the support team should understand the company's compliance requirements in the following areas:

◆ System access

◆ High-level company legal disclaimers upon system access

◆ Transaction authorizations

◆ Separation of duty

◆ Disaster and contingency planning

◆ Data integrity and security

◆ Regular business area review of system security measures

◆ Change control and management

◆ Design control and methodology adherence

This list might be only a subset of the audit controls that are important and measured in your company. The goal is to ensure that, from a support standpoint, your team can demonstrate the appropriate levels of control and consistency. If this is achieved, then your team can rest assured that the business needs are being met, the systems are secure, and audits are not a cause for undue anxiety or last-minute preparation.

 NOTE

ISO is the recognized name of The International Organization for Standardization, located in Geneva, Switzerland. Since 1947, ISO has been responsible for delivering internationally agreed-on quality standards for products and services. Although the standards published by ISO, developed through the active participation of industry professionals worldwide, are not mandatory for business use, they do serve as facilitators to product and service quality and allow reliable and active product and service trade on a global basis. Companies can choose to adopt ISO standards and, therefore, become officially ISO certified. ISO certification is considered desirable in business partnerships and customer relations. Certification proves that a company can demonstrate control and consistency in providing its products or services. As you may have guessed, ISO certification is awarded upon successful auditing of a companies facilities and operations, and annual certification renewal is only awarded after passing annual ISO audits.

The other topic to discuss here is ISO compliance. The goals of ISO compliance are similar to the goals of audit readiness, but the focus of ISO is more quality centric. The support team can achieve ISO certification only if control and consistency of administration can be demonstrated. ISO auditors are typically looking for repetitive actions that yield the same result with each iteration. If consistency can be proven, then it is logically deemed that a company can reproduce products or services with consistent levels of quality and adherence to specification. ISO certification is currently approaching the state of being mandatory; certification was previously only a matter of voluntary action. However, world trade is becoming stricter and more exacting, and some companies have agreed to only work with or purchase from companies that are consistently ISO certified.

Cleaning Up the System

Finally, support team members should review their respective business area elements for cleanup opportunities. (Many will turn up.) The implementation effort involved a lot of design, development, and experimentation. During those phases of the project, many process approaches were probably tried, and some became the live processes the business is currently using. Many others, however, were abandoned and might not have been cleaned away during the implementation effort. If any developmental residue was not identified as damaging to the final process execution, it could have remained in the instance in a sort of orphaned state; by all rights, it should have been cleaned up, but implementation pressures might have caused some non-critical clean up to be delayed. If not all cleanup was achieved prior to the implementation, some orphaned programs, customizations, and master data settings could be resident in the Live Business instance.

Non-critical cleanup is probably more opportunistic in nature. It wouldn't necessarily be a top priority task for you or your team, but a dirty instance can prove to be cumbersome to work through at times. For example, you might need to perform client comparisons between your Live Business instance and your QA/Test instance. This common activity occurs when a support team member needs to determine whether the QA instance is in sync with the Live Business instance. Assume a comparison of table entries could yield a series of values, some of which are actively used by the business areas. However, you may also discover many unused and unneeded values that only lengthen the effort of performing a valid comparison. It's a simple matter of housekeeping, and housekeeping is one of the support team's publicized services. Therefore, give special consideration to the cleanup of the following potentially unused system elements:

- Any unused customer-defined screens or transactions
- Unused customer-defined data elements, domains, tables, or data structures
- Unused or unscheduled customer-defined ABAP programs or reports
- Unused or invalid customer-specific master data values
- Unneeded SAP-provided sample master data values

During your cleanup efforts, be careful about the deletion of SAP-provided information. The last item in the previous list denotes the sample master data values that SAP provides as guidance to a company when customizing their instance. If the area or table where the data is found also includes a company-specific value that your instance contains, it's probably safe to remove the SAP-provided value. However, take care that your deletion activities follow the same methodology and data linkage that is resident in SAP. Some table values are linked to one another, and customization activity needs to follow a careful and deliberate progression. Deleting a table value out of logical order can make it practically impossible to remove additional unneeded data within the system. If the logical linkage has been broken out of order, you may not be able to perform some data deletions. These situations might not necessarily prove devastating to your company's use of SAP, but they will leave some unneeded data values in the system or require unscheduled data restoration to restart and complete the cleanup effort.

Also, never delete standard SAP programs, transactions, or screens. Remember that your company might have chosen to implement a subset of SAP functionality within the various business modules. Other resident functionality, though not yet enabled at your company, might be needed at a future date. Focus your cleanup efforts only in those processes and business modules where the implementation team's efforts were concentrated. The support team will be able to keep busy for the time being.

Finally, be sure to effectively communicate and validate your intentions to delete any elements within the system. Be sure the other support team members are aware of your intentions and have had the opportunity to understand your proposals and have verified that the deletions will not adversely affect any processes that they might be supporting. It's an integrated system, right? Take the extra time to be certain before you act. Checking first could save you considerable recovery time if you act in haste. Since it's a proven good practice, document your clean up efforts.

Of course, you should test any possible deletions in the development instance first. SAP, you will find, can be a bit quirky in its methods of data selection, retrieval, and removal—especially when involving customizations. You may find a bewildering array of system messages, pop-up windows, and so on. Be sure you understand how SAP will interact with you, and you with it, as you perform any intended deletions. Go back and verify that your deletion activities were successful. Then be sure to perform an appropriate level of regression testing, ensuring that any processes that may have accessed the area or table where data was removed are still functioning satisfactorily. The QA/Test instance can be a secondary opportunity to practice and verify your actions before moving on to the actual Live Business instance.

Summary

With this discussion, support is back in business and back in control. So much of the automated environment has changed, and it's been a long road back to this point. This chapter's main goal was to show you and your team how to regain environment control and return to the full-time business of supporting the system and your business customers.

This chapter pointed out the prime areas where you need to establish the support team's domain of responsibility. These prime control points are key to providing assurance to the company—made up of the different business areas—that the system and data are under control and reliably managed. Through the efforts described here, you and your team can successfully demonstrate the security of the new environment, the appropriate separation of duties, and the safety net that exists in the form of disaster and contingency planning readiness. Further, the secure environment you are maintaining helps your team successfully meet audit requirements and obtain ISO certification.

With this chapter, you exit the transition stage of the SAP life cycle. SAP is live and functioning well in your environment. The metamorphosis is complete. The next Part of this book focuses on the mechanics and tools of SAP that you will use in supporting the new environment. If you've made it this far, congratulate yourself on a great accomplishment.

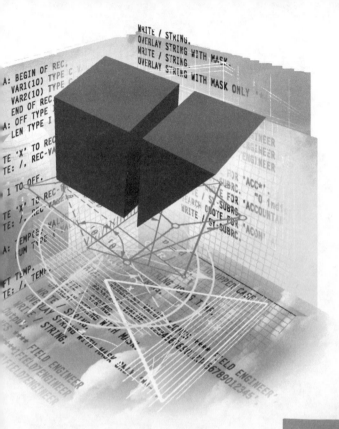

PART IV

Supporting the Live Environment

15 **Maintaining System Security**

16 **Creating and Maintaining Background Job Schedules**

17 **Resolving Common Problems**

18 **Managing Changes in the SAP Environment**

19 **Supporting Customizations in the SAP Environment**

20 **Supporting Reports**

21 **Transaction and Performance Support**

22 **Developing and Maintaining User Confidence**

23 **Disaster Recovery Planning (DRP)**

24 **Archiving SAP Data**

25 **Documenting for Support**

26 **The Evolution of Support**

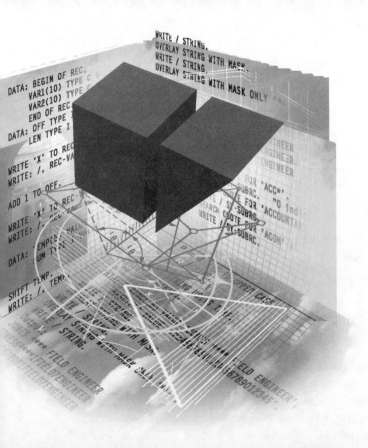

Chapter 15

In This Chapter

- ◆ Developing System Security Policies
- ◆ Establishing a Controlled and Consistent Security Process
- ◆ SAP Logon IDs
- ◆ Passwords
- ◆ Protecting User Logon IDs and Passwords
- ◆ Creating Model Logon IDs
- ◆ Reviewing and Maintaining Logon IDs
- ◆ Understanding the Authorization Profile
- ◆ Additional SAP Security Tools
- ◆ Sharing Security Ownership with the Business Areas

When starting any discussion on system support and maintenance, the first topic to address is security. It is important to understand the need to limit access to the system that maintains the company's business information. The information needs to be protected from unauthorized access and also needs to be protected from any unintentional modification or corruption. System security is more than roadblocks and access denial. It is the aspect of control that protects a company from unexpected and costly data mishaps and loss.

But it's necessary to understand that system security policies and measures are the enablers that allow business and support teams access to the SAP environment in a manner that promotes effective business activity. Security methods ensure that the appropriate business users can create, modify, and review business information and transactions for which they are responsible. Security ensures that a business area's information isn't accidentally affected by other users who are not directly responsible for particular data and who may not understand the proper methods of working with the data or transactions. As well, security methods provide useful boundaries to business areas and the users within them. These boundaries provide logical points of focus and control for the business users themselves.

This chapter begins by discussing the need for security policies and how those policies can be appropriately modeled to support the SAP environment. Security policies and methods are the keystone to ensuring a reliable and consistent environment for your business's use. The policies drive how the different users and support personnel work within the environment. They are also the proven and documented control points that demonstrate your company's internal stability and ability to successfully conduct consistent business activities.

This chapter then discusses the mechanics of creating SAP logon IDs and explains the sorts of information that you will find necessary and useful in maintaining the system's user base. This topic includes discussions and examples of logon passwords and their control. You'll see the most important feature of SAP logons—authorization profiles. Authorization profiles were introduced to you earlier in this book. This chapter, however, shows you more of the details of the profiles and, most importantly, how to develop a process that effectively helps you maintain your SAP profiles.

Besides access to SAP, you'll also learn about many other tools and methods by which you can better ensure a secure environment. Many examples are provided, showing you how to use some of these tools to support and enhance your company's security policies. And you'll discover how your partnership with the business areas can work as a vital security tool as well. You'll see how a solid working relationship with the business areas and the shared ownership of SAP elements, ensure that the security policies are robust, complete, and consistently applied.

Developing System Security Policies

Good system security for any type of automated environment begins with a solid and reasonable plan for applying control. In its best applied sense, control both enables and restricts. In other words, the application of control tactics and methods allows activity within an automated environment, but provides a useful and meaningful way to prevent unchecked and potentially damaging activities and information access. Proper development and use of system access helps business users focus on their particular piece of the business flow and enables them to easily recognize when activity and information are out of their business jurisdiction. Contrary to some popular opinion, control and limits are desirable and helpful to a company's organizational teams.

When it comes to SAP, it is important that the basics of security policy are reviewed, refreshed, and reapplied. What once worked well in a legacy environment might no longer apply in the SAP environment, especially when the element of integration is as prevalent as in the SAP environment. Therefore, security policies within an SAP environment must include the following specific points of concern:

◆ The policies are clearly representative of the SAP environment, architecture, and business area application.

◆ The policies are enforceable in a manner that maximizes the value of SAP integration without compromising business and information effectiveness and integrity.

◆ The policies clearly demonstrate a company's control and maintenance of a reliable, consistent, and functional automated SAP environment.

◆ The policies are applied in a manner that are useful and user-friendly, avoiding the temptation to circumvent them in any way.

◆ The policies are applied with thoughtful understanding and knowledge of the positive impact that SAP can have for a company; the policies are not limiting in an unnecessary or uneducated manner.

With SAP still being relatively new to most businesses, security must receive the appropriate attention by focused support and business resources. As a company works with SAP in the early stages of a new installation, it must monitor and modify the security controls on a potentially regular basis. To this end, your team should have a designated Security Administrator to represent the security needs and respond to issues that may require modifications to present security policies.

As business activity is repeatedly conducted in the SAP environment, small nuances in business processes or information call for the loosening of some controls and the tightening of others. As mentioned in Chapter 3, business users are the most thorough team of system and process testers you will work with. If problems arise that pertain to security policies, the company must understand and resolve them as quickly as possible to avoid any bottlenecks or mishaps elsewhere in the integrated processes.

> Remember the anecdote I shared in Part II in which the one business user "pushed buttons to see what happens." That is the exact sort of situation that calls for good security policies and boundaries of user access within SAP.

The Security Administrator should exhaustively document the security policies. This documentation works as the support team's source of information regarding current security policy, serves as a means of training additional resources in security administration, and serves to demonstrate the company's level of environment control to other interested parties such as auditors or ISO certification review teams.

To help you identify key areas in the SAP environment that should be controlled by published security policies, consider the following:

◆ SAP logon ID administration

◆ SAP authorization profile administration

◆ Global SAP control parameters

- SAP database table controls
- SAP transaction controls
- SAP control policy review methods

These are the most pertinent areas that should be appropriately understood and addressed from a support perspective. Each point is covered in the following sections. One additional area to note is that of business process control. Although the support team usually cannot have a direct influence here, this chapter explains why you should partner with the business area representatives to address this equally important aspect of control.

Establishing a Controlled and Consistent Security Process

Before this section's discussion of some of the actual mechanics of SAP security begins, it's important to clarify that control will ensure a reliably safe environment and can be applied in a consistent method. An SAP environment is not very amenable to a one-shot approach of maintenance, either in tactical or strategic fashion. That is, a single effort to establish control policies is not likely to keep the environment very secure; similarly, implementing a policy that is applied, documented, but then not enforced will be a useless endeavor. The SAP environment lives and grows as your business does; it changes as the support and business teams become more familiar with it and work more of its features into daily activity.

Therefore, the control policies you establish must be dynamic and able to change as the business climate and user needs change. You'll need a focused Security Administrator to manage this activity. Assess the size of your installation and then size the security administration role appropriately. You can usually begin with a single individual in your team to be identified as the Security Administrator. The administrator's responsibilities should include the following:

- Understanding all active security tools being utilized in your SAP environment
- Maintaining open communication with support team members regarding the effectiveness of security methods
- Reviewing additional security opportunities within SAP through training and research
- Establishing documentation that clearly details each security tool and method being used

♦ Quickly identifying and reacting to any potential security holes or breaches

A dedicated resource performing in this capacity basically assures you that security will be maintained and can evolve as situations arise. The biggest responsibility, and key to establishing consistency, is to create useful and complete documentation that details security methods and practices. The support team management should review this material on a regular basis, other than just before audits, to ensure that the Security Administrator is adequately performing his or her role. When in doubt, encourage additional training for the administrator or enlist the services of a resident consultant who may be well versed in this area of SAP. Be sure that each change or evolution of security administration is carefully understood, tested, and documented. The best way to ensure policy confidence and thwart the anxiety of an audit is to have your policies ready to review and proven to be accurate at any time.

SAP Logon IDs

Remember that SAP security and control all begins with the SAP logon ID. You established and managed logon IDs during the implementation and transition phases of the SAP life cycle. However, here you learn how to apply the different features of the logon ID—the additional user information that is associated to the logon ID. But, the creation of any SAP logon ID must be initiated by receipt of an authorized request. A good security practice is to initiate some formal method of SAP logon ID request. The request should include the name of the user as well as his or her business area, physical location, phone number, manager name, and any other information that is useful in identifying and potentially contacting the user. The user's manager should approve the request, either by signature or by some form of electronic mail forwarding. And managers should be aware of all user IDs that are enabled and active in their business area. The same process should be in effect when changes are requested to user IDs. With appropriate approval and information at hand, you can begin to establish the new logon ID. Figure 15-1 shows the initial logon ID creation screen.

As you can see, here is where you determine which logon ID you will be creating (or modifying). SAP currently provides 12 characters for logon IDs. This example uses first initials and last name. You might choose to use last name and first initials or user initials and phone number. Whatever format you choose, try to keep it intuitive and easy to understand. Cryptic acronyms and character significance can really just be cumbersome to manage and difficult to repeat. When your user base eclipses 200, you'll understand what I mean. Keep it simple.

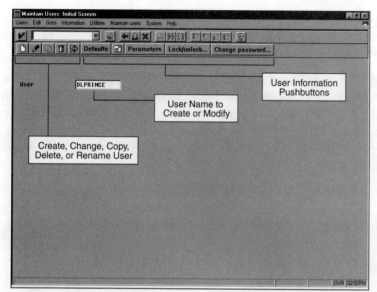

FIGURE 15-1

Logon ID creation begins at the Maintain User: Initial Screen.

In this screen, you'll see some recognizable buttons that facilitate creation or modification functions. You'll also see a collection of textual buttons that branch to screens where additional ID information is entered. The icons are pretty straightforward in their functionality. For more icon information, refer to Appendix B of this book. For now, it's important to explain the additional information screens that accompany the logon ID, as shown in Figure 15-2.

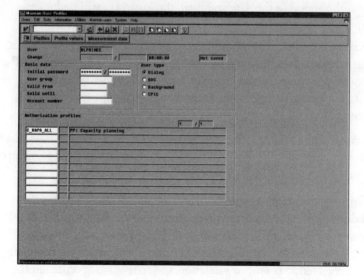

FIGURE 15-2

Maintain User: Profiles screen

When you press the Enter button on your keyboard or use the green check mark icon on the SAP screen, SAP displays the screen you see in Figure 15-2. This is where initial logon ID information is established.

In the Basic data section of the screen, you are required to establish an initial password for the logon ID. This required field allows a user to enter SAP for the first time using the new logon ID. At this stage, the initial password can be of any format because it is usable only for the SAP entry screen. (The following section covers longer-use passwords.) The following fields in the Basic data section are optional but useful:

◆ **User Group.** Allows you to categorize users into customer-defined user groups, for example, by business area. This feature also allows for the subdivision of logon ID maintenance. Additional Security Administrators can be identified to manage a particular user group, and an authorization check can be enabled on the administrator's own logon ID to ensure that the administrator can modify only users within that group.

◆ **Valid From.** Allows you to enable a logon ID for future use. This feature could support the effort of establishing users in advance of their actually being able to initiate an SAP session, for example, a user who will join the business area at a predetermined date.

◆ **Valid Until.** Allows you to specify a future date at which a user ID becomes unusable. This feature is especially useful if your company hires temporary employees or consultants for specific time periods. Upon the arrival of the date specified, the logon ID will no longer grant access to the user. The ID can be deleted at a later time.

◆ **Account Number.** Allows you to associate an account ID with a user. This feature is usually of use when the user is established in the SAP accounting system. In this case, the Account Number field should contain user's cost center (expense account) or company code as the account ID.

The next section of the screen is the User type section. It consists of four selections that are designated by use of a radio button. Radio buttons in SAP permit you to choose one item from a list. The user type can be one of the following: dialog, BDC, background, or CPIC.

◆ **Dialog.** This user type is the most common type of logon ID. It allows for SAP access, navigation, and activity in a usual, interactive manner within SAP by an authorized user. Dialog users are automatically subjected to password validation and renewal as specified in the system password parameters.

◆ **BDC.** This special user type simply checks the logon ID and associated authorization when submitting a batch input session, that is, the processing of data records in an automated manner without any interactive user activity. This type of ID cannot be used in a dialog manner. This type of user is not subject to password verification or renewal.

◆ **Background.** This user type is for the authorization check of submitting batch (background) job or report processing. This type of ID cannot be used for dialog transactions, and is not subject to password verification and renewal.

◆ **CPIC.** This user type identifies a logon ID that is used only during the execution of CPI-C function calls. This type of ID cannot be used in a dialog fashion nor is it subject to password verification and renewal.

The final section of this screen is the Authorization profiles section. This is where the actual profiles that your team has designated are applied to the logon ID. Some IDs contain only a single profile designation if that profile meets the transaction needs of a particular business area. Other IDs might require several profiles. A good example that illustrates the need for multiple profiles is a support team member who is in charge of supporting a specific business area.

It might be useful for the support team member to have authorization to perform system maintenance activities—possibly defined by several profiles—as well as having some level of access to the business transactions of the team he or she supports. Only you and your team can make this determination in accordance with the security policies that you will establish. At this point, the logon ID can be saved; it is ready for use.

By itself, the logon ID information that was established in the previous example is of limited value. Therefore, SAP provides some additional screens for more useful and pertinent data entry (see Figure 15-3).

This screen is accessed by selecting the envelope icon in Figure 15-1 or by using the toolbar menu path Goto, Address. The information to enter in this screen is pretty self-explanatory, but it shouldn't be overlooked. Consider a situation when the support team identifies a runaway SAP session—one that is endlessly and wastefully using massive CPU time. If a logon ID of SMITHJ has initiated the activity and your company has more than one J Smith, identifying the correct employee might be tricky. Fortunately, this address screen can contain enough information to identify the user associated with the logon ID. You might also want to note an additional contact name with each logon ID, such as a business area manager or team lead. The next information input screen is the Maintain User: Defaults screen shown in Figure 15-4.

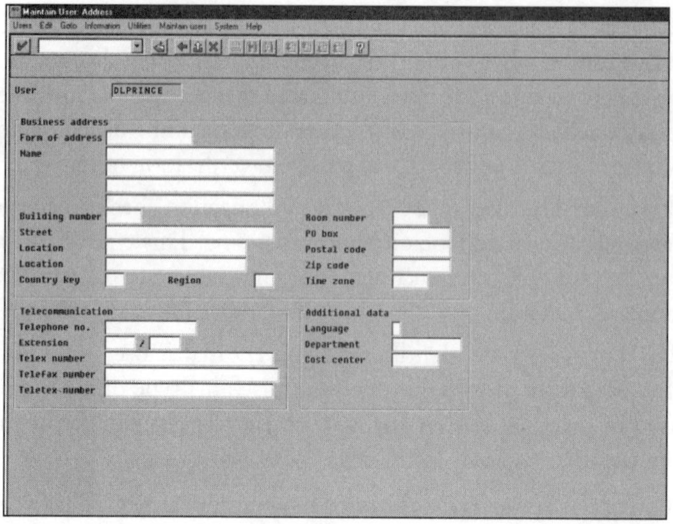

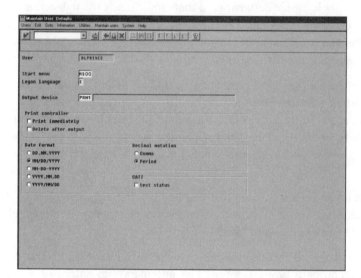

FIGURE 15-3

In the Maintain User: Address screen, more information can be established that provides a better description of who will be using a logon ID.

FIGURE 15-4

The Maintain User: Defaults screen allows entry of user-specific default (automatic) values.

In this screen, SAP allows for the specification of some useful parameters and values that can be associated to a logon ID. These values can be established at the time of logon ID creation, or they can be specified later by the user from the toolbar menu path System, User Profile, User Defaults (this menu path can be accessed from any SAP screen). Within this screen, the following user default values can be established, affecting the presentation of information in the user's session:

◆ **Start Menu.** This entry allows you to specify a defined SAP menu as the starting screen upon accessing the GUI. For example, if a user will commonly need to access the Purchasing menu of activities—accessed via the path of Logistics, Materials Management, Purchasing—the Purchasing activity menu in SAP, in this case being menu ME00, can be specified as the desired starting point for that user's logon ID. This method alleviates the need to traverse the SAP main screen to get to the desired menu. A menu ID can be determined by accessing System, Status from the GUI's toolbar. The menu ID will be displayed in the Program (GUI) field on the status screen (see Appendix B for more information about using the SAP Status screen).

◆ **Logon Language.** Just as the name says, this identifier allows you to specify the language to be used when displaying textual information in the SAP GUI. The English language is designated by E; the German language is designated by D (Deutsche).

◆ **Output Device.** Designated output device identifiers, enabled in SAP's Output Device Administration area, can be set as default printers for user output.

◆ **Print Controller.** Print Immediately does just that. The alternative is to create a print spool request, but not send it to any output device until manually effected. Delete after Output removes the spool file from SAP's spool controller. For incidental output created by a user, this option should be enabled; it avoids cluttering up the spool output controller. However, the best way to manage large output, perhaps generated by a custom program, is to not delete the spool file after output. This method allows reprinting of the output without having to actually reprocess the information within SAP.

◆ **Date Format.** This entry allows for localization of date formatting per the norms and standards of the geographic area in which SAP is being used. European date format typically is shown using the DD.MM.YYYY format as opposed to the U.S. standard MM/DD/YY format.

◆ **Decimal Notation.** Again, this entry allows for localization of the information display. European decimal notation is managed using the comma as opposed to the period.

◆ **CATT.** This flag enables the Computer Aided Test Tool within SAP. The flag can be left unchecked (disabled) if your team is not using this tool.

Next up is the Maintain Users: Parameters screen, shown in Figure 15-5.

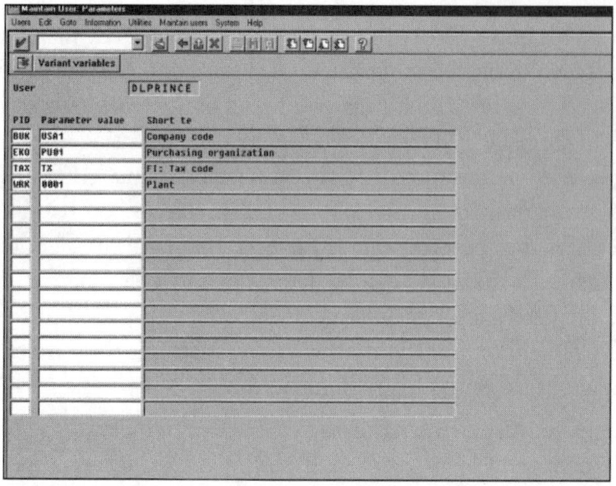

FIGURE 15-5

The Maintain User: Parameters screen allows for even more specification of logon ID attributes.

This screen allows some customization of user session parameters as associated with their logon IDs. If an organization chooses, some logon ID parameters can be set at the time the ID is initially established. The user also has direct access to this screen from the toolbar menu path System, User Profile, User Parameters. Within this screen, you can add the following session parameters:

- ◆ **PID.** This entry is the parameter ID that has been associated with a designated SAP data element. The parameter attribute must be specified in SAP's Screen Painter development in order for the field to be managed in this way.

- ◆ **Parameter Value.** This entry is the desired default value that will populate an identified data field during the user's SAP session.

- ◆ **Short Text.** This entry describes the parameter ID.

The last two items to discuss here are the two textual buttons you can see in Figure 15-1: Lock/Unlock and Change Password.

- ◆ **Lock/Unlock.** By depressing this button, you can check the lock status of a logon ID. Usually, the system will report that the ID is not locked. However, IDs may be locked if the ID is no longer to be used but is not yet deleted. In this case, the Security Administrator can choose to lock the logon ID by using this button and selecting the lock icon as shown in Figure 15-6. Most often, though, it will be necessary for the Security Administrator to unlock user IDs due to incorrect password specification during attempts to access SAP. SAP utilizes high-level system parameters in a central UNIX file. This file contains two parameters that control the number of logon attempts that can be attempted before the system takes automatic action. The first parameter, *fails_to_session_end*, allows you to specify the number of access attempts that can be made before the session is automatically killed. The other parameter, *fails_to_user_lock*, automatically locks a user ID after a specified number of total unsuccessful attempts are made to access the system. In this case, such as a user forgetting his or her password, SAP automatically locks the ID if the specified number of unsuccessful attempts is reached. This option protects the system and the organization from hacked efforts to access SAP with unauthorized use of an established logon ID. Only the Security Administrator can unlock the ID, as shown in Figure 15-6.

◆ **Change Password.** This pop-up screen works just like the initial password that was established when the logon ID was created (see Figure 15-7). It allows the user to gain initial access into SAP. However, immediately upon use of an initial password or changed password, SAP prompts the user to specify a new password as his or her regular password for subsequent sessions. Passwords usually require changing in this manner when users forget their password and, potentially, lock their ID trying to guess what the password might have been. Within SAP, user-specified passwords cannot be displayed anywhere, not even by the Security Administrator. If the user forgets his or her password, the only recourse is for the administrator to unlock the ID, if necessary, and change the password to allow initial access by the user.

Passwords

Initial passwords and password changes performed by the System Administrator are essentially the same; they both provide entry screen access to a user wanting to use SAP. Immediately upon use of this password, the system requires the user to choose a new, longer-term password, as shown in Figure 15-8.

The user is responsible for determining his or her own long-term password, choosing it within the password parameters that have been set in SAP. Common parameters include a default password length as well as an additional check that prevents a password from being identical or very similar to the user ID. For example, if my logon ID is DLPRINCE, my password could not be DLPPASS. The first three characters must differ. Your security policy should incorporate password rules that include the password conventions. Two other password control parameters that are worth men-

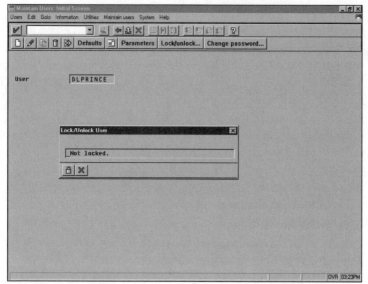

FIGURE 15-6

The Lock/Unlock User pop-up screen will allow the Security Administrator to unlock logon IDs.

tioning are the password expiration limit and the password cycling. These parameters work together. The expiration limit, which is set by your team, determines how many days a user's long-term password is valid. If the limit is 180, then a user is automatically prompted after that many days to change his or her password. Password cycling ensures that a user does not choose the same password twice within a cycle of five

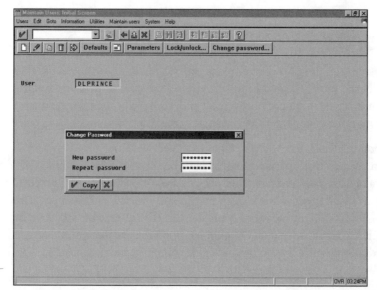

FIGURE 15-7

The Change Password pop-up screen is accessed by the Security Administrator.

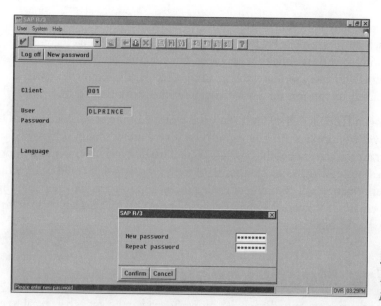

FIGURE 15-8

Initial long-term password prompt

password changes. After five cycles, a previous password can be reused. Once again, users are responsible for their own passwords. The Security Administrator cannot see a user's password. If a password is forgotten, the administrator must reset it with another initial password. The user then has to create another long-term password after initial logon.

Users also have the option to change their passwords between the established password expiration limits. That is, when logging on to SAP's main screen, the user can choose the *New Password* button to change his or her password without being prompted by the system. Users sometimes try to use this technique when they want to reuse their favorite password after being forced to change it. However, SAP has an additional parameter that controls the frequency with which a password can be changed, such as only one password change being allowed in a single day. But this functionality allows users to control their passwords, especially if they suspect that someone else is trying to use their password to log on without permission.

Protecting User Logon IDs and Passwords

In most companies, users work together within their department and across departments. Much trust and respect is developed in these working relationships, sometimes encouraging users to share their SAP logon IDs. For example, one user may have authorization to review certain information that another user, perhaps in a different area, may not. When users work together, they need to understand the data that each other is responsible for. Users who decide to share their logon ID and password with coworkers should be aware of the potential unwelcome result. SAP logs the user ID for every system transaction that occurs. Therefore, the owner of the ID is ultimately responsible for any activity performed with that ID.

Your logon ID policy should not allow the creation or use of generic logon IDs to be used by the business areas. The logon ID is a very useful tool in helping the support team track the activities of the business users. This task includes monitoring for unauthorized business access or monitoring system processes that could be affecting system performance—the running of several inefficient information queries at the same time, perhaps. If a generic logon is used, it is impossible for the support team to determine who the exact user is.

Creating Model Logon IDs

Now, at the risk of contradiction, it's proper to explain how it is beneficial to create a type of generic SAP logon ID for use by the support team and Security Administrator. This ID is known as a *model user ID*. It is of use when testing business user authorizations as well as when creating new business user logon IDs.

The model user logon ID should be created in a way that will reflect the intended settings, profiles, and business use of a business user. Using the BUYER logon as an example, this model user ID would be established as a dialog ID with authorizations that reflect the authorized activities that a business user in the purchasing team would perform. This model ID enables the support team to perform SAP transaction testing to determine whether the authorizations are appropriate for this type of user. Of course, all testing occurs in a Development or QA instance, not in the Live Business instance.

The Security Administrator can also use the model user ID when he or she is creating new logon IDs for users in the same business area. For example, if a new buyer needs access to SAP, the Security Administrator could begin with the BUYER logon ID—it is tested and verified to be appropriate for the purchasing activity in SAP—and create a copy of it when establishing the new user logon ID. The copy activity could include agreed common default and parameter values for this type of user as well. The address information, of course, would need to be modified to be unique to the business user. For security purposes, the Security Administrator should lock the model user IDs to prevent their unauthorized use. They could easily be unlocked when the support team wants to conduct any testing.

Reviewing and Maintaining Logon IDs

Another aspect of system security is the periodic review of logon IDs. Many users need to be established, but as organizations shift and change, some IDs could become inactive or require verification that they are still appropriate to the user's duties. Part of system security revolves around basic housekeeping to ensure that system access remains limited to approved users in an approved manner.

Start by reviewing logon activity. Consider conducting a regular quarterly review of all SAP logon IDs, looking for those that do not appear to have been accessed for an extended period of time. Using the General Table Display transaction (SE17), conduct a search on the user information table USR02. Look for the last activity date that is greater than three months. If you find entries in the selection criteria, contact the users for whom the IDs had been created and notify them that these IDs will be deleted unless the user provides good reason why they should not.

Another good idea is to conduct a table search on the Valid Until parameter. This sort of search is probably most effective if done on a monthly basis. Using the same USR02 table, look for IDs that expire within the coming month. Notify those users and their managers of the pending deactivation and determine whether that deactivation should remain effective or whether an extension is necessary. If the deactivation is to proceed, you can delete that ID after the date has been reached. If the access is to be extended, try to enter the new deactivation date before the user is prematurely locked out.

Finally, it's a good idea to review logon ID change activity. This check should also be performed on a monthly basis. This test is a good way to monitor how IDs are being changed and which logon ID is effecting the changes. This review ensures that logon ID changes remain isolated to only a few team members within the support team. Any unauthorized changes can be traced to the ID used to make the change. If an unauthorized ID had access to change other IDs, that situation can be quickly reviewed and remedied. This information is especially important when you are reviewing changes made to a logon ID authorization profiles.

Understanding the Authorization Profile

The *authorization profile* is SAP's method for establishing controls and parameters at the system transaction level. The profile enables you to customize access to SAP activities according to your business and control policies. Although the intention is not to present a full dissertation about the creation of a profile, this section covers the overall construction and use of profiles from a support perspective.

Authorization profiles are constructed in a tiered fashion. That is, smaller components are identified and developed and then they are collected in meaningful groupings that apply to common activity within SAP. The approach reinforces the business module and business area architecture. The groupings are then used to create useful profiles that will enable a business user to perform SAP activity when logged on to the system using their logon ID.

Figure 15-9 shows the basic building block approach to creating authorization profiles. The following explanation of each block and its function begins with the simple components at the bottom and moves up through the construction process:

- ◆ **Fields.** This block is where you identify an SAP transaction and specify the capabilities within that transaction for the particular user who would have access here. SAP uses a common field identification convention when identifying transaction capability: 01 activity allows creation access of documents or data entries, 02 activity allows change access, and 03 allows display access. Therefore, using this approach, a user can be limited to whichever activity is necessary to perform his or her job duties. Fields are the basis of SAP activity control.

- ◆ **Authorization.** The next block up determines which transactions a user should have access to. If it's not appropriate for a user to enter a transaction screen, that access can be controlled at this level. For example, if a purchasing user could be blocked from reviewing sensitive

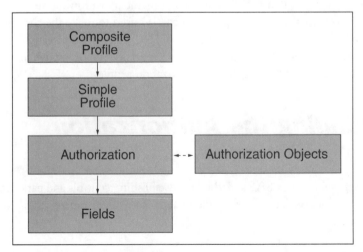

FIGURE 15-9

Authorization Profile components

financial information. If the user attempted to access that information, SAP would deny the access.

◆ **Authorization Object.** The authorization object is actually the template or grouping of related SAP authorizations. This component is a bit tricky to understand because it is not directly related in the profile creation ladder, as shown by the dotted line in Figure 15-9. However, the authorization object is a key for SAP programming and reporting; authorization objects are the elements used in programming to check access authority of any program a user is executing. If present in the code, an authorization check will be made using an authorization object. If the logon ID profile contains the necessary authorization object, the test passes and activity continues. If not, the test will fail and the user will be denied access.

◆ **Simple Profile.** The simple profile is the next logical collection of authorizations that pertain to related activities within SAP. For instance, it is a good idea to create simple profiles that enable major SAP functions, such as purchasing document creation and maintenance. Within this simple profile, you could include access and activity authorization for a collection of purchasing activities that a buyer is likely to perform—purchase orders, purchase requisitions, request for quotes, and so on. However, this collection would probably be only a subset of overall SAP activity that a buyer would have access to.

◆ **Composite Profile.** The highest level of the authorization profile is the composite. In this level, you bring together all meaningful and approved simple profiles to create an applicable user profile that accurately reflects the business activity and information access that a particular user will need in a company. For example, a buyer would have a composite profile that contains simple profiles allowing purchasing document maintenance, master data maintenance, related information access, and so on.

The question, then, is how to develop your business' authorization profiles. You can start with the composite profiles that are included with the SAP instance. SAP provides a series of composite profile templates that are designed to encompass the system activities relevant to a business area and business module. By reviewing these and the authorizations contained within them, you can begin to understand the proper construction of composite profiles that will enable activity within SAP.

The next step is to work with the business areas to determine the key business transactions that are required for each business user. By reviewing the SAP-provided templates, you will find the authorizations for these business transactions. At the same time, you will also find transactions that you don't need. Each company requires different degrees of control and business duty separation. Therefore, expect to leverage the SAP templates to create your own, customer-defined simple and composite profiles that accurately meet your business needs. This approach will provide you with the desired level of access and control and help you and your team become intimately familiar with the construction and administration of SAP authorization profiles.

Administering Authorization Profiles

Separation of duty continues to be a major requirement in any business, from the business user to the support team. Adherence to good separation-of-duty practices will ensure control and security to your automated environment and will provide proof of control at times of review. Because authorization profiles are so powerful within SAP, your team should have a clean separation of duty for profile creation and profile assignment. It's recommended that the individual in your support team who is responsible for the creation and maintenance of profile composition not be the same individual who assigns the composite profiles to the logon IDs. This extra measure eliminates the potential for unauthorized profile creation and assignment within your SAP environment. A good separation and review method consists of a business representative who specifies authorization access, followed by a support team member who creates the necessary profiles and a Security Administrator who, upon business testing and approval, assigns that new profile as required. The inherent checkpoints in this sort of team approach ensure that proper and useful access is provided.

Additional SAP Security Tools

As you can now see, the SAP logon ID is the first major key to your environment security. However, you can employ two other tools to secure the environment you are supporting. These tools, working in part with the logon ID and authorization profiles, ensure additional control of the SAP environment. The first tool is the Transaction Code maintenance screen (see Figure 15-10), accessible via the menu path Tools, Administration, Administration, Tcode administration or transaction SM01.

In this screen, you have access to all of the SAP and customer-unique transaction codes. You can also see the executable transaction code, the program or module pool that uses the code, the screen, identified by a screen number that is displayed upon execution of the code, and the title bar or transaction text associated to the code. By simply checking the check box to the left of any transaction code—*tcode* for short—

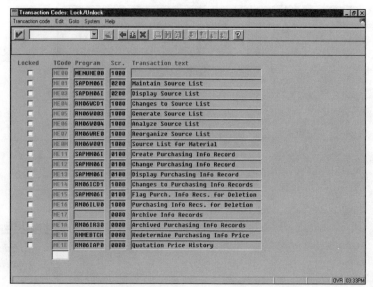

that transaction is locked and not be accessible to any SAP user. This tool is useful when particularly risky activities are associated with a tcode and you determine that it is best to eliminate all access to the transaction, either intentional or accidental. This tool is also helpful when you are updating the SAP system. If a support team member is in the process of modifying SAP functionality that is accessed by a tcode, it is sometimes a good idea to lock the code during the update process. This technique ensures that no users will access the code while the update is occurring. After the update has been successfully completed, the lock can be removed.

The other tool that will be of use in controlling the SAP environment is table logging. With this tool, you can specify when and where you would like to create database logs of changes made to the entries within a particular database table. Therefore, much like reviewing changes made to logon IDs or profiles, you can also choose to log changes to critical tables that should be closely monitored for any change activity. This procedure could apply to any table your business and support teams decide has critical or high-risk information. Table logging is enabled in two steps. First, an overall table logging parameter, *rec/client*, needs to be present in the instance profile when the system is started up. This parameter tells the system to enable recording (logging) of table changes and can be controlled on a client-by-client basis. The second step is to ensure that the specified SAP database tables have logging enabled within their technical settings. See Figure 15-11 for an example of setting the table logging function.

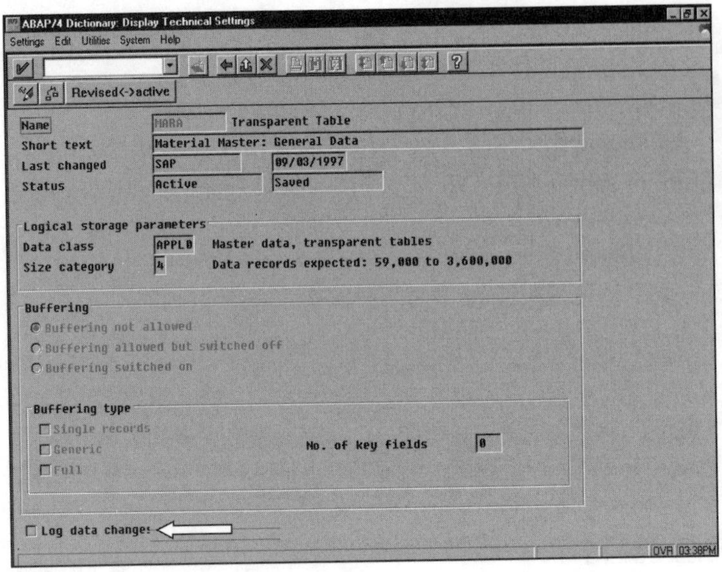

FIGURE 15-11

Table administration—enabling table logging

With logging enabled, you can review changes to the table data at your discretion. By utilizing the SAP transaction SCU3, you may select the table you want to review, as well as the period of time that you want to review. You can even choose to perform a comparison of a table's current data with that of a previous version by selective date. See Figures 15-12 and 15-13 for illustrations of this functionality.

Sharing Security Ownership with the Business Areas

Because so much of your successful support of an SAP environment derives from a good partnership with your business teams, system security and control also benefit from this sort of working relationship. The integration in SAP spreads ownership further across a company's internal organizations and business areas than ever before. Therefore, the business areas, especially business analysts, can provide input and feedback about user access within SAP and any perceived areas of security exposure.

Already you have seen how the business area is fully engaged in authorizing the creation or modification of SAP logon IDs. However, to ensure the capabilities of users are in accordance with the business area activities and business controls, business area managers should become very familiar with the access awarded to the users. This approach is something of a shift from the legacy days. Then, access to an application typically allowed access to those specific functions for which the application was

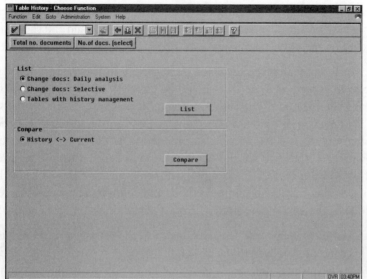

FIGURE 15-12

*Table History—
Choose Function
screen*

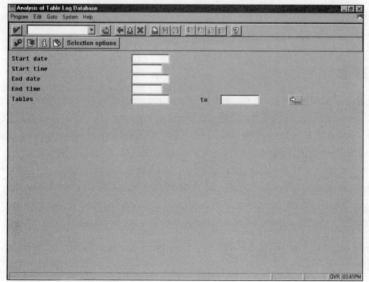

FIGURE 15-13

*Analysis of Table
Log Database screen*

designed. Authorization and capability really existed at the application access level. With SAP's architecture, though, business managers should take a more responsible role in understanding the authorization needs of their team members. Ultimately, it is a department manager, the one who authorizes the creation and authorization of an SAP logon ID, who is responsible for the activities of his or her team. To this end, the business area manager should be able to review business user access and capabilities within SAP on a regular basis. Most likely, this activity would and should emerge as a standard business control practice.

Similarly, the business areas are key in identifying those critical transactions that users need access to as well as those that should be closely restricted. This activity took place during the creation of the authorization profiles. However, the business teams can be instrumental in monitoring daily activity and informing the Security Administrator if access is too restrictive or too loose. As the business areas continue to work with SAP, they will see and develop working trends. Business requirements and controls will also evolve and change. Their involvement in this area is of highest benefit in ensuring that the business methods and controls are properly represented and guarded by the appropriate system access and authorization of the users.

Finally, the business teams can be very valuable in the testing of authorization and access. This concept goes back to the earlier discussion of separation of duty. By their involvement, the business users can ensure that new or revised authorization profiles provide the proper level of access and control within SAP. By partnering with the support team in this effort, both teams gain greater understanding of business, technical, and overall security-related issues.

Summary

As you can no doubt see from the information presented in this chapter, security is a big deal. The most useful method of security begins with the SAP logon ID itself. If properly authorized and constructed, the access to SAP will be managed in a manner that ensures appropriate users gain appropriate access to SAP functionality. Once inside SAP, additional tools and reviews are available to monitor user activity. This approach may sound a bit like policing, but it isn't intended to be. However, with a system like SAP and its integrated architecture, so much more information is accessible through a single logon ID that user activity must be properly controlled.

The following list summarizes the key points of support activity in relationship to security:

- ◆ Review and understand your company's security needs, wants, and desires; ensure that ideals in this area will fully support a controlled environment and protect your business from any exposure of protected business data or potential for data loss and corruption.

◆ Capture all security requirements in controlled documentation of some sort (electronic, printed, web pages, and so on); determine who can best represent the creation of security documentation and be sure the information can be regularly reviewed and updated as required.

◆ Identify a Security Administrator within the support team who can provide a well-focused approach to creating and maintaining security policies and can consistently apply the concepts.

◆ Create a process that will enable the timely establishment of SAP logon IDs for business and support team members; be sure each ID is appropriately authorized for creation, and capture the appropriate amount of user information for easy review and contact of the user when necessary.

◆ Be sure your environment has appropriate logon ID parameters set at the system level; be sure to control length of passwords, cycling of passwords, and lockouts for repeated unsuccessful attempts at system access.

◆ Keep your environment clean; enable regular review of logon IDs for inactivity or expiration; do this in a proactive method to ensure that your system stays clean and users are not prematurely locked out of SAP.

◆ Establish your own SAP authorization profiles as leveraged from SAP templates; be sure your profiles contain access only to transactions and other activities within SAP that has been enabled an managed within your business environment; make use of the varying levels of profile generation for easy modular profile creation and maintenance; ensure that you have adequate separation-of-duty between profile creation and profile assignment.

◆ Enable additional security measures such as transaction locking or table logging according to your business needs.

◆ Be sure to partner with your business areas to ensure that you share a common understanding of security practices and requirements; work together to uncover areas of exposure or undue constraint.

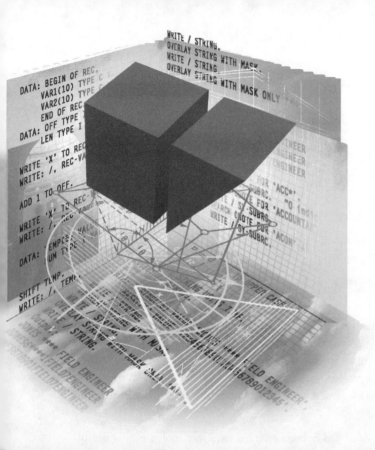

Chapter 16

Creating and Maintaining Background Job Schedules

In This Chapter

- Job Scheduling: An Overview
- Job Scheduling Tools
- Job Schedule Status
- Monitoring Job Schedules
- Securing Job Schedules
- Job Alerts and Notifications
- Recovering Job Schedules
- Best Practices for Job Scheduling

Background processing is a very common and useful functionality in any automated business system. Its name implies that information gathering, calculation, and updating can be performed outside of an interactive dialog session. Background processing, sometimes referred to as *batch processing,* allows for the utilization of system resources at times when user activity is lessened and data contention—the locking of data records—is less of an issue.

This chapter introduces the SAP Job Scheduler. This dynamic tool is highly useful in managing your business processing activities in a regular, repeatable manner. The Job Scheduler supports various triggering methods and provides very usable job logging that will help you monitor the activity and completion of your job schedules.

In addition to the Job Scheduler, this chapter also introduces other ways to perform background job processing. It explains some good practices to apply when utilizing background processing and handling processing problems that may arise. Because these jobs are conducted in your Live Business instance, the chapter also discusses background job security.

Finally, you will learn about developing background job processing. You need to know when to run a job in a dialog session and when to run a job in background mode. You also need to be sure that the time and manner you choose to run the job is efficient and does not cause any disruption or problems for other SAP processes, including the activities of other users.

Job Scheduling: An Overview

Simply put, *background job scheduling* is the process by which you can instruct SAP to execute an ABAP program automatically. You can control the program timing, frequency, execution's and triggering. If the program provides any sort of output, you can tell SAP whether to send the output to a printer device or to hold the output in a spool file. In essence, the Job Scheduler lets you create a profile of information and conditions that you might specify when executing a program in an interactive session.

Background scheduling is also called *batch scheduling*. By this definition, you can surmise that a schedule can consist of multiple programs with multiple criteria—a veritable *batch* of processing that you want to occur in an automated, background (non-interactive) manner. Therefore, you can create job schedules to conduct a chain of linked processing functions that result in a logical, progressive manipulation of information. For example, you can schedule jobs that will retrieve and upload data files within and outside of SAP. Then you can follow with jobs that filter, sort, and concatenate the data as you require. Finally, you can use the new data to update SAP database tables in a background manner, resulting in business information that is more usable by the business areas than if data were presented in any sort of raw, unprocessed form. All of this could be done in a single, larger program, but the Job Scheduler lets you create component jobs that can be shared among several background job schedules or that can provide logical stopping points if special data review or intervention is required.

Background scheduling can also be performed in dialog sessions—interactively. At any time, an ABAP program can be executed in a dialog session. By this method, the SAP session is rendered busy until the processing is complete and the result is available for review. While busy executing the job, your session is unavailable for use until the job is completed, at which time the session is released from the busy status. In some instances, lengthy processing can cause a session time-out. That is, some SAP parameters terminate dialog sessions if they have been processing a functionality longer than is deemed effective by CPU management standards. However, background processing can be enabled during dialog sessions, freeing up the session GUI for additional activity and eliminating the potential of session time-out—background sessions are exempt from the session-timing restrictions.

So what's the best method to determine when a job should be run in dialog mode or when it should be deferred to batch mode? The best indicator is the expected time it takes the program to process. If the program has very restrictive parameters, you might be able to get a small amount of required information relatively quickly. This job is a good candidate for dialog-session processing. However, if the program you are executing is accessing, reviewing, and manipulating large amounts of data—especially if the selection parameters are quite broad —you'd probably be better off choosing a background execution.

Job Scheduling Tools

To begin, it's best that you first be given a demonstration of the method by which a job (program) can be submitted for background processing via an interactive (dialog) SAP session. In this scenario, assume a user chooses to execute a program for data review and selects background processing so he or she may continue to use the current session. Also, since users' sessions are subject to processing time-out, background job processing alleviates program termination if the designated processing time is longer than the standard dialog session parameter.

First, start by accessing the point where a job can be executed. There are two methods by which a user can select and execute an ABAP program. The most common method is to use the ABAP/4: Execute Program screen (SAP transaction SA38). The entry screen, shown in Figure 16-1, prompts you to enter a valid program name.

In this screen, you can choose to execute the program directly or by using a program variant. A *variant* is a predetermination of program parameters or conditional criteria.

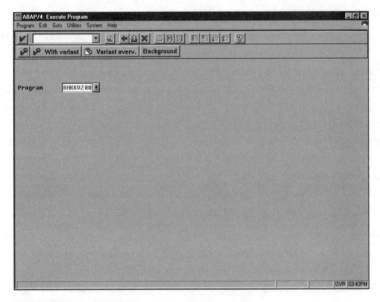

FIGURE 16-1 *ABAP/4: Execute Program entry screen*

If you choose to run a program with the same range of vendor numbers each time, you could create a variant for that program that consistently submits the same information as the conditional criteria. If you do not want to use a variant, you need to enter the conditional criteria at the time of execution (see Figure 16-2).

At this time, you will enter the conditional criteria that the program uses to retrieve the desired data or perform whatever function it is programmed to perform. The need for conditional criteria that narrows the program's span of data interaction cannot be overemphasized. This technique reduces processing time, reduces the time a job session is active within SAP, and lessens the impact of data being locked (if data is being updated) from other users or processes that may need to use it. If you run a program that reports on material documents created in SAP, but do not specify any selection parameters, the program runs for an extended time. It may run so long that it could hang in the system or require a system administrator to cancel

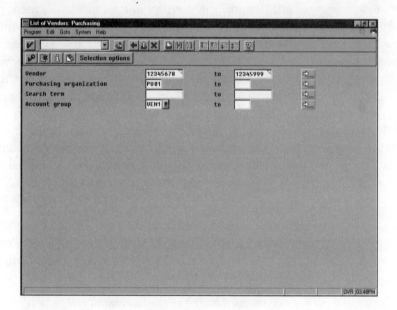

FIGURE 16-2 *ABAP/4: Program Criteria Selection screen*

it. If, however, you restrict your selection to a given time period, maybe only a single month's worth of data, then the processing can take place more quickly and you get your result faster and with greater reliability.

So what about background processing? Well, at this point, you can click on the Execute icon and let the processing occur and put your session in a busy status. But you can also choose to execute the program in the background by choosing the toolbar menu path Program, Exec. in Background. If successful, the system returns a message that your background session has been submitted. All you need to do is retrieve the output or view the result online later.

The other method of submitting background processing is through the use of job schedules. In the previous example, your job submittal required you to access the job execution screen, enter your job plus any conditional criteria, and select the Exec. in Background command. This approach is fine for jobs that run in an ad hoc manner, which can be infrequent and potentially inconsistent in the conditional criteria to be used. However, if the job is executed on a regular basis—daily, weekly, or monthly— and the conditional criteria are always the same, then a background job schedule is the better method. The reason is that, within a job schedule, you can select the job or jobs you want to run, when you want to run them, how often you want to run them, which conditional criteria you want to use during their execution, and where you want to divert output. This information needs to be set up only one time. In a support role, you make extensive use of the Job Scheduler to execute regular business reports and other processing. This method is especially effective to allow execution to take place during nighttime hours or in your absence. Once the job is scheduled, SAP takes over.

Before you can start to create background job schedules, you need the proper authorization. Background job scheduling is a controlled-access activity, and for good reason. As a support team member, you need to work with your teammates to ensure that your job schedules run at optimal times, allowing for open job scheduling sessions and without inflicting situations of data contention.

Data Contention—*When two processes, background or background and online, attempt to access and update the same data.)*

When creating a background job schedule, the SAP authorization object, Background Processing: Background Administrator, must be present in your composite profile. This authorization should be relegated to the support team members. It is generally not advisable to allow business area users to access the Job Scheduler. They do not have access to information that lets them know the best times or methods to schedule jobs. They could also potentially schedule the same job multiple times if they do not clearly and effectively communicate. Job scheduling should be maintained by the support team, based on the input provided by the business areas.

To begin, access the Job Scheduler via the Define Background Job main screen. To access it, you can use the toolbar menu path System, Services, Job, Job Definition, or you can use the transaction code SM36. Either method gets you to the Job Scheduler definition screen, as shown in Figure 16-3.

In this screen, you start by entering a job schedule name. It's a free-text field, and your job name can be whatever you wish—up to 32 characters in length. If possible, try to choose a name that is meaningful and easy to identify when you are reviewing a list of job schedule names at a later date. Try not to name a schedule the same as a program name that might run within it. It typically isn't very relevant to the support team, especially if one team member is reviewing the schedules of others. Within this screen, you also need to establish the additional parameters:

◆ **Job Class.** This parameter is a classification category that is used within SAP for job prioritization. Job classifications are A, B, or C, with A being the highest priority. This option is useful if many jobs are running on an SAP server, and several become queued up waiting for an opening processing session. In this case, SAP executes queued up *A* jobs first, and so on down the line.

◆ **Target Host.** In this parameter, you can specify a host system (server) upon which your schedule will run. A host system must have background

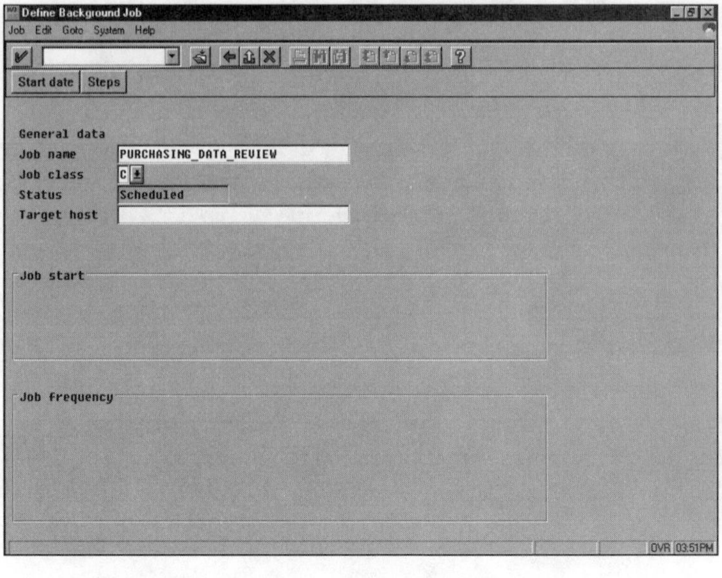

FIGURE 16-3

Job Scheduler: Define Background Job main screen

processing enabled in order to run a background job on it. If several host systems are present and are enabled to execute background processing sessions, you may manually specify which host your process uses. Normally, this field is blank. SAP automatically assesses the available background processing host systems and chooses which system has the most available background processing sessions. This, of course, assumes that your SAP landscape includes more than one database server; additional *application servers* can be specified to allow the utilization of additional server hardware to balance system activity.

You also see two other areas on this screen, Job Start and Job Frequency, which are blank at this time. The corresponding button, Start Date, is used to specify values for these areas. By clicking on this button, you go to the Start Time dialog box, shown in Figure 16-4.

Here you have several options for determining a timing and frequency for your background job. If you choose Immediate, as represented by the corresponding button, you can enable the execution of your background job immediately upon saving a completed job schedule. If you choose this option, the dialog box is updated to reflect your choice, as shown in Figure 16-5.

Another option you have in the Start Time window is the choice of the Date/Time button.

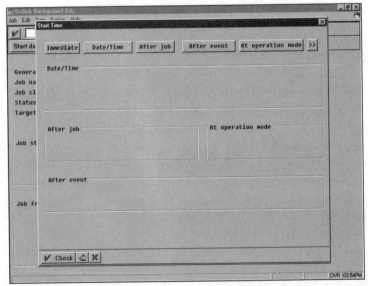

FIGURE 16-4

Job Scheduler: Start time dialog window

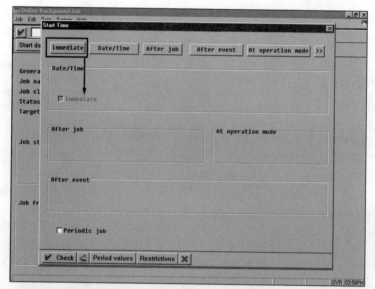

FIGURE 16-5

Job Scheduler: Start time selected for Immediate

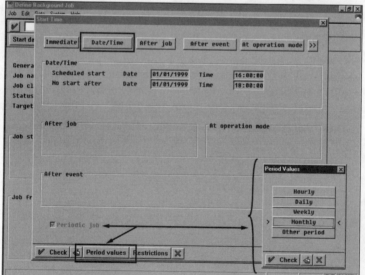

FIGURE 16-6

Job Scheduler: Start time defined using Date/Time selection.

This option lets you specify starting dates and times, job avoidance dates and times, and job frequencies. In this window, dates are depicted as defined in your logon ID defaults. Time is depicted in military time—01:00:00, 12:00:00, 14:00:00, and so on—and is displayed according to your user logon ID defaults. The Scheduled Start date is quite straightforward. However, SAP also provides a No Start After date and time, which can be especially useful if your job must execute within a certain time window. If, for some reason, the job is unable to execute on time, it will not execute if the job has not started and the No Start After date/time parameter is reached.

 NOTE

Be sure to consider the impact of geographic time zones when using the No Start After date/time parameter. Jobs that start after some sort of user interaction could be affected adversely if time zone differences are not considered when setting this parameter.

In this window, you can also specify a job frequency (repetition) period. Selecting the Periodic Job check box and depressing the Period Values button opens an additional dialog pop-up window that enables you to select the job frequency of a job. In this instance, if you select a start date of July 1, 1997, and then a period value of Monthly, your job runs again on August 1, 1997, and on September 1, 1997, and so on. If you chose a different calendar day for the first job execution, the repetition repeats by reference of the first execution. Weekly jobs occur on the same day of the week as the first job executed. Also within this window, you can click on the Restrictions button, as shown in Figure 16-7.

In the illustration, you can see that the dialog box lets you choose the restriction of Execute Only on Workdays. If this option is chosen, you must tell SAP what to do if a situation occurs where the scheduled start date is not a workday. From the list of selections, choose whichever option you want SAP to exercise. To make the

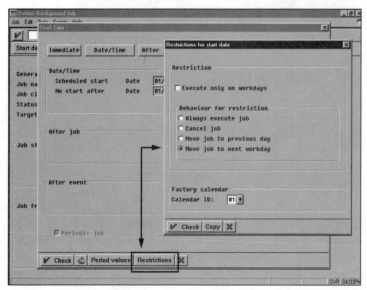

FIGURE 16-7

Job Scheduler: Start time defined using Date/Time selection and enabling the Restrictions function.

restriction setting complete, you must specify the Factory Calendar that you want SAP to reference when checking job executions against this restriction. Factory calendars are specified by your company to take account for weekends, national holidays, and company holidays. After all parameters have been established, you can use the Save icon in the Date/Time dialog box to save your settings. Your job schedule will look like the example shown in Figure 16-8.

Using the Date/Time specification will probably be the most common manner in which you specify start criteria for a job schedule. However, other options are also available:

- ◆ **After Job.** You can use this criterion to specify another job that SAP should complete before your job begins execution. SAP checks for the successful completion of the predecessor job before beginning your job. This setting is useful for sequential job execution in data processing. For example, if one SAP job schedule collected and collated data into a file, it could be a predecessor to your job, which uses that file for follow-on processing.

- ◆ **After Event.** Events are triggers in SAP that can be raised by SAP ABAP programs, external programs, or manually within SAP. For example, if the previously mentioned data file creation program also raises a flag to indicate that the file has been successfully completed, that flag can be raised as an event that triggers the execution of your job schedule.

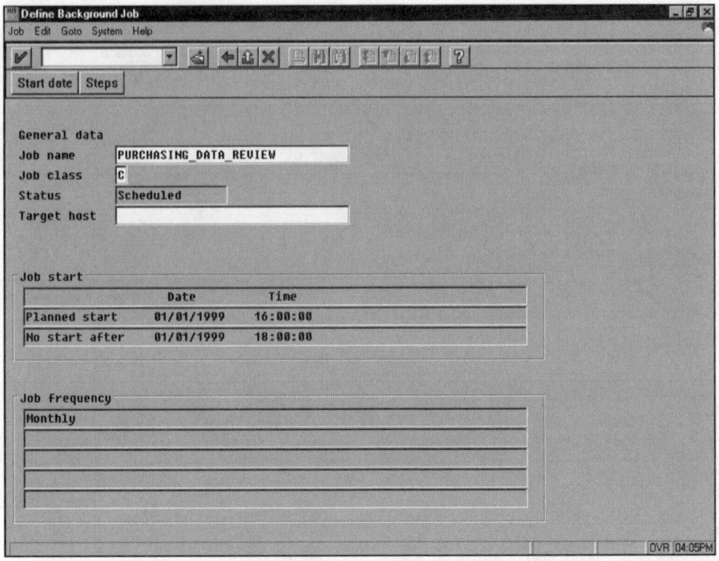

FIGURE 16-8

Job Scheduler: Start time defined and saved.

You can see that you have other options available to determine when and how your job schedule should be executed. But this is only half of the equation. You must now tell SAP which programs to process within this schedule. Job schedules can contain a single program or several related programs. They can even contain several executions of the same program, but using different program variants (conditional criteria). To specify the programs to be run in a job schedule, press the Steps button in the Job Scheduler's Define Background Job main screen (see Figure 16-9).

In this screen, you enter the ABAP programs and the related variants you want to execute when the job schedule is executed. You can enter as many programs as you like, or you can enter the same program multiple times with as many different variants as you like. If you are uncertain of the available program variants, press the Variant List button. You are provided with a list of existing program variants from which you can choose.

Figure 16-9 also shows that you can schedule External programs, or processes that might exist in a UNIX system. With the external program functionality, you can enter a UNIX path, pass a runtime parameter, and specify the target host machine. This option is especially effective for managing processes and data manipulation between SAP and legacy environments.

If you have chosen to run an SAP ABAP program in your schedule, the next step is to identify the output print parameters by pressing the Print Specifications button. As you can see in Figure 16-10, you can enter many variables to specify the output parameters for a program's output.

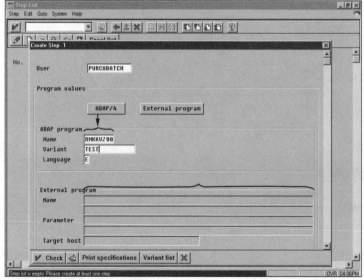

FIGURE 16-9

Job Scheduler: Job Step editor screen

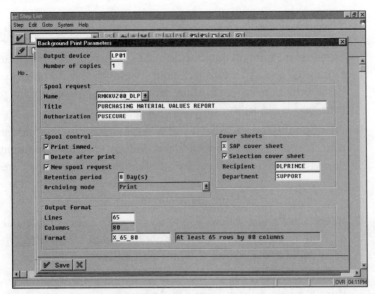

FIGURE 16-10

Job Scheduler: Job Step print specifica-tions editor screen

Some of the variables are self-explanatory. The following list highlights those that are the most useful from the support perspective:

◆ **Title.** This entry is a report title that will print out on the output cover page. Believe it or not, many programs are executed and output is generated, but it is often unidentified and sometimes can get lost, misplaced, or recycled. Choose a meaningful title for program output to help ensure that a recipient or any business user can determine the content of the output.

◆ **Spool Control.** The three check boxes you see in this area are quite effective:

◆ **Print Immed.** Sends the output to the specified output device immediately upon completion of the program. You can opt not to print output immediately and can retrieve the output from the SAP spool controller later. If the output can be easily reviewed online, then this option is a good way to save paper.

◆ **Delete after Print.** Deletes an output spool file from the output controller immediately after the print request has been completed. This option is useful for keeping the output controller clean. However, it's generally a good idea to deselect this check box, as output is so often lost, misplaced, or recycled. If the output is required for regular business use (for example, standard data output required by the business areas), then it is a good idea not to delete the spool file after the initial printing. If an output is lost, you can easily access the output controller, locate the spool file—using the meaningful output title makes locating a file easier—and reprint the spool file. This technique relieves the need to reprocess the information, especially if the information is a "snapshot in time" and is needed for time-stamp analysis.

◆ **New Spool Request.** Allows you to append program output to an existing spool request. Appending is done by ensuring the output device, name, number of copies, and format are identical to a previous output request. Typically, this box is checked, creating a separate request for each program's output.

◆ **Retention Period.** Allows you to specify the number of calendar days (up to eight) that a spool file not marked as "delete after print" will be stored in the Output Controller.

◆ **Archive Method.** Allows you to select the program result to Print, Archive, or both Print and Archive.

◆ **Cover Sheets.** Allows you to specify whether you want to attach a cover sheet to the output. Using cover sheets is a good practice and helps identify the content of the output. Make good use of the Recipient and Department values here. The recipient requires the input of a valid SAP user logon ID—another reason that the ID should easily identify the intended business user of the output. The Department field is a free-text field and can be populated in an appropriate manner. Both of these values print on the cover sheet, further helping to ensure that the output gets to the intended owner.

When you have completed the entry of your job steps, choose the Save icon to display your list of steps. Go back to the Define Job Schedule main screen and save once more. SAP will inform you that your job has been scheduled.

Job Schedule Status

Job schedules have four different job statuses. These describe a job's current state of readiness, activation, or completion. The different job statuses are as follows:

◆ **Scheduled.** The job has been created, but has not been authorized for execution.

◆ **Released.** The job has been authorized for execution and will do so upon reaching the specified start date and time or event trigger.

◆ **Ready.** The job has reached its start criteria and is ready to execute. When a batch processing session is available, the job execution commences.

◆ **Active.** The job is currently executing.

◆ **Finished.** The job has successfully completed all job steps and is now complete

◆ **Canceled.** The job experienced some error during processing one of the steps. If a job has multiple steps, and any step aborts, the following steps will not execute.

Monitoring Job Schedules

From a support role, one of the key elements of your job is to ensure that data processing and reporting is executed to the business requirements and that the processing executes successfully. The business users' expectations are that information will be available to them at the time they need it and in the format they need. Information availability ensures that the users can continue their regular job activities.

To ensure that the users have their information as they need it, you need to consistently monitor the job schedules to verify that they are operating correctly and as scheduled. In the case of special job schedules or exceptionally risky or critical jobs, users may need confirmation from the support team that their job has completed successfully. The easiest method to review SAP job schedule activity and status is to use the SAP Job Overview monitor. This monitor can be accessed from any SAP screen by using the menu path System, Services, Jobs, Job Overview, or you can use SAP transaction SM37 (see Figure 16-11).

Enter the job selection criteria you want to use. If your jobs have been created with the same user ID or a common job title prefix, you may use a wildcard search. Determine the date and time range for your search and select the status of the jobs you want to have reported as a result of the search. You can search for only completed jobs, canceled jobs, or any of the other combinations. Set your criteria and press Enter, as shown in Figure 16-12.

In this next screen, you can see the listing of the jobs that matched your search criteria, including the status of each. To review details about any of the jobs, double-click on one of the listed entries.

If you prefer a more graphical depiction of job schedule activity, you can use SAP's Graphical Job Scheduling monitor. This monitor provides a GANTT chart representation of job activity within the system. Using select and click methods, you can

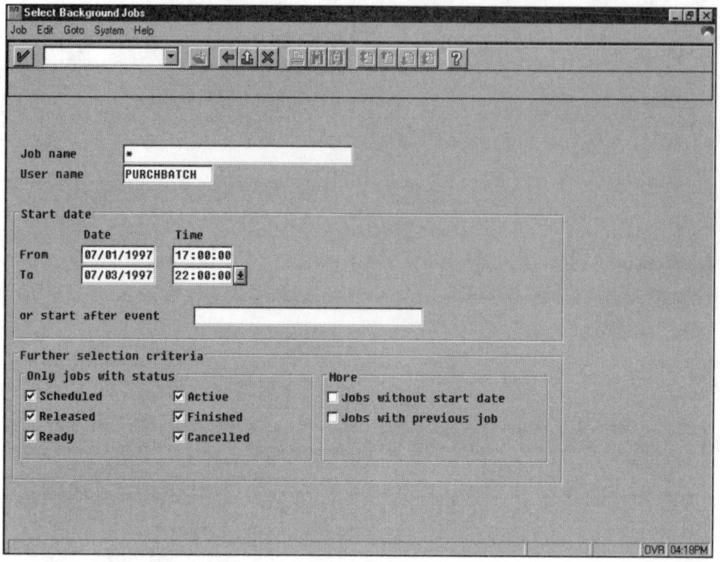

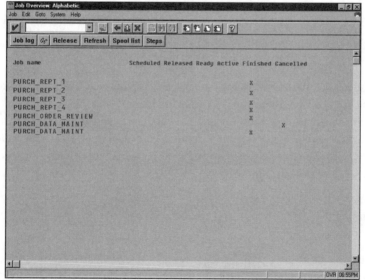

FIGURE 16-11

Job Overview Selection screen

drill into the bars on the graphical display to retrieve more information about completed jobs and pending jobs. You can access this functionality through the toolbar menu path Tools, Administration, Computing Center, Management System, Control, Job Scheduling (see Figure 16-13).

FIGURE 16-12

Job Selection search result

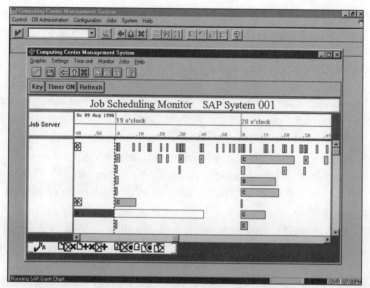

FIGURE 16-13

SAP's Graphical Job Scheduling Monitor

Securing Job Schedules

Background job scheduling is a very effective method of managing data processing in your SAP environment. You and your team should take advantage of the Job Scheduler functionality as much as possible. However, you should be sure that the job scheduling activities remain within the support team. Any user with valid SAP access can create background jobs with the proper authorization. But, experience shows that background processing is best carried out when the support team controls job creations and submissions. The support team has the best opportunity to view the overall job scheduling landscape and, as a more compact team, it can identify points of processing contention or inefficiency. Business area users are usually not afforded the same sort of overall processing view and might end up submitting the same jobs from desk to desk. For this reason, SAP provides adequate job scheduling authorization objects.

♦ **S_BTCH_ADM.** This object should be granted to the Basis administration (Infrastructure) team member of the support team that manages batch processing at the system level. This authorization allows the *Batch Administrator* to review batch processing on any and all servers and clients associated with your SAP instance. This authorization also allows the batch administrator full capability in creating, modifying, reviewing, and deleting batch jobs.

◆ **S_BTCH_NAM.** This object performs a user ID check to ensure that the batch job request being made can be performed by the user specified. That is, if your team establishes unique user IDs for batch processing—those containing the appropriate authorization for a batch job creation and submission—then that is the user name that should be specified during job schedule creation. At the time of batch session execution, SAP checks for this authorization before allowing the batch session to commence.

◆ **S_BTCH_JOB.** This object provides authorization for a user to release jobs that have been created under his or her user ID. This object does not allow for the releasing of jobs that have been created by other users.

◆ **S_ADMI_FCD.** This authorization object allows access to Basis administration functions such as spool maintenance, trace functionality, and debugging. This authorization should be granted only to the Batch Administrator and other appropriate support team members.

The use of batch authorization objects ensures that unauthorized users do not create background job schedules that are ineffective or that could be executed at inappropriate times of system usage. Authorization checks can also be enabled at the background job execution level. That is, a user may elect to process a job in the background, but if he or she does not have adequate authorization to *release* a background job, it will not execute until another user or support team member with adequate authorization releases the job for processing. The authorized user can change start times prior to releasing a job for processing. This procedure ensures that jobs do not execute at inappropriate times or in a manner that could lock data during regular times of online activity.

Job Alerts and Notification

When programs abort, as they sometimes do, it's usually important to know about the situation as quickly as possible. Failed jobs can obviously delay your data processing and cause setbacks for the business areas. But some failed jobs can cause troubles for downstream processing as well. If data collection or manipulation is incomplete or inaccurate, it's possible that another process—background or interactive—could make use of the faulty data, causing unknown problems further in the process. The sooner you are made aware of problems, the sooner you can halt further problems and correct the situation.

SAP provides an Alert monitor that is useful in tracking a variety of R/3 functions, including errors in ABAP program execution. The Alert monitor is actually a component of the Computing Center Management System (CCMS) of SAP. Most likely, this area is managed by your Basis Administrator. The administrator can keep the Global Alert Monitor active on his or her PC workstation, having it automatically refresh to ensure all R/3 processes are running normally.

When an error or warning is experienced in SAP, the Alert monitor records the instance server where the trouble has occurred, provides a textual description of the problem, and graphically displays a control panel with either a yellow (warning) indicator or red (alert) indicator. As you can see in Figure 16-14, the Global Alert Monitor is actually a collection of informational rows that are buttons. These buttons, when pressed, provide further details of the activity on any instance. Naturally, a green (normal) indicator is desired.

The detailed view of the Alert monitor in Figure 16-15 shows the various activities and alerts that may exist on a server. In the example in Figure 16-15, you can see the status of different activities that occurred on the server. The buttons at the left side of the display can be pushed to get more details about the particular problem. In the case of an ABAP program problem, you can review the job log to investigate and resolve it.

To access the Global Alert Monitor, use the menu path Tools, Administration, Monitoring, Performance, Alerts, Global, SAP System, or use the transaction AL01. Remember that the Basis Administrator may have exclusive access to the monitor's response functionality.

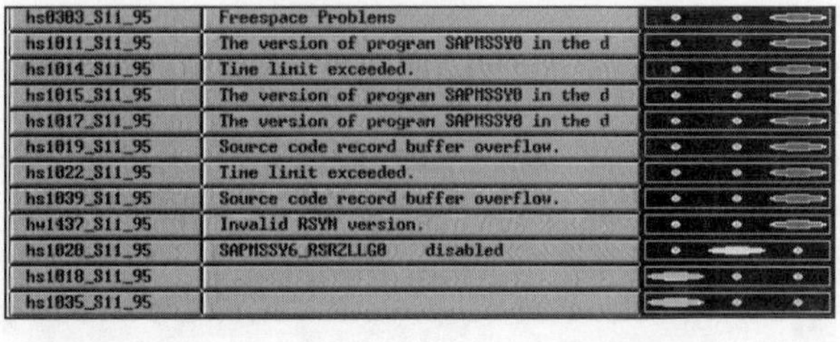

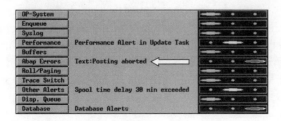

FIGURE 16-14

SAP's Graphical Alert Monitor

FIGURE 16-15

SAP's Graphical Alert Monitor: detail view of a server's activity

The Alert monitor is a good tool for notifying an administrator of problems in SAP. However, it lacks a certain element of true notification ability. Checking for problems in SAP as just described requires constant attendance and review of the Alert Monitor. If you are creative, you might consider developing a custom error notification system that uses e-mail messaging or pager notification. Some support teams use automated notification systems that scan the SAP job log for canceled job schedules (status = A [Abend]) and, upon detecting a schedule in this status, invoke an external UNIX program. The program can call a script that contains an e-mail command such as "export EMAIL="<email address> for email"" notification. For more critical aborts, as you determine them, consider use of an e-mail command that can be used for pager notification with the popular "<pager #>@mobile.att.net." This might be a preferable sort of true autonotification. In this manner, aborts can be identified and routed in a more real-time basis. If you want to create this sort of notification process, your solution should include the following features:

- Customer-defined tables (using Z-type naming conventions) that can store job schedule names and criticality indicators

- A regularly executed custom ABAP program that searches the SAP job overview tables looking for canceled job schedules

- An external program that, upon notification, can invoke UNIX scripts that create standard e-mail messages or pager notification; be sure this program passes pertinent data regarding the job schedule, time of abort, and so on

Work with the other support team members and create a custom solution that best serves the needs of your team and business areas.

Recovering Job Schedules

If your job schedule errors or aborts, recovery is quite simple. If the job schedule normally runs at a predetermined date and time, you need to copy the failed job schedule and restart it (again, authorization objects will control job scheduling activity). In the Job Overview screen in SAP, place your cursor on and select the failed job. Using the toolbar, select the menu path Job, Copy. A pop-up dialog window will appear in which you can rename the job schedule for your copy. It's a good idea to retain the same name or one very similar and to include some notation such as Redo, Rerun, or some other text that will let you or any other support team member know that this schedule was manually recovered or executed. Save the new schedule name, and you'll now see your entry on the Job Overview screen in the status of Scheduled. Simply choose the new schedule and use the toolbar menu path Job, Change. The screen you see is identical to the one you saw when you first created your job schedule. Choose the Immediate start time and save the change schedule. The Job Overview screen shows that the schedule is in the Ready or Active state, depending on the availability of a batch session.

Best Practices for Job Scheduling and Supporting Job Schedules

Now that you have examined the mechanics of working with background jobs, I'd like to share my perspective of some of the best ways to manage your background jobs. First and foremost, you will always find it easier to manage background jobs if you develop a method of consistency in your approach. To this end, your job names should be easy to decipher and bear a resemblance to the programs that are being executed within the job. If you will be managing a collection of purchasing jobs, give your job schedules names that begin with PURCHASE, PURCH, PUR, or any similar naming convention. This suggestion applies to the other work area job schedules as well. This naming convention makes it easier to perform wildcard searches within the job overview monitor, allowing you to enter the prefix followed by the wildcard asterisk. This technique is also useful to other support team members, who will undoubtedly encounter your schedules in their reviews. No one likes to spend time trying to decide what job schedule just aborted and who might be responsible for it.

You might also determine a series of authorized batch user logon IDs to use when executing batch schedules for the various work areas. User IDs like PURCHBATCH and PLANBATCH make wildcard searches easier. This approach will also make the identification of job schedules easier, allowing for quick identification of which business area is being represented by the job schedule. Application of authorization objects is also facilitated and should not require alteration when using this approach. If an actual user ID is used for executing batch jobs, you might have to make authorization changes if the individual changes responsibilities. In this case, the job schedules for which he or she was responsible would all need to be updated to another authorized user ID.

From the support perspective, a good practice is to review the Job Overview screen daily. If you have jobs that execute nightly for which you are responsible, begin each day by determining whether all processing from the previous evening has completed successfully. Investigate any jobs that aborted or that seem to have been delayed for any reason. Good support practices dictate that you notify your business teams of any problems with job execution as quickly as possible. This is especially true if processing completes, but some part of the process does not behave properly. If a result or output is delivered, users should be notified immediately that the data with which they are working is suspect.

Finally, consider keeping a spreadsheet of your regularly scheduled jobs, including start times, job steps, print parameters, and variants. This activity may seem redundant, but consider what could happen if the job scheduling tables become corrupt in any way. A spreadsheet with the pertinent information eases the recovery effort and ensures that all schedules are precisely recreated. What's more, a job schedule spreadsheet is an excellent tool for reviewing overall job scheduling activity. It can describe the attributes of your job schedules well enough for other support team members to use the information. The spreadsheet can also be used by another support team member in the event of your absence.

Summary

This chapter explained the mechanics of creating and maintaining job schedules. The SAP Job Scheduler is an invaluable tool to the support team. With it, you can effectively manage background data processing at times that will not collide with regular user activity. In addition, the scheduler will not unduly stress the system processing sessions at times of peak online usage.

Job schedules are a major component of the support task set. The business areas rely on the regular processing of information and reports. The Job Scheduler helps the support team achieve the data processing activities in a regular, automated manner. Managing the job schedules becomes easier when the activity can be established one time and then executed repeatedly by SAP. The pertinent support aspects related to this chapter's subject matter follow:

- ◆ Job schedules are your best bet for managing information processing off-hours or for processing large amounts of data.
- ◆ Ensure that your team has enabled the appropriate amount of security to keep job scheduling activities accessible to the support team, or other authorized individuals, only.
- ◆ Create your job schedules using a method of consistency and commonality in naming conventions, authorized batch user IDs, and so on; job schedules that are easily interpreted and searched will save you and your team valuable time.
- ◆ Make full use of SAP's output controls and print parameters.

◆ Monitor your job schedules daily, even if aborts haven't been reported; a few minutes spent here will assure that all processes are working normally and data integrity is not at issue.

◆ Ensure that your team has a well-functioning process for monitoring job cancellations and enabling timely investigation and recovery.

◆ Keep an up-to-date matrix of your job schedules for use as reference by other support team members or in case of any sort of job schedule detail recovery.

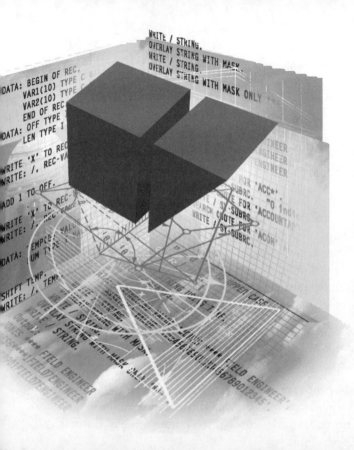

Chapter 17

Resolving Common Problems

In This Chapter

- ♦ Categorizing Common Problem Areas
- ♦ Responding to the Situation
- ♦ Useful Basis Tools

In your support role, you will maintain the SAP environment and work with your partners to ensure that the system behaves well. Depending on the level of stabilization within your environment, system problems can be relatively few and far between, or they can be frequent and out of control. In any event, as you respond to the problems, you will find trends in the problems that point to a root cause. Your goal, naturally, is to drive to the root of the problems and resolve them as quickly as possible.

In the SAP environment, problems arise that will lead you to believe that "it's always something." Granted, peculiarities will spring up, but most situations can be pegged to one of the common problem categories introduced in this chapter.

This chapter begins by providing the common problem categories that exist within the SAP environment. You'll see how problems manifest themselves and how they are reported by the business teams. In this discussion, you'll learn some of the best methods to troubleshoot these problems.

Finally, you'll find out about to some helpful Basis tools that are useful for categorizing, troubleshooting, and resolving some of these problems. The Basis area of SAP is where the general system and database administration activities occur. This area of SAP administration is cross functional, not pertaining directly or uniquely to a particular SAP module or to your company's business areas. Although the focus here is not to go into deep Basis administration, this chapter covers enough of the tools so that you will be aware of their availability and basic use. Depending on the structure of your team's system authorizations, however, some of the tools might not be readily available in your environment.

Categorizing Common Problem Areas

In the support role, problems come to you from many directions. Your job schedules abort, processes hang up, the system runs slow at times, and users may complain that there "must be a glitch in the system."

> I really dislike the term glitch. In the technical world, it has arisen as a catch-all, blame-all term that assumes problems with information systems are always due to some mysterious glitch. In my experience, 99.999 percent of all information system problems have a solid reason. A glitch is usually an easy way for someone to throw a problem at you without having conducted some reasonable amount of investigation first. We'll have no more glitches, please.

Sometimes, you might think the job is nothing but problem after problem. To help you maintain some sanity, you should notice trends in the problems you are responding to. This information will help you resolve situations more quickly and give you a better feeling of understanding and control. If you can determine problem areas or trends, you can work more proactively within the SAP environment, heading off the problems before they occur.

Because SAP is integrated, it's often possible and probable that an error in one area of processing can exacerbate additional problems with downstream processes or interactive data manipulation. Finding the problems, identifying trends, and drilling down to the root cause can facilitate the recovery effort. Any data corruption that occurs as a result of an upstream problem needs to be overwritten, backed out, or deleted. Understanding the trends and reacting to the core problem will save you and your team countless hours of additional recovery time and general user dissatisfaction.

The following five major categories of SAP environment problems will be discussed throughout this chapter:

- System access and authorization problems
- Data access and contention problems
- System performance and resources problems
- Data integrity problems
- Program and process specification problems

System Access and Authorization Problems

System access and authorization problems are the most obvious problems you will manage. You will find several kinds of access or authorization problems within the SAP environment. However, once you have identified them, you can easily ensure that other such problems are alleviated. I assume that a new user wanting access to SAP is not a problem, just an administrative need. New logons should be handled by the Security Administrator. Using the model user logon IDs, a new user should be created in reference to the model user and its verified authorization profiles (as discussed in Chapter 15).

A user might call you and report that he can no longer access SAP using his authorized logon ID. He might also report that the ID was working just fine until this day. You might review the ID and find it exists and has the appropriate authorization profile attached. However, look closely to see whether the user has been locked or whether a Valid Until date has been reached. Both of these situations will keep a user from accessing SAP.

If a user is affected by an authorization problem, SAP will display an error message banner at the bottom of the screen that might read, You Do Not Have Access to Transaction XXXX. This banner is the most direct method for determining an authorization problem. You must then review whether the user should have access to the activity and whether the user profile should be modified. Using SAP transaction SU53 within the same screen the error banner is displayed in, another screen appears that informs you exactly which authorization object was being checked and which object the user did not have access to.

But not all authorization problems are so easy to determine. Often, you will find users reporting that they have requested reports to run in the background, but never received the output. Sometimes this situation will prompt them to run the report again, maybe several times, before they contact you. Check to see whether the user truly has authorization to submit background processing sessions. You can review the background job queue (SAP transaction SM35) and inspect a comprehensive listing of background session activity, including sessions that are waiting to be authorized for release. Here you may find the waiting user's background session.

Authorization and access problems can also occur within the support team's processing environment. Often, job schedules abort because the user ID chosen for executing a background session does not have adequate authorization to perform the task. Additionally, file access has caused the aborting or delay of processing tasks. Don't forget to check file authorizations, such as UNIX file permissions, when you are attempting to resolve why files are unavailable or inaccessible. This situation is particularly pesky when the processes always executed properly in the past and now do not. Inquire whether file permissions were changed or system authorization masks were put in place by UNIX system administrators.

Access and authorization problems arise most often during times of system house-keeping, which is often spurred by a systems audit. Access to systems might loosen during the course of business, but hopefully not in any manner counter to your security policies. Even if your system is quite secure and well regulated, the onset of an audit might cause administrators to insert additional security measures. Don't be afraid to ask whether some security changes were recently made. You may not have been in the information loop prior to the change. Don't waste time laying blame; just work to resolve the problem quickly and then determine if a process needs to be improved for security maintenance, an additional method of communication needs to be established, or the current methods need to be properly utilized.

Data Access and Contention Problems

Data access problems can be very much related to general authorization problems. Your organization might have chosen to limit data access to certain members of the organization, either within the business areas or across the entire company. This sometimes occurs with financial information or purchasing contracts and pricing information. This information can be very sensitive, and it might not make sense for all users to have access to the information. If this type of case arises, the best method of resolution is to refer the situation to the business areas. Most likely, this condition is a business control, and the access restriction may be there for a reason. Again, your good partnership with the business areas comes into play. Working with the business teams, determine whether the data restriction is appropriate. If so, this issue may be one of process training for a user. If not, you may have an area where undue restriction exists. Find the authorization object that is being checked and revise and test the user profile until access is more representative of the user's duties.

Usually, the more serious problem arises as a form of data contention. By definition, this situation implies that data that is trying to be accessed is locked by SAP because an update task is underway. If another process or user attempts to access the data in an effort to change it, his or her access will be denied. The user is notified by a warning banner that the data is already being processed and that display-only review is available. To an ABAP program, this situation will result in a job abort. Data locked in this manner, known as *lock entries*, is a common occurrence in the SAP system. When data is being manipulated, it is appropriate to deny all other maintenance until the first manipulation is complete. However, if the system crashes or hangs in any way, locked entries could result and may not be properly cleared when the system is brought up again. Also, if a user has a pending update session that is left incomplete and unattended, the lock entries will exist and prevent other users or processes from accessing the information if their task requires the data to be updated.

To review lock entries, use the SAP Lock Entries utility. You can access this utility via the toolbar menu path Tools, Administration, Monitoring, Lock entries or with the transaction code SM12. On reaching the utility, you will be prompted to enter a search criteria, as shown in Figure 17-1.

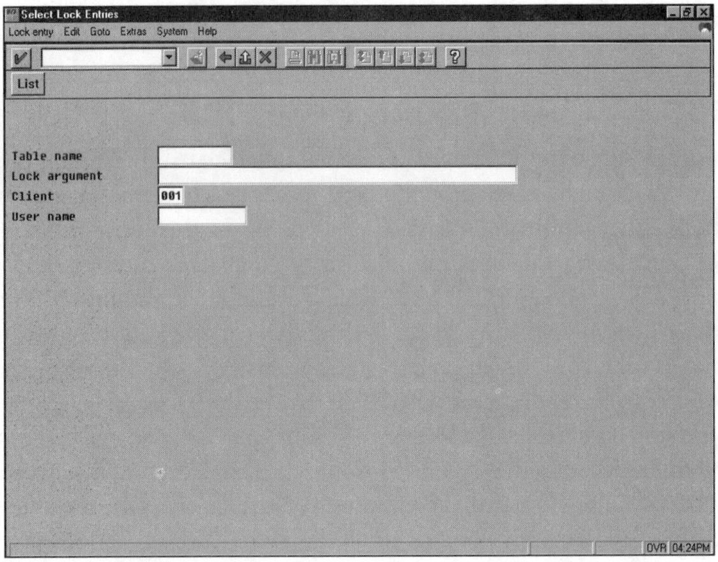

FIGURE 17-1

*Select Lock Entry
main screen*

Searching for lock entries can be a bit tricky. If neither you nor the person you are working with knows exactly what is locked, you may wish to perform a relatively open search. Lock entries do not take very much time to search, so you're pretty safe if your search criteria is somewhat loose. Also, a lock entry does not necessarily have to occur in the particular area or table of SAP in which the user is working. Because SAP is integrated and makes use of relational elements of key data, finding the lock entry is like trying to find a needle in a haystack. Therefore, specifying only the client to search is usually adequate. Click on the List button, click the green check mark, or press the Enter key. If any lock entries exist, they will be listed on the next screen (see Figure 17-2).

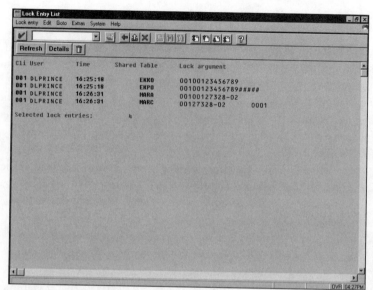

FIGURE 17-2

Lock Entry List

This list displays the user ID that initiated the lock entry, the time the entry was locked, the table that the entry is stored in, and the actual data that is locked as shown in the *lock argument*. With this information, you can do several things to resolve the lock entry. First, you should contact the user whose logon has the entry locked. There may be good reason for the entry to be locked, such as pending interactive processing. Or perhaps the user left the session unattended for some reason and isn't aware that the entry is in a locked status. Notify the user to release the locked data as quickly as possible. Sometimes, the user who calls to report a lock entry can actually be the cause of the delay. If a user is running multiple SAP sessions, he or she may data lock in one session and attempt to modify the same data in another session. In this case, it might be a good idea to review how many sessions a user has operating. In this second method of resolving lock entries, use the System Monitor to determine whether the user is currently running multiple sessions. If a user's session aborted for any reason, it may have resulted in a lock entry. If the user reports not having any multiple sessions, delete the sessions that are not active in the System Monitor. This action sometimes clears the lock entry. The final method of resolving lock entries is to actually delete the entries in the Lock Entry List. You should take this step only if you are sure that the lock entry is not the result of valid active updating. If you are certain, select the entry and choose Lock Entry, Delete. You will be warned of the dangers of deleting lock entries. Because you are certain that this action is appropriate, confirm the warning and proceed. The entry will be deleted, and the user or process requiring use of the data should now be able to continue. Understand that deleting sessions and clearing lock entries is typically reserved for the Basis Administrator.

System Performance and Resources Problems

System performance and system resource problems are usually managed directly by the Basis Administrator. However, as a support team member, you may be contacted by the business users who report that the system "seems slow today." This symptom could have a number of causes, so begin with understanding the process they are attempting to execute. If they are running a program, it could be the culprit. Inefficiently written ABAP takes a long time to process. However, if the user is merely attempting to perform standard SAP activities, you could work with the Basis Administrator to determine whether the system is operating at maximum efficiency. The Basis Administrator should check the following items:

- ◆ **System workload monitor**. Helps determine how well system processes are being distributed across the various application servers.

- ◆ **Operating system monitor**. Provides useful statistics regarding CPU, memory, and disk utilization.

- ◆ **Buffering**. Allows the interim storage of SAP data so that it is immediately available to the local server. Buffering helps reduce the amount of actual database server access that is required for SAP activities.

- ◆ **Database monitor**. Database problems can sometimes be the culprit of poor system performance. The database is the core server that operates your SAP instance. For a database server to behave correctly, it must have a large number of database locks, much like lock entries, available to secure information processing. No process can execute without the appropriate number of database locks. If some process has run awry, it's possible for all locks to be used, preventing further processing. The database monitor is useful in determining the current health and availability of database locks and activity.

- ◆ **Network monitor**. Helps track the availability and activity of any network connections to and from SAP. It could be useful in tracking down a failed network connection.

Data Integrity Problems

Problems with data integrity are sometimes the most difficult to resolve. Business data is managed mainly by the business teams. In many instances, business teams have specified and tested programs to process large amounts of business data automatically—this is the series of job schedules that you might manage. Data integrity is completely reliant on the accurate interpretation and processing of business information, either directly by the business users or as specified in background processing sessions.

You'll walk a fine line when you work with data integrity issues. Problems with the SAP data might initially be assessed as some sort of system or programmatic bug. Your first action is to determine the business process that has been affected and what activity or upstream process might have preceded the problem. Sometimes, data not behaving properly or reports not capturing the appropriate information can be due to small flags, settings, or other nuances within the process or data management. You should gently make users aware of the situation and teach them how to correct the problem in the future.

Program and Process-Specification Problems

Other times, processing of data is truly inaccurate, and the problem can be traced to the specifications used to develop a data processing program. Naturally, any incorrect specification is never intentional, but it is important to review the original specification with the original process and program designers, if they are available, to determine whether the specification had always been incorrect, whether the specification had since changed, or whether the testing of the program had been incomplete or inconclusive in any way. The intent of this investigation is not to lay blame—that never solves anything—but to determine whether areas of communication gap or design process inefficiencies need to be addressed for future design efforts. Usually, this type of situation results in a code or customization change of some sort. The goal is always to fix the problem as quickly as possible and to document the findings and new specifications within the support and/or process documentation.

Responding to the Situation

As always, your response to any system or processing problem will set the tone of how committed you are to supporting your business area. The sooner you can respond appropriately to a situation, the more potential damage—either informational or business, partnership oriented—you can mitigate. Your response should be swift, direct, and include the appropriate investigation to ensure that you have all pertinent details before you act.

If you have developed a method by which you are able to recognize problem trends, you might also be able to develop response individuals or teams, such as the Security Administrator or Basis Administrator, that can be involved for appropriate problem resolution. Since they would have the focused expertise in such areas, they would be the best team members to further assess a problem, enable the fix, and determine if a core problem still exists and requires additional investigation.

Immediately on the realization of a problem, ensure that you communicate properly to the business users and the rest of the support team. Business users should be informed of any potential problems that could affect their activities or the reliability of the data with which they are working. If you can notify the users as quickly as possible, you can save them the effort of rework if data integrity has truly been compromised. They may be inconvenienced in the beginning while the problem is being sorted out, but they will always thank you for notifying them immediately to make them aware of the situation. Never hold back information that could affect user activity, nor should you try to cover up any mistakes – especially yours! In SAP's integrated environment, the sooner a situation is communicated, the sooner processes can be held up to ensure that the problem, like a virus, doesn't spread any further than necessary.

Inform the support team members of problems quickly, too. They can be instrumental in helping to troubleshoot a situation, and can recognize other areas that might be impacted. Working within your team, you can more accurately assess a problem in the SAP environment and work to resolve it quickly. If additional business areas might be affected, the various support team representatives can engage their business users by informing them of the situation.

But, finally, be sure you communicate any problems calmly and concisely. No one likes a panic, especially the users. If you are in the habit of "alarming" the users when there is a potential problem, they will alarm one another in turn. Then, the process analysts are alarmed, and often problems are quickly escalated to management. Your role of effective support in this situation is to react quickly, calmly, and clearly. Provide only the information that is necessary at the time, and don't make assumptions that you cannot yet validate that could cause user anxiety. Most users only need to be made aware of a "potential problem that we are investigating." Let the user know the situation will be characterized as quickly as possible and they will be kept informed.

Useful Basis Tools

Although you might not be directly responsible for Basis administration in your support team, it is helpful to know of some of the tools and utilities that can be invoked to help monitor the system and resolve problems. Chances are you will have some access to these Basis tools to help you become more self-sufficient when supporting your users.

Update Monitoring

Normally, all SAP update activity is automatic and does not require your intervention. However, in some instances, table or database problems are present that do not allow a successful update task to complete. Although the task can process information, that information is unavailable for further use. SAP usually provides the following information message banner: Information Already Being Processed. When the update task is complete, the data is available for further use. One of the most notable indicators of an update task error occurs during the creation of a document (purchase orders, financial documents, or material documents) within SAP. SAP assigns document numbers when the information is posted. If a user reports that the document number he or she just received is not found in the SAP system, you might suspect a problem with the update task. In this case, you can use the Update Monitor to find the record, usually designated with the ERR notation in the status.

Update Monitoring Tool—Ensures that all information updates are executing properly.

Update errors can be drilled into by double-clicking on them for further information. You will find pertinent information to help you identify the source of the update problem. While an update is active, you will be able to monitor its progress. You'll see pending update status of INIT or AUTO, both which indicate that processing is not yet complete. If all update tasks have completed and have done so successfully, the Update Monitor is empty. You can access the update monitor by the menu path Tools, Administration, Monitoring, Update.

System Log

The system log is a collection of information that provides useful analysis of SAP system transactions and events. The system log can record local (server specific) or central activities.

In the system log, you can review all activity or limit your review to errors and aborts. The system log is a file of rolling information. It is designated to be of a certain size, and when the maximum size has been reached, the system automatically begins recycling the entries from the back of the file—from oldest to newest.

The system log allows you to search for entries based on various criteria that will more closely suit your analysis needs. Reported log entries can also be sorted. Each reported log entry can be drilled into to get further details about any particular transaction or event in your SAP system. You can access the system log by using the menu path Tools, Administration, Monitoring, System Log.

Dump Analyses

The dump analysis is the detailed information about the conditions of an ABAP program abort. When an ABAP program aborts, a short dump is created. If the program is running in an interactive session, the short dump will be displayed on the user's screen. The system error will be captured in the system log as well as in the dump analysis. In the dump analysis, you will find information that is an actual snapshot in time of the ABAP program and the error it experienced. You'll find information about the time of the error, the cause of the error, SAP's initial classification of the error, the data being processed during the error, and the actual line of code where the error occurred. As you might guess, this tool is useful in tracing programmatic errors in ABAP processing. Dump analyses can be viewed during interactive program executions via the system log or by using the menu path Tools, Administration, Monitoring, Dump Analysis.

Output Controller

The output controller provides information about processed spool (output) files. It was first introduced to you in Chapter 16 as a repository of spool requests that may have been deferred from immediate printing. The output controller provides a listing of all spool requests that have been selected for temporary archival as well as the status of each request. If the request encountered any problems—spool completion, device access, and so on—the output controller will report the file as being in the Error status. Drilling into the reported line, you can find additional information that will help you determine the cause of the problem. If the error has been corrected, the spool file can be reprocessed for output within the output controller. This step alleviates the need to reprocess the actual program that originally created the request. To access the output controller, use the menu path Tools, Administration, Spool, Output Controller.

Summary

As with any automated business system, problems occur that require your fast response. In a new SAP environment, the level of problem occurrences can vary and can seem quite overwhelming at first. A stabilizing environment will incur frequent problems as each of the systematic and business processes is exercised and refined. Expect a degree of tuning. Over time, many problems will have been found and fixed. Because businesses operate on repeatable daily, weekly, and monthly cycles, many problems can be resolved in a relatively short time.

During the settling period, you will find the common problem trends discussed in this chapter. If you are paying close attention, you'll begin to recognize the types of problems that can arise, allowing you to react quicker to solve them. By anticipating the problem trends, you can proactively seek out root causes of problems and cure them in an effort to save recovery effort in the future.

SAP, as you have seen, provides many tools that can be of use in the investigation, categorization, and resolution of common problems. If you and your team make good use of these tools, you can maintain the stability of your environment. Work closely with your business partners and users to determine when problems are purely systematic, data related, or a combination of both. Through quick and informative responses to processing and system-related problems, you can ensure that the business areas will develop trust and confidence in you.

Briefly, here are the main support points to consider from this chapter's discussion:

◆ Expect problems to occur, especially in the early weeks and months of an SAP implementation. Have faith that many or most will be resolved through the repetitive cycles of a business's activity.

◆ Identify noticeable trends in problems that are occurring. Categorization of problem trends will lead to quick resolution and proactive error reduction.

◆ Be sure to respond quickly and calmly to problems. The environment might be new to the whole organization. Your calm and informed responses to problems will instill greater confidence in the business areas.

◆ Make good use of the SAP Basis tools. They will assist you and your team to discover, track, and resolve problems.

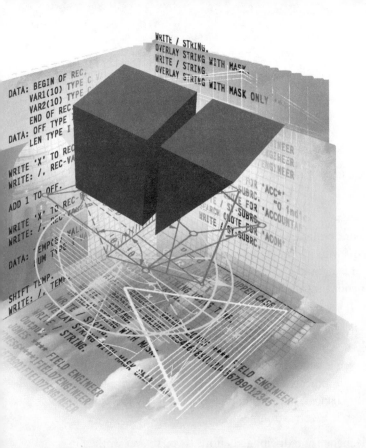

Chapter 18

Managing Changes in the SAP Environment

In This Chapter

- ◆ Developing a Change Process
- ◆ Different Kinds of Changes in SAP
- ◆ The Transport Tool
- ◆ Communicating Changes

One thing you can always count on in an SAP environment is change. Sometimes changes are a result of problems with the programs or processes. Sometimes changes are spurred by the desire for enhancements. Sometimes they are simply the result of not having all settings or functionality available as originally planned. Whatever its cause, you and your team are in the business of managing change.

Changes in SAP can come in the form of program code fixes and updates, customization changes, master data changes, or even upgrades and fixes delivered directly from SAP. To be effective, you'll want to enable changes quickly, yet sensibly. Remember, in an integrated environment, any changes you make can have a significant impact. You shouldn't fear changes, but you should be able to fully identify and represent their impact within your SAP environment.

Managing change is a very deliberate and disciplined effort. If you've ever worked in an automated environment, you're aware of the rigors that must be exercised before any change can be safely implemented. These rigors include full investigation of changes that are proposed; verification of the business need and effect; evaluation of the impact to all business areas and processing routines; and testing, testing, testing. Even seemingly small changes can have an impact within the automated processes, especially those of an integrated SAP environment.

To help you succeed in managing changes to your SAP environment, this chapter begins by discussing the need for a change management process. If you've previously supported an automated environment, you might have a process that addresses change management. However, in this chapter you'll learn how a former change process might no longer apply in an SAP environment. You'll see the necessary elements of a robust and dependable change management process and steps you can take to ensure that you can manage changes with relative ease and confidence.

This chapter then discusses more about the types of changes. You'll see the most common types of changes that you can expect in your SAP environment and the degree to which they will require your time and effort. Because changes can range from master data updates to major program code repairs, this discussion will help you understand how to scale your change management efforts to correspond to the changes you are working with. Some changes are easier than others, but all require your dedicated adherence to a change management process.

To help you achieve your changes, you'll be introduced to the most essential and effective change management tool in SAP, the *Correction and Transport System*. SAP has done a good job in providing for the eventuality of change and this tool is an extremely effective source of change control.

Finally, the discussion concludes with the aspect of communicating changes. This topic sounds like such an obvious ingredient of any change management process. However, you'd be surprised—or maybe not—at how often changes and related activities are not well communicated in an automated environment. SAP has some useful communication tools that you'll discover in the final section of this chapter. In addition, you'll see the tools that allow you to explore other possibilities for communicating changes within your environment.

Developing a Change Process

A change process or methodology needs to be developed for your new environment to ensure that changes are appropriate, timely, and made with high levels of result certainty. To develop a beneficial change process, you'll first need to understand the life cycle of changes to your SAP environment. Briefly, changes stem from the identification of a need for a fix or enhancement to an SAP business solution. The change can range from simple to complex. Your change process should accommodate this inherent spectrum of difficulty associated with changes. Your change process should facilitate quick changes (for example, simple code fixes, simple customization changes, and simple master data modifications). However, your process must also be rigorous enough to properly capture and guide complex changes and enhancements (for example, new customer-defined solutions, changes that affect multiple business areas, and changes to SAP-provided program code). This balance is difficult to achieve. If your process is too complex, the support team will find ways to effect simple changes in more direct methods that might circumvent the change management process. In this case, you lose a degree of control, communication, and a certain portion of your audit trail of the modification. On the other hand, if your change process is too liberal, it might allow significant changes that have a widespread effect and, if not properly controlled, could bypass critical testing and review. Therefore, it is recommended to establish a change process that does the following:

- ◆ Forces the logging of all changes made within the SAP environment
- ◆ Ensures that changes to SAP objects are properly controlled by appropriate authorization access
- ◆ Ensures that all changes can be traced to the originator of the change as well as the initiator of the change request

◆ Enables a method by which changes to be made can be reviewed by management and prioritized according to business and technical needs

◆ Forces the use of the SAP instance landscape: Development, QA/Test, Live Business

◆ Ensures that testing and verification are required as the change progresses from instance to instance

◆ Provides repeatable and reliable steps to ensure that changes can made quickly, yet completely

◆ Ensures a hook into change documentation and support documentation creation or modification

Because changes in the SAP environment can have a significant impact, you'll want to be sure that your change management process is as robust and controlled as your system security policies. In some respects, this environment can be an offshoot of system security—you want to be sure that only authorized individuals can enable changes in your SAP environment. As mentioned in the discussion about support transition earlier in this book, ensure that your system is properly protected from direct updates in your Live Business environment. Begin with visiting the System Change Options (SAP transaction SE03) and be sure your Live Business environment is adequately locked down.

The business teams as well as the support team must understand your change process. Many of the change requests come directly from the business users or business analysts. Because they work repetitively with the business solutions within your SAP environment, they will become aware of areas of error or useful enhancement. The business teams should work with you in managing and effecting change in the system. Be sure that the business team representatives (users or analysts) can accurately explain the change requirement and the activity or situation that identified the need. At all opportunities, re-create the situation that led to the need for change. This activity can usually be accomplished in the Development instance without fear of inappropriate data manipulation of live business data. Some situations, though, can be directly tested in the Live Business environment. With care, you can take a business process or SAP transaction to the point where the situation is manifested without actually modifying information or posting transactional data. Again, take care when using the Live Business instance for testing, and do so only if the information you need is not available in a Development instance.

When re-creating the situation, you can also verify with the initiator of the change request the exact specifications of the desired change. Be sure you both fully understand the intent of the change so that the result matches the requirement. If the complexity of the change is of enough significance, capture the intent of the change in properly documented specifications.

When a solution has been enabled in a development environment—no open development in the Live Business instance—review the revised functionality with the change initiator to prove the solution's completeness and effectiveness. If this unit testing succeeds, the change should be effected in the QA/Test instance for a more Live Business-like test. When that succeeds and is properly approved, the final step is to move the change to the Live Business instance.

Be sure your process includes embedded check and authorization steps, such as user testing and verification. Again, this step is an outgrowth of the system and environment security policies. In fact, change validation and authorization should be considered a key element of the security and control policy. In this manner, you can be assured that all changes made are verified by both a support team member and business area initiator to ensure the change is appropriate for the business needs. Neither individual can work independently and in an unauthorized manner to effect changes to the environment.

Not all changes are initiated by the business areas, and you must ensure the same level of control and authorization for changes that are identified and driven by the support team directly. Often, the support team members initiate changes that enhance data manipulation, processing efficiency, or overall system performance. Changes of this sort should require review and verification by other support team members and the potential authorization by the support team management. Again, this system ensures that changes are appropriate, effective, and cannot be implemented in any sort of independent fashion.

Different Kinds of Changes in SAP

SAP is a collection of objects—ABAP programs, data tables, data elements, screens, and transactions. In any of these objects you can expect the need to make changes, sometimes out of necessity—bug fixes—and sometimes out of choice—enhancements.

As you now know, the SAP environment is quite configurable to your company's needs. SAP enables you to make the environment truly yours, eliminating the need to force-fit SAP functionality into your automated environment and reducing the need to try plain vanilla and out-of-the-box solutions that may come from other ERPs. Consider, then, the following types of objects you might support and change within the SAP system:

◆ SAP-provided ABAP programs, screens, transactions, and data dictionary elements

◆ Customizations

◆ Master data elements

◆ Customer-defined objects

SAP-Provided ABAP Programs, Screens, Transactions, and Data Dictionary Elements

SAP is a collection of ABAP programs, screens, transactions, and data elements, and modifications to any of these elements are probably the most powerful, yet potentially risky, changes you can make in your SAP environment. Although modifying SAP source elements is not generally encouraged—especially by SAP—the option is available. All elements in the SAP system are identified by their date of modification or delivery and the owner of the change or delivery. For SAP elements, these are usually identified as being owned by *SAP* with a user ID. SAP keeps track of its elements when providing upgrades or fixes to customer sites. When SAP provides a modified element to a customer, it provides an electronic packet—a *transport*—that contains the modified object. When the packet is installed in your system, the SAP object is automatically updated.

If an object has been changed uniquely within your environment, then any changes you make will not be known to SAP and can be overwritten at the time the object is updated. This factor explains why changing these objects is risky. If you do need to change an SAP object, SAP provides a method of registering the change. This registration is done via an SAP-generated registration tool known as the *SAP Software Change Registration* (*SSCR*). With this tool, SAP is able to register all manual changes to code or dictionary objects that may have been made at your site. All such changes are recorded within your SAP system. If a situation requires SAP first-level support, managed by SAP employees, the registered changes can be reviewed as potential areas of investigation.

The SSCR also provides a built-in level of security that you and your team will find useful and beneficial. To make a change to an SAP-owned object, the SSCR requires the individual attempting the change to be properly identified as a *development user*. In this way, the SSCR checks to ensure that the user attempting the change is registered with a valid *developer's key*. The developer's key works as a one-time registration process that yields the assignment of a unique identifier to be associated with the development user. At the first attempt to modify an SAP object, the system requires the entry of the developer's key. Then the development user is granted authorization to proceed with the modification. Future modifications to SAP objects by the same development user do not require the key. The SSCR requires the key only when the development user is not in the valid list of authorized development users.

Coupled with the development key is the *object key*. Much like the developer's key, the object key must be registered within the SSCR and yields a unique object identifier. This key is required when the first change is made to an SAP-owned object. Future modifications do not require the key. Both the developer's and object keys are assigned through the use of SAP's *Online Service System (OSS)*. The OSS is where these keys can be created and registered. The OSS system can be accessed from anywhere in SAP using the transaction code OSS1. In addition to registering new objects, you can request an overview to see which developer and object keys have already been registered. Figure 18-1 shows the OSS Registration screen.

Although it sounds like a lot of red tape, the use of these keys is actually very effective. Any user in your SAP clients will require the appropriate authorization profile to effect object changes, but these developer's and object keys further limit change access. Because changing SAP-owned objects is not the most preferable activity to engage in, this method of registration ensures that unauthorized developers are not allowed to change such objects in an unauthorized way. It's usually a good idea to manage the assignment of these keys through a central support team contact—the Security Administrator, perhaps. In addition to preventing intentional unauthorized changes to SAP-owned objects, these keys can prevent accidental updates. The dialog request for the key is an immediate signal that an SAP-owned object is at risk of being changed.

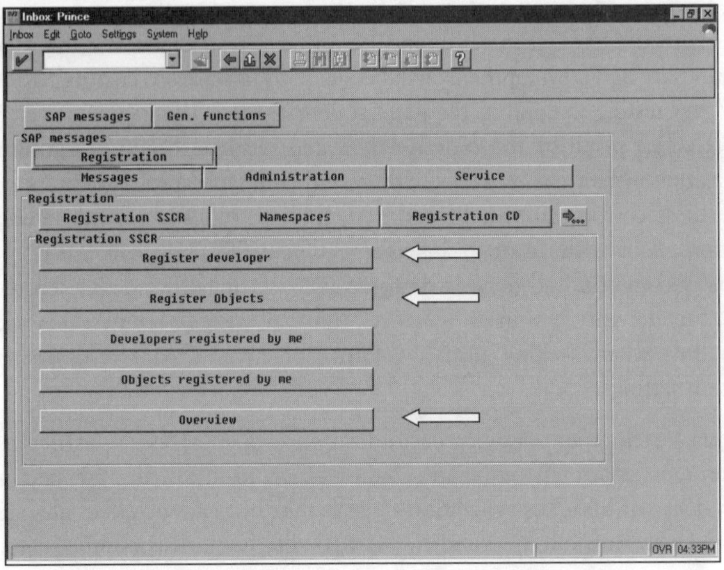

FIGURE 18-1

OSS Registration screen

Sometimes you might consider alternatives to modifying SAP-owned objects. The moment a customer modifies an SAP-owned object, SAP is no longer legally liable for that object's operation or interaction within the SAP system. And, as already mentioned, changes to SAP-owned objects require additional review and management if SAP provides updated versions of that object, either via a system upgrade or fix. An alternative, then, is to create a customer-defined object, using the Z-class naming convention. Sometimes, for a very simple and low-impact change, the SAP-owned object can be copied and modified. In this case, be sure your object title or embedded documentation points to the original SAP-owned object that was used as reference. This information is critical in the event of a fix or upgrade later. You'll want to apply any SAP-provided changes to your custom object. The downside of this approach, however, is you also need to change references to the new object if called by other areas of SAP. Investigate the need for the change carefully, determine the impact of either method, and proceed with appropriate documentation of your decision and outcome.

Customizations

In most cases, changes you make to customizations will have a lesser impact than other objects such as ABAP code or data dictionary elements. However, customization changes will affect the manner in which SAP solutions operate and respond during use. Don't let their simplistic nature fool you. Clicking a single check box in a customization screen can shut down a business process before you realize it. Customizations should be treated with the same respect and change control as other objects. Review and test all customization changes in a Development instance before progressing to a QA/Test instance and Live Business instance. It's also a good idea to ensure that your Development instance includes a separate customization master client. After testing is done in the general development instance client and verified in the QA/Test instance, the proven values and settings should be captured in the customization master client. This client is your company-specific reference for all of your business customizations. In addition, SAP provides a general reference customization client with all of its instances—Client 000. You can use this client to review very common and generic customization settings that enable basic business solution functionality within an instance. You may wish to refer to this client from time to time when seeking further information about SAP's recommended customization settings.

Like other development activity, customization change access is restricted to users with the appropriate customization authorization profile. Most general users can review values within a customization object table, but cannot effect changes or the creation of new entries. As noted in the SAP life cycle discussions, customization access should be restricted to a limited number of support team personnel, possibly aligned by business team association. As during the implementation, this team should have exclusive maintenance authorization over customizations, working with other support team members and business area representatives to review, test, and establish customization settings. A special process should be implemented to enable the team to properly receive, manage, and document customization changes. The following discussion revisits an illustration of this process that was introduced in Chapter 7.

Master Data Elements

Master data elements are entries in SAP database tables. They are the table values that contain your company's identity, basic business control parameters, and product or service values. These elements are often the most changeable elements within an SAP environment. In fact, these elements are often so fluid that SAP often does not capture them in any formal change management process. If table logging is enabled, changes can be reviewed in that manner.

Nevertheless, master data changes can have a far-reaching impact within SAP. Recall the discussion about integration in Chapter 2. Changes to master data can

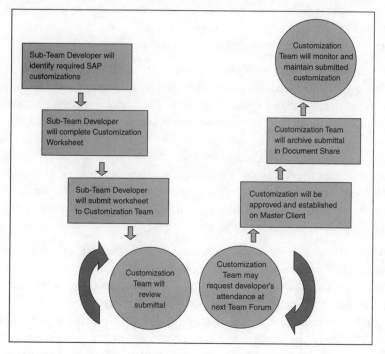

FIGURE 18-2 *Customization communication and change management flow*

immediately effect other processes within SAP, across multiple business modules. If you plan to make changes to master data, perform a variety of table searches, especially where the data you are changing is a key element. Be sure to consider the impact of a change or deletion in a master data table. You may need to clear other data elements (transactional data elements, for instance) before you can proceed with your intended changes.

Customer-Defined Objects

These objects have been defined specifically for your company's SAP environment. With these objects, you have the most liberty in managing change. However, integration still applies and must be understood before changes are carried out.

The Transport Tool

With all this talk about elements subject to change within SAP, as well as the change management process you will develop for your business, it's time to introduce the main SAP tool that helps you effect change into and out of your various instances. At the time you make a change to ABAP code, data dictionary objects, customization tables, and select master data tables, SAP requires you to capture your change in the change packet called a *transport*. The transport is the vehicle that captures your modifications and makes them *transportable* (movable) to other instances.

When you attempt to save a change to an element in SAP, the SAP *Correction and Transport System (CTS)* requires you to identify a *correction* or *repair* to use as the reference packet for the changes you are making. The correction is your actual change task. In other words, the correction is the modification you made in the Development instance that you saved to the task packet. The repair is much the same, but it is reserved to denote change tasks that affect SAP-owned objects. Customization changes also cause the creation of corrections, but they are classified as customization objects. As you work through your change activities, you can use the same corrections to capture progressive change. You can also use corrections as collective packets, capturing multiple changes made to multiple objects.

When your change activity, including testing, is complete, you will release your correction. Before the release of your correction, SAP had created temporary locks on all objects that are included in the correction. This approach prevents others from modifying the objects before you can transport them to another system. This system is good and bad. It protects your objects from parallel modification but can also unduly lock objects required by others if your correction is not moved along in a timely manner. To prevent the latter situation, you will want to transport your correction to another instance for further testing or final usage in a Live Business instance. Each correction has a corresponding transport request. The transport request contains the correction and its objects that have been modified. After the correction is released, you need to release the transport. Then your transport will be the vehicle to move the objects along to their destination instance. In your support activities, you will be managing a large amount of corrections and transports. Outside of authorized direct instance changes—in an instance that is enabled for direct updates—the CTS is your only method of moving modifications along.

Managing the transport activity occurs at the UNIX level of your SAP environment. Using the UNIX command *tp import*, your transport is brought from the source instance into the destination instance. This activity is best managed by the Basis Administrator, the Security Administrator, or a specially designated Transport Administrator. Running the tp import command invokes a serial process. Any other tp import activities are delayed until the one in queue is completed. For this reason, it is a good idea for a central individual to manage the transport/import activity for the team. Imports can be performed at any time, but it's wise to wait for times of reduced user activity. As you know, changes being imported into a source system, especially the Live Business instance, can have adverse affects if the object being updated is actively in use by a business user or other company individual.

TIP

It's usually a good practice to review system activity (use transaction SM51) to ensure that items being transported won't be in direct conflict with any process that is actively being used.

Each transport that is imported will create a *transport log*. The transport log is available to document the success of the import. Each step of the transport import is captured in the log.

The log gives each step a status of completion and success:

- ◆ **0000**—Indicates a transport step that was successfully completed with no errors.

- ◆ **0004**—Indicates that the transport incurred some warning situations such as objects that may have been deleted from the source instance tables (possibly intentional). The transport step, however, has completed successfully.

- ◆ **0008**— Indicates that an error has occurred and the transport step did not complete. Review and modification, either to the original correction contents or the content attributes (for example, syntax errors in

ABAP code) are required. The object then needs to be transported again.

♦ **0012**—Indicates a truly fatal error, usually related to the well-being of the system, that is typically not attributed to the transport steps.

Communicating Changes

The final element that makes your change management process the success that it should be is a good method of communicating your activities. From a support perspective, you need to be sure that your other team members are aware of any modifications to the SAP environment. The degree to which you communicate may depend on the impact and complexity of a change, but always communicate. In addition to ensuring that others are aware of and ready for the modifications, this approach prevents anyone from accidentally overwriting or corrupting your work. More important, the business users need to be aware of any changes that may require additional knowledge or changes to the way in which they perform their jobs.

Beginning with the support team, be sure the team communicates regularly to discuss the activities of the members. Whether they are performance driven or business driven, changes are always happening, and everyone should be aware of how the activities might have an impact on other efforts. Use regular forums, electronic mail messages, voice mail messages, or whatever suits the need for your team.

For the business areas, change communication needs additional attention. Although *you* may fully understand the impact of changes you are planning, the using community probably won't. Be sure that any change you plan, whether initiated by the business areas or not, is communicated well in advance. System and functionality availability is critical to the using community, and any changes to system uptime affect the timing of the business area activities. If, for example, the system or a solution is going to be temporarily unavailable, let the users know so they can manage their work around the event. Last-minute notification rarely goes over well.

How you communicate to the business area is as important as when you communicate. If major changes are coming, visit the business area forums to inform them of the event and then remain to answer their questions. Use voice mail distribution extensively to remind users of the change event and if any schedule adjustments have been made to the original plan. If the change takes more than a day, provide several voice mail messages to advise them of the progress. Believe it or not, users are curious about what you are doing and how well your plans are executing. If any problems occur, the users will want to know so they can make any appropriate adjustments on their end.

Then, when you are ready to begin, use SAP's *System Messages* feature to provide inter-SAP notification. This feature enables you to create pop-up messages in a dialog window. These messages are displayed as users log on to the system and must be acknowledged before they can maneuver through the GUI. If users are already logged on to SAP, then the next navigation step they make after the message is released will prompt the pop-up dialog window. It's a terrific tool and allows you to communicate directly within the GUI. A common system message is illustrated in Figure 18-3.

Summary

So, change is inevitable. You will face it under favorable and not-so-favorable conditions. It can be in the form of wonderful new enhancements to the SAP business processes, or it can be in response to a problem within the system. Whichever, understand the reasons and need for change in your SAP environment. You'll want to monitor the rate of change to determine whether it is a signal that control is at risk. But you'll also want to purposefully introduce change if your team or the business areas perceive the processes are at risk.

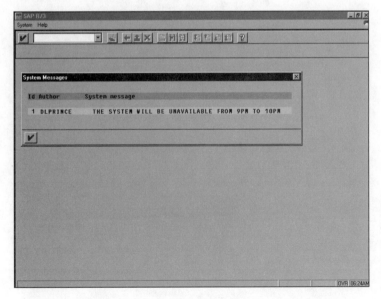

FIGURE 18-3

A system message can be used to communicate change activity to the SAP users.

You've seen the kinds of changes you can expect to work with and the tools with which you will effect change. Most important, you have realized the need for a viable change management process that will help you successfully enable changes. It's a very deliberate process and critical to the stability of your SAP environment.

To further summarize, here are the key support points when managing change in the SAP environment:

- ◆ Change control and change management are closely linked to security control.
- ◆ Changes to the SAP environment must be enabled by appropriate authorization only.
- ◆ Changes can be very simple or very complex; SAP tools exist that are adaptable to the level of change complexity.
- ◆ SAP provides additional levels of authorization when changes are being initiated to system objects that are provided directly from SAP.
- ◆ Communication of changes must be timely and thorough; tailor the communication content to the intended audience (support or business users).

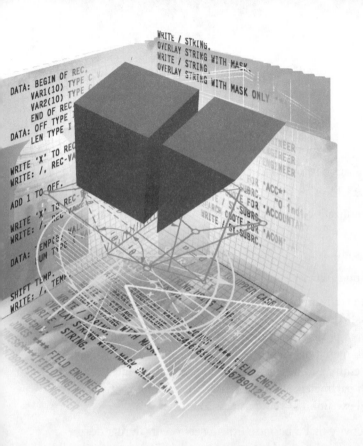

Chapter 19

Supporting Customizations in the SAP Environment

In This Chapter

◆ SAP Customizations: A Support Overview

◆ High-Level Customization Management

◆ Customization Update Tools

◆ Using Existing Customizations and References

◆ Transporting Customizations

◆ Using Naming Conventions

◆ Tracking Customization Activity

As you should now understand, customizations are a key to SAP's inherent adaptability to your business needs. SAP was never designed to be a one-size-fits-all solution. Any ERP that would attempt that would most likely fail. So during the implementation phases of your SAP migration, you learned about SAP customization and how your company's unique entity and business information could be entered into SAP to set the environment's parameters and boundaries. These customizations are key elements in the successful execution of your business solutions.

Most of the customization activity that a business experiences occurs during design and development of your business solutions. However, you will still need to manage customizations in the Live Business environment. The need to perform customization work can stem from inaccuracies or problems in your business solution functionality. Usually, like other initial changes to the environment, these will surface during the initial weeks of a new implementation. But you may also perform additional customizations as a result of enabling additional functionality within your SAP environment. This activity could be large or small in scale, but be sure you again have a process for close tracking and control of customization changes.

This chapter starts with an overview of customization activity as it pertains to the support realm. Because these customizations are as important as the ABAP code within the SAP system, you must understand the impact of supporting them in a live environment. Although you might not always be modifying customizations, you will need to support the understanding and review of customizations in your regular support activities.

Next, you'll learn about the common tool set to use for actually changing or creating new customizations. In the implementation discussions, you'll find out about the presence and need for customizations when preparing a new SAP instance. This chapter goes into more detail about actively maintaining customization settings and values.

The discussion then turns to the best practices for identifying customization values. Much like using naming conventions for ABAP programs and data dictionary elements, you can help yourself by working with established naming conventions that make it easy to recognize your company-specific settings and values. You'll see some common customization areas where you can do just that.

Finally, you'll discover how to track your customization activity. To properly support the customization aspect of an SAP environment, you must monitor the actual activity of customization work within the system. If this requirement has the familiar ring of *documentation*, you're right on the mark. Documentation will help you maintain your customizations. You'll see some good methods for documenting your ongoing customization activity.

SAP Customizations: A Support Overview

To properly set the stage for supporting live customizations, a bit of review is in order. Looking back to the implementation effort, the implementation team began working with customizations. During that time, you determined that a select team of individuals who would be able to best represent, understand, and test proposed customization settings should manage those customizations. That team became a core element of the implementation team as far as filtering the business requirements into the areas of customization activity. Given the appropriate authority by the implementation team, the customization team was responsible for maintaining established customizations and working with process designers and developers to investigate and implement additional settings in support of the business processes. As the team worked in this role, it started a habit of documenting customization decisions and settings so that others could understand them. More important, the customization documentation served as the base reference for system builds. Otherwise, the instance and client builds would need to rely on memory of previous settings or start over from a generic base of SAP sample settings.

At the time of support transition, you'll remember that documentation was a major deliverable of the transitional knowledge transfer effort. All customizations that were established and documented were passed along to the long-term support team. To a certain degree, these are vital keys to SAP. As you might expect, it is advisable to maintain customizations via a dedicated team of support representatives, much as was done during the implementation effort. This approach lets the team develop core expertise in the maintenance of customizations.

Specific authorization objects control customization access so that only identified personnel can make customization changes within the SAP environment. Access can be limited to customization maintenance capability within a single instance client, or it can include access to client-independent customizations. As the name suggests, *client-independent customizations* affect all clients on a particular SAP instance (recall Figure 6-6 that illustrated multiple clients on a single instance). Great care should be exercised in allowing access to this functionality. As a checkpoint, SAP will display a dialog pop-up window when a client-independent customization is being accessed in maintenance mode. The restriction of customization access is a good idea because some customization settings, often as innocuous looking as a simple check box, can be easily set or unset while traversing through the screens. A team member who wants to review a screen could accidentally enable or disable settings. It's best to prevent this potential occurrence altogether.

The focused customization team members can also act as internal consultants to other support team members as well as to the business teams. Customizations can be a bit elusive at times, and it's useful to have a team that is familiar with the location of customization screens and the logic behind establishing the settings. Moreover, a key role of this team is to provide helpful insight to current customization settings and the decisions that were made in establishing them.

This team can operate to fulfill the following duties and services:

◆ Participate in development or enhancement of business processes requiring customization

◆ Monitor customization activity and report any potential conflicts or security holes

◆ Maintain an up-to-date repository of customization documentation

◆ Assist other company sites or entities in developing a similar SAP environment

High-Level Customization Management

For customization, the tools of the trade can be found within SAP's *Business Engineering Workbench* (*BEW*), which can be accessed via the menu path Tools, Business Engineering, Customizing. This path takes you to the Customizing entry screen. Proceeding into the *IMG* via the similarly named button, you will gain access to the *Implementation Guide* (IMG) hierarchy. There is where you will drill into the business module areas to make the actual customization changes or settings.

NOTE

IMG is a tool that assists companies in implementing customizations that will adapt SAP use to their particular business needs. The IMG allows a structural approach to identifying and setting customizations within SAP. With the IMG, you can use SAP's prescribed approach to establishing customization settings in a logical and linked manner; some settings need to be established or enabled before successive customizations can be made.

Figure 19-1 shows the structure of locating and setting customizations within SAP. To a large degree, you can see that the same business module logic is used in the IMG structure. This helps a support team locate and enable necessary customization settings that will enable business module functionality. Sometimes, though, customization settings are a bit difficult to locate. The assignment of customizing screens within this IMG structure is not always the most intuitive. For example, some settings you need to make for the purchasing area might actually exist in the corporate structure branch (used during the establishment of a new instance/client). You can spend quite a bit of time and effort endlessly searching through branches and screens looking for your customization.

Searching for customizations can be especially difficult when the activity involves locating a single customization screen; probably the sort of activity that will be experienced within the support team. The IMG is well designed for taking a team

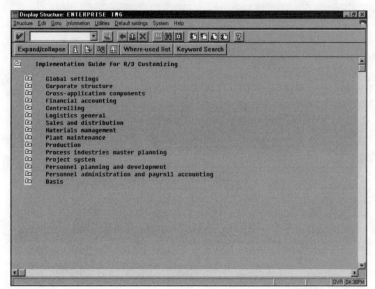

FIGURE 19-1

IMG customizing structure overview screen

through the progressive customization process—starting from the essentials of establishing an instance/client and progressing through the supporting customizations that follow. However, if you need to find a single customization area, out of any sort of sequential flow, then you may have your work cut out for you. You can ease the anxiety of finding a particular customization by using the IMG search utility (see Figure 19-2). With this, you can enter a text string that will hit on matches within the particular customization descriptions.

Depending on how you designated the return result, you can either get a pop-up window of all matching hits (see Figure 19-3), or you can choose for the search function to take you directly to the first hit, within the customizing substructure, that is found. And, although this utility is very useful, it works well only if you know the proper type of SAP customization terminology to search for.

Because finding customizations can sometimes be difficult, even with the use of the IMG search utility, it might be useful to develop an alternative form of documenting your customizations. During the implementation phase, it was suggested that you create an archive of customization submittal documents. These helped the designer or developer understand and communicate his or her customization needs, but also helped the customization team and other implementation team members to understand the intent of the proposed customization. At the time of support transition, that documentation was handed off to you and the other customization support team members. With this documentation, it is useful to create a matrix to track the delivery and availability of the customizations that were established as well as their supporting

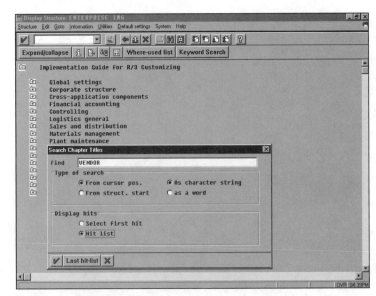

FIGURE 19-2

Customization find utility

FIGURE 19-3 *Customization search hit list and direct hit destination options*

documentation. This method was actually started during the implementation effort, and the matrix grew as the project progressed. Several times, other team members were asked to review this matrix to understand the customizations. Within the matrix, each customization referred to the actual SAP description/title of the customization.

That convention helped in cross referencing to the IMG structure. The matrix also included a pointer to the customization documents, those being reviewed extensively by others as well as yourself, throughout the implementation effort and into the support phase. Sometimes the customization document was the quickest method to locate the customization path and transaction code. (See Figure 19-4 for an example of a customization matrix.)

If a matrix like this appears rather simplistic, that's because it is. If you spend some time in SAP's IMG, you will find that it also provides areas for customization status and documenting. This environment, of course, promotes a fully integrated approach to managing your business. However, you might find that your documentation would be more reliably accessible if it is kept elsewhere. Consider a situation where your SAP system is unavailable—perhaps for a backup or hardware upgrade. In a situation

Business Area	Description	Document Filename	Tested/ Documented By	Date Submitted	Date Approved	Correction Number	Status/Comments
MM	Purchasing Group	purgrp.doc	DL Prince	2/5/97	2/10/97	K00912345	Complete and Approved

FIGURE 19-4

Sample customization matrix content

like this, you may be unable to retrieve your documentation. Consider also where other support documentation is to be stored. More than likely, you will have other pertinent information—organization charts, project plans, business strategies—stored elsewhere.

It might be preferable to keep all support-related documentation in a central repository if at all possible. Suppose, for example, that you maintained the customization matrix as an HTML document. The referenced customization document file names could be enabled links to the actual document on an Internet or intranet server. Consider taking a copy of the IMG structure, creating an HTML file with that content, and creating links there. Your HTML reference structure could be modified slightly to make finding the customization a bit more intuitive. Also, you could create a search utility for searching document content on an Internet or intranet server based on a key word. Use your imagination. Sometimes it is good to break out of the confines of the SAP system. Not always, but sometimes.

One last suggestion is to develop a customization management tool that allows you to freely and easily share your environment information with other company sites or entities. Companies often establish an SAP environment at a primary—a.k.a "beta"—site to determine the overall effort, effectiveness, and return on investment. If the project is a success and the business prospers in the new environment, other sites will probably follow suit. Your efforts now become the company-specific roadmap for these other sites. You spent a considerable amount of effort discovering the different areas of customization. From a company perspective, it would be unwise to make another team redo your work. Think of the relative ease a sister division would have in using your documentation to customize its SAP instance in an accelerated manner. Because you and your team have a good documentation strategy—the Web strategy works especially well in this situation—you can provide the matrix and supporting documents, or a URL to that Internet site, to make the sister division's effort quicker and more direct.

Customization Update Tools

If you are now familiar with the IMG and the SAP Procedure Model (first introduced in Chapter 5), you'll recognize that SAP provides guidance to system customization in ways that are more suited to an implementation effort. Naturally, most

> Once fully established in the support realm, I found that customization activity actually dropped off significantly. This was good news and bad news. The good news was that the decrease in activity signified a more stabile environment. The bad news was that it became quite easy to forget your way about the customization transactions and menu paths. As I said earlier, some of those customization screens are tucked away quite neatly and can be difficult to dredge up again, especially after a time of not working so closely with the customization structure. Again, I found a good trail with the matrix and the customization documentation to be extremely helpful.

customization takes place during the implementation phases, and most of it does not change—company codes, tax codes, entities, and so on. However, the SAP tools are not very direct in helping you understand that it is necessary to support these customizations outside of the implementation effort. A method to help you establish a customization support team and methods to find and manage customization areas outside of an implementation has already been discussed. If you've gotten this far, you are ready to support additions and changes to customization settings.

This section explains more about the actual mechanics of creating or changing customization settings. The intention here is to help you understand SAP's customization tools and methods, not to teach you everything about customization activity. This discussion will help you understand the technical aspect of supporting customizations and what sort of investment might be required when establishing your long-term customization team.

To begin, you must understand that SAP customizations are structured and maintained in three different styles—*view-led customizations, special customization transactions,* and *view cluster customizations.* View-led customizations are designed to allow the display and maintenance of related setting values in a single screen or transaction. The interesting thing about these is that the values you see are actually stored in various data tables. A *view* in SAP is an actual grouping of similar data tables that simplifies managing the information within those tables. Figure 19-5 shows a view of the Purchasing Group data.

In the small pop-up window, you can that purchasing group maintenance entails customizing two different tables within the view—the purchasing group value and the associated printer value. From the pop-up window, you can access either of the views you want to manipulate. This example uses the SAP table maintenance transaction SM31. When you select the first view the customization screen appears (see Figure 19-6).

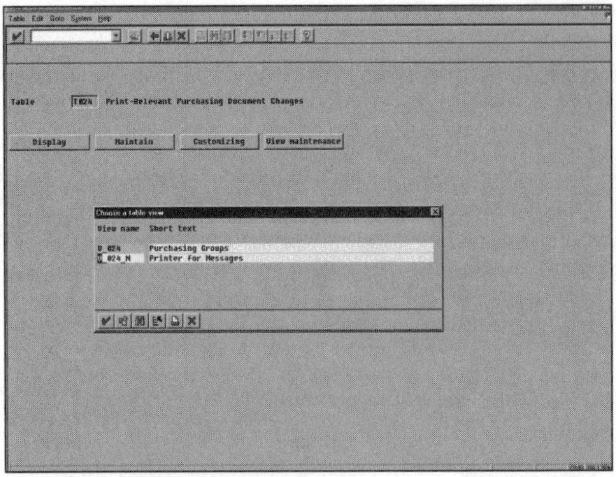

FIGURE 19-5

View maintenance of Purchasing Group customization values

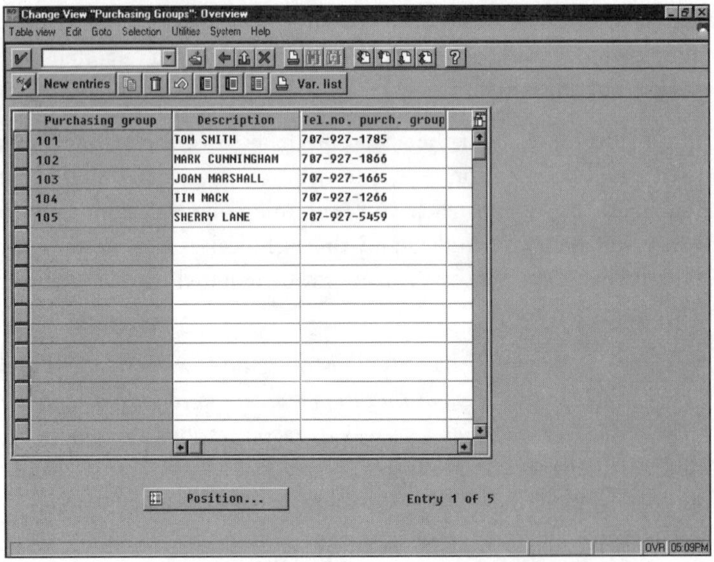

FIGURE 19-6

Purchasing Group customization screen

Within view-led customizing, there is another dimension to the actual customizing activities. The example in Figure 19-6 is what is known as a *single-level process*. In this type of customizing, the work occurs within a single screen. Here you can manipulate the values of an entry in the table, delete a record entirely, copy an existing entry, or create a new entry.

The other type of customizing uses the *two-step process*. In this method, your customization work begins with an initial *list* screen, and the values of the record are maintained in a follow-on *detail* screen. Values can be updated in both screens.

Regardless of the process style, view-led customizations are the simplest type to maintain in SAP.

The next type of customization is the special customizing transaction. This type of customizing process was developed to maintain more complex customization settings and related table updates. A *document type* customization is a good example of a customizing transaction—to make document types fully functional in SAP, multiple complex table settings must be maintained. A view-led process that attempts to display the updateable values in a single-screen view could not manage this sort of customization. Therefore, special transaction codes have been established to maintain the different values that need to be established for proper functionality of the customizations in support of the business process represented. Each special transaction takes you to a single-level process, a two-step process, or a dialog box in which you will make the actual customizations.

The last type of customization is view-cluster customization (see Figure 19-7). This type of activity is similar to the view-led customization except that the different steps required to complete the customization are presented in a hierarchical fashion. This customization is accomplished through a navigation window that leads you through the different parts of the overall customization.

Each level of the hierarchy leads you to a separate area to perform the related customizing tasks. The overall hierarchy represents the sum of all customizations that need to be maintained to render the functionality useful.

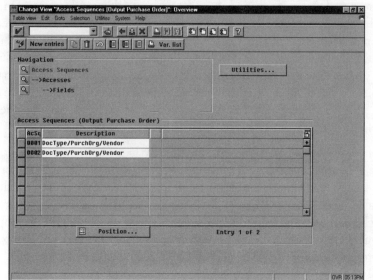

FIGURE 19-7

View-cluster customization navigation window

Using Existing Customizations and References

A useful feature for supporting customizations is the ability to create additional customizations with reference to those which already exist. Simply put, you can copy customizations that have already been set in SAP. By selecting an existing entry, it's frequently possible to copy the characteristics to a new value; you need only to change the key value and description of the new value. This method allows you to take advantage of previous investigative work. Often, you will find the need to create more values in a given customization area of SAP—material movement types, for example. Your team, through arduous investigation and testing, already determined the characteristics for the creation of a movement type in your company's SAP environment. But perhaps you now have the opportunity to add a new type to better manage flow of material in a certain portion of the process. By using a reference to an existing movement type, you can copy and create a new type; then just fine-tune some internal pointers such as reconciliation accounts. This activity in SAP is termed creating with reference. The same terminology is used to create business documents within the various business modules. The process is quite simple.

You can display a customizing screen—view-led, cluster-view, or special transaction—and select an entry that will be the basis for your new entry. You may find the Copy icon on that screen, but, if not, you can also use the menu path Edit, Copy as to perform this task (see Figure 19-8). SAP copies the entry and places you in the same screen as if you were creating the entry without reference. Here you can review the copied values and make any adjustments that are necessary for your new entry. If you attempt to copy an entry to another that already exists, SAP warns you about the unintentional duplication. Once you have completed your setting input and validation, all you need to do is save the entry. SAP will provide a message on the status bar that confirms the number of entries that have been successfully copied. Be aware, though, that you must copy view-cluster entries at each level of the hierarchy. Sublevels are not automatically copied.

Another tool involves comparing customization values from client to client, either within the same instance or to a remote (separate) instance. The comparison functionality allows you to check your customization entries with those in a different client or instance. This tool is useful when your team has secured a customization master client. If you ever need to know whether clients are out of sync, a comparison to the master client can help you to understand where differences might exist and require reconciliation.

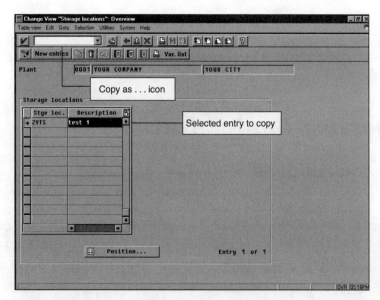

FIGURE 19-8

Example of customization copy

To compare two clients within the same instance, use the menu path Tools, Business Engineering, Customizing, Tools, Table Analyses. Enter the name of the customizing table that you want to compare and click the Compare button. When asked for the client that you want to use for comparison, enter its name and click the Continue button. SAP will provide a side-by-side listing of the table values in each of the clients for you to review and reconcile (see Figure 19-9).

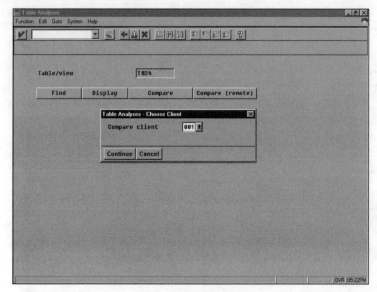

FIGURE 19-9

Customization table comparison between clients (same instance)

Conducting comparisons between clients on two different systems—a remote client comparison—is very much the same as comparing two clients within the same instance (see Figure 19-10). This time, however, you will be prompted to enter a valid instance identifier.

Transporting Customizations

Chapter 18 briefly touched on the concept of transporting customization changes via a customizing request. This sort of request captures the changes you made in a customizing table for import in a designated target instance. At this time, because you now understand more about the manipulation of customization values, you need to understand more about the customizing request, its transport and import, and the options regarding how you manage the customization changes you will make.

First, however, it's important you understand the different levels of customization effect. As you know, customizations can be client specific or they can be client independent. *Client-independent customizations* affect all clients on a given instance—any settings made in a client-independent customization updates those tables on all clients with that SAP instance. In contrast, *client-specific customizations* apply only to the client in which they are being specified. Therefore, customization table entries in one client instance can be different from customization table entries on a different client within that same SAP instance. This concept is important to understand when talking about transporting customization changes because client-independent changes cannot be transported to different clients within the same SAP instance. The table in Figure 19-11 lists the characteristics of customization elements and indicates whether they can be transported.

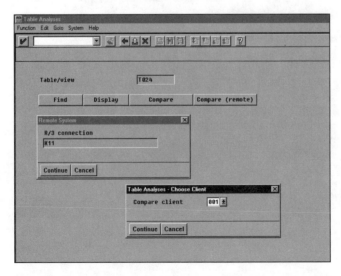

FIGURE 19-10

Customization table comparison between clients (remote instance)

	Between two SAP systems	Within one SAP system
Client-specific table entries	yes	yes
Client-independent table entries	yes	no
Client-specific tables	yes	yes
Client-independent tables	yes	no
Whole client	yes	yes
Note	yes	no
Documents	yes	no
Implementation guide	yes	no
Hierarchy structure	yes	yes

FIGURE 19-11

Customization element transport conditions

The following section describes how your changes are recorded and managed in transportable customizing requests. Customizing requests consist of two elements: the request itself, which is the transportable element, and the task. The *task* is the companion element that is actually used to log and capture the customizing change entries into the request. To capture your customization changes, you will need to create a customizing request (SAP creates the task automatically at the time of the request creation). Use the menu path Tools, Business Engineering, Customizing, Tools, Transport. You will see a familiar hierarchy structure display. This example creates a request using the selection Transport to Another System.

Upon selection, you can get to the request detail screen. This screen, accessed also via the transaction SE10, is where you can review the status of other requests you may have created. Specify your query to be limited to Modifiable status and Customizing category. Press Enter to display the Customizing Organizer screen (see Figure 19-12). You may use the icon to create a new request, provide a title for it when prompted, and save your work (see Figure 19-13). You will be provided with a new request number that you may refer to when saving customization changes.

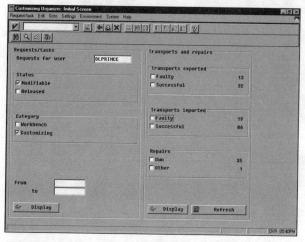

FIGURE 19-12 *Customizing Organizer: Initial Screen*

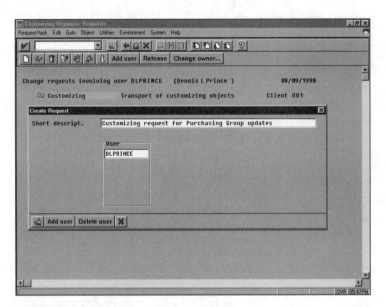

FIGURE 19-13 *Creating a new customizing request*

Now, with a new request available, you can reference it when you save your customizing changes. In addition, you can create customizing requests on-the-fly. In other words, you can access a customizing screen, make the desired changes, and create a new customizing request when you save (see Figure 19-14).

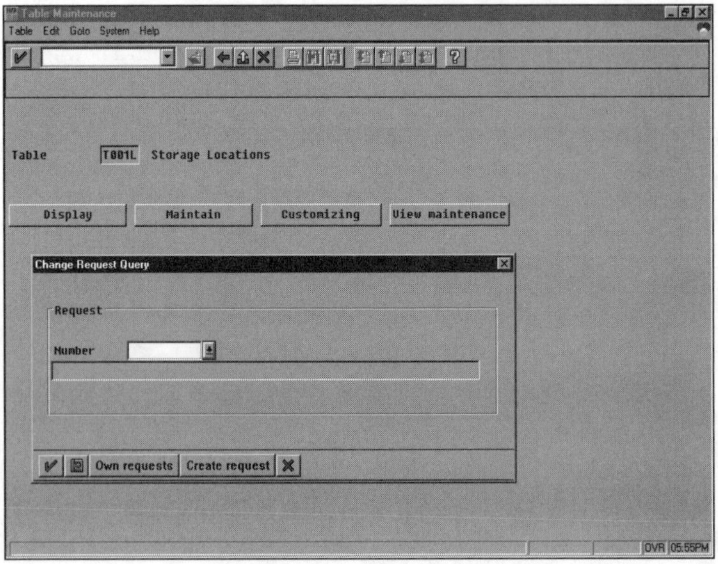

FIGURE 19-14 *Creating a new customizing request during customization activity*

Any customizing changes that you want to include in the same task and request can be saved with reference to a specific task number (see Figure 19-15). When all of your customizing activity is complete, you can return to the Customizing Request Organizer screen (SE10) and release your elements for transport. The task within the request is released first, followed by the request itself. Then, as with other object transport requests, the items are unlocked in the source system. The request can now be transported to the destination of your choice.

When the customization request is transported, the values and settings within the request completely replace all entries in the destination instance/client. But, as mentioned before, you do have other options for changing customization settings across clients and instances. The first option is to copy entries from other clients or instances, which is actually an extension of the comparison functionality described earlier. From within the customizing screen where you are working, use the menu path Utilities, Compare, Other System. As with the compare, you select the system you want to use as the source of your copy.

Then SAP provides the same side-by-side listing of the values. When you find one you want to copy into the client in which you are working, select the entry and click the Copy Entry button. Save your changes, and you're done. This method is usually good when you are synchronizing a few entries between clients or instances. Larger-scale work would probably be best served through a customizing request.

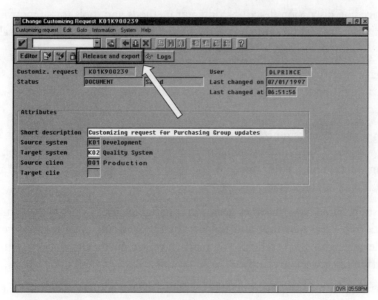

FIGURE 19-15 *Releasing a customizing task/request for transport*

There is always the option of manually entering customization changes in the different systems and clients in your SAP environment. Sometimes this method can be viewed as a fast way to make changes, avoiding the transport process or the comparison process. Use this method with discretion, though. Manual work can introduce the element of typographical or other human errors. It can also lead to development and test instances being out of sync with your Live Business instance.

Using Naming Conventions

Try to remain consistent when creating or modifying customization values and settings. In the case of table entries, work within the naming conventions established when the SAP environment was implemented. Hopefully, the customization team in the implementation effort conducted a good amount of investigation to develop naming conventions that would serve your business and have a long-lasting value. If this is the case, stay within those naming rules. It will ease your efforts and the efforts of others when reviewing customizations in the future. Consistent values are easier to support.

Tracking Customization Activity

The preceding discussion described different methods and tools for supporting customizations. This section summarizes the unique tracking methodology of each tool.

First is the IMG. Searches on the IMG will help you find areas where customizations have been performed. The IMG also includes some internal status screens and document input screens that you may elect to use. This, of course, is at your own discretion.

Then you have the customization matrix. As an alternative to the IMG, this matrix (refer to Figure 19-4) contains references to customization documents, submitters, dates, and status notes. With this tool, you have a working checklist of customization activity, both completed and pending.

The customization request comes next. This tool can be used not only to capture customizations for transport but also to view the status of any open requests you may have. Reviewing this screen helps you manage your requests and release them when your customizing work is complete.

Another tool for tracking customization activity is client comparisons. Using a secure reference environment such as the customization master client, you can check the customization values in different clients and instances as required. If the master client is truly being used properly, you should be able to rely on it as the source of synchronization.

Any differences you may encounter will reveal either work in progress or a breakdown in the process of master client utilization.

Finally, although not discussed directly in this chapter, you can use SAP's table logging feature to track customization activity. Table logging will help you see changes made to the customizing tables. By reviewing the logs, you can monitor changes to the values and settings as you see fit.

Summary

From this chapter's discussion, here are the main elements of customization support:

- ◆ A focused subset of support individuals should provide customization support.
- ◆ Customization support activity is typically less intensive than the activity when working through an implementation effort. Still, support activities are necessary.
- ◆ A strong customization support process includes appropriate authorization control, process methodology, documentation, and a simple and direct information retrieval and review method.
- ◆ Customization changes can be managed through a variety of tools. Some available tool should fit the scope of just about any customization change effort.
- ◆ The use of the customization tools also helps ensure a viable method to track change activity.

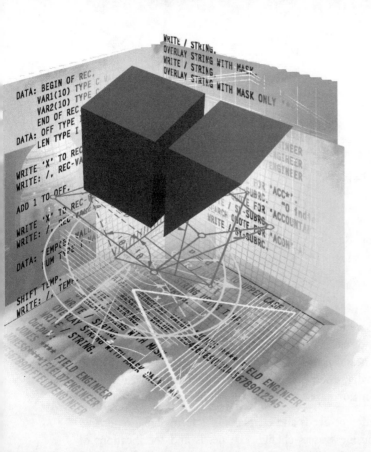

Chapter 20

Supporting Reports

In This Chapter

- ◆ Informational Needs and Scale
- ◆ Determining Useful Reports
- ◆ Reporting Tools
- ◆ Report Elements
- ◆ Working With Report Results
- ◆ Matters of Efficiency
- ◆ Supporting Reports
- ◆ Additional Resources

Reporting is one of the most prevalent activities that occur in a business. This activity enables the analysis of information and trends as related to business goals and deliverables. Reports tell businesses how well they are operating, where they should concentrate their efforts, and what troublesome situations might exist. To the support team, supporting reports is a major staple of the overall job responsibility.

This chapter discusses the different needs and elements of informational reporting. As the analytical needs of business users change, the needs and specifications of reporting also change. So the first hurdle to jump is understanding the informational need and how to best satisfy it. Reporting can be managed through a variety of means, and within SAP reporting can be extremely simple or extremely complex. The trick is to match the solution to the real need.

Once the need is understood, then it is appropriate to ensure that the right information is available. Too little information can cause the wrong action to occur. Missing bits of detail can misrepresent the situation and cause a user to react in a totally inappropriate manner. But too much detail can cloud the picture, and a user may become so overwhelmed with sorting through a mountain of information that good decisions will elude him or her. Your goal is to find the right balance of informational quantity and quality.

Just as informational needs can range from simple to complex, so too can the methods to retrieve the information from SAP. This chapter describes tools that you can use to quickly and immediately begin extracting the information you need, scaling the solution to the complexity of the information requested.

The discussion of reporting tools extends to handling the result your reporting provides. You have several options, and you will need to decide on the best way to use a report's output.

The chapter closes with a discussion on aspects of reporting efficiency. Reports can be useful tools to business teams, but as a matter of good report writing practices and good housekeeping, you'll want to be sure that they can operate well within the SAP environment. The final section suggests some additional sources of information on good reporting practices and style.

Informational Needs and Scale

In gathering and reviewing data, it is easy to get caught up in getting information as fast as possible rather than taking a few moments to really understand what information is really needed. This situation often stems from an ambiguous request at the outset. If your manager says, "I want to see a record of our sales this year," you might jump and start sorting a huge database with thousands of records. You later find out that the manager wanted only domestic sales. Then it was actually sales within the western region. Further, it was really only sales that contained orders for a particular series of products, and so on. Now, this example is extreme, but the point is valid.

Too often, activity is spurred by a very ambiguous request that really required tailoring at the outset. No one is well served by a report that contains too much data to be logically reviewed or information that cannot be logically sorted to arrive at any sort of decisive outcome. Some individuals have a difficult time expressing what they really need. Often, they are reacting to some sort of situation and haven't given enough thought to determining the best response. On other occasions, the belief is that a report or some sort of business automation is the answer to a problem. Again, if the true business need and response isn't well thought out, no form or report or functionality can truly effect a positive influence. And data for data's sake and reports for report's sake are not of much use.

So as you support reports and retrieval of information, you actually become a business consultant to your customers and partners. They have a need because a situation arose. You want to ensure that, before you even begin thinking about a solution—which is difficult for some of us to refrain from—you want to have a meaningful conversation with the requestor to truly understand the nature of the request. Use the knowledge you have about the relevant processes and duties within the business to help the requester see other perspectives or sources of information. If you don't understand some aspects of the situation, ask the requestor questions until you have a clearer picture. If neither of you really understands an important piece of the puzzle, find someone who does. This preparation period will pay off immensely for both you and the requestor. You will gain greater understanding about the business process you are supporting, and the requestor probably will, too. The requestor will also gain further understanding about sources of business information within SAP and which ones are best suited for the desired results.

Once the need is well understood, then the scope of information is to be considered. In this, you will determine how much data is required to provide the result the requestor is looking for. Here is where you find the balance between the right information to search and the right amount of it.

Be sure you can identify proper sample sizing of the information to be extracted. The more you access, the longer it will take. If 1 month's amount of data will provide the same trend analysis as 12 months then scale the solution appropriately. Your understanding of business information can help you provide the best product to your requestor.

So when determining the proper need and scope of a report request, be sure you have clear answers to the following questions:

◆ What is the end result or decision that the report will help achieve?

◆ What exact information is needed?

◆ How current does the information need to be?

◆ What is an appropriate size of information sampling that will yield the result desired?

Reporting Tools

Once you have determined which information is needed and how much, you can look at which tool might be best to fulfill the need. You want to be sure to use the best tool for the job. You also want to be sure you don't overengineer a solution that only requires a simple amount of data. The following sections describe some tool options you have at your disposal.

One-Dimensional Table Extracts

Always look for the most direct path available when extracting SAP information. Some requests are quite simple and can be fulfilled through a direct table query. This case occurs when the information that is requested is all contained within a single table definition. For example, if a user needs to see all of the assigned purchasing group values and which users were assigned to each and their phone numbers, you would find that information quickly available in the T024 table. Therefore, using the SAP *General Table Display* (transaction SE17) or *Data Browser* (SE16), you can access the information that is needed, and print the result, download it for other uses, or e-mail it. If the information is not of an extremely sensitive nature, business users should be able to perform this sort of quick and simple query themselves using SE17. Information selected with SE17 or SE16 can be restricted to applicable criteria as supported by the actual table contents. Therefore, date restrictions can be used in a table search for a table that contains a date element. For most other fields, you can specify range options to select the information that you want to view in either alpha or numeric fashion. This method is applicable only to single-table searches, though. That is, if the information requested is in multiple SAP tables, there is a better tool to manage those requests. Figures 20-1 and 20-2 provide further illustration on how to use the Data Browser and General Table Display functionalities.

ABAP/Query

This tool is found within SAP and is, for all practical purposes, a hybrid of data browser functionality and full-blown ABAP coding. Unlike a simple table search,

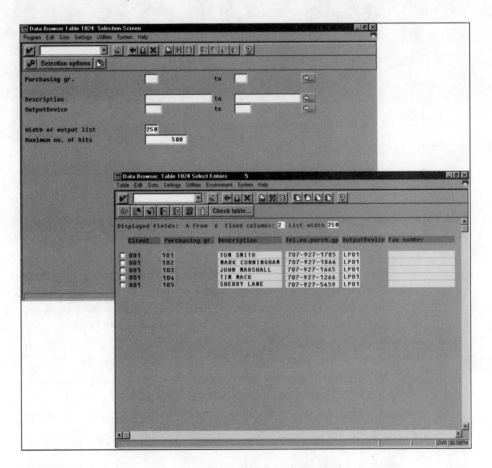

FIGURE 20-1 *Data selection and result using the Data Browser (SE16)*

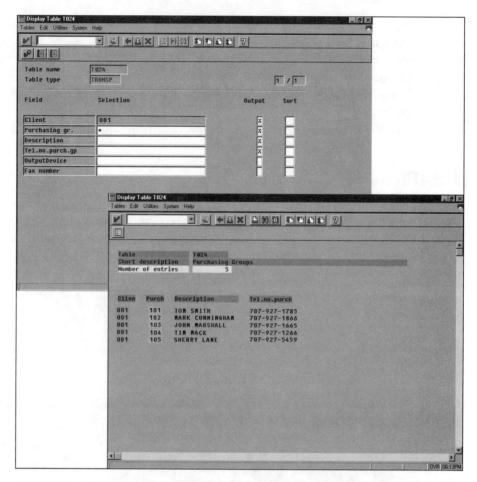

FIGURE 20-2 *Data selection and result using the General Table Display (SE17)*

which yields information from that table's contents only, ABAP/Query allows you to specify multiple tables from which you can obtain information from several data tables within the same query. The main feature of this tool is that the query specification can be developed from an interactive GUI screen. Unlike writing a complex ABAP program, ABAP/Query enables both users and support personnel to create more complex reports through the use of easy-to-understand screens, developed with the same look and feel as the rest of the SAP GUI environment. The result is a useful query that is actually converted *into* ABAP code based upon your selections.

With the ABAP/Query tool, you can create the following sorts of reports:

◆ Standard information lists
◆ Calculated lists

◆ Sorted lists based on information ranking specifications

◆ Combination reports

As you might imagine, the ABAP/Query tool allows access to a lot of SAP information—so much so that extremely deep and system-resource-intensive queries can be developed. Because of some of the informational access and system processing concerns, use of ABAP/Query can be restricted through several different means. First, an authorization object, S_QUERY, controls ABAP/Query definition and changes. S_QUERY must be present and properly enabled for a user to create and maintain queries. Second, ABAP/Query has a unique feature known as *user groups* that limits the use of certain information queries. Each SAP user belongs to a particular user group, and information queries are identified by the user group they serve. These user groups coincide with the business activities of each business module within SAP and the manner in which business users are assigned to managing those business functions. Some activities in SAP span modules, and therefore some users might be assigned to multiple user groups.

Before queries can be created and used, the support team must complete certain administrative tasks. First, functional areas need to be created within the tool to which new queries can be associated. The functional areas are actual definitions of subset table and data structures that logically associate to the different business modules within SAP. Without functional areas, query developers would need to see all database tables and structures when constructing a query. Subsets provide only those tables and data structures that pertain to the business area being addressed. From this point, you continue your definition of a functional area into functional groups and data elements. SAP's extremely customizable functionality allows you to work with only the tables and elements that will yield the results that the business areas need. Functional areas and groups can be modified as required.

Once the ABAP/Query functional areas have been defined, new queries can be created to extract information needed by the business areas. In supporting ABAP/Query, you may need to modify the functional area definitions if data requirements are not being satisfied. You will also have the opportunity to fine-tune the queries that have been developed for greater operating efficiency. Although well-trained users can be enabled to create their own queries, the support team should expect to be instrumental in creating queries.

To access the ABAP/Query functionality, general business users can use the menu path System, Services, ABAP/Query (see Figure 20-3). For administrative purposes, the support team can access the ABAP/Query administrative areas using the menu path Tools, ABAP/4 Workbench, Utilities, ABAP/Query.

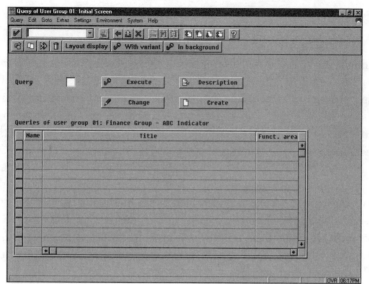

FIGURE 20-3

ABAP/Query main screen

ABAP/4 Programs

The next consideration is the actual coding of reports using SAP's ABAP/4 programming language. This method will yield the most elaborate reports possible within SAP. The technical duty of coding reports requires significant familiarity with the rules and conventions of the ABAP/4 language. You can use ABAP to create reports that derive data from multiple SAP tables, create areas of working storage for further comparison and manipulation, and include a host of calculation and reporting functions. ABAP code can be leveraged from need to need, creating new reports from existing reports or using modular segments of ABAP code in multiple reporting situations. ABAP-programmed reports can be designed to prompt for different ranges of selection criteria when the program is executed. ABAP reports can also be associated to background job schedules and preset to run at certain times using different variants of selection criteria. Actually, the capabilities of ABAP-programmed reports are so great that it's not feasible to provide a full account of the possibilities in this chapter. To learn more about ABAP programming and its use in creating reports, please refer to Prima Publishing's *Introduction to ABAP/4 Programming for SAP, Revised and Expanded Edition.*

Third-Party Query Tools

It's also worth mentioning that several third-party tools are designed solely for use in database extraction and reporting. Each tool has its own administrative needs and functional offerings. These can be used as an alternative to using SAP-based tools. If you want to use a third-party tool, choose one that can perform complex data extractions and manipulations within a user-friendly interface. Also be sure to clarify which company organization will be responsible for the expertise and maintenance of the tool and its functions. Your team will have to decide whether a tool like this should be supported by the support team, or directly by the business users.

TIP

A few examples of third-party solutions are FOCUS Six from Information Builder's Inc., Cognos Accelerator from Cognos Corporation, and various products from Interactive Software Systems Inc.

Report Elements

For a report to truly have significance, you'll want to be sure it contains the proper elements of standard report output, meaning both printed matter and onscreen displays of information. A collection of data values is useful only if it is arranged in a usable and legible manner. A good report contains the following elements:

◆ Date and time values for when the report was executed

◆ The program name

◆ A descriptive title

◆ The user who executed the report (sometimes found on a cover sheet)

◆ Progressive page numbers

◆ Header lines that describe the different text elements

◆ Separator lines or page breaks that improve readability

◆ Summary values

Determining Useful Reports

So now you have the most excellent report ever conceived. It's truly a work of informational art. But how do you know how useful it really is? After all, it will only be as good as the degree to which it is used. To do some initial checking, ask the following questions:

◆ Why is this information needed?

◆ How often is this information needed?

◆ Who will use this report?

◆ How long will this report be needed?

These basic questions should be answered during the initial investigation conducted with the report requestor. His or her specifications of the report's use and content should provide strong reasoning for the report's creation and ongoing support. If, however, you are unclear on any of these points, you might have missed the original goal.

Revisit the requestor's needs to ensure that the data elements you have captured are truly indicative of the result that was intended. Sometimes, only a portion of a data element is required (for example, descriptions). In this case, report only that information. If cumulative information is the main point of the report, be sure yours has totaling, tally lines, and a summary page. Often the summary is all that is needed, but sometimes it helps to provide detailed information as well.

When considering printed reports, real estate—the space available on a page of output—gets very valuable. Above all, keep the information easy to read and easy to understand. Simplicity is the goal. Too much information is just that—too much.

When determining the elements of your report, be sure you have a good understanding about who the audience will be. Tailor the information presented to the report user's needs and expertise. Don't be quick to include more than what the requestor asks for. In fact, unless the report is otherwise incomplete, give the requestor just the information for which he or she asked. The requestor might not share your analytical interests.

There are two real indicators of a useful report. First, if the report enables appropriate and decisive action that improves a business situation, then the report has succeeded. A report that is well-used, well-worn, and well-traveled is a well-designed report.

The second indicator is simple: How quickly is the report thrown away, and how many users understand the use and intent of the report? If you ask a user about a report and he or she responds with complete bewilderment, then something is amiss. Perhaps the report didn't meet the true need. Perhaps the report was too cumbersome to understand. Perhaps the use of the report wasn't well communicated. The bottom line, though, is how many warm reports—those fresh off the printer—find their way into the recycling bins before the ink is fully dry. This comment may sound a bit glib, but it is true that many reports can run for months and years without intended recipients ever knowing why. If you suspect a report may have outlived or missed its purpose, try this test: Stop running the report and see who notices. If users jump up and exclaim they haven't received it, the report is still useful. If no one mentions it, leave the report turned off.

Again, this is an area where your business user partnering skills come into use. Sometimes, business analysts specify and design reports on behalf of the using community that is intended to receive them. Be sure the analyst's intent matches the user's needs. This is not just to isolate analysts; some more experienced business users can also over-specify a report's content. You'll need to work hard, yet diplomatically, to separate one person's analytical vision or personal style from the true needs of an audience for a report.

Working with Report Results

You now have the opportunity to determine what you will do with the result of a report. The pat answer is usually to port the output to a printer and distribute it. This action is very valid and useful for many reports. However, these days it is increasingly important to consider paper usage and the need for printed reports. Forests are leveled daily in the name of information reporting. Ask yourself if you can use the information in any other way.

SAP is exceptionally adapted to working with online screen displays of report results. When displayed, some reports can contain elements that make them more useful online than in printed form. SAP, through ABAP functionality, can provide color-coded online report displays that guide a reader through the meaning of the output. For example, red text can alert a user to take action, whereas green text can indicate that all is well.

Even more useful is SAP's capability to create reports whose output actually works like other interactive SAP features. Reports can be generated that provide lines of results. Using advanced ABAP functionality, those reported lines can actually be links to other areas of SAP. In this manner, an online report can be a working list that enables a user to manage activity in a real-time, online environment. No print delays or lost pages with a solution like this.

Matters of Efficiency

A good reporting method is one that is efficient, which means that your information selections are logical and properly focused. Using selection criteria is the most important means of selecting the data you wish to retrieve. Much the same as when you pared down the actual data requirements, the selection criteria of your search should get just the information you need in the most direct and efficient manner. Each tool described earlier uses selection criteria. Take full advantage of that feature, and you will be pleased with the results you get—in terms of information returned and processing speed.

A good ABAP report can provide excellent information for business use. However, a poorly constructed ABAP report can tie up system resources and even be aborted. ABAP programs work on two levels of selection criteria. The first is with the request for input criteria on which the program is to gear its data search. The programmer is responsible for providing useful selection parameters that help a user narrow down the window of relevant data. If the specifications of the report are communicated and understood well, selection criteria can be specified in a well-thought-out manner. The programmer is also responsible for providing efficient programmatic searches and retrievals of data. This entails the actual coding of the program, and the manner in which the programmer employs the user-provided selection criteria to access tables and extract information. Efficiency also includes a narrow selection of information based upon the criteria provided and using internal tables to manipulate information.

For new programmers, it is probably a good idea to have a more experienced programmer review your code for efficiency. The two team members should work together to highlight areas where modification and tuning can be applied to make the program run better and more efficiently. With practice, new programmers can quickly learn methods to streamline their code and achieve the best result, both in output and operation time.

Supporting Reports

So, with all of this said, what does it truly mean to support reports? First, you need to understand what methods to employ when an informational request comes to you. You need to work with requestors to understand their needs and perhaps even guide them to the best sources of the information they seek. Sometimes you will know of supporting information that will help them achieve the result they truly seek. This expertise, of course, comes from having a good understanding of the information query's purpose and having a solid set of specifications from which to work.

Some of your support work will come from investigating areas of information storage of which you might not be entirely familiar; for example, if you have to cross over to information in a business module that you infrequently work with. These opportunities to broaden your knowledge of the information that is being stored within SAP will reinforce your understanding of the integrated information flow.

In this area of SAP support, you will be supporting reports and programs that have been written and developed by others, which can be difficult. Programmers tend to have their own particular programming style, which includes the way they structure their programs, the internal processing options they use, and the conventions they use for internal data variable and table naming. Your best bet is to identify core segments of ABAP language and then to compare the program's structure to another that you understand better—maybe one of your own. Once you understand the original programmer's style, do everything you can to follow it if you will be making changes to the piece of code. The only thing more confusing than another programmer's style is finding a program that incorporates several different programmers' styles. Once you've identified a programmer's logic and naming conventions, work within that style rather than against it. Otherwise, you're probably better off recoding the entire program, time permitting. But if you work with and understand a programmer's style, you'll be more apt to recognize it in other situations. With familiarity, you will be able to work with differing styles quite well. The methods other programmers use might not necessarily be the best in your mind, but it's not always feasible to rework code to fit your particular likes or thought processes. Otherwise, other programmers will be doing the same when they have to work with your code.

Supporting reports means that you will want to be familiar with SAP's ABAP/4 language. The logic, for the most part, is pretty straightforward and follows the common logic conventions of most programming languages. Work with code and follow its logic through so you can understand the program as it executes. If you will be supporting a particular set of reports or programs, you want to understand them well in case any problems arise and require you to verify the functionality of the code.

Additional Resources

SAP has extremely well-written help text throughout most of the GUI screens. You can also find very useful information on data extraction and reporting on the help utility CD-ROM. In addition, check out Prima Tech's *Introduction to ABAP/4 Programming for SAP, Revised and Expanded Edition*. Finally, refer to Appendix D of this book for information regarding SAP training courses.

Summary

Dealing with requests for information is a large portion of your support activities in the SAP environment. Businesses thrive on data. Their needs are never ceasing, and you want to be in a position to help them better define those needs and follow-through with a solution that exceed their expectations.

To summarize, here are the key points of support discussed in this chapter:

◆ Before any data collection activity commences, be sure you and the requestor can fully and consistently explain the need for the information.

◆ Be sure you can understand the complexity of the information required and choose the right tool to match the complexity; many queries can be conducted directly by the requesting users.

◆ When developing any report, be sure you understand the audience that will receive it and tailor the presentation of the data to their needs and skill level.

◆ Be sure your reports contain the minimum elements described in this chapter.

◆ Get yourself trained in the use of ABAP/4; you'll work more efficiently when responding to user requests and potential reporting problems.

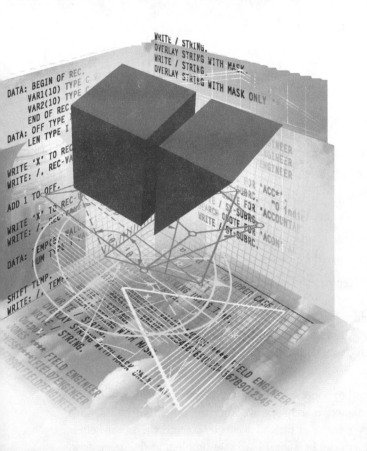

Chapter 21

**Transaction and
Performance
Support**

In This Chapter

- ◆ What Is Transaction and Performance Support?
- ◆ Reviewing the Work Processes
- ◆ Data Contention Revisited
- ◆ SAP Performance Tools and Methods
- ◆ Maintaining Ease of Use in SAP
- ◆ When to Enable Automated Processes

In the support role, you will often hear, "The system doesn't seem to be working well today," or "Boy, that system is really slow!" These are valid comments, and they deserve your response. The fact is that your SAP system will experience peaks and valleys of response efficiency. Although it is not always directly related to SAP itself, there are some things you can check within SAP to determine whether a problem or bottleneck exists.

In the support realm, you need to concern yourself not only with system availability but also with system performance. If users are working through SAP transactions that are taking extremely long periods of time to access or execute, then your help is needed. Sometimes the problem can be a local hardware problem at the user's desk, a problem with inefficient programming within SAP, or larger problems with the SAP instance hardware or network activity. Although you may not resolve these problems yourself directly, you will need to understand the contributors to undesirable performance conditions.

This chapter looks at what your role is in regard to supporting transaction activity. It starts by showing you how you can understand performance problems and what basic troubleshooting you might conduct to potentially resolve a simple problem. If the problem eludes your expertise or span of control, then you'll learn when it's time to get someone else involved.

Another look at data contention might be in order, which was a consideration when managing batch job schedules. Here, you'll see how data contention occurs and how to help correct such situations.

The overall ease of use in the SAP system is discussed next. When the system responds well, processes run smoothly and consistently. Ease of use is actually a key enabler of any good business solution, and it works well with the integrated architecture of SAP. However, when performance is down, ease of use suffers and process accuracy can be impacted. You'll see what can happen when processes get bogged down and why you'll want to stay on top of the usability factor in the SAP environment.

Finally, the discussion closes with the topic of using automated processes. Granted, SAP is an amazing automated system, but many of the functions you can manage within it can be executed manually. At some times, manual execution is a good approach; at other times, a manual process slows productivity and flow in the system. You'll learn how to tell when a process is better suited for automated processing rather than manual processing.

What Is Transaction and Performance Support?

Transaction and performance support can be defined as the monitoring and assurance of good system response time and ensuring that the users are successful in conducting their business within SAP. These days, as processing power is higher than ever before, we are all interested in speed. We want to conduct business transactions almost as quickly as we can conceive them in our minds. If we can think of the solution quickly, why must we wait for a software application to interpret and respond to our thoughts? With so much more activity taking place at each employee's desk, rapid response and reaction from the business tools is of highest importance. Slowdowns or limiters are frustrating and can cause errors and missed opportunities.

Your role, then, in assuring good transaction response is to continually be aware of system performance. It's actually as easy as working with the system yourself. As you maneuver through SAP in your daily support activities, you'll notice when response seems to be waning. Sometimes it is simply a hiccup—perhaps a large processing event just completed—but you'll want to be aware of any situation that is sustained.

If you experience a slowdown, it's possible that your business users are experiencing the same thing. To make a quick determination, branch over to their business module activities in SAP. Truly poor performance will manifest itself just in navigating through the business transactions of the system. Perform some simple data searches or display some business documents. If it's taking longer than usual to get the desired results, it's time to do some further investigating. Your analysis is still rough, so don't sound off the alarms just yet.

Reviewing the Work Processes

Your next step would be to review the overall processing activity within SAP. To do this, you will need to use the *Work Process Monitor* (see Figure 21-1). Here you can find work processes that may have experienced problems, or you can find out if so many work processes are simultaneously executing that new processes are waiting for a free session. To access the Work Process Monitor, use the menu path Tools, Administration, Monitoring, System Monitoring, Processes, or you can use the SAP transaction SM50.

Work Process Monitor—An overall server (instance) monitor that gives a quick view of processing activity taking place within SAP.

In SAP, the work processes are responsible for managing system activites such as user dialog sessions, update processing, lock management, and background processing. Therefore, you can see why this screen is a good place to begin your investigation. In this screen you'll see the different processes are executing, the status of those processes, some run-time statistics, and how many work processes that are free for use. As you look at the process overview, you will see the following information:

◆ **No.** The internal number of the process used for assigning system messages.

◆ **Ty.** The type of work process that is executing: DIA indicates a dialog user session; UPD and UP2 indicate update tasks; ENQ indicates an enqueue task that manages data locks; BTC indicates a background process; SPO indicates a spool (print) process.

◆ **PID.** The process ID indicator as established by SAP. SAP establishes the PID, but it is manifested at the UNIX level of the server. This is useful because, if a process cannot be terminated directly within SAP,

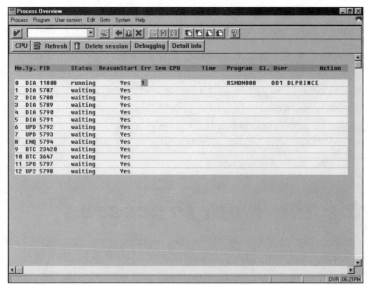

FIGURE 21-1

Work Process Monitor overview screen

the Basis Administrator can access the PID within UNIX and terminate the session from the database level.

◆ **Status.** The current of the current process: Running indicates that the process is currently active; Waiting indicates a free process that is waiting to be assigned to a work task; Hold indicates that a session is in reserve for a user; Killed indicates a session that has aborted and been canceled.

◆ **Reason.** The reason for a process in the Hold status.

◆ **Start.** Indicates whether an automatic restart should occur after a process abort.

◆ **Err.** Provides a numeric representation of the number of times a process has aborted.

◆ **Sem.** The number of the semaphore upon which the process is waiting.

◆ **CPU.** A cumulative value of CPU time that has been expended in executing the process. This indicator can be updated with the Refresh button.

◆ **Time.** A companion to CPU, this indicator shows the actual clock time that has elapsed since the start of the work process.

◆ **Program.** The name of the ABAP program that is being executed within the work process. This name can change as the process executes, as most processes branch to different ABAP programs to complete the business task.

◆ **Client.** The client that was used when executing the process.

◆ **User.** The user logon ID that started the work process.

◆ **Action.** The action (for example, sequential read, direct read, update) that is currently being executed within the work process.

◆ **Table.** If the work process is accessing a database table, the table name is displayed here.

As you can see, this informative screen can provide you with most of the information you would want to know about currently-executing work processes. In this screen, pay special attention to seemingly duplicate sessions being executed by the same user. This situation could indicate that a user has started the same program multiple times. Also, be especially aware of the situation in which *all* available work processes appear to be executing. In this case, no additional processes can execute until some of the existing work processes free up. And, of course, if you see processes running that have an error status or have been running for an extremely long time, then those will require further investigation.

Understand that work process monitoring is actually a direct responsibility of the Basis Administrator. You should have access to review the process monitor, but that might be the extent of your capabilities. If any processing looks suspicious or like it might require action, contact the Basis Administrator immediately.

In addition to work process review, you can conduct a user overview within SAP. Much like the work process overview, a user overview allows you to monitor the different user sessions and determine whether a particular user is running a session inappropriately or has multiple sessions running and is locked from further processing. To access the user monitor (see Figure 21-2), use the menu path Tools, Administration, Monitoring, Users, or you can use the SAP transaction SM04.

In this screen, you can see which users have active sessions running in the SAP instance or application server that you are reviewing. If you employ multiple application servers in your SAP environment, choose the server that is assigned for the users' business area use. But when reviewing this screen, you have access to the following information:

- ◆ The logon ID name assigned to a user
- ◆ The number of sessions running under a user logon ID (signified by multiple entries under the same logon ID)
- ◆ The current SAP transaction being executed by a user
- ◆ The time of the last dialog activity initiated by a user in a session

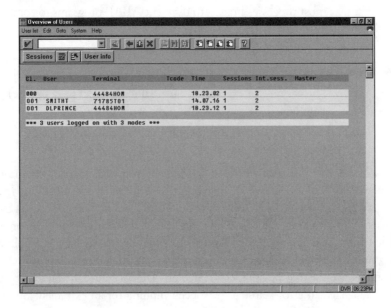

FIGURE 21-2

User Session Monitor overview screen

Within the User Session Monitor, you can review user session activity and perform the following functions:

◆ Terminate a process operating within a user session

◆ Put a user session into debugging mode for analysis

◆ Take control of a user session

◆ Delete stale user sessions

Again, the Basis Administrator may be responsible for these controlling activities. However, the user overview screen is another excellent tool to help you understand more about what the user is trying to achieve and which SAP utilities the user is already executing.

Data Contention Revisited

With the discussion of reviewing user sessions, it's good to reaffirm the need to avoid data contention situations. Data contention occurs when certain information within the SAP tables is locked for update by a user dialog session or a background process. The locked information, displayable in the Lock Entries utility, cannot be used by other users or processes until the pending processing is completed and the locks are removed.

In some instances, locked data will be reported back to a user's GUI. SAP often provide san error message that indicates the data is locked for update, and sometimes will even provide the logon ID that is currently locking the information. Other times, the error message will only report that the data is locked but might not list the logon ID that is locking it. This condition usually occurs when a background process or update process has the information locked.

The point to be made here is that all dialog users are allowed up to six SAP sessions to be running simultaneously from a single logon. This feature is a terrific benefit to users because it allows them to review and manage information quickly and easily by toggling between the sessions. However, running multiple SAP sessions under a single logon is often a significant contributor to data contention issues. If a user has a problem accessing information because it is locked, a review of the Lock Entries overview can sometimes reveal that the user has locked the data. A follow-up review of the user's active sessions will reveal that a session exists that has locked the data. If, for some reason, the session terminated, it's possible that the lock was never cleared. In this case, the session should be deleted first. If the lock doesn't release after that, then delete the lock in the Lock Entries overview.

NOTE

Sometimes it might be necessary that the Basis Administrator delete a lock entry at the UNIX level if it cannot be deleted directly within SAP.

SAP Performance Tools and Methods

You've seen how to conduct some investigative research within SAP when performance is of issue. Here, then, are some ways to address some of the performance issues your users might be experiencing. These tools are largely controlled by the Basis Administrator, as is most of the system performance responsibility. However, because your interaction is directly with the user experiencing the problems, it is a good idea for you to become at least familiar with some of these performance options.

User and Process Load Balancing

Load balancing is the method by which the SAP system automatically distributes work processes across the various servers available for SAP activity. Within SAP, you can establish *logon work groups* and assign them to different application servers. This approach allows you to designate servers to match the processing needs of a particular business area. For example, it might be appropriate to assign an application server with improved response time to a business team that has very mission-critical duties. Within each logon work group, it's a good idea to establish at least two application servers. This method allows SAP to automatically disperse the users between the servers to maintain the best possible response time. When a user logs on, SAP can determine which application server to use based on response time statistics and the number of users already logged on. In addition, the use of backup servers also ensures that no user is denied a logon because all defined dialog sessions are in use.

Synchronous and Asynchronous Updating

Another opportunity to improve user response and activity within SAP is to consider the manner in which ABAP programs perform database updates. You have two methods to choose from. *Synchronous updating* means that an executing program or a user's dialog session is kept busy and unusable until the update has successfully completed. For long transactions or when system performance is not peak, this technology can mean noticeable delays to the user. The option, then, is to make use of asynchronous updating. In *asynchronous updating,* the updating task is given to the SAP Update Manager functionality. The update is carried out in the background, and the executing program or user dialog session continues to other tasks.

Within SAP, most update transactions are carried out asynchronously. When any update errors occur, a record is written to the update log. When customer-specified ABAP programs are developed, you should understand the amount of information that is being updated and the expected time it will take for an update to complete. These factors should be considered when determining whether to program with synchronous or asynchronous updating.

Database Locks

Database locks are the method by which your SAP application communicates with the database server to secure exclusive access to information being updated. The lock ensures that information is not accessible by other users or processes while your update is taking place. Once the updating is complete, the lock is removed. Much like the work process availability, activity within SAP cannot continue if it cannot secure database locks. This situation may be rare, but runaway processes can essentially consume all available database locks (although usually thousands or more are enabled). In this case, SAP processes will experience terminations and the display of ABAP short dumps. If you become aware of mass termination of user sessions, check the database lock status immediately with your Basis Administrator.

Database Performance Tuning

Database performance tuning is another area of Basis concentration, but performance tuning can occur in many areas. Although you probably won't be directly able to perform the tuning yourself, here are a few of the areas that can be modified:

◆ Shared memory allocation

◆ Virtual memory usage

◆ SAP table reorganization

◆ Dbspaces

◆ Buffer use and allocation

Maintaining Ease of Use in SAP

System performance determines the speed at which processing occurs. In addition, response speed can be of extreme importance to the business. Take the example of customer orders. It is necessary for a business to be able to enter customer orders, either automatically or manually, in a reasonable amount of time. Customer order numbers need to be system generated in some cases, and customers may actually be on the telephone awaiting confirmation of their order. Nothing discourages a customer faster than waiting for a company representative who is waiting for information to be processed, possibly explaining their dissatisfaction with the system. This situation gives the impression of an inefficient process. The same is true for retrieving customer order information at the request of a customer.

But aside from the speed at which the information is processed, good system performance is also important from the standpoint of the flow of business processing. A slow system will slow down the work that users are trying to accomplish. Immediately, their productivity has been impacted. If others are waiting for the upstream process to complete, then their productivity is also impaired. And, while waiting for a process to complete, users may begin to work on other activities and then must remember where they left off with the original job when the system began performing badly. This situation often causes missed or incomplete process steps. This isn't to say that slowdowns will never occur or that business users are incapable of managing multiple tasks at a time. However, the more quickly a process can run from end to end, the more likely it is to run smoothly and to completion.

When to Enable Automated Processes

Automated processing isn't always the answer to data manipulation activities. Much of a business's processes are best managed in an interactive mode, allowing for human interaction and complex decision making. The manual process should be left alone as long as it continues as a benefit and not a hindrance to business activity. However, consider automated processing when you consider issues of system performance. Complex processing that is system resource intensive should be analyzed for the timeliness of its execution. The fact is that some processing, such as order management and manipulation, requires large amounts of system resources. Look at processes that consume large amounts of processing power and determine whether they can run off-hours. If so, include an automated process in a background job schedule. Schedule the processing during the nighttime or weekend hours. Your goal is to keep as much CPU as possible available during the daily dialog activities of the business users.

Another consideration involves streamlining business processing. This topic isn't directly related to system performance issues, but it warrants your consideration. If a simple and repetitive business process is managed manually, explore the possibility of automating it and run it in a background process. If it is not resource intensive, it could be executed during regular work hours, providing updated information throughout the work day. The automation of the process alone will improve efficiency and accuracy of the data manipulation.

Summary

The system is only as good as its performance. Grand solutions that can do just about everything for a business are useless if they can't operate in a timely and consistent fashion. As support, you will need to watch the overall performance of SAP to ensure that the business solutions are operative and can be conducted in a reasonable amount of time. Business activity is continually speeding up, and the automated processes that power a business have to support the demand for information processing.

In performance monitoring, you might be able work with some of the Basis tools that are designed for this purpose. Become familiar with them if you can. They'll give you a better understanding of the overall SAP architecture. As well, knowledge of performance issues and what affects performance can help you make better decisions about process solutions and enhancements.

The key support points to remember from this discussion are as follows:

- ◆ It is important to monitor the users' successes in performing and completing regular SAP activities; they will inform you of problems and will want to know that you are working to make the system respond appropriately.

- ◆ From your support role, you should be able to perform initial investigations into situations and causes of poor system performance.

- ◆ Become familiar with some of the SAP performance and activity review tools; you might not have direct ownership or full authorization to use them, but familiarity with their use will help you serve the business users.

- ◆ Provide further advice and guidance to business users regarding the good use and misuse of multiple SAP sessions; help them to clearly understand what data contention is and what they can do to minimize it.

- ◆ Monitor business processes carefully and determine when opportunities exist to choose automated processing over interactive processing.

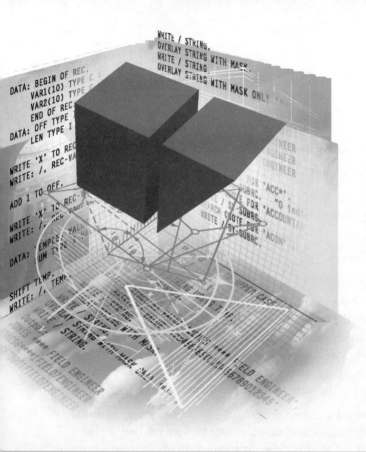

Chapter 22

Developing and Maintaining User Confidence

In This Chapter

◆ Determining Your Customer Base

◆ Establishing and Maintaining the Partnership

◆ Communicate!

◆ Helping Users Help Themselves

◆ Engaging the User Base

◆ Grooming Expert Users

◆ Damage Control

At this time, it's good to break away from SAP tools and mechanics for a review of your role and relationship with the business team you support. It becomes so easy to get caught up in SAP functionality and activity. But you need to remember that your job is to help the business users who work with business processes (which, of course, are the essence of the business). Regardless of how strong or bulletproof your solutions are, they are only as good as the team that is using them.

The new SAP system has caused a certain amount of anxiety and unrest with the business teams. What was once familiar and commonplace to them has been replaced by an entirely new system that has a vastly different approach to managing the business activities. You need to be aware of the impact this change has had upon the users and work with them to soften the impact.

This chapter's intent is to remind you of your responsibility to the users that you support. It begins with the understanding of exactly who the users are and what they are doing. In turn, they need to know who you are and what you are doing. Your goal is to develop a business familiarity with them and begin to build a partnership.

Communication, which has been strongly advocated earlier in this book, becomes a recurring topic of discussion. You'll see how important it is to have good communication with users so you can establish and maintain your working relationship with them. You'll learn some methods by which you can communicate with users in an open fashion.

Then the discussion shifts to how you can best enable the users to be more self-sufficient within SAP. Access to information within SAP can be something of a mystery, but some simple tools can enable your users to become more competent. You'll learn about some of the tools that business teams can use to meet their daily needs.

Throughout this discussion, you are actively exposing your business users to the styles and usage of SAP. Although all of them will grow in their SAP knowledge, some will acquire a greater grasp of the system, the processes, and the possibilities that exist within this new automated environment. These are the users with whom you will want to work even more closely.

Your goal is to enable the users to become more comfortable and effective with SAP. If you can achieve this goal, you will instill them with more confidence, and they will develop more confidence in you as their support representative.

Determining Your Customer Base

You've already learned about the alignment of support team members to the business areas and users that need to be supported. You understand how you will most likely support core business functions such as finance, purchasing, warehouse, inventory. During the implementation effort, business users were identified and established within SAP. As the system went live, you recognized who used the solutions and how successful they were—the solutions and the people using them. Then, during the transition period, you may have received full ownership of support responsibilities for one of the major business user groups. By all rights, you should clearly know the users who work within the business area you support. Maybe, and maybe not.

During an SAP migration, business activity is brought into a bubble of focused activity. To make the migration a success, business must perform to some sort of measurable boundary of regularity. Sometimes confining business activity into a predictable process boundary can work as a constraint to the business areas, but locking the activity down to a certain degree is necessary to ensure that the SAP migration can be effected successfully and in a manner that supports the main business requirements. After the migration, though, the business areas are eager to once again spread their wings and begin exploring and working in new directions. Quite often, one of the first indicators of a return to full business activity is the fluctuation of business users within the system.

If you have a good, controlled support methodology, you will know when new users come on board even if you are not directly responsible for enabling SAP logon IDs. The support team always needs to know when a business area is expanding its base of users. In turn, they can make any necessary modifications to the processes (program variants, report distribution, and so on) to include the new user in daily processing activities. In fact, it's preferable for the business area support team member to receive all requests for new user logons as well as any changes to existing user authorizations. The support team member could potentially receive a request from the finance team that a new user needs access. The support team member will understand what the new user's activities will be, and determine what parameters, settings, and report processes need to be modified to enable the new user's activity. Of course, the support team member will pass the actual logon ID request to the Security Administrator, but in this fashion the support team member is acutely aware that his user base has just changed.

Further, you'll want to casually monitor what the different users are typically doing in the system. It's important to notice which business processes are utilized most often. You'll see whether there is an even disbursement of activity or whether the balance is a bit weighted. This information helps you understand which processes appear to be the most critical, most used, and potentially most problematic. Equally, understanding the different users' activities will help you understand how effective and successful they are within SAP. For example, if you notice a particular user having a high incidence of data errors, you might want to investigate further. Perhaps the individual never received proper training to use the solution; perhaps the solution hasn't been working properly for anyone; perhaps an entirely new solution is required for a business requirement that was previously unknown.

You'll also want to keep in close contact with new users. Try to establish contact with them as soon as you can. They'll appreciate knowing who you are and how you can help them. They might have difficulties early in their assignment, and you'll want to monitor their progress to ensure that their work is fruitful. Knowing that you are available and approachable should encourage them to contact you and ask questions, as opposed to experimenting within the system on their own.

Also be aware of geographically dispersed users. More and more, businesses are making use of virtual organizations and groups to manage business activity in a single automated environment. *Remote users*—those in a different geographical area than the rest of the business team—can sometimes feel left out or forgotten. Be sure you can establish good working relationships with them to ensure they are getting the output they need, that their activities are progressing well, and that they understand the policies and processes that govern the overall environment. Be sure these users understand the proper procedure for logging problems—the help desk or direct contact, whichever model your team has adopted.

Knowing who your users are is sometimes as important as knowing some of the processing intricacies of the SAP environment. No matter how much automation you can program, there will always be business users who will interact with SAP. Once a business settles into its SAP environment, users tend to relax and begin to venture out in creative ways to meet their business needs. Your job is to know your users and what they do.

Establishing and Maintaining the Partnership

Your first step to establishing the business partnership was in understanding who your users are, and their understanding of who you are. If your user base is responsible for key processes—which they typically are—be sure you can understand the constraints under which they work and can help them meet their business requirements. For example, a flurry of activity usually occurs at the last minute before the calendar changes and a new month starts. Work with your users closely during these times, and look for inhibitors or potential roadblocks that could prevent them from meeting their deadlines. By acting as their proponent, you will learn more about your users' needs and duties and will also show that you are dedicated to making their goals achievable.

However, be sure to share with your business partners the policies and controls under which you are working. Last-minute effort is always a reality, but you should explain how large amounts of data processing or ad hoc requests can bottleneck everyone's efforts. Encourage proactive and distributed processing to smooth out the business activities and ensure that system performance doesn't become compromised or emerge as a delaying factor. Work with your users to also explain how knee-jerk changes—those that come about because a situation arose and a quick fix is requested, often without proper investigation—cannot be properly managed in the integrated environment. This news may be something of a disappointment at first, but over time the business team will learn your schedule and working conditions and will work with you to make sure that everyone is successful.

What has just been described is the embodiment of support and business advocacy. Each team understands the other, each is knowledgeable about the other's processes, and each needs to work out mutually beneficial agreements. But, since you are in a service role, don't expect the users to bend over backwards to accommodate you. After all, your job is to work to meet their needs. It's not so much that you will be taken advantage of, but business needs must come first because they are more directly involved in the profitability of the company.

You'll find, though, that your partners will sympathize with some of the odd requests to which you have to respond and some of the odd hours you have to work. They'll even develop a greater appreciation for what you do and may be more conscientious about the requests they make, weeding the unnecessary ones from those that are truly critical.

It all sounds good at this point, and you're all one happy family. But you should always be prepared for problems. The worst news you ever have to deliver to your users is that their information is lost and that they will have to redo some of their work. You may also have to tell them that the system will be unavailable for an extended period. This news adds to the already frantic pace that business users sometimes operate in. In the support role, sometimes the messenger does get shot. However, if the partnership exists, then you might gain a little patience and understanding. Always prepare for the rainy day, and if it comes, work your hardest to get your users back on track. Trust me, they'll notice.

Communicate!

The key to any good partnership is the communication that exists between the partners. The more you know about each other, the better you'll be able to find that common ground that binds you. When you step back, you realize that you're all working for the same company.

Develop methods to communicate regularly. Visit the business team forums when appropriate and just act as a fly on the wall during their discussions. You'll gain a great amount of insight as you watch team members converse among themselves and interact with their managers. You'll find the natural leaders in the team and see the skills and expertise that each member brings to the team. Watch for personal styles, mannerisms, and emotive triggers. Learn the best way to communicate with your users through watching them communicate with others. Then establish opportunities to meet with the team or representatives to discuss joint efforts between your team and theirs. Let them know of your plans and the plans of the support team.

Give them insight to your activities and how the sometimes-nebulous work that you do behind the scenes actually benefits the business areas. Undoubtedly, the business team will have requests for problem fixes and process enhancements. Work collectively to understand the needs, develop good understanding of the benefits, and work together to develop specifications and a plan that will enable the solutions to work better.

Allow for impromptu communication with the business team. Without losing all of your working time, keep yourself open for the users to tell you of SAP problems they are having or to ask you questions. Take time to show them how to work through the system. It's time well spent because the more users know about SAP, the more successful they will be and the fewer problems will emerge.

Through all of this communication, be sure you can take a passive stance and truly *hear* what is being communicated to you. If you've spent the time and effort to get to know the users better, you'll be better equipped to understand the underlying needs and motives when users come to you with questions or problems. Some users have trouble expressing exactly what they want. Some may be overwhelmed with their current responsibilities and may come to you in an aggressive manner when a problem occurs. If you can work to understand what the problem is and what the consequences might be, you can show them that you understand the situation and then can share how the two of you can rectify it. This investment and interest in their needs will diffuse their anxiety and will show them you truly do hear what they are saying.

Finally, be sure you can provide good methods of communicating the status of your activities. Users are always interested in what is busying you and are frequently well served by knowing what you are up to. Especially when you are working on an issue that directly affects them or their business, regular status updates affirm that you are still working on resolutions and are conscientious enough to take the time and share your progress. Sometimes you will have no progress to report, but as long as you continue communicating, they'll know you haven't abandoned them. Good communication tools you can use here are

- Regular e-mail distributions
- Voicemail messaging
- Web pages with special project status sections
- Frequent status meetings and discussions

Helping Users Help Themselves

It's a common tenet that nobody likes to depend on others. Dependencies on others add to the anxiety about being able to complete tasks on time. Dependencies cause people to not trust their own capabilities and instincts. Overall, the result can be a less effective workforce.

Clearly, most of your support activities cannot be handled directly by the using teams—even if they had the skills, business controls and security policies will not allow it. Still, there are some activities that you do on a routine basis that the business users can accomplish themselves. What you might take for granted in your own skill set might be a true enabler to a business user. Consider sharing with the users what you know about the following tools and methods:

- **General table display.** All business users should have access to SE17 to review table information. Any user can perform this safe search, and it will enable them to review information that they may have believed was available only through the development and use of a complex ABAP program. Show them how to use criteria restrictions and sorting capabilities. Then show them how information can be printed, saved to a file for distribution, or downloaded for direct use in a spreadsheet application.

◆ **Job status overview.** Frequently, users will become familiar with the background processing activities that you manage. You make it a regular habit of reviewing the schedule overview and job logs to ensure that the processing completed as planned. Show the users how to make use of transaction SM37 so they may review job processing themselves. It's not uncommon for users to contact their support team member for verification that a job schedule completed as scheduled— users often work more confidently when they see a positive indicator of activity rather than assume "no news is good news." By enabling the users to make use of the job overview, they can review job activity themselves whenever they wish.

◆ **User parameters and user defaults.** These are settings enabled when users are assigned an SAP logon ID. You probably used a very generic template when making settings here. Show the user how they can access these two screens and make changes that best reflect their daily processing needs.

◆ **Output controller.** Users will also have access to the output controller, although it will probably be restricted to their particular logon ID. Reviewing the information presented in the output controller enables them to monitor the processing of any print requests they have made within SAP.

These tools might be somewhat simplistic, but they are effective, and they put the power of reviewing basic information in the hands of the users. By promoting this activity, you can achieve several things. First, users are more able to provide for themselves in terms of daily information review or regular management of the specific parameters of their SAP sessions. They learn more about the information in SAP— where it is stored, how it is stored, and how it is interrelated to other information within the system. Second, access to and knowledge of this sort of information enables the users to do more for themselves and reduce some of their dependence upon you. Rather than having to call you for relatively simple matters, they can get what they need right away, which eliminates delays and also frees you up for more pressing matters. Third, this kind of activity promotes user self-confidence. Most users tend to understand that data goes into the system and comes out of the system, but they aren't always sure what happens to the data while it is inside of the system. You can help them understand. Achieving this sort of understanding is empowering, and it can breed further curiosity within users to understand more so that they can work more effectively.

> The whole reason I made the transition from business administration to information technology years ago is because I wanted to know what sort of magic was happening inside the system. When I discovered that a lot of it wasn't so magical after all, I wanted to share what I had learned with others. This sort of knowledge can break down the barriers to understanding that keep people anxious about how well they interact with an automated system.

Lastly, having access to SAP information and the ability to initiate small changes to your GUI becomes fun. Once you learn how to work with an application or how to better manipulate information, you actually start enjoying it. It's like a newfound freedom. It allows you to experiment and learn. Upon initial successes, users are usually driven to get even better results and will enjoy unlocking further mysteries within the system.

Engaging the User Base

Now it's useful to review what you've just learned. You've now established good healthy contact with your users, and you know the people who are working with the business processes you support. You've spent time and effort to understand their business conditions and the expectations the company has of them. At the same time, you've made the users aware of your role within the company and, more important, in helping them achieve their business goals. In addition, you've introduced some simple tools that will make users more productive and self-sufficient within SAP. Through all of this communication, you have engaged your users more actively within the SAP environment.

Engaging your users means to include them in knowledge sharing and activity planning. With a new system such as SAP, a core of experts who have a deep understanding of the system will usually emerge. Typically, this group worked the implementation effort and now supports the system. Because of their expertise, others will naturally defer to them in matters of system functionality and solution decision making. However, from a company level, information and knowledge should actively spread throughout the company, especially to the business areas, to ensure that everyone associated with the system is successful and productive. The partnering and engagement of the users is critical to the company's efforts to be as effective and profitable as possible.

When you engage the business users, you immediately demonstrate your confidence in their abilities, as well as your respect for the work that they do. Perhaps it's not as immediately glamorous as developing and implementing a leading ERP system, but what they do enables a company to continue its operation in the business world. All teams contribute to the overall wellness of the company. With that in mind, when you engage the business teams, you also hasten their familiarity with the system and help settle them into using SAP. Once you can get them comfortable and confident with the system, you both can focus on the effectiveness of the business processes. You can help them understand that SAP is sometimes confusing and overwhelming. Share your initial experiences with them as a means to show them that the system can be learned and needn't be a source of anxiety. They just need a little time, understanding, and practice.

Grooming Expert Users

Some folks enjoy working with the intricacies of a system more than others—probably the way you found your role in a support team. So when you see certain users take a more active interest in SAP and the business processes, take note. These folks will become your *expert users*.

Every good business organization should have certain team members who can provide a source of immediate reference to their business peers. Expert users are typically very skilled in business processes and policies; they will also become quite adept at using an automated system in a way that exploits business opportunities and opens new avenues for applying automated solutions. These individuals tend to be more strategically oriented—working with strategies and opportunities—rather than tactically oriented—working with established repetitive processes.

If you find a potential expert user on your business team, recognize the individual or individuals and establish them as such. The expert users should be able to fulfill the following roles:

- ◆ Internal business team source of assistance with SAP and business questions
- ◆ Likely candidate for inclusion on business enhancement teams
- ◆ Likely candidate to help train others, especially new team members

Expert users should be properly recognized by their business colleagues. Their efforts and commitment are valuable to you because expert users can filter basic user questions and provide immediate help. Even more, they are essential as you work to understand current business requirements as well as future trends in the business processes. These experts can help assure that business solutions will remain competitive and even superior to other business' methodologies.

Damage Control

As mentioned earlier, there will be times when things go wrong. Mistakes happen, and their effects will need to be reckoned with. If you've already demonstrated your commitment to serving your users, then you know you will be motivated to reverse any damages that may have occurred—either in processing efficiency, data accuracy, or partner relationships. If a problem occurs and you are the guilty one, all you can do is your best to resolve its impact.

The first thing to do is communicate the situation clearly and completely to the user team. Voice-mail messages sent to a departmental distribution list work well. Try to keep your explanation brief yet representative of what has happened. Don't belabor the details, especially those that are very technical. But be sure you communicate clearly enough so that those affected understand exactly what the problem is, how it will affect them, and what your plans are to resolve it. If you don't yet have a clear understanding of the full impact, explain that and give a time when you will follow up with more details. By all means, be sure to follow up. Everyone makes mistakes, but if you have been diligent in the development of your business partner relationships, you should be able to recover from the situation relatively unscathed, although perhaps a bit wiser.

Summary

This whole chapter has been about working with your business users in an effort to involve, educate, and empower them. It has been included in this part of the book as a subtle reminder that you need to stay in contact with your business teams, especially as you become engrossed in the technical aspects of supporting SAP. As you can see, there are many opportunities to strengthen your working relationship with the users, and the paybacks will be rich indeed. It might seem like a lot of common sense, but the reality is that many of these basic efforts go unnoticed or untried. The introduction of a new system provides an opportunity for your company to reevaluate its styles and methods. Just as the implementation team had the opportunity to rework processes that were known to be problematic and inefficient, you will also have the opportunity to rework business linkages and relationships. From the support perspective, you will probably need to reach out your hand to establish the relationship. If you do, you can quickly develop an engaged user team that will know you are working in its interests and will have confidence in you.

Here are the key support points described in this chapter:

◆ Know who your users are and how they might be expanding or changing as the SAP system becomes more settled in your company.

◆ Reach out to your users to establish a partnership that fosters understanding of their needs as well as yours.

◆ Be sure you have open lines of communication that are easy to use and consistent.

◆ Introduce the users to some of the basic tools of SAP that will allow them to gain access to information that helps them perform their jobs.

◆ Develop expert users within the business team whenever possible.

◆ Respond quickly, concisely, and honestly when problems arise.

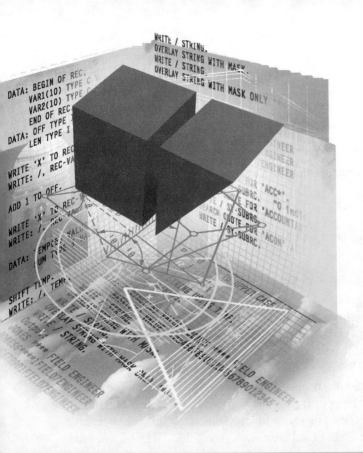

Chapter 23

Disaster Recovery Planning (DRP)

In This Chapter

- ◆ Developing a Disaster Recovery Plan
- ◆ The SAP Instance Structure and DRP Readiness
- ◆ SAP System Backups
- ◆ Backup Retention
- ◆ Locating the DRP Instance and the System Backup Storage
- ◆ Rehearsing the Plan

No one likes to think about the issue of disaster recovery. Few people even believe in the eventuality of a disaster that could truly affect business for more than a couple of days. Some people even jokingly contend that if a disaster were to truly occur, their business infrastructure might be the last thing on their minds. But it's not nuclear warfare we're discussing here. Disaster Recovery Planning (DRP) concerns itself with any extended breaks in business service and overall system environment disruption or corruption. This situation could mean a major hardware failure, breaks in communications links, or any manner of supporting hardware interruptions. Think of it in this manner, and you begin to see the possibility for such situations. Of course, earthquakes, floods, and any other acts of God are always possibilities. Regardless of the cause of the disruption, your organization must be prepared to react in a manner that will maintain business activity.

This chapter discusses the content and need for a usable DRP method. Much like an audit, DRP is a reality that every support organization needs to understand and provide for. In fact, your DRP readiness is a major audit concern. Auditors will investigate to see whether you can respond in times of unexpected emergencies, how well you can preserve the business flow and integrity, and how well you can regain normal operations. To handle a disruption, you need a plan. This chapter looks at some of the basic DRP elements and helps you assemble your plan for emergency response.

First, you will develop your DRP plan by looking at your SAP system backup strategy. This strategy is one of the key components that will govern your responsiveness. You'll discover some pointers on how often and where you should conduct backups. Where you stage your DRP readiness is critical to your relative success of responding to a disastrous situation.

Then the discussion continues with an examination of the timetable that should be enabled for DRP action. How bad is a bad situation, and how long should you wait before executing a DRP recovery? Surprisingly, just as some people don't put much stock in the eventuality of a disaster happening, some also don't know how to recognize one when it's occurring. Here, you'll get some key points to look for to determine whether you have experienced a disaster that requires DRP tactics.

You'll also learn how to gauge your DRP readiness. Every good plan needs to be tested. Just as the implementation team worked hard to ensure that their designs would support the business, you will need to conduct similar testing to ensure that your DRP approach is feasible and complete. It's practically a fire drill. You'll see what environment settings you should simulate to properly test your plan.

Developing a Disaster Recovery Plan

What exactly makes a good disaster recovery plan? Well, first you should be clear on what constitutes a disaster. A *disaster* can be any event that prevents access to or usage of a company's business processes or information technology tools. This condition can include restricted access to a business site—as a result of fire, earthquakes, floods, and so on—or a loss of power or communications. If any situation arises that prevents the normal business flow or restricts critical informational processing or storage, you may need to respond with a viable DRP.

Every business should have a DRP. It can range from simply backing up files to disks and storing them in a bank vault—for very small-scale operations—to establishing temporary working headquarters that are fully capable of continuing a business's activities—usually for a large-scale corporation. Whatever the size of the business, it needs a workable recovery plan. Developing a DRP can occur only if and when the need is properly prioritized within a business's organizational structure. The company's controller and top business managers usually drive DRP development. The plan's development must include full and active participation from the business's senior management, acting as the final point of plan review and approval, plus representatives from the various business areas, property management team, communications and hardware support team, and the information technology (support) team. As stated, no one expects a disaster to occur, but if one does, you'll want to be ready. Therefore, your plan should provide clear answers and logical actions:

◆ Identify business systems, applications, and processes that are critical to business activity

◆ Identify geographic location of business-critical tools (hardware, communications)

◆ Identify situational triggers that will cause a DRP response in times of business interruption

◆ Identify critical teams that will be fully trained and can react appropriately to a DRP situation

◆ Identify communication methods to keep the business users informed of the disaster recovery and expectations for resuming business activity.

◆ Identify methods and measures to resume normal business activity, including alternative processing and functionality

Identifying the Critical Elements

The first component of any DRP is the clear identification of all of the business's systems, applications, and processes, and the criticality of each to the business activity. Within this topic, you should classify each of your business systems, applications, and processes as one of the following:

◆ **Mission critical.** This category is the highest level of importance to the company and could include the fulfillment of critical customer orders or satisfying legal and contractual requirements. An element in this category will probably require some sort of DRP action usually within a period of less than 24 hours.

◆ **Business competency.** This sort of element is usually not immediately critical to the overall business well-being but could have impact on processing competency, consistency, customer satisfaction, and less-critical commitments. This sort of element can usually be affected for a few days before DRP action is required.

◆ **Nominal need.** This category is a lower-effect element. It is typically of least consequence to daily business activity, such as statistical review, reporting, and any other automated process that can be handled manually.

Identifying the Geographic Location of Tools

Of course, you'll need to clearly define the location of the tools that are supporting your company's critical processes. These tools include your information servers (the SAP instance, for example), your central communication hubs, and even geographically-dispersed business teams that are responsible for the fulfillment of high-importance activity. This point may sound a bit obvious, and hopefully it is. However, you might find situations where hardware servers are managed in ad hoc ways and might be running some extremely important processes or housing very critical information. Be sure you can account for all critical hardware by tracing exactly where the high-visibility processes and information services are managed.

Identifying the Disaster Recovery Timetable

The next thing a DRP requires is the identification of business tolerance for interruptions. Interruptions of some sort will always occur at your company—system and process upgrades, planned maintenance downtime, and (hopefully) infrequent system crashes or aborts of some sort. Some interruptions are normal and can be planned for. These occasional interruptions can be recovered within a very short time. But how long does a business wait through a widespread interruption before it realizes business is being affected?

In this step, consider the matter of timing in developing your DRP. Your plan should begin by identifying how long the business can withstand interruption before the impact is unacceptable or potentially intolerable. This time window can only be identified at the company level because each business provides different products or services that entail their own unique levels of interruption tolerance. However, the timing issue needs to be fully understood and agreed to by top management. From this point, your plan can include steps to take to maintain business activity until the environment can be returned to normal. For example, what would the business require as far as resources or information to keep an active flow and completion of business commitments in a 2-day interruption? Then extend that period to 5 days, then 7, then 10, and so on. The longer the interruption exists, the more significant the recovery steps and alternative processes will become. Therefore, your plan should include how long a process can be interrupted over a consecutive number of hours or days before alternative methods (backup systems, manual processing) should be enacted. Be sure you can identify this parameter for each of your critical and required systems and processes.

Identifying the Recovery Team

You've developed an understanding of what constitutes a DRP response, what systems and processes are most critical, and when to enact a DRP action. Now you need to specify who is responsible for identifying the disaster and responding to it. Your recovery team should include the following members:

- ◆ Disaster recovery manager or leader
- ◆ Disaster recovery team members—each able to represent the critical business areas and processes potentially affected (possibly in geographically-dispersed regions)
- ◆ Hardware support technicians
- ◆ Communication support technicians
- ◆ Business area representatives—responsible for verifying that DRP measures are successful

The overall goal of the disaster recovery team is to recognize and assess potentially disastrous situations. It will need to review interruptions, assess their sustained impact, and recognize the need for DRP measures. The team should be relatively lean in membership but large enough to properly represent the potential impact of a disaster. You may choose to construct your plan to call for progressive team involvement as the potential for a disaster grows. But the last thing you'll want is a large, disorganized team that isn't clear on the role of each member. In a disaster, there can only be one true leader.

Identifying the Response Method

This step requires the active involvement of each business area as you identify the different elements of criticality. Your DRP plan must include exactly what resources need to be in place at varying times of disaster. For example, if a team is without system access after 24 hours, it may need to begin working in a manual method—responding to customer orders, for example, with predetermined forms or templates. If the disruption continues, local servers may need to be enabled and loaded with software to keep a team working at a near-normal pace. Only the business team can assess the various impact points and determine which facilities it will need to maintain its business response. Be sure you can clearly determine the needs of each business area in regard to the following:

◆ Work space
◆ Power and connectivity
◆ Tools (PCs, phones, fax machines, printers, and so on)
◆ Applications (including alternative short-term applications)
◆ Process procedures (manual alternatives)

Approval

Your plan needs to be fully reviewed by the company controller and senior management. They should be the driving motivation behind the need for the plan. Therefore, they must understand the DRP steps you propose and assess the plan's ability to satisfy business needs in the time of a disaster.

The SAP Instance Structure and DRP Readiness

Now that you know what the DRP should include, consider again your SAP environment. It is where your instance strategy is of most importance. If you didn't take note before, now is the time to fully understand why it was suggested to maintain the instance landscape that was first introduced to you during the discussions about the implementation effort, and later during the transition period. Figure 23-1 shows the preferred instance landscape.

The Disaster Recovery instance is highlighted in this version of the illustration. This well-maintained and well-protected instance will actually become your *hot swap* instance if the disaster involves the disablement or total corruption of your Live Business instance. Consider the situation where your hardware fails and cannot be recovered for more than a week. If you've been faithful to your DRP instance, you can quickly migrate business usage to the Disaster Recovery instance. The information shown in Figure 23-2 reinforces the need for a DRP instance refresh strategy, ensuring the DRP instance is always in sync with the Live Business instance.

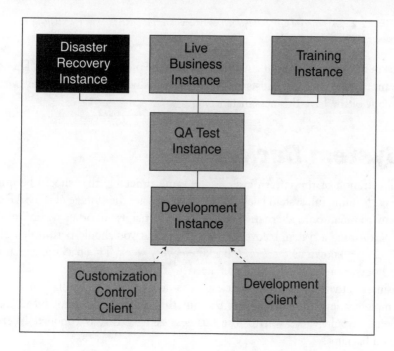

FIGURE 23-1 *This preferred SAP instance landscape provides for DRP readiness.*

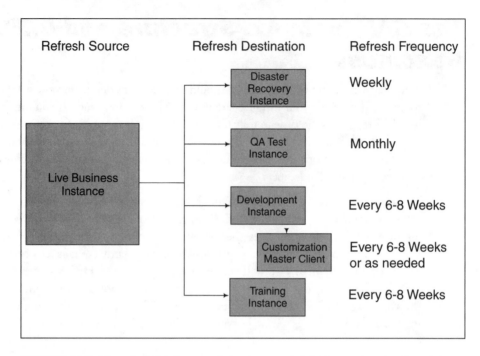

FIGURE 23-2 *The preferred SAP instance refresh cycle ensures the DRP instance is continually ready for use in the event of a disaster.*

Because a disaster can strike at any time, you must be prepared at all times. Therefore, you want to keep your DRP instance *hot* by continually keeping it refreshed with the latest copy of the Live Business instance.

SAP System Backups

The illustration of the refresh cycle is the same timetable that should be utilized when performing full system backups. The backups are the storage of the SAP database environment onto alternative media for potential use in other system refreshes or in performing a system recovery. You can see that you should perform a full system backup—known as the *level 0* backup—every week. This backup, which takes many hours, is necessary if you ever need to recover and restore a week's worth of business activity. Because this backup does take so long, it is usually not feasible to complete a level 0 backup everyday. But this schedule does not mean that an emergency would cause you to lose business activity that is conducted between weekend backups.

SAP is enabled with what is known as a *logical-log file*—also termed a *level 1* back-up—that captures daily business transactions and activity within the system. These logical-log files can fill up quickly, yet SAP provides methods to store the file contents to another media to achieve the essence of smaller backups. In the event of a system restore, the level 0 backup can be applied first; then each logical-log (level 1) backup can be applied, restoring your environment to the state it was in prior to becoming unavailable. Nevertheless, data loss could occur if any of the backups are corrupt or if any business activity takes place after the most recent backup and the beginning of the problem. Hardware administrators and the Basis Administrator typically manage SAP backups.

Backup Retention

A question that bears consideration is how long you should keep your backup tapes. You might think it's only necessary to keep a backup tape until a new one is created. By this method, your storage is minimal, and you would achieve a regular, rolling method of maintaining a backup of your SAP environment. However, just as it's always possible for an unexpected event to strike your SAP system, it's just as possible for a problem to occur with any of your backup tapes.

> It's common to use backup tapes to restore testing and training instances. Unfortunately, I've seen situations where the backups used to restore the information were actually corrupt; a good backup did not exist for that period of time. Further investigation revealed that there was a recurring problem with the backup execution, and several weeks of backups were corrupt and unusable. As you can imagine, this situation can leave a business extremely exposed if a recovery is ever needed.

It is necessary to establish a retention period for your system backups. Consider the following recommendations:

◆ **Level 0 backups: 26 to 52 weeks.** These are your critical backups, and you'll need to ensure you can recover any period of time necessary to restore a working environment. Besides their use for system recovery, these backups can also be instrumental in investigations that concern shifts in business activity that might relate to inappropriate data management methods within the automated processes. Level 0 backups can be restored to test systems from any time period to conduct further investigations that reflect the system status at any questionable moment.

◆ **Level 1 backups: 7 to 14 days.** You do not have to keep the daily logical-log file backups for extended periods. Each level 0 iteration recaptures this information.

Locating the DRP Instance and the System Backup Storage

Your choice when locating your DRP instance and the storage of your backup tapes is of utmost importance. For example, if you keep the DRP instance and the Live Business instance in the same data center and a disaster strikes that building, then, technically speaking, you'd be *hosed*.

Disaster recovery resources should always be reasonably dislocated geographically. You might want to consider locating your DRP instance and your Live Business instance in different states. Because natural disasters typically strike within a geographic region, you want to be sure that a single weather event does not affect both machines. The same holds true for your backup storage. Locate it in some offsite location to preserve its safety and security. Many companies do nothing more than manage offsite retention services for your critical backup media.

Rehearsing the Plan

When your plan is complete and all considerations have been addressed, it's time for the test. Until you've exhaustively tested your DRP, it's really only an unproven theory. You will need to develop a test scenario that can virtually simulate the events of an actual emergency or disaster.

If you have an SAP instance landscape like the one previously shown, the largest component is already in place—the DRP instance. Because SAP is the point of concentration in this text, it is the environment that must be available and immediately usable. But SAP is only one component of your test. You will need to work with the disaster recovery team to conduct your DRP rehearsal. The first task of the team is to develop your scenario of disaster simulation. Although you don't have to actually deconstruct your working business environment, your DRP instance allows you to conduct your rehearsal parallel to the unaffected Live Business environment. Your test could include the following exercises:

◆ Stopping and restarting your DRP instance.

♦ Applying the last level 0 and any incremental level 1 backups to the DRP instance; this exercise includes verification of the backup process to ensure that the backup media is free from corruption.

♦ Restoring UNIX communications used by your SAP environment (scripts, config files, data directories, and so on).

♦ Monitoring the turnaround time of the restores to SAP and rebuilding of the UNIX environment.

♦ Staging and monitoring the contact and response time if network communications need to be reestablished.

♦ Verifying the online SAP business information.

♦ Simulating business activity in the restored system by executing job schedules, reporting, and interactive business transactions.

You should plan to conduct this sort of DRP rehearsal every 8 to 12 months. Your organization might require this activity more frequently or less frequently. However, consider more frequent testing if your rehearsal did not yield the desired results or if significant change has occurred in the DRP team membership.

Maintaining Your DRP

Of course, a DRP is not something you develop once. Much like the support environment, your DRP needs to change and grow as your business environment and technical infrastructure undergoes modifications. The DRP is a documented and reviewable action plan. Your DRP needs to be revised to reflect any new environment elements and the additional steps to take if recovery is required.

As new modules are enabled, they are deserving of DRP measures. The disaster recovery team, lead by the disaster recovery leader, needs to monitor the business and technical environment for significant change. While your company is undergoing the SAP transformation, you might want to review DRP readiness on a six-month interval. Of course, the ultimate choice will be up to your company's leaders.

Summary

In this chapter, you've examined the need for a strong DRP for your business. This important element sometimes gets forgotten during the excitement and newness of the SAP experience. However, it is possible that your business is at more risk initially during the early stages of SAP operation than after the system has stabilized. So much of the system is new, and the backup strategy and recovery methods might be significantly different from those of a previous legacy environment. Be sure to give this very important aspect of your new environment the attention it truly deserves. It's really a case of "pay me now, or pay me later." I think you'll find that it's preferable to pay up front.

Here are the major support topics covered in this chapter:

- ◆ The development of a DRP should be initiated at the highest levels of company management.
- ◆ Your DRP should include a clear description of which systems and processes are mission critical and their thresholds of disruption tolerance
- ◆ A DRP should be constructed and managed by a dedicated disaster recovery team.
- ◆ Your SAP instance should be equipped with a regularly refreshed *hot* instance that could be used in the event of a disaster.
- ◆ Your team should have a reliable and regular SAP backup and s torage method.
- ◆ Your DRP should be rehearsed as directed or as needed to ensure that it works.

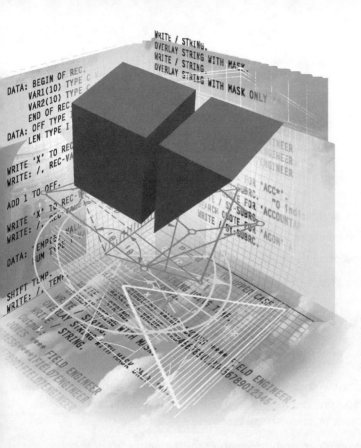

Chapter 24

Archiving SAP
Data

In This Chapter

- ◆ Why Archive?
- ◆ Developing Your Archiving Strategy
- ◆ SAP Archiving Tools
- ◆ Additional Archiving Considerations
- ◆ Third-Party Archiving Solutions
- ◆ Determining the Appropriate Elegance of Archiving

Somewhat akin to the topics of disaster recovery and audit preparedness is the issue of archiving. When you approach archiving, you are approaching more than just the issue of removing information from your database. You are also approaching the issue of information availability and usability. This subject involves matters of business standards, legal requirements, and of course, storage costs. Your business can generate thousands upon thousands of records and transactions every year. Practically everyone who works in a business will need to refer to historical information, but a time comes when the information repository you are sorting through is so cumbersome that the information in your business system devalues.

Archiving is sometimes seen as an opportunistic venture for businesses when they decide they should enforce data retention requirements and business management obligations. However, with SAP, archiving is an issue that rears its head quickly and requires a thorough investigation and plan sooner than some might expect. Therefore, this chapter presents you with an overview of what goes into an archiving plan's development in relationship to the SAP environment.

This chapter starts by answering the obvious question: Why archive? You will learn about some of the trials and tribulations you might experience if you are not preparing for regular archiving activity. It can creep up on you in the form of poor system performance, high data storage costs, and increased overhead required to manage a fast-growing information repository.

The next topic is the timing of your archiving activity. You should be thinking about what your online data storage threshold might be and how to know when you're approaching it. Rather than waiting for performance degradation, you can look at some key areas within SAP to determine your system's archiving needs. Oddly, even with the adverse affects of not actively archiving, you'll probably find that it's difficult to rally support for archiving efforts. Archiving is a subject that never gets the appropriate attention until something drastically goes wrong.

Then you consider what to archive. Getting an answer to this delicate question might be the step that will require the most effort from you and your team. Again, knowing the integration factor within SAP, you can surmise that data archiving must be conducted carefully to ensure that information remains consistent within the system. Developing a strategic archiving plan that works from a data storage standpoint—and without compromising the information value within SAP—requires coordinated efforts from the support team and the business teams. The complementary discussion includes determining how *elegant* your archiving method is and what sort of retrieval and off-system review capabilities will be necessary. Archived data is useful only if it can be retrieved and reviewed. The issue to deal with here involves determining what potential needs the business could have for the archived information and to what degree the information needs to be searchable.

The chapter ends with an overview of SAP's Archive Development Kit (ADK). You'll learn about some of the basic archiving functionality within SAP, which should provide a starting ground for your archiving investigation and planning.

Why Archive?

The information that your company keeps online is of great importance. However, there comes a time when stored information is no longer accessed or has become obsolete. In these situations, the information becomes a burden. Excessive data storage can have unnecessary and even adverse affects on your daily business operation. Consider, then, the following key reasons to archive:

- ◆ To retain a manageable environment
- ◆ To reduce the consumption of disk storage space
- ◆ To improve system performance
- ◆ To simplify and speed up information query results
- ◆ To protect historical information from accidental corruption or loss
- ◆ To comply with general business requirements according to legal stipulation, record-keeping standards, and potential reuse of business data (for example, numbering schemes)

Information archiving is one of the basic tenets of business management. Information must be stored in ways that are appropriate to its usefulness. A good business operation will maintain an environment in which the right data is available in the right way at the right time. Archived information is usually more difficult to access, but the infrequency of need supports the delay in availability.

Developing Your Archiving Strategy

To develop a good archiving strategy, consider each of the following key points, which will be discussed in further detail throughout the chapter:

◆ What to archive

◆ When to archive

◆ Understanding business requirements for archiving

What to Archive

You will have two different archiving classes (methods) in your SAP environment:

◆ **Database-specific archiving.** Concerns issues of reducing database storage volume with a focus on storage capacity, storage cost, and access efficiency.

◆ **Application-specific archiving.** Concerns issues of storing business information and transaction records for historical, legal, and usability purposes.

Database-specific archiving activity is usually driven by the Basis Administrator or infrastructure support subteam. They will be monitoring information tables, files, and directories for consistent low usage and will investigate whether an archiving eventis suitable. Their role, after all, is to maintain a good working environment. Application-specific archiving activity is driven by the business areas. They should determine how long business information must remain active on SAP and at what point data can be archived to a secondary storage location or medium. Each business area will probably have unique requirements for data availability, and you should expect each archive specification to differ somewhat in scope or timing.

When to Archive

Timing is the most interesting aspect of an archiving plan. Consider that you are in the realm of SAP's integrated business information architecture. Because so much of the information works together, you need to ensure that you maintain the logical linkages to avoid breaking the data chain.

For example, if you determine that you should keep purchase order information for a period of 12 months and the inventory team determines that material document information needs to be kept for only 6 months, you have a potential collision. Review of a purchase order includes the availability of related material receipts. If the material documents have been removed from the system, there will be a hole in your purchase order data. To assure that no business area will be inadvertently deprived of necessary information, archiving timetables must be developed in an integrated manner. The best suggestion here is to work with all archive requirements, find the overlapping linkages, and choose the longest retention time as a basis for archiving activity.

Understanding Business Requirements for Archiving

In order to begin your archiving detailed planning, you'll need to start with the business requirements. Archiving goes hand in hand with retention schedules. These are the conditions that dictate how long business information must be kept available in any form. Just as you must keep your tax returns for a minimum of seven years, the business areas will need to retain proof of business activities for a certain period of time, usually dictated by law. But retention requirements differ from archiving requirements in that archiving typically refers to electronic storage and retrieval means. Retention comes into play after the archive period has expired, but the retention period has not. Sometimes, the storage method will be the same. However, with such rampant changes in technology, records that have been archived and retained over the past 10 years have probably been managed through a variety of different media types. Whatever the situation, you'll want to work directly with representatives of the business teams to

- Identify the business data and business documents that are to be managed by archiving and retention policies
- Identify the business archiving period for online information availability
- Identify the hand-off method when archiving expires and retention comes into play

From a technical standpoint, you'll want to translate these requirements into an archive plan. Try not to overwhelm the business area representatives with the technical details of archiving. The key deliverable to you is the understandable data archiving requirement. But be sure you reach an agreement with the business area regarding how long-term retention will be managed. This plan includes possibly transferring archived information to a different media for long-term storage and a method to properly destroy records after the retention period has expired. In most cases, the proper and timely destruction of information is as important as the proper archiving of it.

SAP Archiving Tools

SAP's archiving tools enable a business to set up an archiving program that is suited to the type of information that is being managed. For example, some information needs to be captured and collected in a meaningful way so that it can be retrieved and reviewed later. Some information can stand alone, being useful when viewed in a singular fashion. Other information is not needed in any long-term review manner. That data can be deleted immediately without any backup or archiving activity. Whatever the need, SAP provides a methodology to assist you and your team to manage your online information.

SAP Archive Overview

As you should now understand, SAP contains both master data—the permanent information that helps operate your business—and transactional data—information about business events within the system that could be more temporary in nature. The role of the archive process in SAP is to deliver a method by which superfluous information—aged transactional data or flagged master data—can be removed from the system. In the case of unneeded master data, the process can be as simple as deleting the records and reorganizing the data tables. On the other hand, transactional data, which records your business activity, must be captured in a manner that will preserve its meaning and integrity, removed from the database, and stored in a holding area for possible review later. SAP has developed a tool set that supports this clean up and storage activity.

Each business application area has defined parameters that allow information to be copied from the active database to an archive file. Then, upon validation of the successful archive event, the original objects are deleted from the database tables. This activity is usually managed with background processing. The archiving activity is quite customizable, allowing you the control you desire over the archiving events.

After information is successfully written to an archive file, you may choose to leave it in a designated file structure, direct it to another storage media, or pass it to another tool called *ArchiveLink*.

ArchiveLink—Links SAP to optical archiving systems for the recognition and manipulation of optically archived items such as drawings, business documents, or output lists. ArchiveLink is covered in more detail later in this chapter.

Archiving Authorization

As with most other SAP functionality, access to archiving functionality is restricted. To prevent unauthorized activities, SAP archiving processes require the presence of the S_ARCHIVE authorization object. Users will be denied access to the archive functionality if the S_ARCHIVE object is not present in their authorization profile. Within the object, you can control the level of access to the archive tools, which include writing archive files, deleting archived data, reading archive files, and reloading archived data. Access may be controlled to allow complete capabilities, only change capabilities, or only display capabilities, much like many other authorization fields within SAP. Also note that archiving activity is client independent. As you enter the archiving management screens, SAP displays a pop-up warning stating this fact.

Archive Objects

The archiving tool set begins with the archive objects. Archiving in SAP is an *object-oriented* activity. In other words, objects are identified within SAP that will consist of hooks to various database tables in a logical manner. For example, within each object—in this case, one that is to be used for the archiving of purchasing documents—the archive object will be defined and constructed to reference the different tables that contain information that make up the header and detail information you'd find when reviewing a purchasing document. This approach supports the concept of relational table structures and the use of key data elements. In this way, the archiving object, sometimes referred to as an archiving *handle*, enables you to lift relational data out of SAP and store it in a way that will provide a complete representation of the information that has been archived—in this example, a purchasing document. To access the archive objects, use the menu path Tools, Administration, Administration, Archiving or use the transaction code SARA(Figure 24-1).

The pull-down arrow provides a view of some of the standard SAP archive objects. The archive object is customized to refer to the various tables that are to be accessed when creating the logical gathering of information to be archived. The archive object is the handle that represents all of the tables that support the application information to be archived. To give you an example, look at the following listing of tables associated with the MM_EKKO archive object:

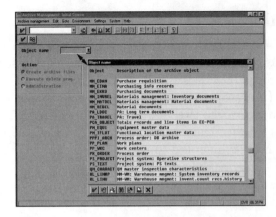

FIGURE 24-1

Archive Management: Initial Screen

Table	Table description
EKKO	Purchasing document, header
EKPO	Purchasing document, items
EKKO	Purchasing document, header
EKPO	Purchasing document, items
EKPV	Purchasing document, shipping data
EKBE	Purchasing document, history
EKBZ	Purchasing document, delivery costs history
EKAB	Release (order) documentation
EKKN	Purchasing document, account assignments
EKET	Schedule lines
EKES	Confirmations
EKAN	Addresses for once-only vendors
EKUB	Index, stock transport order
KONV	Document conditions
KONH	Master conditions, header
KONP	Master conditions, items
KONM	Master conditions, quantity scale
KONW	Master conditions, value scale
A016	Master conditions, outline agreement, items
A019	Master conditions, outline agreement, header
A068	Master conditions, outline agreement, plant conditions
EKPA	Partner roles
RESB	Reservations
SADR	Delivery addresses
NAST	Message records
EIKP	Import data, header
EIPO	Import data, items

As you can see, an archive file with object representation contained in these related SAP tables would provide a usable representation of the original business transaction.

Archive objects are also customizable. Customization here lets you specify the parameters and procedures to be used when the archive object is executed. You can even create and customize your own archive objects for any specific needs or tables you may have implemented within your company-specific SAP environment. The following table contains the useful transaction codes for managing SAP archive objects.

Tcode	Tcode Description
SAR1	Structure of an archive object
SAR2	Definition of an archive object
SAR3	Archiving: Customizing
SAR4	Definition of the archive classes
SAR5	Assignment of archive classes
SAR6	Archive events: Generation program
SARA	Archive management

Archive Management

Archive management allows you to schedule the archiving activities of each defined object. Each archive object is defined for use with an actual archive program written in ABAP. SAP provides standard programs to manage these activities. Within archive management, you define how you want your archive object to be controlled, how often you want it executed, and how to direct statistical results of your archiving event. Using transaction SARA, you will specify your archive object, then specify the parameters for archiving events and spool output (Figure 24-2).

As you can see, the look and feel of the archive management functionality is very similar to the look and feel of the SAP job scheduler. Once an archiving event is complete, you can perform an archiving event overview (similar to a job overview) that provides statistics on the completion of the archiving event.

Archive Development Kit (ADK)

Built into the archiving methodology is the identification and inclusion of important archive identifiers. These identifiers capture information about the environment and structure in which the data once resided as well as the archiving method used during the creation of the archive file. This umbrella approach used with SAP's archive tools is referred to as the *Archive Development Kit (ADK)*. Within SAP, the ADK works as

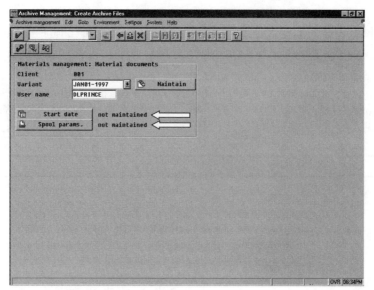

FIGURE 24-2

Transaction SARA lets you schedule archiving event parameters.

an interpreter that can communicate and operate a handshake (linkage) between the application areas in which SAP data is found and the eventual archive file where it is deposited. The ADK's job is to capture the hardware-dependent information about the archived file, which identifies the structure and storage method of the information when it is later retrieved, possibly within a different hardware environment.

ArchiveLink

ArchiveLink is an interface that archives and retrieves optically archived objects from within the R/3 application. This feature supports the direct access and use of archived documents, lists, and so on from within the various SAP business applications. ArchiveLink's user interface gives the business areas direct access to important business documents by linking to a program that displays the optically archived document. ArchiveLink maintains the linkages between the SAP business module objects and the archived elements, including linkages to helper programs that provide the proper viewing of the archived document.

ArchiveLink can be enabled through the customization of archive objects. With this, you can automatically hand off archived information to the interface at the time of the archive event. You can also move information to ArchiveLink manually as well.

Additional Archiving Considerations

You should, by now, have a fully defined plan for archiving information from your SAP instance. You should have a clear specification about what, when, and how you need to archive. But in addition to those elements, you should also consider some alternatives to archiving. First, consider whether you are archiving because of database constraints, but at the cost of truly needed information. If the archive schedule hinders access to information that is relatively active and regularly used by the business teams, you might be better off increasing your database storage capacity. It's very easy from a technical standpoint to arbitrarily determine that three or six months of data "should be plenty." However, if you're failing to truly understand a real business need, then the archiving actions will create more problems than solutions. Hence the participation of business teams in developing the archiving plan is extremely important. Likewise, when you consider performance, it might be necessary to upgrade your server hardware.

Another archive-related consideration is to recognize that the archiving process leaves gaps in the tables, but the index indicators still exist. To get the most from the archiving/delete effort, reorganize and reindex tables to ensure that future table use and access will be optimal.

Third-Party Archiving Solutions

Archiving is something of a commitment, and businesses are shy to use the first archive tool that becomes available—including SAP's integrated ADK. Because of this uncertainty, several non-SAP vendors—including iXOS (actually in a partnership with SAP to develop and deliver archive solutions), Filenet, and Documentum—are offering other solutions to the archiving dilemma.

The merits of each of these alternate solutions cannot be fully discussed here (and they are only a small representation of the different alternate solutions available). You should conduct your own careful assessment of the archiving solutions and options available and choose the one that can meet your company's unique archiving needs.

Determining the Appropriate Elegance of Archiving

Elegance will become a key factor in your archive strategy development. Simply put, you need to determine exactly which data you require and by what method you need to retrieve it in the future. Your archiving plan should be a matter of true need. In other words, it would be inappropriate to enable the very best, cutting-edge archive environment if archive retrieval activity is negligible or very simple at your company. The point is, be sure that your archive solution meets the true needs of the business. You won't get extra points for delivering an overengineered solution. Chances are it will cost your organization more than you could possibly recover from its use.

> So here's the real story from the man on the streets: I am not aware of any significant developments or experiences with SAP archiving in the industry at large. That's not to say that all SAP-enabled companies are not archiving. Rather, I've been astounded at how many professionals have not yet exercised a regular archiving process. I'm frequently asked the question, "Are you guys archiving yet?" I'm not sure why this is, and I cannot even share experiences of my own with a regular archiving effort.
>
> But I have seen a sharp rise in the concern over archiving issues, especially as company servers quickly fill disks of information that needs to be managed. I think that archiving is an area of general business management that needs to return to basics. Starting with company or corporate objectives and mandates, archiving and retention strategies need to be completely revisited and revised before significant archiving activity can commence with confidence.

Summary

The need to clearly understand archiving and retention strategies is increasing, and businesses need to conduct significant up-front work to properly address the archiving issue. No matter how many tools and methods are offered, no confident work can begin with archiving until the ultimate need is clearly stated and understood by all involved.

Following are the key support points discussed in this chapter:

- An archiving strategy must exist before any data displacement activity can begin.
- The support team should be deeply involved in understanding the *exact* business requirements for archiving, including what to archive, when to archive, how to archive, and how long to maintain what has been archived.
- Be sure that your archiving strategy properly reflects the business's archiving needs; don't overdesign an archive methodology.

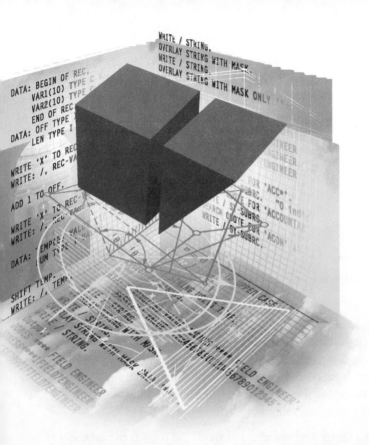

Chapter 25

Documenting for Support

In This Chapter

- ◆ Why Document?
- ◆ Types of Documentation
- ◆ Establishing a Documentation Habit
- ◆ Documenting Code
- ◆ Documenting Business Rationale and Alternatives
- ◆ Creating and Maintaining the Support Reference Guide
- ◆ Document Storage, Reference, and Sharing Techniques
- ◆ Measuring Successful Documentation

The merits of documentation have been expounded throughout this text. With about every point of discussion, there has been reference to some sort of supporting documentation that should be completed. Essentially, you are making history—if only from the standpoint of your business activity—through your actions. What you learn, what you do, and what you implement should be properly documented to ensure that others will understand the reasoning and motivation behind your actions.

If you have ever worked with a legacy environment and were hard pressed to find the original and complete support documentation, you know the frustration of painstakingly retracing the steps of your predecessors. When you consider an SAP implementation and the eventual support of the SAP environment, the reasons for providing good documentation should be glaringly clear. Take this opportunity to leave a superior and completely reliable documentation trail.

Documentation is valuable not only to others—teammates, business analysts, successors—but also to you. Depending on your particular SAP support responsibility, it can practically be guaranteed that some of the things you do will be quickly forgotten. In my years of SAP experience, I've worked with some great developers, yet even they sometimes have trouble remembering the exact location of some menu or where to make tiny system settings. Clear documentation can help you master SAP's vast size and scope.

Why Document?

It's true—documentation is not only difficult to write, but it's difficult to write well. How can you possibly capture everything you know about a program or process that would really make it useful information. Besides, you already know the ins and outs of the solution, so why document what you already understand?

First and foremost , you should learn that documentation is a source of freedom. If you don't document what you know and do in your daily support duties, then how can you ever pass those duties along to another person or even take time away from the office without receiving calls? If you don't have a clean method for others to follow what you have done, how can you ever be free from it? Eventually, you will want to move to other job opportunities, and, as experience shows, full job duty documentation and knowledge transfer are key prerequisites that must be fulfilled.

Without these, you might eliminate your own chance for cross-training and advancement. To improve your cross-functional knowledge is to build your worth to the organization. But if you can't cleanly depart from one area of support because you haven't prepared adequate documentation to ensure the success of your followers, then you are only denying yourself.

> On the day that this is being written, a support team peer was overheard lamenting the need for documentation. "I hate documentation," he said. "It's boring, and no one uses it." It's funny because just two days earlier he received support responsibility for a business solution that was new to him. One of his early remarks during the support handoff was, "Where's your documentation so I'll know what to do with this?"

From the perspective of your company, documentation is important because it preserves environment knowledge and understanding. An organization is at tremendous risk if it cannot easily replace an individual who may depart unexpectedly. These knowledge silos (recall that term?) put the continuous business flow at risk. Any individual who wishes to identify him- or herself as the only one who knows about a program or process is a danger to the organization. The SAP market is hungry for experienced individuals. It is easy for an individual to be lured away from a company by a competitor who desperately needs that individual's knowledge and expertise. In business, there is sometimes no loyalty. Your team must reduce the risk of knowledge silos by requiring full documentation for all solutions in the automated environment. Good documentation can also serve as a reference for other company sites or entities. Your good efforts can be put to immediate use at sister divisions or branches to assist in their maintenance of an SAP environment. Your company won't have to invest the same amount of time and resources as it did for the initial implementation and stabilization if its own documentation can jump start the process at a fledgling site. You'll be surprised at how quickly the same achievements can be realized.

And because it is such a recurring concern to any business or technical team, you must prove your audit readiness to internal and external firms. They will be grading your team on its demonstrated business controls and proof of knowledge retention. Anything less can jeopardize the quality and consistency of a product or service that a company provides. These audit report cards are shared with your top management and the industry at large. Good current documentation and good documentation habits will prove that your company's interest in its resident knowledge is protected and that customer satisfaction will not be compromised.

Finally, following on the heels of the audit topic, there is the more recent need and desire for companies to become ISO certified. ISO is a set of quality standards developed by the International Organization of Standards in Geneva, Switzerland. These quality standards, known as ISO 9000, were developed to ensure consistent adherence to common quality practices for manufacturers and service providers across the globe.

To some companies and customers, ISO certification is a stringent requirement before any business agreements can be reached. ISO standards are based on the ability to perform business activity in a standardized and repeatable manner that will assure consistent levels of quality in a company's products. A key element for certification is controlled documentation to ensure the adherence to the standards set forth.

Types of Documentation

This book has introduced many different documents, templates, and forms. Each item supports a building block approach to the long-term support of your SAP environment. Each new document, or iteration of a previous document, leverages heavily from previous efforts, reducing the need to recreate or reestablish information and avoiding the costs associated with recreating what already exists.

The documentation evolved as the SAP life cycle progressed and should provide a good historical background of the activities, investigations, and decisions of you and your team. Your documentation provides an excellent reference trail for the long-term support team. So to be sure you have adequate documentation for successful SAP solution support, check that each of the following elements is available:

- ◆ **Business specifications**. Every solution that is being supported by you or your team should be properly tied to the business requirements that drove its creation. Business teams are responsible for clearly indicating the business input and output needs and parameters and what risks are involved with failure of a solution. These specifications should also clearly identify any crossover impact to or from other business areas.

- ◆ **Technical specifications.** As directed by the business specifications, every solution must have complete technical specifications that can describe the exact tools and techniques used in satisfying the stated business needs. Technical specifications should include full data descriptions and dependencies, programs and programming elements employed, nonstandard elements in the solution (such as, interfaces to legacy systems, bolt-on solutions, or tables).

◆ **Solution flow and interdependencies.** This information is key in the integrated SAP environment. Every solution should be identifiable in a high-level business process flow. The flow should represent the business activity and should illuminate the areas of dependency, potential bottlenecks, and critical process elements.

◆ **Recovery instructions.** Every solution should include instructions that will help a support team member properly identify problems and execute a reliable and complete recovery.

◆ **Background processing schedules.** All solutions should have easy-to-follow documentation that captures all background processing needs. Documentation of background processing should enable a support team member to follow the logic of specific job processing events and aid the team member in the complete recovery of background process creation in the event of systematic information loss.

◆ **Maintenance requirements.** The regular maintenance requirements of each solution should also be identified. Maintenance includes table additions, data reorganizations, authorization maintenance, and so forth.

◆ **Identification of original developers.** Each solution should clearly identify the original designers, developers, and other major contributors to the solution. If the solution intent is unclear, it could be necessary for the support team member to contact any one of these individuals for additional information.

◆ **History of revisions.** As a point of version checking and demonstrated control, each solution must have a documented history of all its changes (fixes or enhancements). Revision history can be maintained in a single location for the entire solution or within the individual components.

Establishing a Documentation Habit

Documentation is difficult to maintain. It is usually the last thing to be completed when solutions are finalized or modified. However, good documentation habits are necessary to avoid the potential pitfalls as described earlier. This is why you were continually introduced to the documentation needs throughout the entire implementation effort. In addition to being critical for good solution design and delivery, the regular expectation of documentation deliverables helps develop the habit of including documentation creation and maintenance activity throughout the SAP life cycle and beyond.

It's understandable that technical developers are not always the best individuals to write supporting documents. If necessary, team these folks with business representatives or other support team members that are adept at capturing the details of a process in such a way that will make it more supportable. Developmental information is highly valuable to you and your team, and you want to ensure that you can capture every bit of it.

The best way to ensure good documentation habits is to make the delivery of high-quality documentation a measured activity. The truth is, if the documentation doesn't appear to be high on the list of measured results, it's usually doomed to be one of the lowest priorities on everyone's list. People perform to the standards set before them. Therefore, the team management needs to clearly display the need for documentation and monitor its availability and reliability on a regular basis.

Documenting Code

Within SAP, you can insert comments as in any other programming language. Some programs found within support organizations are documented beautifully, which makes them easy to read and interpret. Equally, some code can be found that has little identifying information—especially the name of the original author—and it makes code review more tedious and less effective.

If you want to ensure that your ABAP programs are well documented, start your team out with a standardized ABAP template. This template works as the starting point for all new code and will clearly document each section of a program. A standard template might look like the following example:

```
*_____*

* Program name :                        *

* Description  :                      *

* Author    :                      *

* Date    :                      *

* Specification :                    *
```

```
*                                          *

* DESCRIPTION  : This program will ...       *

*                                          *

*_____-*

* Revision History:                         *

* 02/05/1997 DLP  Added 'description' to write statement*

*              per change #77112           *

*_____-*

REPORT ZZTEST MESSAGE-ID 01.

*_____—Table Declaration————————-*

TABLES: MARA,           "Material Master Table

        EINE,           "Info Record Table

        ZZTEST.         "Test Information Table

*_____-Controls——————————*

CONTROLS: TC_9000 TYPE TABLEVIEW USING SCREEN 9000.

*_____—Data Declaration ——————————*

DATA: WS_LINES   TYPE I,

   WS_DOCNO   LIKE ZZTEST-MATNR,

   OK_CODE(4)  TYPE C.

*_____—Internal Table Declaration————————*

DATA: BEGIN OF TAB_9000 OCCURS 0.

DATA: SEL_MARK.

    INCLUDE STRUCTURE ZZTEST.

DATA: END OF TAB_9000.
```

```
*———————————Selection Screen—————————————*

SELECT-OPTIONS: S_MATNR FOR ZZTEST-MATNR.

*————————————Start-of-Selection Event——————————*

START-OF-SELECTION.

 SET PF-STATUS 'LIST'.

* Authorization check

 PERFORM AUTHORIZATION_CHECK.

* Select data to be processed

 PERFORM SELECT_DATA.

* Process data

 PERFORM PROCESS_DATA.

END-OF-SELECTION.

*————————————End-of-Selection Event —————————————*

*

*

*————————————User Command Check———————————————*

* In this step, the program will check to determine if the user has  *

* chosen to ...                                        *

*———————————————————————————————————————————

*

AT USER-COMMAND.

 CASE SY-UCOMM.

  WHEN 'CHNG'.

   CLEAR ZZTEST. REFRESH TAB_9000.

   ...
```

```
ENDCASE.


*————————————————Subroutine Forms——————————————*

*

*——————————————————————————————————————————————
.*

*    Form AUTHORIZATION_CHECK

*——————————————————————————————————————————————
.*

*    This form will check for the required authorization object.*

*——————————————————————————————————————————————
.*

*

FORM AUTHORIZATION_CHECK.

  AUTHORITY-CHECK OBJECT 'Z:TSTCHK'

      ID 'ACTVT' FIELD '02'.

  IF SY-SUBRC <> 0 .

  ...

ENDFORM.                   " AUTHORIZATION_CHECK

*

*——————————————————————————————————————————————*

*    Form SELECT_DATA

*——————————————————————————————————————————————*

* This form will use the selection criteria entered by the user in

* the selection screen and ...

*——————————————————————————————————————————————
```

```
*

*

FORM SELECT_DATA.

  SELECT * FROM ZZTEST WHERE MATNR IN S_MATNR.

   WRITE: / ZZTEST MATNR,

       10 ZZTEST-DESC.            " Change #77112

         ...

  ENDSELECT.

ENDFORM.                  " SELECT_DATA
*_____*

*_____*

*   Module USER_COMMAND_9000 INPUT

*_____*

*    This module will check the command entered by the user. *

*_____*

*

MODULE USER_COMMAND_9000 INPUT.

  CASE OK_CODE.

   WHEN 'BACK'.

    CLEAR OK_CODE.

    SET SCREEN 0. LEAVE.

   WHEN 'SAVE'.

    CLEAR OK_CODE.

    PERFORM UPDATE_RECORD.

    SET SCREEN 0. LEAVE.
```

```
    ENDCASE.

    ENDMODULE.              " USER_COMMAND_9000 INPUT

    *

    *END OF PROGRAM
```

Asterisks in SAP ABAP code signify comment lines. These lines of code are not executable. Also notice the double-quote marks within lines of valid ABAP code. The double-quote mark allows you to include inline comments that are also not executable. Notice how an inline comment is used to show the change that was made per the Change #77112. This method allows you to cite your change reference number in the Revision History block in the beginning of the code and directly call attention to it at the actual point of modification.

Maintaining the Support Reference Guide

The support reference guide was the key support document described during the support transition period discussion (see Chapter 13). The support reference guide is a culmination of key informational elements from the design and development effort and includes information that would be useful if a problem with the solution ever arose. The support reference guide is known as your *living* documentation.

To keep this support reference guide alive, it must be fully reviewed and tested first. Support reference guides are excellent tools for carrying out a knowledge transfer. You should be able to read through the guide with the recipient of the solution in a manner that proves the document's informational flow and completeness. The review of the support reference guide is also a good method to check the grammatical aspects as well. Essentially, the support team member who uses the guide will read it thoroughly and certainly let you know if any errors are found. The new supporter of the solution may come back to you with questions regarding the document's content, especially when he or she is faced with problems. Work together to resolve the issue and identify additional information that is needed in the guide.

The heart of the support reference guide is the *troubleshooting and recovery* instruction section. Each time an error or problem occurs with a particular solution, be sure to document the situation in this portion of the guide. Be sure to include useful text that explains the situation, any testing or investigation that was helpful in the resolution, and the final steps to be taken to recover from the problem. If the same or similar problem should occur again, the support person, or a designated backup, could refer to the recovery section of the document for full recovery instructions. If you keep this document updated, you will have a "living" guide for support.

Document Storage, Reference, and Sharing Techniques

Your documentation is only as good as your ability to find and make use of it. How many times have you toiled to find a document or memo that you apparently mis-filed? If you weren't able to find it, you needed to rewrite it, hoping you could recall all the information it captured. Your documentation storage system needs to be logical, easy to use, and secure. Storage of documentation doesn't have to be elaborate to be effective. A simple networked file structure is suitable for this purpose. You can restrict access to a file *share* like this to members of the support team or extend access to additional business partners. You can establish permissions and passwords on the individual files, but don't create too much complexity in accessing documentation.

If you want to get a bit more up to date, consider the development of an Internet Web page within the confines of your company's access firewall. Because Web usage is so prevalent these days, it's only natural to harness the qualities for your business support activity.

You can link your documentation page to other related support information, such as project updates, system availability schedules, and department meeting announcements. One especially fine feature of publishing your support documentation in HTML format is that you can embed links to related documentation in the body of the document text. This approach enables a reader to access branches of reference information, then to return to the original page where the link appeared.

Web solutions are also very useful when you are supporting geographically dispersed sites. Authorized company sites can gain immediate access to your support information. This technology eliminates the need to mail physical documents or to create large e-mail transmissions. A Web solution often reduces the need for travel because users at different locations can share information almost immediately.

Measuring Successful Documentation

And how do you tell if your documentation efforts are truly paying off? Well, begin by reviewing how many of your supported solutions are fully documented and reviewed. A high level of completion indicates that the support team is motivated to ensure documentation deliverables are complete and available for use wherever and whenever needed. Low levels of completion might indicate that the priority for documentation is not being communicated and measured adequately.

Also, review document-revision activity. You should expect that much documentation will require revision as an ongoing activity in the support team. Changes to solutions will occur, or new problems will present themselves. If the documentation is being managed properly, updates are taking place and the documentation is being kept *alive*.

Support team members should also be polled to determine when they used the support documentation—either during periods of backup support or to enable knowledge transfers. An effectiveness study should assess how well initially delivered documentation met the support criteria and enabled reliable support transition. Take this opportunity to look for weaknesses in the support documentation. Be sure to monitor the usefulness and applicability of documentation styles and standards. Support team members should regularly review documentation styles and standards to continually improve documentation use and effectiveness.

Summary

By this point, you should be fully convinced of the importance of good documentation in your SAP environment. Every element, nuance, and decision that went into the creation of your new environment will be of highest value to you and your team. The SAP system is extremely complex, and it's virtually impossible to commit all aspects to memory. More importantly, consider the expense your company invested to migrate the business to SAP. Everything that was experienced and learned is of utmost use to other efforts. By being a good steward of documentation, you not only help increase your company's return on its investment but also write the history of your company's leap into the future of an SAP-managed environment.

The key support points discussed in this chapter follow:

◆ Documentation gives a team the freedom to step away from its daily activities, either on a temporary basis or in pursuit of other opportunities.

- Documentation helps in the retention of critical knowledge and development.
- Documentation enables successful audit events and enables companies to achieve ISO certification.
- Documentation preparation is a habit that should begin early in the SAP life cycle; it needs the continual encouragement and prioritization from the support team management.
- Documentation should be reviewed and updated whenever solution specifications change or problems are encountered.
- Documentation should be reviewed to ensure that it is meeting its intended goals; adjustments should be made to maintain high-quality documentation.

Chapter 26

The Evolution of Support

In This Chapter

◆ Looking Back

◆ Recalling How SAP Will Change Your Work Environment

◆ Developing Confidence in Yourself

What this book has attempted to do is tell a story about SAP, a company's migration, and the growth of the individuals involved. The book's full content won't be reviewed in this chapter—you can reread any of the chapters you wish. But the point of the book is based upon the belief that the onset of SAP has had a major impact to the business industry in our day. Growth of business methods and the technology that enables them has been nothing short of explosive—sometimes so much so that just trying to keep up becomes a full-time job.

As hungry as SAP can be in consuming resources to manage it, individuals like you are also hungry to devour as much information about SAP as possible. But in your quest for continuing knowledge and expertise, it's easy to concentrate more on what you don't know, rather than to take account of what you do know. It's healthy to take account of where you've been and how you've grown as you continually strive to provide the best support you can in the new SAP environment.

This chapter will briefly revisit the manner in which SAP's architecture and methodology has required changes in the way teams support the business environment. Although the approach is quite logical, it has probably caused a certain amount of organizational upheaval in your company—or soon will—and that isn't always easy to deal with. However, if you and your team can rise to the occasion, the payoff will be well worth the investment. Once the new foundation is in place, you'll be thrilled and amazed at the opportunities that await you as you rebuild a better operation to take you into the new millennium. After all, if enabling SAP was an easy thing to do, everyone would have done it by now.

So, take a cleansing breath, lean back, and turn off that GUI. This chapter will bring you full circle in this adventure. Let's look at where we've been and where we've ended up. It's quite a ride, and one that will probably change your professional outlook from this day on.

Looking Back

It's interesting at this point to think back to when someone first mentioned that the company was investigating the implementation of a new business application called SAP. At that time, you weren't sure if you should spell it, or say it. It probably even sounded like another one of those business fads that make project teams prolific for a time, only to spiral away in missed opportunities and excuses. You might have even shrugged your shoulders and turned away, slightly amused, yet relatively indifferent—until you found that you were on the team.

The implementation effort—the "SAP life cycle," as you came to know it—was like no other you had participated in. The endeavor that this team was undertaking was huge. How does a team feasibly disable the core automated system that a business operates on, replace it with an entirely new and methodologically different one, and never miss a beat throughout the whole process? Sure they said you were crazy—and just crazy enough to make it happen. Implementing SAP can often appear as a near-impossible task. The overwhelming idea of SAP implementation has to be one of the biggest sticking points for SAP and for organizations that are courting the idea of switching over. The application is well conceived and extremely powerful, but the logistics of getting it into place is quite awesome. Market leadership and market position are fleeting statuses, and forward thinking is more important today than ever. Because of the fickle marketplace, businesses must take every opportunity to improve their standing by continually improving their internal processes.

So, assuming you were up to achieving the impossible, and after months of learning, investigating, digging, toiling, testing, testing, and testing, your team developed the solution that would implement SAP. All egos were checked at the door, and all closed minds were opened as you worked to develop a virtual business that operates on the SAP platform. Now you just had to sell it to the folks who would need to use it day in and day out. That, you may have found, is quite a challenge. Remember, you are asking business professionals to drop their familiar and comfortable automated environment and take up a new approach. It's not an easy situation for anyone—you or them. Along the way you probably endured some of the slings and arrows of the naysayers, but the mission was still on track and the project was destined to complete. Your only hope was to empathize with the anxieties of the users and assure them that the entire implementation team would be behind them every step of the way.

Now all your milestones have been met and approvals have been granted; S-Day has arrived. The legacy systems processed their last transactions, information was written to the old data structures for the last time, and the business completed what was seemingly just another day of work. And as the door closed behind the last of the users who called it a day, you and your team sprang into action. Working feverishly yet methodically, you pulled apart the legacy environment, tossing it aside like so many spare parts, and wheeled in the shiny new SAP system. You worked around the clock, like so many technicians maintaining the theme park after hours.

And then they came back. The users had returned and were ready to get back to work. Of course, they were aware of your recent activities, and there was a noticeable buzz of excitement and anxiety. You and your team members swarmed through the business areas, ensuring that the users were accessing SAP and were moving about as they had during the training sessions.

Your hope was that all would go well because this was the real thing. The work they were doing was now in the live environment, as opposed to the laboratory environment where "Oops" might be accompanied by a chuckle and a shrug of the shoulders. Some of your greatest anxiety was felt during these first few days of a live SAP environment. You had a backup plan—a return to the old legacy environment—if anything truly went wrong. You were determined, though, that wouldn't come to pass.

At this point you can really appreciate why you and your team members had spent so much time and effort reviewing, discussing, testing, and documenting—until you couldn't bear to look at another design specification. You were already an expert in your area of concentration, and now you were rapidly becoming an emerging expert on SAP. That's a big accomplishment.

The story continues as the new environment stabilizes and regularity returns to the work place. The system is settling in, the users are settling in, and the early problems have been understood and addressed. The darn thing works, thanks to the efforts of people like you.

Getting the environment back into the hands of the long-term support team is the last hurdle to clear in this major event. Some of the implementation team members decided to become members of the new support team. Some of the other implementation team members, though, may have found other opportunities. Before you let them go, you made sure they transferred their knowledge to a support team member. And here came the virtual, and literal, reams of documentation. Don't lose that documentation. Rest assured that you'll be looking at it sometime in the near future.

Now you are *support*. You're working to maintain the most popular ERP on the market today. You're working with tools and functions that help you serve your users as they work with SAP, and you are always learning about new features of the system. Equally, you have established yourself as the advocate for the business area that you are responsible for. The users are no doubt pleased and impressed with your accomplishment, and you should be, too. Wasn't that fun?

Recalling How SAP Will Change Your Work Environment

Recall, if you will, how the architecture and integration inherent in the SAP design was described. It's a methodology that works, but it's probably considerably different from most legacy environments. So much change is required to truly get the most out of SAP, you must adopt a welcome attitude to change in order to make the effort a success. Some organizations try to work SAP into their existing processes and methods. This approach might maintain a level of comfort within the company but will never allow SAP to do what it was designed to do. A company could easily discredit SAP, stating that it did nothing spectacular. But SAP is only as effective as you allow it to be. When SAP is used with the term *reengineering*, you need to be sure that you are reengineering your business processes and not attempting to reengineer SAP.

The fear of change is real and should be reckoned with. The nice thing about SAP is its modular design. This feature allows companies to ease into the application's use and build their expertise gradually. The return on investment might be slower with this approach, but it might be a more palatable introduction for some. Others, though, choose to jump in with both feet and want to harness the beast for all it's worth. This approach is fine, too, but it does pose increasing levels of risk. This book has proposed a gradual migration approach, to the extent that the introduction of SAP will noticeably replace logical portions of legacy operations without introducing a change so sweeping that it could completely halt a business's activity should something go awry.

It is true that SAP's architecture calls for change in an organization's internal structure. However, while an implementation team is working to develop a parallel working business environment, it can also develop a parallel organizational environment. This book spent a good amount of time elaborating on the aspects of an implementation team's membership, mixed skill level, and physical structure. The development and activity of the implementation team was also a rehearsal for a new support organization that was to emerge. A well-poised company will take full advantage of the benefits of the laboratory environment.

Perhaps the biggest impact you can expect from the support perspective in the new SAP environment is the call for a return to basics. In other words, the introduction of SAP in a business environment can often put everyone back on the same level of knowledge and expertise. The users are now equally matched in their understanding of the system, although some may not like playing on this sort of level field. Learning new tools is welcomed by some and shunned by others. Your job is to reestablish yourself as the strong support advocate whom the users can rely on. Whereas familiarity may have created contentment in the old environment, now so much is new and different. You'll want to practice good old-fashioned customer service with your business teams. Their ultimate success will determine the overall success of your company's SAP migration. If you don't closely care for and feed this effort, it will wither and die.

Developing Confidence in Yourself

Now you should take a look at yourself and consider the road you have been traveling. As you'll recall, it was strongly encouraged that anyone reading this text should leap at the opportunity to work in an up-and-coming SAP environment. ERPs are the future of business management. SAP is the front-runner in the ERP market and seems to be gaining in its lead. Just being associated with an SAP effort is a recognizable achievement—you possess the experience and aptitude to help manage a company through the complex migration.

The SAP application is extremely complex, and the scope of its capabilities can be overwhelming. You might become easily discouraged if you cannot keep up with the amount of information coming your way, or you might continually feel lost to some extent within the system. For your benefit and reassurance, look back and recognize how much you *do* know about SAP; you probably understand more about it than you give yourself credit for. By reading this book, you have become more aware of SAP architecture, integration, and functionality. Apply this new knowledge to what you might already know or use the knowledge to begin maneuvering about within the application. Take credit for your achievements and build on them. Work with others and share tips, methods, and experiences. Once you're in the system and beginning to get comfortable, you'll be learning at an exponential rate.

But how, you might ask, are you ever going to feel confident supporting SAP when there is so much you don't know? Easy. You're going to find out. Reading this book was one step, and Appendix D lists many more resources. Remember, though, that good support begins with the dedication to help your customers. That doesn't always mean that you can answer their questions immediately. It does mean, however, that you are committed to finding answers to their questions so they can continue to be productive while you continue to learn and grow.

Above all, relax with SAP. Don't fear it. Just learn how to approach it. Remember that you are not alone. Work closely with your teammates and customers to better understand some of the intricacies of the system. Rely on support documentation and any resident consultants. Visit user conferences and other events focused on SAP methodologies (see Appendix D again). You'll learn firsthand what other business professionals are trying to understand about SAP. You'll probably find out that you know as much or more than some of your industry peers. The secret is that *everyone* is still learning about SAP. You'll learn something new about it every day. Recognize your opportunity to learn, take that opportunity to your best advantage, and enjoy the experience. Best of luck. Everyone's rooting for you.

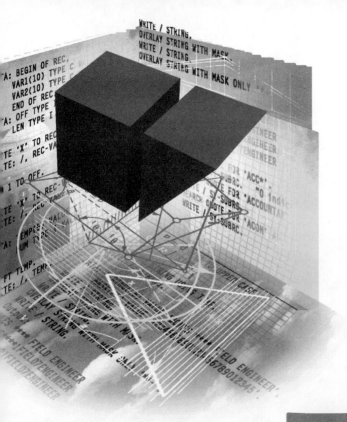

PART V

Appendixes

A **A Brief History of SAP**

B **An Overview of the SAP GUI**

C **Additional Tips, Tranactions, and Tools**

D **Finding Additional Information**

E **SAP Training Programs and Facilities**

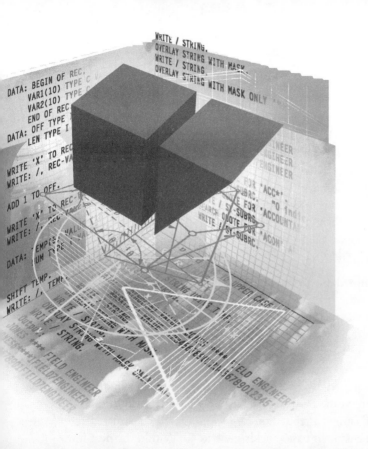

Appendix A

A Brief History of SAP

The purpose of this appendix is to provide more information about SAP, the company. Now that you know so much about the R/3 application and its functionality, you might also be interested in learning about the company's origin, history, and customer base. Although the intention here is not to *sell* SAP, you will undoubtedly be impressed with the company's fine track record. In 1972, five systems analysts began work on a business application that utilized real-time data within an integrated architecture. Working nights and weekends, these five former IBM employees (based in Mannheim, Germany) developed *Systemanalyse and Programmentwicklung* (which translates to Systems Analysis and Program Development).

The initial product was limited by technological constraints: Computer storage capacity was too limited for the real power of integration to be unleashed as it is today. However, although input and output rates were slow and the scale of the product was correspondingly limited, the company signed its first customer, the German ICI subsidiary in Ostringen. The company had grown to nine employees and, although off to a modest start, reported a first-year profit of DM 620,000. In the following year, the company signed two additional customers—Roth-Handle and Knoll. These customers adopted the financial accounting solution developed by the fledgling company, and SAP earned a reputation for providing well-constructed and consistent applications. The customer base quickly grew to 40. Within the next few years, profits rose to nearly DM 4 million; the employee count grew to 25.

In 1977, five years after its inception, SAP became a closely held corporation and changed its name to *Systeme, Anwendungen, Produkte in der Datenverarbeitung* (Systems, Applications, Products in Data Processing). At this point, the company moved its headquarters from Mannheim to Walldorf. When it attracted the first foreign customers during the same year, the customer base soon grew to 100 clients and the employee count doubled.

SAP's real breakthrough came in 1979 when it released its first fully enabled Enterprise Resource Planning (ERP) product: the R/2 system. Sales had climbed to DM 10 million, and SAP headquarters continued to expand. Throughout the 1980s, SAP continued to grow and to work closely with its customers. The R/2 application was continually tuned and modified to meet the demands of a growing customer base. During this same time, SAP expanded into other countries and continued to acquire new customers. By the middle of the decade, SAP sales exceeded DM 100 million.

In 1988, SAP became a publicly held corporation, and stock began trading in the German securities exchange. The following year, SAP stock was being traded on the Zurich exchange, and the number of employees rose to 1,000. SAP continued to expand in additional foreign markets.

In 1992, the company released the first open client/server system: R/3. With the release of this product, and from this point on, SAP's growth and revenues soared to the surprise and delight of the stockholders. The record growth continued through the next two years; the company's capital reached the DM 500 million mark, and the stock split 1:4.

Today there are approximately 1,400 active R/2 installations and an impressive 15,000 R/3 installations. Currently, SAP is in the company with—and leading—several other major client/server ERP development companies. Figure A-1 shows SAP's standing in the ERP market.

As you can see, SAP has clearly taken the lead and continues to stay in front of the pack. Its growth has been nothing short of astounding.

- ◆ SAP employs more that 15,000 people.
- ◆ SAP dedicates 55 percent of its resources to customer service.
- ◆ SAP focuses 24 percent of its resources on research and development.
- ◆ SAP focuses 21 percent of its resources on sales and marketing.
- ◆ SAP has offices in more that 50 countries.
- ◆ SAP provides solutions for 15 major industry sectors, including oil and gas, health care, automotive, and high tech and electronics.

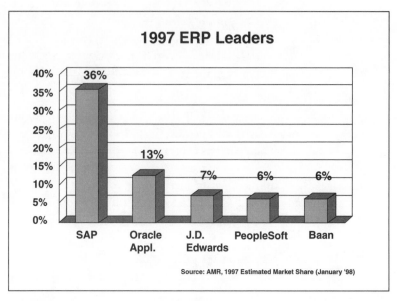

FIGURE A-1 *Leading ERP providers (1997)*

- ◆ In FY97, SAP achieved a 62 percent increase over FY96 revenues.
- ◆ In FY97, SAP R/3 sales rose 63 percent.

SAP is currently used by more than 7,500 customers in more than 90 countries—with live SAP installations at more than 13,000 geographically dispersed customer sites. The list of SAP customers reads like a Wall Street "who's who" list of world market leaders. SAP customers include the following companies:

- ◆ Chevron Petroleum
- ◆ Chrysler International
- ◆ Random House, Inc.
- ◆ Hewlett Packard
- ◆ Reebok
- ◆ Deutsche Bank

Now you can understand why SAP is recognized as the fourth-largest independent software supplier in the world and why it ranks as the global leader in business-application software.

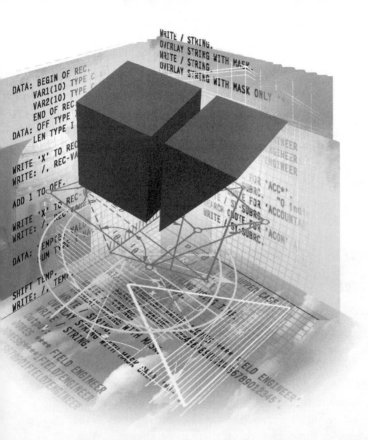

Appendix B

*An Overview of
the SAP GUI*

This appendix provides a brief overview of the SAP graphical user interface (GUI). To effectively work with SAP, you need to be familiar with its on-screen look and feel. R/3 is a Windows-based GUI, and it responds much the same as other Windows applications. It employs many different drop-down menus, buttons, icons, and hot spots. You have probably already had some exposure to the SAP GUI. Therefore, this discussion omits the most basic maneuvering instructions.

The SAP Main Screen and Issuance of Transaction Codes

Figure B-1 shows the top portion of the main SAP screen. This screen is identifiable by the toolbar selections (Office, Logistics, Accounting, and so on) as well as the presence of the Dynamic Menu button on the menu, which enables users to customize a menu of selections that they have assembled themselves. From the main screen, you will also notice the Command field, which is the white keyboard entry field just above the Dynamic Menu button. The Command field is where you enter SAP transaction codes. The code in Figure B-2, SM37, provides direct access to the Select Background Jobs window. In this menu, you can enter a transaction code, always four characters long, by referencing its four-character designation alone.

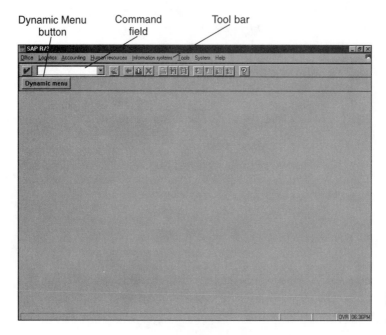

FIGURE B-1

SAP main screen

Elsewhere within SAP, you need to precede the transaction code with a */n* prefix. This prefix tells SAP that you want to initiate a new (/n) screen transaction. To find a screen's transaction code, choose System, Status from the toolbar drop-down menu. The transaction code will be reported in a screen similar to Figure B-2.

The Data Table Selection and Result Screens

Because system data is what you will be reviewing, analyzing, and sometimes managing, you should be familiar with the methods by which you can review data within the database tables.

There are several ways to review table data within SAP. One of the more useful to you in a supporting role is to use the SAP Data Browser (transaction code SE16). Figures B-3, B-4, and B-5 show the screens you will manipulate when you use this method to search for and extract data.

Commonly Used SAP GUI Icons

Within SAP, as you probably noticed in some of the preceding figures, you will encounter numerous icons that effect different actions within the system (see Figure B-6).

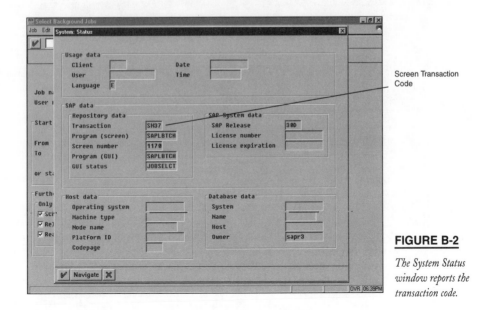

Screen Transaction Code

FIGURE B-2

The System Status window reports the transaction code.

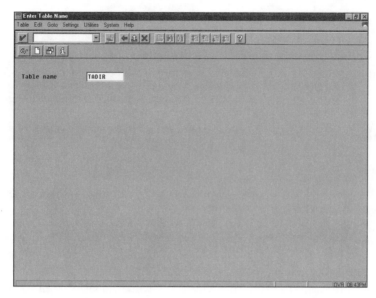

FIGURE B-3

Transaction SE16 (Data Browser) entry screen

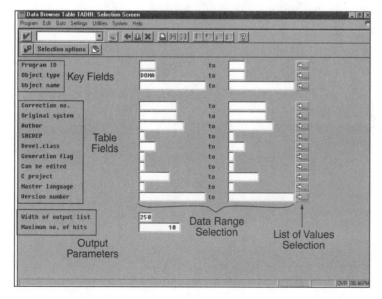

FIGURE B-4

Transaction SE16 (Data Browser) selection screen

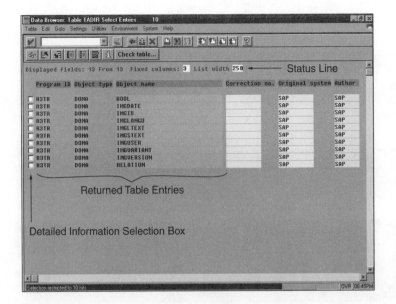

FIGURE B-5

Transaction SE16 (Data Browser) results screen

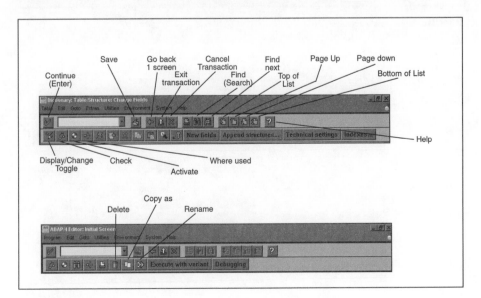

FIGURE B-6 *Commonly used SAP icons*

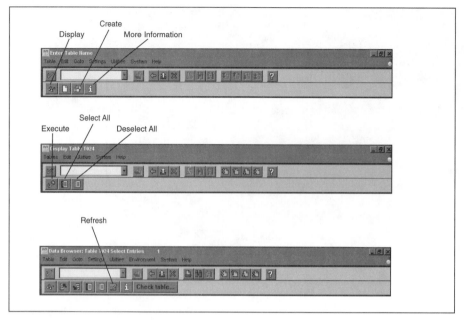

FIGURE B-6 *Commonly used SAP icons*

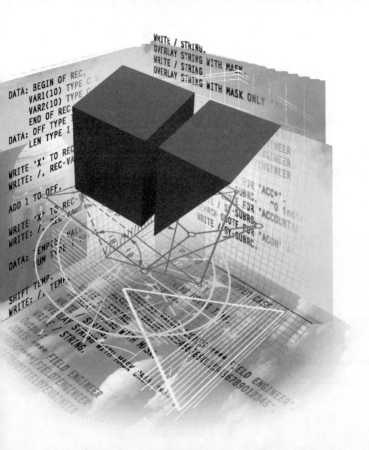

Appendix C

**Additional Tips,
Transactions, and
Tools**

Throughout this book, you have been provided with various methods and functions that you can use to support the SAP environment. So many different tools are available in SAP that it's not feasible to capture them all. However, this appendix will provide you with some more helpful hints and useful tools that will help you support your SAP environment.

SAP Transaction Code Quick Reference

You'll want to increase the speed with which you can access different areas of SAP. A support team member will usually make good use of direct SAP transactions. Here is a listing of some of the most commonly used support-related transaction codes.

Tcode	Program	Screen	Description
AL01	RSRZALM1	0000	SAP Alert Monitor
AL02	RSDB0000	0000	Database alert monitor
AL03	RSHOST20	0000	Operating system alert monitor
AL04	RSSTAT85	0000	Monitor call distribution
AL05	RSSTAT26	0000	Monitor current workload
AL06	RSEFA900	0000	Performance: Upload/Download
AL07	RSPERF10	0000	EarlyWatch Report
AL08	RSUSR000	0000	Users Logged On
S002	MENUS002	1000	Menu Administration
S@E	SAPMSSY3	0001	Debugging
SA38	SAPMS38M	0101	ABAP/4 Reporting
SA39	SAPMS38M	0102	SA38 for Parameter Transaction
SAR0		0000	Display Standard Reporting Tree
SAR1		0000	Structure of an archive object
SAR2		0000	Definition of an archive object
SAR3		0000	Archiving: Customizing
SAR4		0000	Definition of the archive classes
SAR5		0000	Assignment of archive classes
SAR6		0000	Archive events: Generation program
SARA	SAPMAADM	0001	Archive management

(Continued)

Tcode	Program	Screen	Description
SARL		0000	Call of ArchiveLink Monitor
SARP	SAPMSERP	0100	Reporting (Tree Structure): Execute
SART	SAPMSERP	0100	Display Reporting Tree
SCAL	SAPMSFT0	0100	Factory Calendar with CUA Interface
SCAM	SAPMSCAM	0200	CATT Management
SCAT	SAPMSCAT	0100	Computer Aided Test Tool
SCC0	SAPMSCC1	0100	Client Copy
SCC1	SAPMSCC1	0111	Client Copy - Special Selections
SCC2	SAPMSCC1	0120	Client transport
SCC3	RSCCPROT	0000	Client Copy Log
SCC4		0000	Client administration
SCC5	SAPMSCC1	0112	Client Delete
SCD0	SAPMSCD0	0100	Change Documents for Utilities
SCDN	SAPMSNUM	0100	Change Documents for Number Ranges
SCDO	SAPMSCDO	0100	Display Change Document Objects
SCOM	SAPMSCOM	0100	SAPcomm: Configuration
SCPF	RSCMPFKT	0000	Generate enterprise IMG
SDW0	MENUSDW0	1000	ABAP/4 Development WB initial screen
SE01	RDDM0004	0100	Transport and Correction System
SE02	RDDM0007	0100	Environment Analyzer
SE03	RDDTOOL	0136	Transport Utilities
SE06	RDDCUSTR	0100	Set up Workbench Organizer
SE07	RDDSTR01	0100	Transport System Status Display
SE09	RDDM0001	0100	Workbench Organizer
SE10	RDDM0001	0500	Customizing Organizer
SE11	SAPMSRD0	0100	ABAP/4 Dictionary Maintenance
SE12	SAPMSRD0	0100	ABAP/4 Dictionary Display
SE13	SAPMSEDS	0010	Maintain Technical Settings (Tables)
SE14	SAPMSGTB	0100	Utilities for Dictionary Tables
SE15		0000	ABAP/4 Repository Information System
SE16	SAPLSETB	0230	Data Browser
SE17	SAPMSTAZ	0100	General Table Display
SE30	SAPMS38T	0100	ABAP/4 Runtime Analysis
SE32	SAPDSTXP	0100	ABAP/4 Text Element Maintenance
SE35	SAPMSDIA	1010	ABAP/4 Dialog Modules

(Continued)

Tcode	Program	Screen	Description
SE36	SAPMSLDB	0100	ABAP/4 Logical Databases
SE37	SAPMS38L	1010	ABAP/4 Function Modules
SE38	SAPMS38M	0100	ABAP/4 Program Development
SE39	SAPMSCMP	0100	Splitscreen Editor: Program Compare
SE40	SAPMSEUN	0100	MP: Standards Maint. and Translation
SE41	SAPMSEU3	0100	Menu Painter
SE43	SAPMSEU3	0200	Maintain Area Menu
SE51	SAPMSEUS	0100	Screen Painter
SE52		0000	Parameterized screenpainter call
SE54	SAPMSVIM	0050	Generate View Maintenance Module
SE55		0000	Table view maintenance DDIC call
SE56		0000	Table view display DDIC call
SE57		0000	Table view maint. delete, extern
SE61	SAPMSDCU	0100	R/3 Documentation
SE80	SAPMSEUE	0000	ABAP/4 Development Workbench
SE81	SAPMSEU8	0000	SAP Application Hierarchy
SE82	SAPMSEU9	0000	Customer Application Hierarchy
SE84		0000	ABAP/4 Repository Information System
SE85		0000	ABAP/4 Dictionary Information System
SE86		0000	ABAP/4 Repository Information System
SE87		0000	Data Modeler Information System
SE88		0000	Development Coordination Info System
SE91	SAPMSMES	0400	Maintain Messages
SE92	RSLGAD00	1100	Maintain system log messages
SE93	SAPLSEUK	0390	Maintain Transaction Codes
SERP	SAPMSERP	0100	Reporting: Change Tree Structure
SM01	MSTTSTC	1010	Lock Transactions
SM02	SAPMSEM1	0500	System Messages
SM04	RSM04000	0000	User Overview
SM12	RSENQRR2	0000	Display and Delete Locks
SM13	RSM13000	1414	Display Update Records
SM21	SAPMSM21	0200	System log
SM23	SAPMSSLG	0200	System Log Analysis
SM30	SAPMSVMA	0100	Call Up View Maintenance

(Continued)

Tcode	Program	Screen	Description
SM31	SAPMSTBM	1000	Table maintenance
SM32	SAPMSTBM	1000	Maintain Table Parameter ID TAB
SM33	SAPMSTBM	1000	Display Table Parameter ID TAB
SM34	SAPMSVMA	0200	Viewcluster maintenance call
SM35	SAPMSBDC	0100	Batch Input Monitoring
SM36	SAPLBTCH	2050	Batch request
SM37	SAPLBTCH	2070	Background job overview
SM38	SAPMSQIO	0100	Queue Maintenance Transaction
SM39	SAPBTCPE	0000	Job analysis
SM49	RSLOGCOM	0020	Execute Logical Commands
SM50	RSMON000	0000	Work Process Overview
SM51	RSM51000	0000	List of SAP Servers
SNRO	SAPMSNRO	0150	Number range objects
SNUM	SAPMSNUM	0100	Number Range Driver
SOA1	SAPMOPTA	0101	ArchiveLink: Early Archiving
SOA2	SAPMOPTA	0102	ArchiveLink: Late Archiving
SOA3	SAPMOPTA	0111	Early Archiving Maintain Settings
SOA4	SAPMOPTA	0112	Late Archiving Maintain Settings
SOA5	SAPMOPTA	0103	ArchiveLink Simultaneous Archiving
SOA6	SAPMOPTA	0113	Simult. Archiving Maintain Settings
SP01	RSPOSP01	0100	Spool Control
SP03	RSPO0048	0100	Spool: Load Formats
SP11	RSTS0012	0100	TemSe directory
SP12	RSTS0010	0100	TemSe Administration
SPAD	SAPMSPAD	1010	Spool Management
SU01	SAPMS01J	0200	Maintain User
SU02	SAPMS01C	0113	Maintain Authorization Profiles
SU03	SAPMS01C	0111	Maintain Authorizations
SU05	SAPMS05W	0100	Maintain Internet users
SU10	SAPMS010	0100	Mass changes to User Master
SU11	SAPMS01C	0111	Maintain Authorizations
SU12	SAPMS010	0200	Mass Changes to User Master Records
SU20	SAPMS01D	0060	Maintain Authorization Fields
SU21	SAPMS01E	0060	Maintain Authorization Objects
SU22	SAPMS012	0000	Auth. object usage in transactions
SU23	SAPMS01F	0000	Load tables in TAUTL
SU30	SAPMS01S	0100	Total checks in the area of auth.
SU50	SAPMS01J	0500	Maintain User Defaults

(Continued)

Tcode	Program	Screen	Description
SU51	SAPMS01J	0510	Maintain User Address
SU52	SAPMS01J	0520	Maintain User Parameters
SU53	SAPMS01G	0000	Display Check Values
SU54	SAPMS01K	0000	Maintain User Menu
SU55	SAPMS01T	0000	Start user menu

Using the Command Field

The Command field is where you enter your SAP transaction code for immediate navigation to another SAP screen (refer to Figure B-1 in Appendix B). From the SAP Main menu, enter a transaction code directly (for example, SU01). From any other screen, you will need to add a prefix command to the transaction code (for example, /nSU01). The prefixes tell SAP how you want to leave the screen you are already in. Use the following prefixes as described:

◆ **/n**—Leave current screen session and start a new screen session.

◆ **/o**—Open a new SAP session (GUI) without leaving the current session.

In addition to screen navigation, you can use further commands in the Command field to perform other activities:

◆ **/I**—Exit your SAP session after a dialog prompt from SAP.

◆ **/o** (without a tcode)—Show a dialog box of all current sessions you have running.

◆ **/e**—Exit your SAP session without a dialog prompt from SAP.

◆ **/nex**—Another method to exit your SAP session without a dialog prompt from SAP.

◆ **/h**—Engage SAP's debugging mode for all following activity.

The small pull-down arrow to the right of the command field is a transaction buffer that records approximately 13 of your most recently executed commands. The buffer works much like a Web browser; just click on an entry to select it; then press Enter to open that particular transaction screen.

Custom SAP Job Link to Job Schedule Location Program

There has been significant discussion about background job schedules in this text. Unfortunately, SAP does not provide a tool that enables you to search for the active usage of job steps (programs) in relation to job schedules. Therefore, the following custom ABAP program is presented; it allows you to perform a veritable "where used" listing of ABAP programs in relation to the job schedules where the programs are actively used.

```
REPORT ZZJSFIND .

* written by Gareth M. de Bruyn, 1996

TABLES: TBTCP,

         TBTCO.

PARAMETERS: W_PROG LIKE TBTCP-PROGNAME.

DATA: BEGIN OF INT_JOBS OCCURS 0,

         JOBNAME LIKE TBTCP-JOBNAME.

DATA: END OF INT_JOBS.

SELECT * FROM TBTCP WHERE PROGNAME = W_PROG.

MOVE TBTCP-JOBNAME TO INT_JOBS-JOBNAME.

APPEND INT_JOBS.

CLEAR INT_JOBS.

ENDSELECT.

SORT INT_JOBS BY JOBNAME.

LOOP AT INT_JOBS.

      ON CHANGE OF INT_JOBS-JOBNAME.

          WRITE INT_JOBS-JOBNAME.

      ENDON.

ENDLOOP.
```

Echoing Sessions in SAP

Another important tool is the session-echoing functionality within SAP. This tool is especially useful for tracing errors or demonstrating onscreen activity when working with your business users. Essentially, if a user is working with you over the phone, you can echo your SAP onscreen activities to his or her terminal, or vice versa. Much like a sharedX session in UNIX, this feature enables the two of you to view the same screen when investigating a problem or clarifying proper SAP usage. To enable an echoed session, do the following:

1. From within the User Overview screen (SM04), find the user session to which you want to echo.

2. Select the session to which you will echo your onscreen activities.

3. Use the menu path Edit, Echo Session On.

4. The recipient will see a screen that mirrors your activities. You will be the master session, and the recipient's session will be the slave.

5. When you no longer need the echo session, return to SM04, select the slave session, and use the menu path Edit, Echo Session Off.

Customizing the Data Browser

If you've noticed, when you engage the SAP data browser (tcode SE16), the selection screen provides only a few fields that exist in the table you are searching. Often the field you wish to use for your sort isn't displayed. However, your use of the data browser is customizable. From the data browser, use the menu path Settings, Selection Criteria. A pop-up screen enables you to select and deselect the table fields you want to display on the selection screen. You can also use the functionality from Settings, User Parameters to change the manner in which the selection information is provided to you. For example, a toggle switch allows you to display the field descriptions or actual SAP field names as you begin your search selection.

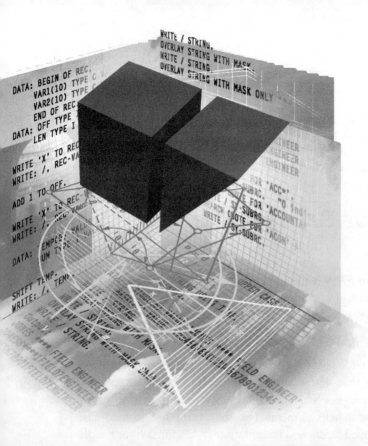

Appendix D

Finding Additional Information

This appendix provides additional sources of SAP information. A lot of people out there are talking about SAP, and you can travel many avenues to learn more about SAP and what it can do for your business. Information ranges from independent Web sites, business user groups, conferences and events, and consulting firms.

Official SAP User Groups and Organizations

There are a variety of different SAP-dedicated user groups in existence today. A few of the more prominently known groups are listed below.

Americas' SAP Users' Group (ASUG)

ASUG is an independent, not-for-profit organization that exists to combine the collective knowledge of its more than 450 member companies. Members are volunteer representatives from the vast range of SAP's corporate and small-business customers. ASUG's primary missions are to help all members better utilize SAP in their businesses; to provide a friendly open forum and presentation-style approach for the discussion of core topics that revolve around SAP architecture or business modules; and to communicate the collective needs of the group directly to SAP in order to help guide SAP's development efforts. ASUG conferences are usually held semiannually. For more information about events and registration contact:

ASUG

401 North Michigan Avenue

Chicago, IL 60611

Phone: 312-321-5142

Fax: 312-245-1081

E-mail: asug@sba.com

URL: www.asug.com

Multinational User Groups

Many multinational SAP user groups are also in existence today. These user groups focus on regional support, as well as issue-specific support. For the most up-to-date listing, visit the following Web site: www.sapfaq.com/#institutions-and-contacts. worldusers. Here, you'll find user group names, contact names, and current e-mail addresses.

SAP Labs, Inc.

Formerly known as SAP Technology, Inc., this organization develops software and add-ons to the SAP application. It is officially recognized as an extension of the SAP Walldorf headquarters. Of immediate interest to companies considering SAP implementation, SAP Labs offers an R/3 Simplification Group whose charter is to provide tools and methods to streamline SAP implementations.

SAP Labs, Inc.

3475 Deer Creek Road

Palo Alto, CA 94304

Phone: (650) 849-4000

　　　　(800) 485-9800

Fax: (650) 849-4200

URL: www.saplabs.com/saplabhm.htm

Conferences and Expositions

Conferences and expositions, much like the user groups, are staged events that bring together SAP representatives, partners, consultants, and business users. In years past, these were more sales and marketing events. However, as the solution has evolved and more users have gained experience with the application, the agendas for these events have become more focused and results oriented. Although several multinational events are held, the following two events are the most important.

Sapphire

Sapphire is the biggest and most widely attended exposition devoted to SAP. It attracts literally thousands from around the world. Here, SAP representatives, business partners, and customers join to discuss current SAP usage, business trends, and the future of SAP application opportunities. It's a huge event, and you might walk away with more questions than you brought. Sapphire is also a terrific opportunity to make some networking and partnering contacts with other SAP users and professionals. Events have been held in Japan, Amsterdam, Canada, the United States, and Spain. For more information, visit www.sap.com/sapphire/.

SAP Technical Education

Often referred to as Tech Ed, this conference offers SAP professionals an opportunity to meet with other SAP technical people and work with SAP solutions in a hands-on environment. This conference focuses on out-of-the-box solutions and add-ons to the SAP R/3 application. In addition, many workshops instruct and inform attendees about different ways to maximize and extend SAP functionality. For more information, visit www.sapteched.saplabs.com/teched98/homeV3.htm.

Consulting Organizations

Consulting firms are more full service in approach as opposed to what you might learn piecemeal from expositions or user groups. Essentially, a consulting firm will contract with your organization to send SAP-knowledgeable resources to your site for an informational overview, training, recommendations, or even full-fledged SAP implementations. Obviously, this assistance comes with a rather hefty price tag. As mentioned in Chapter 5, it's often a good idea to have consultants on hand during the design and development phases of an implementation.

Ernst & Young LLP

Ernst & Young is a consulting service that provides business advice and solutions to a variety of businesses using a variety of business solutions. Ernst & Young employs a sizable workforce of SAP consultants and can help your team make major progress and achieve success in your SAP migration. Ernst & Young offices are located throughout the United States and Puerto Rico. For an office in your region, visit the company's Web site at www.ey.com.

Deloitte and Touche Consulting Group/ICS

Deloitte and Touche Consulting is one of the leaders in the industry of providing consulting services to industries interested in migrating to SAP usage. They are powered by over 13,000 employees worldwide and provide many flexible approaches that will help businesses implement SAP. You can find out more about the many services Deloitte and Touche Consulting provides by visiting their Web site at www.deloitte-ics.com.

CaRD America Inc.

CaRD America Consulting boasts an experienced staff that has effectively helped companies implement SAP R/2 and R/3 on four continents in commercial, government, and manufacturing settings. They are recognized by SAP as a National SAP Implementation partner.

CaRD America, Inc.

Headquarters

420 Peninsula Avenue

San Mateo, CA 94401

Phone: (650) 340-9973

    (800) 573-CaRD

Fax: (650) 340-1239

E-mail: info@card-america.com

URL: www.card-america.com

Origin

Origin is a multinational information technology (IT) services company; it delivers assistance to companies looking for help with applications that range from desktop solutions to ERPs. Origin has offices in more than 100 cities in 31 countries. To find an office near you, visit Origin's Web site at www.origin-it.com.

Bureau van Dijk

BvD, as it's known, is a consulting firm that focuses on the various aspects of SAP use. This firm's mission is to provide knowledgeable consultants to work with a business, not only in terms of installing SAP but also in postinstallation support, business analysis, project management, and training. BvD provides approaches for businesses of all sizes.

BvD

Atlanta office

Five Concourse Parkway

Suite 2875

Atlanta, GA 30328

Phone: 770-395-2833

Fax: 770-395-2836

West coast office

25741 Pacific Crest Drive

Mission Viejo, CA 92692

Phone: 619-673-2155

Fax: 619-673-9809

E-mail: BVDUSA@aol.com

SAP-Related Web Sites

The following Web sites are both useful and informational. Please bear in mind that neither the author nor publisher of this text actively supports any of these sites and, therefore, are not responsible for their content or management.

SAP-AG Official Company Web Site

Of course, start at the top and visit SAP's official site (www.sap.com). Here you will find more marketing information than anything else. However, it is a good site to visit if you wish to know more about the premise and products of SAP. This site includes comprehensive listings of industries served, installed customer base, and geographic proliferation. A nice feature is that SAP has included a generous amount of its own literature and brochures in .pdf (Adobe) format. Download them and read them at your leisure.

SAP Frequently Asked Questions Web Site

This independent site located at www.sapfaq.com is managed by Kaliana Kellye of Michigan and features great information from around the globe. The site provides input from many people involved with SAP. It also has schedules for ASUG expositions and many useful links.

The SAP Fan Club and User Forum

This site at www.sapfans.com is a real grassroots gathering of SAP professionals and users that provides a friendly and informative meeting place. Its basic premise is to encourage the regular and informal exchanging of SAP information, tips, publications, and job opportunities. This site was created and is maintained by Rao Tella.

Appendix E

SAP Training Programs and Facilities

SAP is working with its customers to develop innovative approaches to R/3 instruction. To get the most out of the courses, SAP suggests that attendees begin with a basic overview and gradually move to a topic-intensive focus. This approach is illustrated in Figure E-1.

Traditional Courses

Currently, SAP offers training courses that cover the following business and technical areas:

Application Training

◆ Logistics:

  ◆ Customer Order Management

  ◆ Manufacturing—Discrete

  ◆ Manufacturing—Process

  ◆ Plant Maintenance

  ◆ Procurement

  ◆ Project System

  ◆ Quality Management

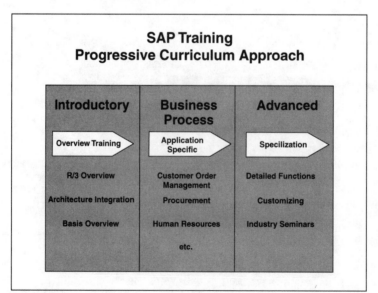

FIGURE E-1

SAP's progressive curriculum approach starts with the basics.

- Service Management
- Accounting:
  - Cost Management and Controlling
  - Financial Management and Accounting
- Human Resources
- Information Systems
- Cross Applications and Business Process Technology
- ABAP/4 Development Workbench (DW)
- Basis Administration

Specialized Industry Solution Workshops

- Automotive OEM Industry Solution Workshop
- Automotive Supplier Industry Solution Workshop
- Apparel Footwear Industry Solution Workshop
- Software Industry—SAP Industry Workshop
- IS-Oil Downstream Workshop
- Promotional Funds Management for Consumer Products Industry
- Retail Overview:
  - Listing and First-Time Purchase Orders
  - Merchandise Procurement and Distribution
- Retail Information System (RIS)
- Configuration and Organization in SAP Retail

To get the most out of the SAP training classes, attendees should have at least a basic understanding of the course material being presented as well as knowledge about the use of the SAP GUI prior to attending the course. Although this advice may sound inconsistent with the intention of a training course, preknowledge of the underlying concepts enables students to focus on the applications of those concepts. To help with this approach, SAP has teamed up with CBT Systems to provide relevant computer-based training. The current offerings include

- R/3 System Overview
- Basis: Archive Management
- Basis: Archiving Applications
- Human Resources

- Customer Order Management
- Procurement
- Financial Accounting
- Manufacturing
- Management Accounting
- Service Management
- Project System
- Plant Maintenance

Additional Training Resources

As SAP is becoming so widely used around the globe, there are continual needs and pressures to provide SAP instruction in a variety of new and innovative ways. Some additional training methods that companies can utilize are listed below.

On-Site Delivery of Education

SAP training teams will basically conduct the training at your business site. On-site training is a good alternative for companies that have many employees to train. The curriculum can range from a single course to an entire suite of programs.

Portable Classrooms

SAP's innovative portable classroom bundles hardware and software and delivers the package to a customer's site on a lease basis. The package consists of a complete SAP R/3 system installed on an NT server; 12 multimedia laptop computers for use as student workstations; and all supporting connection hardware.

Information Database

The information database is another on-site multimedia training tool where all training material is accessible, via customer license, from an R/3-enabled information repository. This approach allows customers to access standard SAP training programs from any location, at any time that is convenient for them.

SAP continues to prepare new curricula for its training programs and to develop innovative methods of delivery. For more information about these or any other SAP training opportunities, contact Education, SAP Americas, at 1-800-777-1SAP (1727).

Index

A

ABAP template, 404–409
ABAP/4: Program Criteria Selection screen, 269–270
ABAP/4 programs and reports, 344
ABAP/Query, 341–343
access policies, 117–118
ADK (Archive Development Kit), 395–396
AEDAT field, 29
AENUM field, 26–27
AL01 transaction, 283
Alert monitor, 283–284
application-specific archiving, 390
ArchiveLink, 392, 396
archiving
    ADK (Archive Development Kit), 395–396
    alternatives to, 397
    application-specific, 390
    ArchiveLink, 392, 396
    authorization, 393
    business requirements, 391
    database-specific, 390
    elegance, 397–398
    handles, 393
    management, 395
    objects, 393–395
    overview, 392
    reasons to, 389
    S_ARCHIVE object, 393
    strategy, 390–391
    third-party solutions, 397
    timing, 390–391
    tools, 392–396

ASUG (Americas' SAP Users' Group), 442
asynchronous updating, 358–359
audit, 232
    compliance requirements, 233
    readiness, 232–236
audit checkpoints, 227
authorization checks, 117
authorization profiles
    administering, 258
    authorization, 256-257
    collections of authorizations related to activities, 257
    composite profile templates, 257
    fields, 256
    highest level, 257
    key business transactions, 257–258
    problems, 292
    template or grouping of authorizations, 257
authorizations
    background processing, 292
    collections related to activities, 257
    data access problems, 293
    problems, 292
    template or grouping of, 257
    user logons, 177–178
automated processes, 360

B

background job scheduling, 266–267
    authorization, 270
    interactive, 267
    timing and frequency, 272–275
background processing, 266, 270

schedules, 403
background user type, 245
backup strategy, 62–63
backups, 180
  corrupt, 383
  Disaster Recovery instance, 66
  interdepartmental, 62–63
  legacy systems, 180
  level 0, 383
  level 1, 383, 384
  reinstating, 230–232
  retention, 383–384
  SAP systems, 180
  system, 382–383
balance, 43
basic support, 13
batch authorization objects, 281–282
batch processing, 266
batch scheduling, 267
BDC user type, 245
BEW (Business Engineering Workbench), 320
blackout, 161–162
bolt-ons, 64, 128
buffering, 296
bug fixes, 64
BUKRS field, 29–30
business
  monitoring technical aspects of, 4–5
  process support, 13–14
  recording transactions, 29
  relationships, 26
  requirements for archiving, 391
  specifications, 402
business areas
  change communications, 314
  determining levels of expertise in SAP, 210
  direct involvement with business process
    maintenance, 194
  expanding, 365–366
  identifying transactions users need to access, 262
  input and feedback about user access, 260
  involvement, 194
  manager familiarity with user access, 260-262
  process support team, 194–195
  sharing security ownership, 260-262
  support team assignment, 216–217
  testing authorization and access, 262
business culture support models, 12
business documents, 29–30

Business Process Scenario for Unit Testing, 146
business systems, classifying, 378
business teams
  change process, 306
  communicating with, 61–62
  development and integration, 38
  implementation support phase, 162
  involving in Quality Assurance (QA) instance,
    65–66
  linkages, 39
  modules, 39
  sharing policies and controls with, 367
business technical support, 12–13

C

call tickets, 9
call-tracking Web sites, 165
CATT (Computer Aided Test Tool), 249
CCMS (Computer Center Management System)
  and Alert monitor, 283–284
Change Password pop-up screen, 252
change process
  development, 305–307
  management, 305–306
changes
  ABAP programs, screens, transactions, and data
    dictionary elements, 308–310
  communications, 314–315
  correction or repair, 312–314
  CTS (Correction and Transport System), 312, 313
  customer-defined objects, 312
  customizations, 310–311
  importing, 313
  master data elements, 311–312
  transport, 312
  transport tool, 312–314
  types of, 307–312
check tables, 33
clean system environment, 67–68
Client 000 customization client, 310
client copying, 142
client-dependent customizations, 320
client-independent customizations, 330
clients, 64, 101
  customization table entries, 330
  instance master, 103
  interface development, 102–103
  process development, 101–102

client-specific customizations, 330
code, documenting, 404–409
common problems
    categorizing, 291–297
    communications, 298
    data access and contention, 293–295
    data integrity, 296–297
    dump analysis, 299–300
    notifying users of, 297–298
    output controller, 300
    program and process specification, 297
    responding to, 297–298
    system access and authorization, 292–293
    system log, 299
    system performance and resources, 296
    tools, 298–300
    Update Monitor tool, 298–299
    update task errors, 298–299
common terminology, 40–41
common tool set, 82–84
communications
    changes, 314–315
    common problems, 298
    with customers, 61–62
    deleting elements, 234
    design phase results, 108–109
    implement support phase, 163
    integrated support team development, 39–40
    issues, 165–166
    need for simplicity, 59
    open line of, 17
    refreshing system, 68
    tools and forums development, 46–47
    with users, 368–369
company culture SAP changes, 227–228
company mission statements, 78
conferences and expositions, 443–444
consultants, 81
    continued use of, 195–196
    dependency on, 217
    temporary reliance on, 216–217
contingency plan, 160–161
controls, 42–43, 86
    changing company culture, 227–228
    checks and balances, 58
    company support for, 227
    corruption, 59
    data integrity, 59
    identifying key points of, 228–229

Logon Administrator, 86
    organizational-chart level, 58
    proper amount of, 58–59
    protecting Live Business instance, 228–229
    removing/restricting implementation team
        access, 229
    restricting access to logon modifications, 229
    SAP logon IDs, 244–251
    security, 59, 241
    security policies, 243
    support and implementation teams, 206–207
copying customizations, 328
core competencies, 8
corruption control, 59
co-support team, 222
CPIC user type, 247
crash and burn machine, 64
cross training, 62–63
CTS (Correction and Transport System),
    142, 312, 313
cubicle environment model, 45
current state, 97
    process flow diagram, 98–99
customer base, 365–366
customer-defined
    elements, 118–119
    objects, 312
    solutions, 128
customers
    basic responsibilities, 17
    commitment to, 17–18
    communicating with, 61–62
    direct interaction with support team member, 8
    emergency contacts, 61
    empathizing with, 17
    how support teams will interact with, 61
    ideas about business and process flow, 62
    knowing, 17
    miscommunications, 17
    open line of communications, 17
    pending changes, enhancements, or system
        unavailability, 61
    problems, 17
    regular methods of gathering information, 61–62
    showing confidence to, 18
    support-team terminology and, 41
customization matrix, 334
customization team, 120–121
customizations, 119–122

BEW (Business Engineering Workbench), 320
capturing changes, 330–331
changes, 310–311
client comparisons, 334–335
client-dependent, 320
client-independent, 330
client-specific, 330
comparison of values, 328–330
copying, 328
creating with reference, 328
cross-functional perspective, 119
customization matrix, 334
customization request, 334
Customizing Implementation Guide (IMG)
    hierarchy, 320–321
customizing request, 330, 331, 332
document type, 325
documentation, 120, 322–324
existing, 328–330
high-level management, 320–324
identifying, 120
levels of effect, 330
manually entering changes, 334
naming conventions, 334
requirements, 119
saving to reference with task number, 332
searching for, 321–322
single-step process, 325
special transactions, 325, 327
structure, 321
styles, 325
support overview, 319–320
table logging feature, 335
task, 330
tracking activity, 334–335
transporting, 330–334
two-step process, 325
update tools, 324–327
view cluster, 325, 327
view-led, 325–326
customizing data browser, 440
Customizing Implementation Guide (IMG)
  hierarchy, 320–321
    searching for customizations, 321–322
    tracking customization activity, 334
Customizing Organizer: Initial screen, 331
Customizing Organizer: Request Detail screen, 331
Customizing Request Organizer screen (SE10)
  transaction, 331, 333

cutover plan
    implementation steps, 159
    when to perform, 158

D

damage control, 373
data
    front-end validation and verification, 33
    integrated, 24–35
    loading into SAP, 129
data access and contention problems, 293–295
data browser, customizing, 440
Data Browser (SE16 transaction), 340
data contention, 270–271, 293–295, 357
data dictionary elements, changes to, 308–310
data elements, migration of, 119
data fields, 248
data integrity
    control, 59
    problems, 296–297
data loads, early, 129–131
data manipulation in legacy system versus
  SAP system, 181
data mining, 25, 27
data recovery in legacy systems and SAP
  systems, 181
data tables
    books, 25
    linked, 27
    master data, 24
    transitional, 25
database locks, 359
database monitor, 296
database software manufacturer, 13
databases
    asynchronous updating, 358–359
    performance tuning, 359
    synchronous updating, 358–359
database-specific archiving, 390
data-verification programs, 130
date formats, 249
Date/Time dialog box, 275
DDT (detailed design tool), 99
decimal notation, 249
dedicated test area, 144
default printers, 249
Define Background Job screen, 271
deleting elements, 234

design iterations, 133–135

design phase

    communicating results, 108–109

    constructing future environment landscape, 103–104

    current system and process analysis, 97–100

    documentation, 109

    early prototypes, 105–108

    establishing Development instance, 100–103

    incorporating project work plan, 96–97

    obtaining approval, 110

    project implementation dates, 96

    project scope and high-level process migration plans, 93–95

developer's key, 308

    OSS (Online Service System), 309

development environment, 82–84

Development instance

    additional clients, 65

    add-on functions (bolt-ons), 64

    bug fixes, 64

    establishing, 100–103

    ideas, 64

    innovations, 64

    instance master client, 103

    interface development client, 102–103

    new functionality, 64

    process development client, 101–102

    recreating change situation, 306

    regression testing, 64

    reviewing and testing customization changes, 310

    testing deletions in, 235

    unit testing, 64

development phase

    customer-defined solutions, 128

    customization team, 120–121

    customizations, 119–122

    data-verification programs, 130

    documentation, 136

    early data loads, 129–131

    early system builds, 116

    freezing design specifications, 135–136

    functional prototypes, 135

    identifying and investigating gaps and issues, 124–126

    interface development, 131–132

    iterations of design, 133–135

    logon and access polices, 117–118

    mapping legacy data to SAP, 123–124

    master data policies, 122–123

    naming conventions, 118–119

    populating with usable master data, 129

    reclassifying elements in SAP terms, 126

    redefining and using existing fields, 126

    reengineering processes, 127–128

    report development, 132–133

    retiring element use, 126

    separation of duties, 117

    solid design, 115

    sound working environment, 115

    strip programs, 129

development user, 308–309

dialog user type, 244

Disaster Recovery instance, 66–67, 381–382

    backups, 66

DMT (Data Mapping Tool), 123–124

document storage, 410

document type customization, 325

documentation

    ABAP template, 404–409

    audit readiness, 401–402

    background processing schedules, 403

    business specifications, 402

    clean-up efforts, 235

    cross-training, 401

    customizations, 120, 322–324

    deliverables, 219–221

    design phase, 109

    development, 220

    development phase, 136

    document storage, reference, and sharing techniques, 410

    documenting code, 404–409

    file names, 88

    good habits, 87–88

    habit of, 403–404

    history of revisions, 403

    ISO certification, 402

    knowledge silos, 401

    legacy environment, 98, 99

    living, 409

    maintenance requirements, 403

    measuring successful, 411

    necessity of, 107

    original developer identification, 403

    passing duties with, 401

preserving knowledge, 401
reasons for, 400–402
recovery instructions, 403
security, 242
solution flow and interdependencies, 403
support reference guide, 220–221, 409–410
technical specifications, 402–403
testing and training phase, 151–152
troubleshooting and recovery guide, 220
types, 402–403
Web pages, 410
documenting code, 404–409
DRP (Disaster Recovery Plan)
backup retention, 383–384
business competency, 378
developing, 377–380
Disaster Recovery instance, 381–382
disaster recovery timetable, 379
geographic location of tools, 378
identifying critical elements, 378
instance, 230, 231
instance structure, 381–382
locating DRP instance and system backup
storage, 384
maintaining, 385
mission critical, 378
nominal need, 378
readiness, 381–382
recovery team, 379–380
rehearsing plans, 384–385
response method, 380
system backups, 382–383
dump analysis, 299–300

E

early data loads, 129–131
early prototypes, 105–108
**setting project scope versus project timeline,
107–108**
early system builds, 116
ease of use, 359–360
EBELN field, 29
EBELP field, 29
EKPO table, 29–30
elements
changes to basic, 308–310
customer-defined, 118–119

deleting, 234
electronic packets, 308
identifying and investigating gaps and issues,
124–126
missed in original discussions, 218
modified, 308
reclassifying in SAP terms, 126
requiring long-term support teams, 217
retiring use, 126
transports, 308
**e-mail and integrated support team
development, 47**
end-to-end testing, 147
entity definition, 26
environment
constructing future landscape, 103–104
need for simplicity, 59
ERP (Enterprise Resource Planning) tools, 76
errors and integration, 35
ERSDA field, 26–27
exceptional support
brief information, 18
defining roles and responsibilities, 17
empathizing with customer, 17
knowing customer, 17
open line of communication, 17
showing commitment, 17
understanding and restating problem, 17
expanded office area model, 45
expert users, 372
external training teams, 150

F

FI (Finance) module, 39
fields
authorization profiles, 256
redefining and using, 126
file names, 88
final unit testing, 144–146
financial chart of accounts, 26
freezing design specifications, 135–136
front-end data validation and verification, 33
full regression testing, 65
functional prototypes, 135
future state diagram, 104–105
future state environment, 104

G

General Table Display (SE17 transaction), 340
General Table Display transaction, 255
generic logon IDs, 254
geography, 26
Global Alert Monitor, 283
global configurations, 120
Global Customization Matrix, 120–121
good documentation habits, 87–88
Graphical Job Scheduling screen, 279, 280
GUI (graphical user interface)
    common icons, 429–431
    data table selection, 429
    installation, 84–85
    issuing transaction codes, 428–429
    main screen, 428–429
    menu as starting screen, 249
    queries from, 342
    result screens, 429

H

handoff
    changing roles and responsibilities, 201–205
    criteria, 201
    developing criteria, 208–211
    issue-tracking matrix, 211
    stabilization, 201
    stabilization metrics, 209–210
    stabilization time frame, 208–209
    stable and ready for, 212
    tracking progress to stabilization, 211
handoff acceptance, 222
hand-off points, 41–42
hardware implementation team, 84
help desk
    call tickets, 9
    questions to ask, 10
    as single point of contact, 9–10
    up-to-date information, 10
high-level customization management, 320–324
high-level process migration plans, 93–95
history of revisions, 403
hoshin, 78
hot line, 9
hot line phone numbers, 165

I

ideas, 64
IMG customizing structure overview screen, 321
implementation support phase
    business teams, 162
    call-tracking Web sites, 165
    communications, 163
    enabling turn-on, 162–163
    evening out system load, 166
    hot line phone numbers, 165
    initiating blackout, 161–162
    live cutover plan, 158–159
    postmortem meetings, 167
    reports, 167
    stabilization period, 166–167
    status line phone numbers, 165
    steps, 159
    tracking, resolving, and communicating issues, 165–166
    viable contingency plan, 160–161
    visible support, 163–164
implementation teams, 75
    ABAP/4 training, 130
    business process activity, 79, 82
    conducting support team training, 193
    defined office area, 84
    formal knowledge transfer, 218
    hardware, 84
    inaccuracies or minor omissions, 204
    mentoring, 206
    modifying code, 204–205
    new role for, 203–205
    project leaders, 79–80
    removing/restricting access, 229
    roles and responsibilities, 82
    SAP consultant, 81
    shared roles and responsibilities, 205–208
    sharing control with support teams, 206–207
    structure and membership, 79–81
    subteams, 82
    technical aspects of system environment, 79, 82
    transition to Live Business, 204
    visible implementation support, 163–164
    walkie-talkies, 164
importing
    changed SAP objects, 228–229
    changes, 313

inbound interfaces, 131
incorporating project work plan, 96–97
Information Already Being Processed message, 299
information and integrated SAP model, 22
informational needs and scale, 339–340
innovations, 64
instance master client, 103
instances, 64, 101
integrated business flow model, 32
integrated data, 24–35
    books, 25
    key data elements, 25–26
    master data, 26–29
    master data tables, 24
    transitional data tables, 25
integrated processes versus isolated processes, 173–177
integrated SAP model, 20, 22–24
    check tables, 33
    front-end data validation and verification, 33
    information, 22
    master data, 26–29
    modules, 22–23
    process linkages, 22
    pros and cons of integration, 33–35
    purchasing goods, 33–35
    real-time responses, 33
    required entries, 33
    scalability, 23
    supply chain, 22
    support, 24
    transactional data, 29–33
    verification process, 30
integrated support team development
    business support assignments, 41–42
    common terminology, 40–41
    communication, 39–40
    communications tools and forums development, 46–47
    controlling access and tool use, 42–43
    cubicle environment model, 45
    e-mail, 47
    expanded office area model, 45
    internal team partnership, 39
    linkages, 39
    Microsoft Chat, 47
    open floor space model, 46
    partnerships, 39
    physical environment, 44–46

    physical interaction, 44
    separation of duties, 42
    team meetings, 46–47
    voicemail, 47
    Web sites, 47
    workload balancing, 42
integration, 173
    development of business teams, 38
    effects of actions in, 34
    errors and, 35
    not properly understood and managed, 34
    real-time information posting, 35
    special attention to, 175–176
integration testing, 147
intercommunication, 61
interdepartmental backups, 62–63
interface development client, 102–103
interfaces
    ABAP/4 support, 102
    as bookmarks, 102
    developing, 131–132
    execution frequency, 132
    inbound, 131
    outbound, 131
    passing data, 131
Introduction to ABAP/4 Programming for SAP, Revised and Expanded Edition, 26
ISO compliance, 232–236
ISO (International Organization for Standardization), 233
    certification, 233
isolated processes versus integrated processes, 173–177
issue-tracking matrix, 211
iterations of design, 133–135

J

job link to job schedule custom program, 439
Job Overview screen, 284, 285
Job Overview Selection screen, 279, 280
Job Scheduler, 267
    accessing, 271
    definition screen, 271–272
job schedules
    batch user logon IDs, 285
    best practices for, 285–286
    job link to custom program, 439
    monitoring, 279–280

naming conventions, 285
recovering, 284–285
spreadsheet of regularly scheduled jobs, 286
supporting, 285–286
job scheduling
ABAP/4: Execute Program screen, 268–269
active status, 278
alerts and notifications, 282–284
background processing, 270
batch authorization objects, 281–282
canceled status, 278
conditional criteria, 269–270
data contention, 270–271
Date/Time specification, 275
defining output print parameters, 276–278
finished status, 278
host system, 271–272
overview, 266–267
prioritization, 271
programs and variants to be executed after, 276
ready status, 278
released status, 278
scheduled status, 278
security, 281–282
start criteria, 275–276
status, 278–279
tools, 268–278
variants, 268=269
junk mail, 47

K

key data elements, 25–26
key elements, 27
key field, 30
knowledge sharing, 48–49
knowledge silos, 63, 401
knowledge transfer, 214–215
documentation deliverables, 219–221
executing, 218–219
formal sessions, 218
handoff acceptance, 222

L

LAEDA field, 26–27
learning SAP, 85
legacy environment, 97–98

legacy systems
backups, 180
comparing to SAP system, 172–183
continued support for, 205
data manipulation, 181
data recovery, 181
data transfer, 174
duplicate data, 174
forgiving nature of, 179
identifying and investigating migration gaps
    and issues, 124–126
individual system maintenance, 179
interfaces to, 175
mapping data to SAP, 123–124
overnight waiting period, 174
redefining or mapping elements, 118
restoring information, 180–181
single applications for business areas, 177
solution leveragability, 182
synchronization of information, 180–181
truncated information, 174
turnaround time, 173–174
level 0 backups, 383
level 1 backup, 383, 384
linked data tables, 27
Live Business instance, 66
implementing change, 307
protecting with controls, 228–229
testing change, 306
live cutover plan, 158–159
living documentation, 409
loading data into SAP, 129
lock argument, 295
lock entries, 357
deleting, 295
resolving, 295
reviewing, 294
searching for, 294
unable to delete, 358
Lock Entries utility, 294
Lock Entry List, 295
Lock/Unlock User pop-up screen, 250
logical-log file, 383
Logon Administrator, 86
logon policies, 117–118
logon work groups, 358
logons
language, 249
new, 292

restricting access to, 229
reviewing IDs, 229
long-term passwords, 251-252
long-term support teams, 215
  associating with business areas, 223
  backup support linkages, 218
  elements requiring, 217
  executing knowledge transfer, 218–219
  goals, 223
  introducing, 223
  makeup of, 210

M

Maintain User: Address screen, 247, 248
Maintain User: Defaults screen, 247, 248, 249
Maintain User: Initial Screen, 245
Maintain User: Parameters screen, 249–250
Maintain User: Profiles screen
  Authorization profiles section, 247
  Basic data area options, 245
  User type section, 245–246
maintenance requirements, 403
manager responsibilities for team actions, 178
MANDT field, 26–27, 29
MARA table, 26–27
master data, 26–29
  business relationships, 26
  data linkages, 145
  element changes, 311–312
  entity definition, 26
  financial chart of accounts, 26
  geography, 26
  native language information, 26
  policies, 122–123
  product catalogs, 26
  tables, 24
  unique product or service information, 26
  warehouse identification, 26
master data control team, 122–123
material documents, 30–31
material type information, 176
materials
  managing, 176
  obsolescence, 176–177
MATNR field, 26–27, 29–30
Microsoft Chat and integrated support team
  development, 47

migration, 75
  data elements and programs, 119
  DDT (detailed design tool), 99
  identifying and investigating gaps and issues,
    124–126
  initiating blackout, 161–162
mission statements, 78
MM_EKKO archive object, 393–394
model user IDs, 254
modules, 22–23
  adding, 23
  balancing, 42
  business teams, 39
  cause-and-effect results, 23
  dividing activities within, 41–42
  hand-off points, 41–42
  independence of, 23
  selection of, 23
  separation of duties, 42
mood and tone of support team, 60
multinational user groups, 443

N

naming conventions, 27
  customer-defined elements, 118–119
  customizations, 334
  job schedules, 285
  Z class of elements, 118
native language information, 26
network monitor, 296

O

object key, 309
one-dimensional table extracts, 340–341
online SAP object check, 217
open floor space model, 46
operating system monitor, 296
organizational data. See master data
organizations, 442–443
original developer identification, 403
OSS (Online Service System), 309
OSS Registration screen, 309
OSS1 transaction code, 309
outbound interfaces, 131
output, printing immediately, 247
output controller, 300

P

pacing, 17
passwords
  changing, 251, 253
  cycling, 251-253
  expiration limit, 251-252
  initial, 251, 253
  long-term, 250-252
  protecting, 253-254
  rules, 251
performance
  database locks, 359
  database tuning, 359
  ease of use, 359–360
  synchronous and asynchronous updating, 358–359
  tools and methods, 358–359
  user and process load balancing, 358
personal transitions
  additional training, 190
  from business team to support team, 189–190
  continuing on implementation path, 189
  educating other team members, 187–188
  existing legacy systems, 190
  extensions of solutions, 188
  as internal consultant, 189
  returning to support team, 187
physical environment, 44–46
PID (process ID), 354–355
pilot testing
  focusing on process reviews, 147
  post-test survey, 149
postmortem meetings, 167
potential business exposure, 227
PP (Production Planning) module, 39
printers, default, 249
printing output immediately, 249
problems, understanding and restating, 17
Procedure Model, 75
process analysis, 97–100
  process flow diagram, 98–99
process analysts, 194–195
process development client, 101–102
process linkages, 22
process migration plans, 92–93
  high-level, 93–95
process prototype script, 105–106
processed spool files, 300

processes
  accelerated throughput, 173
  automated, 360
  automatic restart after abort, 355
  capturing and transmitting solutions, 142
  classifying, 378
  cleanup, 234
  client used when executing, 355
  CPU time expended in execution, 355
  extensions of solutions, 188
  integrated *versus* isolated, 173–177
  internal number of, 354
  load balancing, 358
  number of semaphore waiting for, 355
  number of times aborted, 355
  processing status, 355
  reason for Hold status, 355
  reengineering, 127–128
  testing, 141
product catalogs, 26
products, unique information for, 26
profiles, testing, 144
program and process specification problems, 297
programs
  aborting, 299–300
  changes, 308–310
  classifying, 378
  common tool set, 82–84
  deleting standard, 235
  migration, 119
project charter, 77–78
project charter statement, 77
project migration plans, 94–95
project work plan
  implementation dates, 96
  incorporating, 96–97
  ownership of tasks, 96
projects
  implementation dates, 96
  scope, 93–95
  setting scope *versus* timeline, 107
prototypes, 105
  early, 105–108
  functional, 135
  setting project scope *versus* project timeline, 107
purchase order transaction, 30

Q

Quality Assurance (QA) instance, 65–66, 140, 142–144, 145
    full regression testing, 65
    involving business teams with, 65–66

R

real-time information posting, 35
recording transactions, 29
recovering job schedules, 284–285
recovery
    instructions, 403
    reinstating, 230–232
recovery team, 379–380
reengineering, 126
    customer-defined solutions, 128
    processes, 127–128
refitting support team, 191–192
refreshing system, 67–68
    reinstating, 230–232
regression testing, 64
remote users, 366
reporting informational needs and scale, 339–340
reports
    ABAP/4 programs, 344
    ABAP/Query, 341–343
    additional resources, 349
    developing, 132–133
    efficiency, 347–348
    elements, 345
    implementation support phase, 167
    as interactive features, 346
    one-dimensional table extracts, 340–341
    onscreen displays, 346
    results, 347
    selection criteria, 347–348
    supporting, 348–349
    third-party query tools, 344–345
    tools, 340–345
    usefulness, 345–346
required entries, 33
resolving issues, 165–166
resources, 56–57
responsibilities
    clearly defining, 17
    handoff changes, 201–205

restoring information in legacy and SAP systems, 180–181
retiring element use, 126
reviewing system activity, 313
roles
    clearly defining, 17
    handoff changes, 201–205

S

S_ADMI_FCD object, 282
SAP
    changes to work environment, 417–418
    conferences and expositions, 443–444
    gathering information, 75
    German language, 27
    history of, 424–426
    learning, 85
    naming conventions, 27
    objective for deploying, 76–78
    training programs and facilities, 446
    user groups and organizations, 442–443
SAP architecture
    authorization checks, 117
    clients, 101
    hierarchy, 101
    instances, 101
SAP environment support, 201–203
SAP Labs, Inc., 443
SAP life cycle
    adopting common tool set and development environment, 82–84
    first phase, 75
    first SAP GUI (graphical user interface) installation, 84–85
    gathering information on SAP, 75
    good documentation habits, 87–88
    implementation team structure and membership, 79–81
    learning SAP, 85
    objective for deploying SAP, 76–78
    project charter, 77–78
    project charter statement, 77
    specific areas of control, 86–87
    sponsoring SAP project, 76
SAP logon IDs, 244-251
    account numbers, 246
    background user type, 247

BDC user type, 247
change activity, 255
changing password, 251
CPIC user type, 247
creation or modification functions, 245
dates valid on, 246
dialog user type, 246
generic, 254
lock status, 250-251
model, 254
parameters and values associated with, 247, 248-249
periodic reviews, 255
profiles, 247
protecting, 253-254
requests, 244
reviewing and maintaining, 255
simplicity of, 244
user addresses, 247, 248
user groups, 246
SAP objects
archiving, 393-395
importing changed, 228-229
registering change to, 308
SAP systems
backups, 180
cleanup, 234
compared to legacy system, 172-183
coordination requirements of bringing down, 179
data accuracy, 179
data management, 175
data manipulation, 181
data recovery, 181
description fields, 174-175
differences in security and user groups, 177-178
extensions of solutions, 188
immediate data availability, 174
inaccurate data, 176
manager responsibilities for team actions, 178
restoring information, 180
reviewing activity, 313
solution leveragability, 182
special attention to integration, 175-176
valid data unavailable, 176-177
SAP Workbench Organizer, 228-229
Sapphire, 444
SAP-provided ABAP programs, screens, transactions and data dictionary elements changes, 308-310

SARA transaction code, 393, 395
S_ARCHIVE object, 393
S_BTCH_ADM object, 281
S_BTCH_JOB object, 282
S_BTCH_NAM object, 282
scalability, 23, 39
screens
changes, 308-310
deleting standard, 235
SD (Sales and Distribution) module, 39
SE03 transaction, 306
SE11 transaction, 217
SE16 transaction code, 440
SE17 transaction, 369
security
access policies, 117-118
additional tools, 258-260
adjusting controls, 242
areas, 242-243
authorization profiles, 255-258
controlled and consistent process, 243-244
controls, 59, 241
differences with SAP, 177-178
documentation, 242
logon policies, 117-118
passwords, 251-253
points of concern, 241-242
policy development, 241-243
protecting logon IDs and passwords, 253-254
reviewing and maintaining SAP logon IDs, 255
SAP logon IDs, 244-251
Security Administrator, 242
sharing ownership with business areas, 260-262
SSCR (SAP Software Change Registration), 308
table logging, 259-260
Transaction Code maintenance screen, 258-259
Security Administrator, 242
duties, 243-244
locking logon ID, 250-251
model user IDs, 254
new logons, 292
self-development, 50-51
separation of duties, 117
access restriction, 230
as audit issue, 230
authorization profiles, 258
support team, 229
services unique information, 26
session-echoing functionality, 440

single point of contact, 9–10
single-step process, 325
SM04 transaction, 356
SM12 transaction code, 294
SM31 transaction, 325
SM35 transaction, 292
SM37 transaction, 279, 370
SM51 transaction, 313
solution flow and interdependencies, 403
solution leveragability, 181–182
special customization transactions, 325, 327
specification freeze, 135–136
S_QUERY authorization object, 343
SSCR (SAP Software Change Registration)
 developer's key, 308
 development user, 308–309
 object key, 309
 security, 308
stabilization, 201
stabilization period, 166–167
Start Time dialog box, 272
status line phone numbers, 165
strip programs, 129
subteams and process-specific work plans, 96
supply chain, 22
supply-chain management, 35
support
 basic, 13
 business process, 13–14
 business technical, 12–13
 changes in, 15
 commitment to, 17–18
 defining, 4–6
 exceptional, 16–18
 integrated SAP model, 24
 overlapping arenas of, 15–16
 technical, 12
 today's role, 15–16
support model 1, 7–8
support model 2, 7, 8–10
support models, 6–12
 business culture, 12
 call tickets, 9
 help desk, 9
 hot line, 9
 single point of contact, 9–10
 tier 1 support, 11

 tier 2 support, 11
 tiered support, 11–12
support organization, 4
support partnership development, 47–49
 knowledge sharing, 48–49
support reference guide, 220–221
 troubleshooting and recovery instructions, 409–410
support strategy, 54
 ability to obtain and maintain technology, 57–58
 backup strategy, 62–63
 clarity of directions and priorities, 60
 communicating with customers, 61–62
 company support for, 227
 correct size of support team, 55–56
 cross training, 62–63
 elements of success, 54–60
 maintaining clean environment, 67–68
 mood and tone of group, 60
 natural areas of resource focus, 56–57
 need for simplicity, 59
 proper amount of control, 58–59
 right mix of resource skills, 56
 work environments, 63–66
support teams, 5
 ability to obtain and maintain technology, 57–58
 background processing, 281
 balance, 43, 55
 balance and tuning, 5
 becoming known by users, 49–50
 becoming students of SAP, 205
 blending implementation and business, 201
 brief information, 18
 business area assignment, 216–217
 business customer direct interaction with, 8
 business technical support, 13
 change process, 306
 charter and vision, 61
 clarity of directions and priorities, 60
 clearly defining roles and responsibilities, 17
 commitment to customers, 17–18
 communicating with customers, 61–62
 communicating with users, 368–369
 confidence, 18
 construction of, 6
 continued support of legacy systems, 205
 contributions, 18–19
 controlling access and tool use, 42–43

core competencies, 8

correct size, 55–56

cross training, 62–63

customer base, 365–366

database software manufacturer, 13

deployment, 216–217

Development instance, 64–65

development of integrated, 39–44

embarrassing or admonishing users, 50

empathizing with customers, 17

engaging user base, 371–372

expanding business areas, 365–366

experience-sharing sessions, 194

formal knowledge transfer, 218

geographically dispersed users, 366

grooming expert users, 372

handoff, 200

helping users help themselves, 369–371

how it will interact with customers, 61

integrated real-time system environments, 208

interaction of, 6

interdepartmental backups, 62–63

internal team partnership, 39

knowledge sharing, 48–49

members, 5

miscommunications, 17

monitoring central processing activity of SAP, 191

monitoring users, 366

mood and tone of group, 60

natural areas of resource focus, 56–57

need for simplicity, 59

new users, 366

newest person on, 18–19

notifying about problems, 298

open line of communications, 17

partnerships with users, 367–368

peak periods, 55

personal transitions, 187–190

physical environment, 44–46

physical interaction, 44

preimplementation training sessions, 193

preparing for new environment, 193–194

proper amount of control, 58–59

putting long-term team in place, 215

refitting, 191–192

remote users, 366

responsibilities, 6

right mix of resource skills, 56

role of, 61

S_ADMI_FCD object, 282

SAP focus, 191

SAP training, 193

S_BTCH_ADM object, 281

S_BTCH_JOB object, 282

S_BTCH_NAM object, 282

Security Administrator, 242

self-development, 50–51

separation of duties, 42

shared roles and responsibilities, 205–208

sharing control with implementation teams, 206–207

single point of contact, 9–10

size, 192

stated intent, 61

subdivisions of, 6

system access and authorization problems, 292–293

team ego, 49

team meetings, 46–47

tier 1 support, 48

tier 2 support, 48

tiered support, 11–12

too large, 56

too small, 55

traditional role of, 78

tuning, 43

veterans, 19

weekends and holidays, 159

workload balancing, 42

synchronous updating, 358–359

system

    access and authorization problems, 292–293

    backups, 382–383

    builds, 116

    defining settings, 118

    maintaining clean environment, 67–68

    messages, 354

    performance and resources problems, 296

    refreshing, 67–68

system log, 299

System Messages feature, 315

System Monitor, 295

system workload monitor, 296

T

table logging, 259–260

team ego, 49

technical specifications, 402–403

technical support, 12
technology, 57–58
  tuning, 5
temporary co-support, 206–208
terminology, 40–41
Test instance, 140, 141–144, 145
testing
  dedicated area, 144
  final unit, 144–146
  full regression, 65
  integration, 147
  pilot, 147–149
  processes, 141
  profiles, 144
  regression, 64
  unit, 64
testing and training phase
  building test and training instances, 141–144
  dedicated test area, 144
  documentation, 151–152
  final unit testing, 144–146
  integration testing, 147
  pilot testing, 147–149
  training approach, 149–151
  third-party archiving solutions, 397
  third-party query tools, 344–345
  tier 1 support, 11, 48
tier 2 support, 11, 48
tiered support, 11–12
tp import command, 228, 313
tracking issues, 165–166
training
  external teams, 150
  materials, 151
  support team, 193
training approach
  coordinating training, 151
  preparing training material, 149–150
  where to conduct, 149
  who should conduct sessions, 150
Training instance, 66
  building, 141–142
  generic logon names, 66
training programs and facilities, 446
  application training, 446–447
  information database, 448
  on-site education, 448
  portable classrooms, 448
  specialized industry solution workshops, 447

traditional courses, 446–448
transaction and performance support, 350–357
  work processes, 354
Transaction Code maintenance screen, 258–259
transaction codes, 258–259
  Command field, 438
  issuing, 428–429
  quick reference, 434–438
transactional data, 29–33
  business documents, 29–30
  material documents, 30–31
transactions
  capabilities within, 256
  changes, 308–310
  deleting, 235
  identifying, 256
  recording, 29
  user access to, 256–257
transitional data tables, 25
transport, 312
transport log, 313–314
transporting customizations, 330–334
transports, 308
troubleshooting and recovery
  guide, 220
  instructions, 409–410
tuning, 43
two-step process, 325

U

unit testing, 64
Update Manager, 358
Update Monitor tool, 298–299
update task errors, 298–299
user base, 8
  engaging, 371–372
user groups, 246, 442–443
  differences with SAP, 177–178
user partnership development
  becoming known by users, 49–50
  embarrassing or admonishing users, 50
user profiles, 117
User Session monitor, 356
users
  access to transactions, 256–257
  active sessions running, 356
  associating account numbers with, 246
  BDC, 247

communicating with, 368–369
CPIC, 247
customization of session parameters, 249–250
damage control, 373
dialog, 246
expert, 372
generic logon names, 66
helping help themselves, 369–371
job status overview, 370
knowledge sharing and activity planning, 371–372
load balancing, 358
logon authorizations, 177–177
number of simultaneous sessions, 357
output controller, 370
overview, 356
parameters and defaults, 370
partnerships with, 367–368
providing with SAP experience, 195
reviewing table information, 369–370
sessions activity, 357
training sessions, 66
types, 247

V

valid values, 118
variants, 268–269
viable contingency plan, 160–161
view cluster customizations, 325, 327
view-led customizations, 325–326
views, 325
voicemail and integrated support team
development, 47

W

warehouse identification, 26
Web sites
call-tracking, 165
integrated support team development, 47
work environments
clients, 64
Development instance, 64–65
Disaster Recovery instance, 66–67
instances, 64
Live Business instance, 66
Quality Assurance (QA) instance, 65–66
SAP changes to, 417–418
Training instance, 66
Work Process monitor, 354–355
work processes
action executed within, 355
database table name, 355
name of program executed within, 355
types, 354–356
user logon ID starting, 355

Y

You Do Not Have Access to Transaction XXXX
message, 292

Z

Z class of elements, 118
ZABC customer-defined table, 119
ZABC-FIELD1 customer-defined data
element, 119
ZABCPROG customer-defined program, 119